**This book is to be returned on or before
the last date stamped below.**

1 5 FEB 2005

30/9/05

A HISTORY OF THE IRISH
WORKING CLASS

By P. Berresford Ellis and Seumas Mac A'Ghobhainn:

THE SCOTTISH INSURRECTION
OF 1820

A HISTORY OF THE IRISH WORKING CLASS

P. Berresford Ellis

LONDON
VICTOR GOLLANCZ LTD
1972

MADE AND PRINTED IN GREAT BRITAIN BY
THE GARDEN CITY PRESS LIMITED
LETCHWORTH, HERTFORDSHIRE SG6 IJS

The cause of labour is the cause of Ireland, the cause of Ireland is the cause of labour. They cannot be dissevered.

JAMES CONNOLLY,
The Workers' Republic, April 8, 1916

CONTENTS

Preface

WHEN JAMES CONNOLLY'S *Labour in Irish History* was first published in 1910, it became a classic of Marxist literature, being the first work to record and analyse Irish history from a Socialist viewpoint. Connolly in this work, and in his *Reconquest of Ireland,* published in 1915, dealt basically with a period from the 17th century to the 19th century and did not claim that he had written an all-embracing history of the Irish working classes but merely a clarification of their place in Irish history. The present book is no more than an attempt at expansion and updating, tracing the struggle of the Irish working classes from their original communistic society, through the various stages of their struggle for national and social emancipation.

This volume, essentially aimed at the general reader, deals solely with the working-class struggle in Ireland and makes no attempt to record the part (often a prominent one) that Irish emigrants have played in the working-class movements of other countries. The author is conscious of the many aspects of working-class history which deserve to be dealt with in more detail than he has been able to devote in the restrictions of a general history. For example: the branches of the First International in Ireland; the early history of Irish trade unionism which began in the latter part of the 18th century; the agrarian "terrorist" organisations of the 17th to 19th centuries, and the Irish soviets of 1920-3. All these aspects are deserving of separate volumes. In fact, the labour history of Ireland, apart from Connolly's unique contribution, is largely an unexplored territory. What has been attempted in this volume is a general history of the Irish working class struggle.

Ba mhian liom mo bhuíochas a ghabháil i dteanga na hÉireann le Pádraig Ó Conchúir as ucht na cabhrach agus an chomhairle a thug sé dhom nuair a bhí an obair seo idir láimhe agam.

P. BERRESFORD ELLIS

Chapter 1

CELTIC COMMUNISM

THE CLASH BETWEEN the Celtic communistic social
system and the crushing slavery of the Anglo-Norman feudal
system marked the beginning of the struggle of the Irish working classes. This was the contention of James Connolly in
Labour in Irish History, which referred to "the Gaelic principle
of common ownership by the people of their sources of food
and maintenance." The idea that early Celtic society exercised
a form of primitive communism is one that has been supported
by several writers of Celtic studies. More traditional academic
thought, however, has tended to translate early Celtic society in
terms of a feudal capitalistic system. Even Frederick Engels,
who learnt the Irish language for the purpose of writing his
projected *History of Ireland*, dismissed the clan system as a
"feudal-patriarchal system". The volumes, *The Ancient Laws
of Ireland*, had not been published in their entirety when
Engels began this work in 1869. In 1884, however, in *The
Origins of the Family, Private Property and the State*, Engels
mentions "the English jurists of the 17th century who were sent
across [to Ireland] for the purpose of transforming the clan
lands into royal dominions. Up to this time the soil had been
collective property of the *gens* or the clans . . ." From Engels's
draft of his proposed Irish history, it is clear that he intended to
undertake a more detailed examination of the clan system, land
ownership and the Irish law system.

Connolly was not a Celtic scholar, of course. This has
frequently been raised in criticism of his work. But he relied for
his information and sources upon reputable Celtic scholars. In
1919, three years after his execution and at a time when his
reputation was high in an Ireland engaged in the first year of
her war of liberation, the conservative forces of the Irish
independence movement wanted Eoin MacNeill, a Celtic
scholar of wide repute, to academically destroy Connolly's
theories on early Irish society. MacNeill was to the right of the

Irish political spectrum and, as we shall see in subsequent chapters, had been against the 1916 uprising. Like many others who condemned the actions of the men of 1916 and who played no active part in the insurrection, he cashed in on the nation-wide republican sympathies to be elected to the first *Dáil* in the 1918 General Election. He subsequently rejected republicanism to become a member of the Free State Government in 1921. MacNeill was therefore considered to be the very man to destroy Connolly's radical theories; however, with Ireland engaged in the liberation war and with Connolly recently martyred and a rallying symbol of the emerging nation, it was thought counter-productive to attack him directly.

Instead, in the August and September, 1919, issues of the *Irish Monthly*, MacNeill attacked the scholar P. W. Joyce, whose work, the *Social History of Ancient Ireland*, had been one of Connolly's main sources. Joyce also had a good reputation in his field and had been appointed a commissioner for editing and publishing *The Ancient Laws of Ireland*.

In criticising Joyce's interpretation of early Irish society, MacNeill stated : "The political system of ancient Ireland was no more communal than that of the Roman Republic. It was aristocratic." Having asserted this, MacNeill provides hardly any references in support of his statements and seems to rely on the weight of his reputation to endorse his arguments. Joyce, however, scrupulously provides a copious bibliography to back his arguments. MacNeill admits his analysis of the subject was only "an interpretation". In fact, he also admits that family society could be described as "communes". When in 1921 his articles were printed in book form as part of a larger work *Celtic Ireland* he devoted a chapter to the "Family Commune" insisting, however, that family "community-ism" developed out of private property concepts and was not a remnant of large scale "community-ism". MacNeill finishes his criticism of Joyce by stating :

> The subject invites thorough research, and the interpretation I have offered, while I think it provides an intelligible solution of difficulties hitherto avoided, requires to be tested in view of the whole body of evidence. At all events, I can find no evidence of communal ownership *on a large scale* (author's italics) and I contend that, instead of being survivals of a wider

communal ownership, the small family communes must have
developed out of individual ownership.

In fairness, it may be pointed out that MacNeill was just as
much coloured by his political views of life as was Connolly.

The Irish conservatives were naturally worried at the tremendous growth of support for Connolly's ideology at this time.
Between 1916 and 1920 the membership of the Irish Transport
and General Workers' Union of which Connolly had been
General Secretary at the time of his execution, had risen from
5,000 to 130,000. It is not insignificant, therefore, that in the
same journal publishing MacNeill's attack on Joyce, the Catholic
Church was not so adverse to attacking Connolly's politics. A
series of articles were published by Rev. L. McKenna SJ which
rebuked Connolly for having "allowed himself to be obfuscated
by German philosophical doctrines (i.e. Marxism) which he
either misunderstood or interpreted in a sense different from their
authors."

Connolly, realising that criticism would be forthcoming from
the conservative academics, made a valid parallel of his interpretation of early Irish society with Lewis H. Morgan's radical
work on other ancient societies :

Hitherto the study of social life and customs of Ireland has
been marred by one fault. For a description and interpretation of
Irish social life and customs the student depended entirely upon
the description and interpretation of men who were entirely lack-
ing in knowledge of, and insight into, the facts and spirit of the
things they attempted to describe. Imbued with the conception
of feudalistic or capitalistic social order, the writers perpetually
strove to explain Irish institutions in terms of an order of things
to which those institutions were entirely alien. Irish titles, indi-
cative of the function in society performed by the bearers, the
writers explained by what they supposed were analogous titles in
the feudal order of England, forgetful of the fact that as the one
form of society was the antithesis of the other, and not its coun-
terpart, the one set of titles could not possibly convey the same
meaning as the other, much less be a translation.

Much the same mistake was made in America by the early
Spanish conquistadores in attempting to describe the social and
political system of Mexico and Peru, with much the same results
of introducing almost endless confusion into every attempt to

comprehend life as it actually existed in those countries before the conquest. The Spanish writers could not mentally raise themselves out of the social structure of Continental Europe, and hence their weird and wonderful tales of despotic Peruvian and Mexican "Emperors" and "Nobles" where really existed the elaborately organised family system of a people not yet fully evolved into the political state. Not until the publication of [Lewis H.] Morgan's monumental study on *Ancient Society*, was the key to the study of American native civilisation really found and placed in the hands of the student. The same key will yet unlock the doors which guard the secrets of our native Celtic civilisation and make them possible of fuller comprehension for the multitude.[1]

In studying early Celtic society, the thesis of Connolly and supporting writers, seems totally acceptable. When an Irish clan, or community, occupied a territory it belonged to the clan as a community. The territory was delimited by natural boundaries and it was then divided for the benefit of the community. Sections of land were appropriated by the ruler and the civil service class (*flaith*) in return for the work of their position in society. Every clansman (*ceile*) also received a piece of land to work and develop. A large section of land, called the *Fearann Fine*, was retained for the entire clan as common land which everyone was entitled to use. This was good pastoral and agricultural land, not unuseable ground which no one else wanted. Another section of land, called the *Cumhall Senorba*, was set aside for the maintenance of the poor, the old, and incapable members of the clan. Those who had their own plot were expected to pay taxes for the upkeep of the community, paying for the support of the poor, aged and orphans. If a man fell behind with his taxes, the surviving relatives were not made to pay his debts, for the Irish law humanely stated: "every dead man kills his liabilities".

The land worked by the *ceile*, the *flaith* and chief was not theirs to do what they willed with it. In his study of the Brehon Laws, Ginnell points out "no such thing as absolute ownership of land existed".[2] This is confirmed by Montgomery's study of land ownership in Ireland: "To the original conception of an organisation of this nature the idea of individual property in the land is totally foreign; the rights of the individual being at most merely a more or less temporary usufruct of the soil by consent of the family group, the reversion remaining in the community."[3] The *Corus Brescna* states: "No person should grant land ... unless by the common consent of the tribe, and that he leaves his share of the common lands to revert to the common possession of the tribe after him." Montgomery adds: "The theory of common ownership recognised no right of alienation by the individual of his share of the tribe land, and even in the Brehon Laws this doctrine holds, 'every tribesman is able to keep his tribe land, he is not to sell it, or alienate it, or conceal it, or give it to pay for any crime or contract'." Even the disposal of chattels, such as cattle, had some restrictions. When the man wanted to dispose of any such goods he had to inform the *flaith* and seek permission from his sept or clan.

The idea of common ownership is simply illustrated in the *Senchus Mor's* "Bee Judgement" which states that the owner of bees was by law obliged to distribute a portion of honey among his neighbours every third year "because the bees had gathered the honey off the neighbours' lands." This is similarly practised in the Welsh equivalent of the Brehon Laws, the Laws of Hywel Dda. Irish law treatise declares that the observance of common rules in agriculture is one of the fundamental institutions of Ireland. From both the Welsh and Irish law tracts the practice of ploughing with a large eight-ox plough shows that a co-operative of several interested parties had to be involved.

The principles of Celtic common ownership survived for a surprisingly long time. In Scotland, for example, Skene states: "Yet though the conscious Socialist movement be a century old, the labouring folk all down the ages have clung to communist practices and customs, partly the inheritance and instinct from the group and clan life of forefathers and partly because these customs were their only barrier to poverty and because without them social life was impossible."[4] As late as 1847, says Skene, there were still places in the Outer Hebrides where the land was tilled, sowed and reaped in common, and the produce divided among the workers in accordance with the old Celtic ways. The old feast of *Nábachd* (*Nábaicheachd*—neighbourliness) was still held there when men drew their pieces of land by lot. The produce of certain lots were set apart for the poor, and fines went to a common fund to buy fresh stock. John Rae, writing in the *Fortnightly Review* in 1895, says the communal system was still current in Islay and in St. Kilda where they "distributed the fishing rocks among themselves by lot", while in Barra "they cast lots once a year for the several fishing grounds in the deep seas off their shores". Fines went to a common fund. In Wales, the system, according to Henri Hubert, in *The Greatness and Decline of the Celts*, seems to have survived into the 14th century when feudalism replaced it.

The basic principles of the old system lasted into 19th century rural Ireland, causing Engels, on a visit, to observe: ". . . professors of political economy and jurists complain of the impossibility of importing the idea of modern private property to the Irish farmers. Property that has only rights and no duties is absolutely beyond the ken of the Irishman. No wonder that so many Irishmen who are suddenly cast into one of the modern great cities of England and America, among a population with entirely different moral and legal standards, despair of all morals and justice, lose all hold and become an easy prey to demoralisation."

Ancient Irish society was a class society inasmuch as there were six basic social categories. It was possible, however, for a person to rise from the lowest order of the society to the highest, and likewise fall in the same manner. Ginnell maintains that the criteria for one's position in society was property. "Their complex political, social and military system was avowedly based on the possession of wealth to an even greater extent than the system founded at Rome by Servius Tullius." Here I would disagree with Ginnell and maintain that one's position in society was granted according to one's ability and one's service to the community. By this I do not mean military service, for it is an interesting phenomenon of Celtic society that there are few cases of people achieving military distinction who were rewarded by grants of land from the community. If Ginnell's contention was true, it would have given rise to a society consistently seeking personal property in order to raise their status, a social system totally alien to the Celtic one, and totally contrary to Celtic law of land ownership.

The Celtic class, or social grading, system, beginning at the bottom of the scale, had a grouping which must be termed as the "non freemen". Many historians, "imbued with the conception of feudalistic or capitalistic social order", to quote Connolly, have referred to the "non freemen" as slaves. By trying to find analogous titles in the feudal order historians of many generations have been misled. To describe the "non freemen" as slaves is erroneous. A closer comparison would be to law breakers in recent French law where a penalty of civil degradation was passed by the Chambre Civique. This meant a loss of civil rights, cessation of pensions, prohibition to practise in professions or be employed in the civil service. Ginnell comments: "There being no prisons or convict settlements in Ireland, except where the natural prison afforded by a small island was available, reduction to a species of slavery, permanent or temporary, was considered a reasonable punishment of criminals guilty of capital offences... and of criminals who could not or would not satisfy fines imposed on them." Therefore, the "non freemen" class was basically a convict class serving out sentences imposed on them by the laws of society. The humanism of Celtic society was against taking away the physical freedom of the offender, preferring simply to prevent the offender from being elected to any position of leadership in the society until he had redeemed himself. Offenders were not excluded from society but were placed in a position where they were made to contribute to its welfare.

The "non freemen" class was sub-divided into three. The lowest was the *fuidhir*. This consisted of cowards who deserted their clan when needed, prisoners of war, and hostages, not born in the clan territory. No *fuidhir* was entitled to bear arms or have any political or clan rights. The *saer-fuidhir* could, however, work land on his own, paying taxes for its use, while the *daer-fuidhir*, those who were untrustworthy and in constant rebellion against the system, could not. But Ginnell points out, "the lowest of them were regarded as intelligent persons, as human beings, not mere chattels." The *fuidhir* remained in this state until he redeemed himself by working or, if he were a prisoner of war, until a tribute had been paid. The third generation *fuidhir* was automatically granted full citizenship in the clan, could intermarry and become eligible for election to any office—even that of chief. St. Patrick, the patron saint of Ireland, was a *fuidhir*, having been taken prisoner in his homeland of Wales.

Above the *fuidhir* in the "non freemen" class, were the *bothach* and the *sen-cleithe*. The *bothach* (from *bothan*—a cabin) was allowed to be a crofter or a cow herder while the *sen-cleithe* was a house servant or herdsman. Ginnell believes that these two types consisted of people born in the territory. They had no restrictions regarding who they could work for in the territory. They were not allowed to leave the clan territory, however, except by special permission. Although they had no political or clan rights they were capable of acquiring their own plots of land by contract and by this means returning to their former status as full citizens.

If, individually, a group of "non freemen" could not qualify for enough land to give them a voice as full citizens of the clan, they were allowed by law to form a guild or a commune, and, having cultivated their communal property for a period of time, automatically qualified, electing one man as their speaker in clan affairs. The right to form such partnerships was also given to artisans and others in industry and these partnerships were an important economic feature of ancient Ireland. The idea that these "non freemen" were analogous to slaves is therefore completely ridiculous. The idea of one man holding another in servile bondage was completely alien to Celtic philosophy and, as Ginnell points out, the Brehon Law "was distinctly and uniformly adverse to slavery".

The next step in social grading from the "non freemen" class was freemen, who did not work their own plots of land but who hired themselves to others or grazed their cattle on the communal land. They took part in the clan's military muster as full citizens but, because they were classed as "itinerants", they had little political say. These "itinerant freemen" were extremely few. The next social grading was the *ceile*, the basis of the whole society, the free clansmen who worked a plot of land, paid taxes for the upkeep of the community, and formed the army in time of war. The *ceile* worked out their political decisions and ideas by means of an electoral system, electing local assemblies to administer clan affairs.

Graded above the *ceile* was the *flaith* who has been called a "noble"—indeed, such is the meaning of the word in modern Irish. Again a misconception has arisen by historians trying to equate Celtic terms with terms in a totally alien system. The *flaith*, far from being a "noble", was a civil servant, a public officer elected by the people to carry out the administrative work of the local assemblies. He was assigned land for use while he was alive in return for his duties. These duties were as state receiver of taxes and executive officer for the welfare of the community. He was bound to keep roads and bridges in repair, supervise the running of hospitals, the orphanage, the poor homes, the *bruighen* (public hostel), exercise police duties, maintain the public mill, the public fishing nets, arrange entertainment for visiting dignitaries and, in time of war, organise the army and act as quartermaster general. The *flaith* also had to make sure the farmers were supplied. If a *ceile* had a surplus of stock he had to inform the *flaith* so that if another was short a balance could be kept. Every *flaith* was controlled by the local assembly and, as they were elected from the *ceile* social grading, they could by no stretch of the imagination be termed an aristocracy.

The next social grading was the professional classes, the Druids, Bards, Brehons, Ollamhs (chief jurors), jurors and doctors. The Druids have been erroneously called a "religious caste" who fulfilled not only religious functions but political ones as well. They were certainly not a caste and anyone with aptitude could undertake the strenuous training required to become a Druid. This is not to deny that there were some druidic families in much the same way as some families carry on certain professions today. The function of the Druid was basically as minister of the Celtic religion, which had a complete doctrine of immortality and a moral system. Druids taught that death is only a changing of place and that life goes on with its forms and goods in another world, a world of the dead which gives up living men. Therefore a constant exchange of souls takes place between the two worlds : death in this world brings a soul to the other, death in the other world brings a soul to this one. Julius Caesar observed that this religious outlook could have accounted for the reckless bravery of the Celts in battle, with their apparent complete lack of fear of death. The Druids were also the philosophers of society. In fact, Aristotle states that early Greek philosophers borrowed much of their philosophy from the Celts. Cicero comments that the Druids were also great natural scientists who had knowledge of physics and astronomy applied in the construction of calendars. The earliest known Celtic calendar dates from the 1st century A.D. and has a highly sophisticated five year synchronisation of lunation with the solar year and is far more accurate than the rudimentary Julian calendar or the one in use today. This is the *Calendrier de Coligny*, now in the Palais des Arts at Lyons. It is also by far the oldest known extensive document in a Celtic language. The Druids were also historians and educators : it was they who ran the schools and higher education. They were political advisers, exempt from military service, and were thus allowed to wander the country freely.

The Brehons, Ollamhs and jurors were those trained in jurisprudence, giving judgement on all suits. The Druids, however, appear to have been experts on "international" law, acting as arbiters in disputes between territorial groups. The jurors were men with some legal knowledge and numbered twelve in any legal case. Little is known of their qualifications for office. They appeared to be members of the local assembly and arranged such things as the division of the common lands of the clan. All the professional classes had to go through rigorous training. In law, for example, "no person is qualified to plead a cause in the high court unless he is skilled in every department of legal science", says a Brehon law tract.

The highest social grading was the "ruling class", the chiefs. There was a whole scale of chiefs ranging from clan chiefs, provincial chiefs, to the overall ruler—the Ard Rí, commonly called the High King of Ireland. All chiefs were elected and there were two qualifications: they had to be capable of carrying out the job involved, and usually they were elected from one particular family used to the problems the chief would encounter, but there was no such concept as primogeniture. Ginnell states: "The feudal principle of primogeniture was not recognised by the law in regard to either rank or property. Instead of it, and in contrast with it, the law provided for election to every office, with the addition that the most worthy should be elected." It was difficult for a chief to usurp his power for he was limited and hemmed in by his office, "and so dependent on his clan," says Ginnell, "that it was easier for him to promote the welfare of his people and safer for him to conform to the intention of the law than to become either negligent or despotic." The chief, in strong contrast with the feudal conception of rulers, was not in any sense a law maker but simply an officer of the law established. He was president of the clan assemblies, commander of the forces in war and usually a judge in the public courts. "On the whole the office resembled as much that of a president of a republic," says Ginnell. The idea that the most worthy should succeed as chief and not succession by primogeniture has been frequently misunderstood by many historians who have even stated that the Celtic succession must have been a blood thirsty business, for "hardly ever did a son succeed his father to the throne"!

Before leaving the status of people in Celtic society it must be observed that woman had an important place. Professor Eoin MacNeill states: "The status of women in ancient Irish Law and the social prominence of women in ancient Irish literature have been found remarkable." Certainly the female had a unique place in comparison with other civilisations. She could be elected as chief, lead her clan to battle or in defence of their territory and, in Irish law, the wife remains mistress of all she has brought into a marital partnership. The electoral-inheritance system of chieftainship very often passed through the female line as exemplified in the ancient sagas of the Ulster Cycle. Women were much protected by Law. If a woman died a violent death attributed to malice or neglect of a man various penalties were imposed. Offences against the honour of a woman caused the imposition of heavy fines. The execution of a woman was strictly forbidden, even if she had committed a premeditated murder. Women who killed were exiled.

The basis of the early Irish law, known as the Brehon Law (from *breitheamh*—a judge), first codified in the 5th century A.D., was arbitration. Disputes could only lead to arbitration and compensation. The death penalty for a crime was enacted only in extreme cases. It was for the injured party to compel the injurer to accept the arbitration and under the law there was a custom of ritual fasting as a method of asserting one's rights. The Brehon Law finds its closest parallel in traditional Hindu law. Ritual fasting is, of course, an integral part of Hindu philosophy.

One of the most fascinating and progressive aspects of early Irish society was the attitude to medicine. Among the ancient "barbarian" peoples (such as the Germanic tribes) the sick and feeble were often put to death. Even in the civilisations of Egypt, Assyria, Babylonia, Greece and Rome, there was no provision made for the ailing poor. Though Greece and Rome attained the highest degree of artistic culture, their treatment of the sick was scarcely equal to those they termed "barbarians". Both civilisations regarded disease as a curse inflicted by supernatural powers and rather sought to propitiate the malevolent deity than to organise relief work. It was not until *circa* A.D. 400 that Fabiola is said to have founded the first hospital in Rome. But there were two remarkable exceptions to this state of affairs. One was the Buddhists of Eastern India who, under their leader Azoka, established the first Eastern hospital in 252 B.C., while the second was the establishment of a hospital near Ard Macha (Armagh, Ulster) by the semi-mythical ruler Macha in 300 B.C. Macha has three namesakes in Irish tradition, each a goddess. Although the story belongs to Irish mythology, it is certainly historically true that the Irish evolved a medical service, a European renowned surgery system and a prototype "national health service" whereby sick maintenance (including curative treatment, attendance and nourishing food) had to be made available to all who needed it. Under the Brehon Law the responsibility of providing for the sick, wounded and mentally handicapped was placed in the hands of the clan. The exceptional working of this system was undoubtedly due in large part to the clan system whereby a man was not one of an immense number of citizens in a country—he was a member of a particular clan and the clan made provision for the welfare of its members.

Both the Senchus Mor and Book of Aicill are explicit on the rights of the sick. If, for example, a man incapacitated another (intentionally or unintentionally) he had to provide a physician, food and a stay in hospital, as well as a substitute to carry on the sick man's work. If a criminal, or an aggressor in a fight, was wounded and then submitted to law, the man had to be taken to hospital and his upkeep paid for. If he was found guilty, the payment of the treatment was recoverable from him. From the Socialist viewpoint it is interesting to note that the Law of Torts states "full sick maintenance (must be paid) to a worker injured for the sake of unnecessary profit."[5] The main point of the Brehon Laws on the subject of sick maintenance was that no one in early Irish society needed to fear illness. Not only were they assured of treatment and hospitalisation but the society would not let them or their dependents lack food or means of livelihood.

Because of the advanced Irish medical system, the laws also had to govern physicians. Not only did the Brehon Laws provide protection against a physician who performed an operation which made the patient worse, but the physician was protected from the patient and his attendants who concealed or gave false information about his symptoms. Physicians, usually consultants at the clan hospital, were expected to keep at least four medical students in their house and to teach them the profession by observation. In many teaching hospitals today, the "direct method" is

regarded as the best for making practical physicians and to give
them a good clinical knowledge of medicine. At the same time it
was good for the physician to know that he was on trial before
his keen students who, gradually gaining experience, forced him
to his best efforts.

The early Irish society recognised that a physician should not
be so busy with his practice that he could not study and keep up
with modern techniques. From time to time the clan made a
grant so, in the words of the Brehon Laws, "he might be
preserved from being disturbed by the cares and anxieties of life
and enabled to devote himself to the study and work of his
profession." Irish physicians were acclaimed throughout Europe
and the premier school of medicine, founded in the 5th century,
was at Tuaim Brecain, Co. Cavan. This was the school of the
eminent physician Bracan Mac Findloga.

The Brehon Laws were very explicit on "lawful" and "unlawful" physicians. "Quack" doctors were liable to severe penalties
which were even more drastic among the early Irish than they
are among most of the states of the world today. The Irish recognised that it was rather easy to deceive people who were ill and
who, desperately seeking a cure, would grasp at any straw to
secure it. Large fines were imposed on "quacks" who pretended
to be qualified surgeons. On the other hand, the qualified physician was held responsible for the treatment of his patients and
compensation had to be paid if, for example, a wound he had
healed broke open after a certain time.

Likewise the law was specific on hospital conditions. The
hospital was known as "the House of the Territory" to indicate
that it cared for the sick in a given district. The staff (apart from
the physician and medical students) were volunteers. The Brehon
Laws state that the hospital should be free from debt, should
have four doors and should have fresh water at hand while dogs,
fools and people likely to cause the patients worry were to be
kept away from the hospital. As well as the sick, the feeble,
elderly and orphans were also cared for.

Travellers were afforded the utmost hospitality and each clan
had its *bruighen*, public hostel, which was looked after by a full
time *brughaidh*, public hostel manager, who maintained the
roads leading to his hostel and kept a light burning all night in
accordance with the law to aid travellers. Special emphasis was
placed on education and the Celtic attitude was not to instil

a knowledge into children but rather to foster a healthy hunger for knowledge among them. Padraic Pearse pointed out : "To the old Irish the teacher was *aite*, "fosterer", the pupil was *dalta*, "foster-child", the system was *aiteachas*, "fosterage"; words we still retain as *oide, dalta, oideachas*" (modern Irish for teacher, pupil and education).

Culturally, the Irish literary tradition was an oral one; all the laws, histories, folk-stories, poetry etc. were committed to memory by the druids and bards, hence the long apprenticeship a druid had to undergo before he qualified. The first written form of Irish was Ogam script, consisting of short lines drawn to or crossing a base line. Then the Irish adopted the Latin alphabet and script to Irish. This semi-uncial script, is now called "Gaelic script". The Irish language became the third written language of Europe, after Greek and Latin, and a wealth of literature was committed to writing mainly by monks who tended to Christianise and bowdlerise ancient Irish mythology. Despite their Christian veneer, compared to Greek myths, the Irish sagas still remain a vigorous literature.

Briefly, then, the early Irish society was a highly complexed civilisation which, as Connolly suggested, exercised a communistic system. But Connolly pointed out "communal ownership of the land would undoubtedly have given way to the private owned system of capitalist landlordism, even if Ireland had remained an independent country." Ginnell maintains that the Irish social system started to decay about the 8th century A.D. and states that the reasons were "chiefly contact and friction with non-Celtic elements, beginning with the wars with the Danes, which deranged the mechanism and disturbed the smooth operation of the Gaelic system." He says one of the problems arose from the *flaith* class who, after contact with foreign elements, began to see the personal advantages of an hereditary system in their favour. "In fact, the *flaith* were rather too well provided for, and were so favourably circumstanced that ultimately they almost supplanted the clan as the owners of everything."

Montgomery places the decay of the Celtic system from the time of the introduction of institutionalised Christianity in the country. The theoretical aspects of Christianity were not very much opposed to the older Celtic religious philosophies and the marrying of the philosophies was a fairly easy step. By using

native customs, ceremonies and interpretations, the Church institution which may be termed the Celtic Church, independent of
Rome, became a powerful force. But the orientation of the
Church towards Roman feudalistic institutions caused a rejection
of many of the Celtic concepts. Montgomery writes :

> The Church lands were in the first place probably granted by
> the tribe from the common stock, and the Brehon Law recognises
> to a very remarkable extent the claims of "the tribe of the Saint"
> to support. The most important influence exerted by the Church
> on the system of land holding is that it undoubtedly did much,
> from more or less selfish ends, to aid free alienation of land. The
> *Corus Brescna* shows that in the case of acquisitions the Church
> had made great inroads on the restrictions imposed on alienation
> by the tribal system; and that even in allotments a successful at-
> tack had been made on the original inviolability of tribal posses-
> sion as far as regards alienation to the Church.[6]

Montgomery points out that the Church's ecclesiastical laws
began to mould Irish society's original conception of land ownership. "An examination of the Brehon Laws shows that there
can be little doubt that the growth of this power of alienation
found if not its origin at least its most fostering elements in the
influence of the Church." Under the influence of the Church
and helped by the disruptive influence of the Norse invaders, the
feudalistic idea began to spread in Ireland. Montgomery again
writes : ". . . at the end of the 10th or beginning of the 11th
century the Irish people were in a state of transition from common property to several ownership, the Brehon writers themselves
favouring the theory of private property." He adds : "In addition, a change which took place in the social organisation of
society, namely the increase in the power of the chief, had a large
influence in breaking up the archaic theory of communism in the
soil." The attempted re-organisation of Irish society was necessi-
tated by major military attacks by the Danes. A militarising of
society with greater power to the provincial chiefs, with standing
mercenary armies, began to replace the previous system. Attempts
to change the Celtic social system were, however, generally unsuccessful before the Anglo-Norman invasion of 1172. In 1070,
for example, Toirdelbach Ó Briain was Ard Rí of Ireland. He
tried to force the Tulach Óg, a clan in the north west, to accept
a friend of his, Conchobhar Ó Briain, as their chief. This was a

complete violation of the laws of succession and overrode the elective power of the clan assembly. The clan rejected Ó Briain by armed rebellion. Another ruler Toirdelbach Ó Conchobhair tried to make his son ruler of the Norse-Irish clans of Dublin but he was also driven out. A similar experiment was tried in Meath. These examples show us that, by contact with the new feudalistic ideas fostered by the Church, some of the Irish rulers were trying to usurp their authority but were kept well in check by public opinion. In fact, after the Anglo-Norman invasion, the persistence of Irish Law for centuries after the introduction of fedualism is without parallel in other countries. The reason is to be found in the rooted position of the Celtic communistic attitude in the national culture. Ginnell comments:

> The idea of private property in land was developing and gathering strength, and land was generally becoming settled under it. The title of every holder, once temporary, was hardening into ownership, and the old ownership of the clan was vanishing, becoming in ordinary cases little more than a superior jurisdiction the exercise of which was rarely invoked.[7]

But according to Montgomery:

> It was doubtless the case, nevertheless, that the idea of tribal possession was deeply ingrained in the Celtic race at the time when Sir John Davies commuted the Irish land tenures. However, far in reality the steady march of time has advanced the feudalisation of land, which in Aryan races seems always to have gone hand in hand with increase of population and the growth of the power of the chief, the idea of landlord and tenant was still strange to the Irish mind and its compulsory imposition on an unwilling people was probably a fatal mistake.[8]

Chapter 2

FEUDALISM

THE BIGGEST AND most active agency in preparing the way for the feudalisation of Ireland and the invasion of the Anglo-Normans was the Church. The Celtic Christian Church which tolerated native laws and customs was now being "centralised" to Rome and the Roman ideology was supplanting the Celtic one. The Celtic Church differed from the Roman Church basically by the fact that each abbey corresponded to the clan territory and its influence decreased or was augmented according to the fortunes of the clan. Hayden and Moonan write:

> Each clan had its own bishop, and its own priests, the diocese was merely the district occupied by the clan. There was naturally a great number of bishops . . . and it was not until the 12th century that the present system of definite diocese grouped in provinces, was introduced. The clan alloted to its clergy, for their support, certain lands . . . looked after by an officer who was generally a layman. The clergy of a clan mostly lived in communities under their bishop, so that the church was both tribal and monastic.[1]

This did not, of course, mean a total restriction of influence; scholars or monks sometimes were attracted to a particular abbey from other parts of Ireland or from overseas. Not only in Ireland but in Celtic Brittany also a lengthy struggle took place before the community system was steamrollered into the static territorial Roman system. Although it was the Church which had the historic role of undermining the Celtic social system, the system was fated to be overthrown by a strong centralised system from outside in the light of European social development. To conjecture, the Ard Rí, to prevent the conquest of Ireland, would probably have had to centralise the system at the expense of the provincial chiefs. Similarly, Strongbow, the Norman leader, to establish himself as king and keep Ireland outside Henry II's domain would equally have had to centralise the Celtic system.

The Church in Ireland was dismayed at the lack of a centralised political state ruled by a strong autocrat. The Church was also dismayed that a large number of Irish refused to accept the dogma of the Christian institution and treated its clergy with little respect. For example, while churches within a clan territory were respected, raiding parties were not always too hesitant about plundering one that belonged to their enemies. One of the Irish Church's most zealous reformers was Maelmaedoc Ó Morgair, born in Armagh in 1095. Maelmaedoc, afterwards sanctified by a grateful Church, described his fellow countrymen to Bernard, Abbot of Clairvaux, in the following terms:

> He discovered it was not to men but to beasts he had been sent; in all the barbarism which he had yet encountered, he had never met such a people so profligate in their morals, so uncouth in their ceremonies, so impious in faith, so barbarous in laws, so rebellious to discipline, so filthy in life, Christian in name but Pagans in reality.

In that age the adherence to local and national customs as against the general practices of the Church was often denounced impious and barbarous. One muses whether it is with a faint touch of irony that Bernard wonders how "so saintly and lovable a man (as Maelmaedoc) could come out of such a race." Maelmaedoc was not alone among the Irish Hierarchy in condemning his people. Cellach, Gilla Maic Liac, both of whom held the bishopric of Connor; Gillebert, Bishop of Limerick; Lorcán, Archbishop of Dublin, and Flaithbertach Ó Broicháin, abbot of Derry, were in favour of the establishment of a feudal episcopal state. Professor Curtis writes that the Irish Hierarchy "concluded that the defects and backward state of their Church and nation were justification for subjecting their native land to a foreign king as one destined by Heaven and the Vicar of Christ to reform otherwise hopeless abuses."[2] It would appear that the Irish Hierarchy, who were in close touch with Rome, actually connived at the invasion of their country in order for a more strict feudal Church and religion to be imposed. Maelmaedoc was a prime mover in trying to extend episcopal jurisdiction over the country and uniting the Church in thirty-six dioceses subject to the primacy of Armagh. He paid two visits to Rome, one in 1139 when he was received by Pope Innocent II.

The attitudes and, perhaps, the advice of the Irish Hierarchy was obviously taken into account when Pope Adrian IV granted a Bull Laudabiliter in 1154-5 giving his blessing to Henry II of England to invade Ireland and "enlarge the bounds of the Church, to teach the truth of Christian faith to the ignorant and rude, and to extirpate the roots of vice from the field of the Lord." In return, Henry was to pay an annual sum to the Pope's coffers. The fact that Adrian was an Englishman has been over-emphasised by certain Irish Church historians, indeed some have even denied the existence of the Bull. But Pope Alexander III also "handed over" Ireland on behalf of the Church. That the Irish Hierarchy knew that Rome supported the invaders there is no question. That they had forced their clergy and laity to accept the invasion as the "will of God" must follow. "Nothing else can explain their amazing surrender before the English king," says Curtis. The Irish clergy had therefore embraced feudalism, a system repugnant to the ordinary Irishman, long before it was enforced on Ireland. As Montgomery points out: "The Brehon Laws certainly show a system to which the notion of feudal ownership is completely foreign . . ." The acceptance of the Papal Bull was also an acceptance of the Pope's right to dispose of Ireland and its people as he wished by the belief that the Pope had feudal lordship over the whole earth.

If the Irish Hierarchy, however, had thought the feudalisation of Ireland was going to be an easy process through the Anglo-Norman invasion they were disappointed. It took five centuries to destroy Irish society. As Connolly wrote :

> . . . coming as it did in obedience to the pressure of armed force from without, instead of by the operation of economic forces within, this change has been bitterly and justly resented by the vast mass of the Irish people, many of whom still mix their dreams of liberty with longings for a return to the ancient system of land tenure—now organically impossible.[3]

The immediate cause of the Anglo-Norman invasion was the result of a tussle for the position of Ard Rí of Ireland. Between 1156 and 1166 there were two candidates for the position— Murtough Mac Lochlainn of Ailech and Rory O'Conor of

Connacht. Dermot Mac Murrough of Leinster supported Mac Lochlainn while Tiernán O'Rourke, of Breifne, supported O'Conor. O'Conor emerged triumphant and with Mac Lochlainn dead, Mac Murrough fled from Ireland in August, 1166. He was determined to win back his provincial chieftainship and tried to interest Henry II who, at that time, was too busy consolidating his Angevin empire which covered England, Normandy, Anjou, Poitou and Aquitaine, with claims over Scotland, Wales and Toulouse. Finally, Mac Murrough interested Richard FitzGilbert de Clare, Earl of Pembroke (known as Strongbow in Irish history). Strongbow had fallen out of favour with Henry II and was looking for some new quest to interest him. Mac Murrough promised him the right of succession to the chieftainship of Leinster and the hand of his eldest daughter Aoife in marriage. Eager to get back to Ireland, Mac Murrough took a small army of Normans, Flemings and Welsh, and arrived back in 1167. The Irish under the Ard Rí, O'Conor, attacked this invasion force and defeated it. Two years later, in May, 1169, the Anglo-Norman invasion proper began.

Some 200 knights and 1,200 men-at-arms arrived in Ireland under Strongbow. In August Waterford fell and the south-east was in Norman hands. The Normans marched on to Dublin and the men of Dublin were persuaded to sue for peace by Laurence O'Toole, the archbishop of the city. While negotiations were being carried on, however, the Normans burst into the city and it fell on September 21, 1170. In the spring of 1171 Mac Murrough died and Strongbow, who had married Aoife, now claimed the "kingship" of Leinster by hereditary right. The Leinster clans revolted at this over-riding of their electoral process and promptly elected Murtough, nephew of Mac Murrough, as their chief. The Normans were now beset by large Irish armies under Murtough, Rory O'Conor, O'Rourke, O'Carroll from Ulster and the Norse army of Hasculf Mac Torcail, the Dano-Irish king of Dublin. With their supplies cut off and besieged, Strongbow, whose real wish had been to gain the kingship of Ireland for himself, sent Raymond le Gros to Henry II in Normandy offering him all the possessions he had taken in Ireland as his suzerain lord. In return, he urged Henry to send reinforcements. Before Henry arrived in Ireland, however, Strongbow managed to extricate his beleaguered army and defeat the Irish. In October, 1171, Henry II landed with 500 knights and 4,000 men-at-arms and received the lordship of Ireland from Strongbow.

The same month a Curia Regis was held at Lismore at which council it was stated that the laws of England were accepted under oath by the conquerors. All laws enacted followed the feudal polity, Henry's object being to assert his feudal lordship over the Anglo-Norman barons and Irish chiefs. Montgomery states:

> ... all laws enacted by him when in Ireland followed the feudal polity and the estates granted were in consideration of homage, fealty and military or honorary service; the grantees under tenure then created being tenants *in capite*, examples being the tenure on which Strongbow received the principality of Leinster and Hugh de Lacy the seigniory of Meath.[4]

Having been defeated in the field, the Ard Rí, Rory O'Conor, began to sue for peace and many Irish chiefs submitted to Henry. With the seeming success of the Anglo-Norman invasion, the Irish Hierarchy convened a council of bishops during the winter of 1171-2 at Cashel under the guidance of Christian of Lismore, who became the principal figure in the Hierarchy following the death of Maelmaedoc. Curtis comments that the Irish Church "was now to make the final *rapprochement* with Rome coincide with the extinction of native Ireland." The Cashel Council passed several decrees which were submitted to Henry II for confirmation. As well as purely ecclesiastical matters, such as the observance of marriage, baptisms, and masses, some of the decrees attacked the Irish social system bringing laws in line with feudalism. One decree directs that the Irish pay tithes in corn, cattle and other produce to the Church. Another freed all Church property from the jurisdiction of the clans and freed the Church from having to contribute to the community by giving refection, lodging or gifts of food to the clan which the decree describes as "a detestable practice". Another decree places all clergy above the clan law, excusing them from paying fines if guilty of breaking the law—even the crime of homicide. As for ecclesiastical practices, the Cashel Council decided: "the divine offices shall be celebrated according to the forms of the Church of England." Curtis adds: "The bishops indeed went the whole way to oblige Henry and, if we are to believe reputable chroniclers of the next century, each of them gave him a letter with his seal attached, confirming to Henry and his heirs the kingdom of Ireland."

Satisfied at his progress in Ireland, Henry returned to England in April, 1172. A few months later, in September, Pope Alexander III wrote three letters from Tusculum. One letter was to the Irish Hierarchy ordering them to assist Henry II to keep possession of Ireland and to censure those who broke their oaths of loyalty to him. A second letter to Henry bids him carry on his good work in the "acquisition" of Ireland. The third letter was to the chiefs of Ireland and commends them "for receiving him (Henry) as king of their own free will." Curtis comments:

> The Irish Church had submitted on cosmopolitan and religious grounds and we may call the bishops honest and disinterested, if ingenuous, men. In reformers such as Malachy (Maelmaedoc) and Christian, patriotism had been swallowed up by a zeal for the Church Universal.[5]

In October, 1175, Rory O'Conor and Henry II concluded a treaty at Windsor by which O'Conor was to continue as Ard Rí of the unconquered areas of Ireland under Henry's lordship on condition he would pay annual tribute to him. The Anglo-Norman barons would continue in the areas conquered, which became known as the English Pale. The treaty did not work because Henry could not (or did not want to) restrain the Anglo-Norman adventurers from grabbing more and more Irish land. Also O'Conor had lost the respect of the Irish people and there were moves to oust him even as ruler of his own province of Connacht. In May, 1177, by permission of Pope Alexander III. Henry made his eleven-year-old son, John, lord of Ireland. The Irish Hierarchy gladly accepted this and published his title at a Synod of Dublin. In 1185, John, then nineteen years old, landed at Waterford with 300 knights and 3,000 men-at-arms in order to strengthen the English colonisation of the country. According to Montgomery ". . . the English settlers strove by force to gain possession of the broad lands so glibly granted them and they built castles and made freeholds but no tenures or services were reserved for the Crown." It was John who, by building a castle in Dublin in 1204-15, began the rule by "Dublin Castle" and created a centralisation to Dublin.

Within the English Pale the feudal system was fully followed.

In the Irish Church, according to Curtis, "bishops and abbots in their secular aspect became feudal potentates and barons under the crown." However, the Anglo-Normans were soon making inroads into the Irish Church and by 1216 John directed that no Irishman should be promoted to the chapter of a cathedral church in case he elected Irishmen to the bishoprics. Irish "nationalist" factions formed within the church, angered by the Anglo-Norman plunder of church property and the Anglo-Norman clerics appointed to Irish livings. It is perhaps ironic that the Irish Church, having welcomed the attack on their fellow countrymen to strengthen their own position, now developed "nationalist" tendencies because they were the subject of attack. In 1213 Henry de Londres, Archbishop of Dublin, Papal Legate and Justiciary of Ireland, perpetrated what Sigerson in his *History of the Land Tenures in Ireland*, describes as the first "agrarian outrage". He summoned everyone to come before him with proof, written deeds, to their ownership of lands within the Pale. Having gathered up these deeds he burnt them, it would seem in an attempt to improve his own property holdings. He barely escaped with his life from the outraged colonists.

But English power in Ireland was on the wane and even the limits of the colony of the Pale were diminishing. Montgomery states:

> Slowly but surely, however, the Celtic race had been absorbing to itself and incorporating in its being the descendants of the proud Norman settler barons. Severed from England and tied to the land of their adoption, the subtle influence of the soil and the alteration in the blood by admixture of race, had their natural effect. The amalgamation was aided, moreover, by the wild anarchy of the land.[6]

By the 16th century the colonists were almost all absorbed into Irish nationality and only in a few towns within the Pale was a language other than Irish spoken. It must, of course, be remembered that at the time of the invasion the English nobility spoke Norman-French. Many of the invading troops were Welsh, and therefore spoke a sister Celtic language to the Irish, while many more were Flemings. It was only in the period 1350—1400 that the English language began to oust French in England. Therefore, the varying languages of the invaders made their assimilation all the more possible. With this general assimilation came a revival of law, land tenures and social order. Curtis comments :

> . . . while they retained English feudal tenures, rules of land succession and inheritance and much manorial jurisdiction and custom, they took over, as something too deeply rooted and indeed too suited to the country to be displaced, the old Gaelic communal organisation.[7]

The first parliament of Anglo-Norman barons had been summoned in 1297 in Dublin with French as the official language. At a Dublin parliament in 1541 the Earl of Ormond had to translate a speech from English into Irish so that the Anglo-Norman barons could understand it. The "defection" of the colonists was not tamely tolerated by the Crown in London or its adherents in the Pale. In 1341 a "general resumption of all the lands, liberties, seignories and jurisdiction that had been granted in Ireland not only by Edward III himself but also by his father" was enacted. In 1342 the colonists, now considered Anglo-Irish, were removed from office under the Crown and in 1355 a series of ordnances were passed forbidding intermarriage. However, says Montgomery, "gradually but surely as time went on the power of the Celtic customs made headway against the English laws and the Anglo-Irish became more and more synonymous with the native race." In 1367 the Statute of Kilkenny tried to stem the tide of Celtic influence over the settlers. It was made treason for settlers to accept the jurisdiction of the Brehon Laws, to speak Irish, to intermarry, or adopt any native customs. But by the end of Henry IV's reign the Speaker of the House of Commons, had to admit that "the greater part of Ireland has been 'conquered' by the natives."

During the period of assimilation the native Irish continued to fight for independence in a series of bloody and fruitless campaigns. They came near success when they invited Edward Bruce, brother of Robert who had managed to drive the English out of Scotland, to become Ard Rí in 1316. One of the basic reasons behind this move was the similarity of culture between Ireland and Scotland. Both Robert and Edward spoke the Scottish Gaelic language which is still fairly intelligible to Irish speakers today. Had Edward Bruce managed to organise the

Irish into a strong centralised front, as his brother had done with
the Scottish chiefs, his venture might have been a success. It is
interesting to note the early unity of the Celtic peoples for
Edward Bruce was also invited to lead the Welsh struggle against
the English. Sir Gruffydd Llwyd urged the Welsh to unite with
the Scots and Irish to gain their freedom. This concept of Celtic
unity was expressed as early as the 10th century by the Welsh
author of *Armes Prydain Fawr* (ironically translated as The
Prophecy of Great Britain) which urged that the Celtic peoples
(Welsh, Irish, Scots, Manx, Cornish and Bretons) unite to drive
the English from their countries.

Henry VIII tried to resuscitate the Anglo-Irish lords and
assimilate the native chiefs to feudalism. Henry assumed the title
of King of Ireland and began by bribing leading native chiefs to
give up their lands and be received as feudal tenants. According
to Froude :

> He desired to persuade them to exchange their system of elec-
> tion for feudal tenure, to acknowledge by a formal act of surren-
> der that they held their lordships under the crown ... in return
> they might retain and administer the more tolerable of their own
> Brehon Laws till a more settled life brought with it a desire for
> English common law.[8]

Many Irish chiefs were delighted at the idea of making their
titles hereditary and lands secure for all time but the majority
continued to conform with the immemorial tradition of the electoral system. As late as 1603 it is recorded that Niall Ó Donnell
convoked the clan according to the custom that he might be
elected chief in due form. He was styled The Ó Donnell without
consulting the king or the king's council. Spenser says that in the
year he visited and wrote in Ireland, 1596, the Irish laws and
customs prevailed virtually undisturbed in the territories of the
Irish chiefs. It is also on record that Cromer, Archbishop of
Armagh and Primate of All Ireland, had to obtain a formal pardon in 1553 for giving a ruling according to the Brehon Laws.
Montgomery comments :

> The two systems of land holding, Brehon and feudal, existed
> side by side; but save where the latter had been imposed by force
> of arms it gained no converts from the native race, and failed to
> alter the ideas of the relation of the occupier of the land. On the

other hand the Brehon Law secured many adherents from among the English invaders.[9]

Such a state of affairs obviously could not be tolerated by the Establishment. The English course of action was voiced by the Master of the Court of Wards, Sir William Parsons: "We must change their (the Irish) course of government, apparel, manner of holding land, language and habit of life. It will otherwise be impossible to set up in them obedience to the laws and to the English Empire."

Chapter 3

THE PLANTATIONS

IT WAS DURING the reign of the Catholic queen, Mary Tudor (1553-8) that the English administration devised its policy to change the Irish "course of government, apparel, manner of holding land, language and habit of life". The method chosen was one which had been successfully used by the Greek city states and by the Romans—plantation. English colonists would form settlements driving out the native Irish from their lands and creating a "New England". The counties of Leix and Offaly were chosen for the experiment. Soldiers cleared the area of its inhabitants, the clans of O'Connor and O'More, and the settlers moved in. They held lands on the condition that they imported and employed only English labour. The O'Mores, especially, fought to retain their clan lands from the colonists, yielding only when the clan was exterminated. This "Leinster Experiment" was unsuccessful partly because the Irish fought hard, burning and harassing the colonists, and partly because not enough colonists could be induced to go to Ireland to "swamp" the natives.

In 1579 a rising took place in Munster centred mainly on the religious issues which were sweeping Europe. The Earl of Desmond, head of the southern branch of the Anglo-Irish Fitzgerald family, was a prime mover in the rising. Having crushed this rising with great severity in 1583, the English administration turned their attention to the "plantation" of Munster. Some 574,628 (English) acres were confiscated by the administration. The land was then parcelled out in lots of 12,000, 8,000, 6,000 and 4,000 acres. A colonist could have a 12,000-acre estate for a rent of £33 6s 8d for three years after which double that amount was payable annually. Every "chief colonist" agreed to bring eighty-six families from England to work the property. The condition of the plantation prescribed that no English planter should allow any "mere Irish" to settle on his property, that the head of each settlement be English, and that female heirs marry only Englishmen. The surge of war, confiscation and the driving out of the native Irish from these lands by which the English extended their colonial grip on Ireland, was another blow against the traditional Irish society.

Two famous Munster colonists were Sir Walter Raleigh, who seized estates of 42,000 acres in Cork and Waterford, and the poet Edmund Spenser, who had a modest 3,026-acre estate in Waterford.

The Munster colonisation was unsuccessful primarily because of a lack of colonists. The colonists were quickly assimilated into the Irish way of life, like the Norman settlers before them. Spenser wrote disgustedly "instead of keeping out the Irish, they do not only make the Irish their tenants in those lands and thrust out the English, but also some of them become mere Irish."

With the plantation of Munster under way the authorities turned their attention to Connaught. In July, 1585, Lord Deputy Perrot issued a commission to the Governor of Connaught calling together "all the chieftans and lordes" . . . "to devise how their titles and rights be affirmed." Frightened by what had happened in Leinster and by what was happening in Munster, the chiefs decided to sign away part of their rights accepting the queen as a feudal monarch, thereby swearing fealty to the queen and obtaining confirmation of their estates, introducing money rents in place of the old Celtic system. Sigerson writes:

> The relations of people and chiefs towards each other and towards the land in that province, altered. The clan lost its ancient power of electing to the headship the individual of its choice. The lands held in trust for it by the chief, in virtue of his office, were permanently alienated to his use and that of his heirs. The customary division of the common lands was stayed, so that they could not be let out but were to remain as commons. The custom of the gavel-kind was forbidden and replaced by "the course and order of the law of England."[1]

Indeed, one Connaught chief, Morrogh O'Flaherty, made a will before he died in 1593 recommending his successor and dividing his lands between his sons because he feared, rightly so, that the Irish law would be superseded by that of the English law of primogeniture.

The province of Ulster was now the heartland of the old Celtic social system and the centre of national opposition to the English conquest. In 1595 the chiefs of Tyrone and Tyrconnell led a grand alliance of the northern Irish clans against the English. The Lord Lieutenant Essex, with 20,000 troops, could not suppress the rising of the great Ulster clans. Recalled in disgrace, Essex gave up his position to Lord Mountjoy who engaged in a policy of frightful devastation, destroying all the food, houses, cattle, men, women and children he could find. Starvation and defeat led the Irish to submit as Elizabeth of England lay dying in 1603. The resulting depopulation of Ulster made its plantation more feasible to the English administration.

"To Elizabeth succeeded James I (of Scotland)," writes Sigerson, "and the Irish expected much from a Celtic king." But James, the Anglicised Scottish monarch, was an eager colonist. In 1603 two Scottish lairds, Hugh Montgomery and James Hamilton, had devised a plantation scheme which had received James's blessing. Con O'Neill, a chief whose clan lands were in Down and Antrim, was in prison. Montgomery and Hamilton offered to effect his rescue if he would sign over two-thirds of his lands to them. James even threw in a knighthood for Con, who was then persuaded to sign over the other third of his clan's property. The settlement run by Montgomery and Hamilton had grown to an estimated 16,000 people by 1614. At the same time Sir Arthur Chichester, the English Lord Deputy for Ireland, had taken lands on the coast of Antrim and created another thriving colony. These successful plantations interested the Stuart monarch. In 1605 the law of *Tanaiste* (election of chiefs) and gavel-kind, by which lands descended to all the sons and not by primogeniture, were abolished by a judgement of the King's bench. The Brehon Laws were described as "a lewd custom" and not laws at all. In 1607 the chiefs of Tyrone and Tyrconnell fled from Ulster and in the following year 511,465 acres were confiscated from the Ulster clans.

Six Ulster counties were escheated—Donegal, Derry (then Coleraine), Tyrone, Armagh, Cavan and Fermanagh—a total of 3,785,057 acres. Much of this land was regarded as useless from the colonisation point of view and it is estimated that only a seventh of the total figure was available for settlement. The main colonisers came from Scotland, mainly from Galloway (from Ayr, Dumfries, Renfrew, Dunbarton and Lanark) which, at this time was still to some extent Scottish Gaelic speaking. Therefore the vast majority of colonists, apart from their Presbyterian religion, had few cultural differences from the native Irish. A large number of colonists arrived from Fife. Captain Edward Burt in his *Letters from a Gentleman*, published in 1730, presents evidence to show that Fyfe was practically monoglot Gaelic speaking before 1707. The extent to which the Scottish Gaelic language was spoken in the "Lowland" area of Scotland is still a very contentious subject due to centuries of Anglicisation in that country. One of the best studies is Prof. William Watson's *History of the Celtic Place Names of Scotland*. The Scottish colonists, therefore, were mainly distinguished from the native Irish by their Presbyterian religion.

James G. Leyburn, in his social history *The Scotch-Irish*, points out that a great deal of intermingling took place between the Celtic Irish and Celtic Scots.

> When James I parcelled out the escheated lands of the Irish lords, the native Irish had been neither exterminated nor driven off to other parts of Ireland. On the contrary, as had been shown, some of the Irish gentry were given new leases, and in defiance of the agreement thousands of Irish peasants were employed on the farms of the planters. Here was the opportunity for daily contact, often of the closest and most intimate sort.[2]

In 1610 the ban between Protestant and Catholic marriages, a testimony to the efforts of the English administration to segregate and subdue the Irish, was lifted " to the great joy of all parties".[3] As Leyburn emphasises, if "great joy" existed then it must have been because the wish to intermarry existed. Arguing the case he writes:

> Finally, it is argued, if the Scots lived their faith to any degree and their Presbyterian ministers preached the word assiduously, as they did, it is unlikely that no Irish converts would be made— and with the religious barrier removed, what could stand in the way of marriage? It is equally unlikely that cases of love between a Scots youth and an Irish girl never led the latter to take her husband's religion for the sake of a happy marriage. Practicality can also be adduced; some farmer needing a wife and unable to find one among his own group, might well make a sensible marriage with an Irish woman of worth; likewise, some Irish woman, recognising realistically that the Scots were in Ulster to stay, that Irish land was permanently alienated, that peace was more im-

portant than constant strife, that Scots were, after all, decent fellows, and that Jock himself was an attractive lad, might break
with Catholicism and take steps to become part of the Scottish
community.[4]

It is interesting today to note that the majority of Protestant
Ulstermen bear Gaelic names while strenuously maintaining that
they are "ethnically" different from the "Catholic Celtic Irish".

For twenty-five years after the first settlements in Ulster, the
colony seemed firmly established but there were always rumours
of native uprisings and conspiracies to throw out the colonists. In
1615 one such conspiracy was suppressed quite ruthlessly. In
fact, life for the colonists in general, until 1690, was a series of
crises when the existence of their settlements seemed threatened.
The conditions of the colonists could be compared to those under
which the settlers of North America laboured with the constant
threat of Indian attack.

Religion was the cause of weakening the colonies in 1639
when Thomas Wentworth, Lord Stafford, Lord Deputy of
Ireland, tried to force all the Scottish colonists to declare their
disapproval of a recent Scottish rebellion against the king's episcopal ordinances. The rebellion of the Scottish National
Covenant in 1638 had re-established Presbyterianism in
Scotland. The Anglican Church was, however, the established
church and Stafford had little time for the Presbyterianism of the
Scottish colonists. All who refused to condemn the rebellion were
severely punished and this caused a mass exodus of colonists.
Wentworth continued a persecution of the Presbyterians on
behalf of the Anglican Church and from 1636-70 most of the
colonists' congregations were without ministers, who had been
forced to leave the country. One group of colonists, led by four
deposed ministers, set out to America in search of religious
freedom, according to Robert Blair in his *Life of Mr. Blair
Containing his Autobiography from 1593-1636*. The colonists
now shared another common bond with the native Irish . . .
hatred of English imperial rule.

In 1639 King Charles I planned to invade Scotland to punish
the Presbyterian rebels and Wentworth raised an Irish army of
9,000 to aid Charles in this venture. The army was derived
mainly from the native Irish who did not share the colonists'
religious beliefs and whose economic circumstances made the

venture seem attractive. It was commanded by Lord Ormonde, who although a Protestant was a staunch royalist. Unrest between Charles and his Parliament was growing and he abandoned his invasion. The Irish army was disbanded but it now became the nucleus of an insurgent army aiming to throw out the English and their colonists and seizing the opportunity given by the internal conflict of the English ruling classes.

On October 23, 1641, the Irish rose under the leadership of Phelim O'Neill, who pretended that he was taking up arms to protect the king, forging a royal commission to that effect. Strong points in Ulster were seized and the estates of the colonists confiscated. The colonists themselves were chased towards the protective shelter of Derry and Dublin. Some contemporary writers, such as the author of *A Brief Declaration of the Barbarous and Inhuman Dealing of the Northern Irish Rebels, 1641*, made out that a great massacre had taken place numbering up to 200,000 colonists slaughtered. Nothing could be further from the truth and these reports were simply propagandist essays trying to stir up English hostility to Ireland. The Irish uprising had many causes; the main one was the attempt by the native Irish to repossess the lands from which they had been dispossessed. The leaders, however, like Phelim O'Neill were landowners and, if we are to believe *The Irish Rebellion or a History of the Beginnings and First Progress of the General Rebellion, 1641,* these same landowners "had not long before turned their Irish tenants out of their lands . . . even to starve upon the mountains while they took on English." The statement, of course, could also be an attempt to discredit the Irish leaders.

Sigerson states that while the rising was led by the displaced Irishised Anglo-Irish gentry it was supported "by those native husbandmen who had been ousted from their lowland fertile lands and driven to the mountains." A number of colonists later sided with the native Irish. Apart from the fact of intermarriage, emphasised by *The Irish Rebellion*, the persecution of the Presbyterians by the Established Anglican Church caused colonists to join the native Irish in attempting to smash English rule.

Sigerson states :

It would appear that whilst the Irish and British tenants were brought into amicable acquaintance by a sense of common wrongs, the alien undertaker and Irish chief, new made into a feudal lord, were occasionally leagured by a feeling of selfish interest. Both had usurpations to make and protect. Those of the former have been detailed : those of the latter were in the circumstance of his transformation. The elective chief who had, by benefit of feudal law, been privileged as a despotic master, could not be favourably regarded by members of the clan, his electors, whenever he really sought to show that he was no longer their minister but their lord. Such cases would occur, more especially, when the Irish lord had been an English favourite rather than a representative of the tribe, whose true chief he may have ousted.[5]

Therefore the uprising of 1641, while backed by the clans in order to regain their lands and backed by a number of colonists to achieve religious freedom, was not a "people's rising". The rising was led by men whose major interest was to increase and maintain property on a feudal basis. The Irish insurgent army achieved a rapid success. The Scottish colonists found themselves split. Some had, according to *The Irish Rebellion*, "degenerated into Irish affections and customs" and regarded themselves as natives, while others fought with the natives to gain freedom for their Presbyterian religion. Other colonists found themselves historically against the native Irish. But, as Presbyterians they were against the Anglican Royalists and as the Parliamentarians had ejected Presbyterians from the House of Commons they were against the Parliamentary forces. General Monk, sent to command the Parliamentarian force in Ulster, actually formed an alliance with certain Irish clans against the colonists.

The English had first moved to suppress the rising in 1642 when Lord Wharton raised an army of 5,500 men and marched them to Bristol for embarkation. Whilst waiting to ship for Ireland the English Civil War broke out and Wharton's troops were needed by the king. It was in 1649 that Oliver Cromwell arrived in Ireland and, in one dreadful campaign, crushed the opposition of the Irish and the Presbyterian colonists alike. Leyburn states :

What Cromwell did deserves to be ranked with the horrors perpetrated by Genghis Khan. His "pacification" of Ireland was so thorough that it left scars on that country which have never been forgotten or forgiven.[6]

Sir William Petty, a statistician of the time, wrote in his *Political Anatomy of Ireland* that out of a total population of

1,448,000 some 616,000 perished by sword, famine and plague. Of this number 504,000 were native Irish while 112,000 were colonists. A further 40,000 decided to leave Ireland to enlist in European armies while, in addition, there was the extensive deportation of 100,000 Irish who were sold as slaves to the West Indies and other colonies. By one terrific blow the remains of the communistic clan system, which had shown vitality for more than a millenium, was now destroyed, root, branch and bole.

Following the defeat of the Irish, a meeting in the Speaker's Chamber, Westminster, was held on January 30, 1652, at which a "final solution" to the Irish question was drawn up. An effective plan of colonisation was proposed and an Act of Parliament embodying the plan of plantation was passed by Parliament on September 23, 1653. The English Parliament was to seize three-quarters of Ireland and the populations of Ulster, Munster and Leinster were to be driven into an area west of the River Shannon consisting of Connaught and Co. Clare. They were to be retained there by a line of military forts. Some 2,500,000 acres of Irish land were to be confiscated to pay the Cromwellian troops now stationed in Ireland.

All the Irish from the three provinces were to be removed to Connaught by May 1, 1654, with the exception of women married to English Protestants before December 2, 1650; boys under fourteen years of age and girls under twelve years, who were to be brought up as Protestants; and the final exception being those who remained loyal to the English Parliament during the insurrection. The latter category, while they could live outside Connaught, were not to come within five miles of a walled town on pain of death. Any Irish, apart from the exceptions, found on the "English side" of the Shannon after May 1, 1654, were liable to be put to death.

The Royalists in exile were delighted at Cromwell's thoroughness in colonisation, a project they had failed to complete for five centuries. Their attitude was summed up by Sir Edward Hyde (afterwards Earl Clarendon) in a letter to M. Betius dated Paris, May 29, 1654:

> Cromwell is no doubt very busy. Nathaniel Fiennes is made Chancellor of Ireland, and they doubt not to plant that kingdom without opposition. And truly, if we can get it again, we shall

find difficulties removed which a virtuous Prince and more quiet
times could never have compassed.

Cromwell's plan was greeted with horror by the remaining
Irish population, now 692,000 people, and brought in a spate of
petitions from the Anglo-Irish gentry. Nevertheless, the plantation scheme went ahead but it was a slow process. On March
19, 1655, there was a general search for, and arrest of, all people
who should have crossed the Shannon. Court martials tried them
and some were condemned to death like Edward Hetherington
of Kilnemanagh who was hanged in Dublin on April 3, 1655,
with a placard on his back bearing the words: "For Not
Transplanting". But economics saved thousands from death.
Most of the "non-transplanted" Irish were simply sold into
slavery thus making profits for such people as Sir William Petty,
who reckons that 100,000 Irish suffered this fate. One Bristol
firm was responsible for shipping 6,400 boys and girls to slavery
aided by Lord Broghill of Co. Cork (Later Earl Orerry). It
would also seem from Prendergast's *Cromwellian Settlement in
Ireland* that the authorities were not particular whether those
taken into slavery were, in fact, exceptions to the transplantation
order or poor Irish who unfortunately fell in the way of the slave
traders. Prendergast writes:

> As an instance out of many:—Captain John Vernon was em-
> ployed by the Commissioners for Ireland to England, and con-
> tracted in their behalf with Mr. David Sellick and the Leader
> under his hand to supply them with two hundred and fifty
> women of the Irish nation, above twelve years and under fifty, to
> be found in the country within twenty miles of Cork, Youghal
> and Kinsale, Waterford and Wexford, to transport them into
> New England.[7]

The situation brought forth protests from several
Establishment figures. In 1655 Vincent Gookin, the son of a
colonist and member of the first Commonwealth Parliament of
1653, wrote an anonymous pamphlet against the project entitled
The Great Case of Transplantation in Ireland Dismissed. He
argued, among other points, that transplantation injured the
revenue. The publication roused the fury of the officers of the
Cromwellian army in Ireland. They petitioned Cromwell.

Colonel Richard Lawrence, a leading member of the Committee for Transplantation, formed on November 21, 1653, published an answer entitled *The Interest of England in the Irish Transplantation Stated.* (1655.)

The necessity to keep the rebellious camps in Ireland divided was recognised by Cromwell and he made concessions to the Presbyterians. In 1653 there were only half a dozen ministers in Ulster but within seven years Cromwell had allowed this number to be raised to seventy. At the same time the Catholic Church was suppressed and £20 was offered for the discovery of priests. To harbour them meant death and thousands left Ireland. Others were imprisoned and camps were set up on Inishbofin and Aran where they were held from 1657 to 1660.

The Cromwellian solution for Irish conquest did not work. There were a number of reasons governing this failure. Firstly, it was impossible to clear the country of the indigenous Irish and inevitably intermarriage took place. Sigerson says :

> Nor could the penal enactment of the State prevent the races from again commingling. Intermarriages were of frequent occurrence and where Irish wives only were to be had it does not surprise us to be told that "many of the children of Oliver's soldiers in Ireland cannot speak one word of English".

Then came unrest from the dispossessed Irish many of whom, refusing to be transplanted, simply "took to the hills" forming themselves into small guerilla bands who attacked the colonists' settlements. One of the first recorded attacks occurred in March, 1655, near Timolin, Co. Kildare, when colonist John Symonds and his sons were killed. Rigorous orders were given to eradicate all the Irish in the area. These guerilla bands swept out of the hills and mountains driving off horses, cows and other stock, and rendering the smooth working of the colonies almost inoperative. The name given to these guerillas was *toiridhe*—meaning a pursuer. The anglicisation of the word was Tory and, later on, under James II, the word was bestowed on asserters of the royal prerogative and today means a bigoted or extreme Conservative, a far cry from the dispossessed Irish guerilla bands.

Rewards were posted for the Tories : 40s was the average

price for a Tory while on October 3, 1655, the following rewards were posted for Tory leaders: Donnogh O'Derrick (Blind Donnogh) £30; Dermot Ryan £20; James Leigh £5 and Laughlin Kelly £5. The rewards gave the colonists a new sport —Tory hunting. Many were caught, their heads being displayed on stakes throughout the country. "So sudden and so frequent were the murders of the English planters," observes Prendergast, "that no person was able to assure himself of one night's safety."

In 1695 the authorities granted free pardon to any Tory who killed two fellow Tories and, in 1718, one dead Tory was the qualifying number for a pardon. Parliament passed an Act of 1707 "for the more effectual suppression of Tories". The Irish Tories can be traced through the Statute Book to the reign of George II when Tory hunting finally died out in 1776.

According to Connolly :

Ere long by one of those silent movements of which the superficial historian takes no account, the proscribed people were once more back from the province into which they had been hunted; heartbroken and subdued, it is true, but nevertheless back upon their own lands.

Connolly continues :

In the North the proscription had been more effectual for the reason that in that province there were Protestant settlers to occupy the lands from which the Catholics had been driven. But even there the craving for a return to the old homes and tribelands destroyed the full effect of the Cromwellian proscription. The hunted Ulstermen and women crept back from Connaught and, unable to act like their Southern brethren and re-occupy their own lands upon any terms, they took refuge in the hills and "mountainy land." At first we can imagine these poor people led a somewhat precarious life, ever dreading the advent of a Government force to dislodge them and drive them back to Connaught; but they persisted, built their huts, tilled with infinite toil the poor soil from which they scraped the accumulations of stones, and gradually established their families in the position of a tolerated evil. Two things helped in securing this toleration.

First, the avarice of the new land owning aristocracy, who easily subdued their religious fanaticism sufficiently to permit Papists settling upon and paying rent for formerly worthless mountain land.

Second, the growing acuteness of the difficulties of the Government in England itself; the death of Cromwell; the fear of the owners of confiscated estates that the accession of Charles II might lead to a resumption of their property by former owners and, arising from that fear, a disinclination to attract too much attention by further attacks upon the returning Catholics who might retaliate; and, finally, the unrest and general uncertainty centering round the succession to the throne.

Thus, in Ulster, the Celt returned to his ancient tribelands, but to its hills and stony fastnesses from which with tear dimmed eye he could look down upon the fertile plains of his fathers which he might never again hope to occupy, even on sufferance.

On the other hand, the Protestant common soldier or settler, now that the need of his sword was passed, found himself upon the lands of the Catholic, it is true, but solely as tenant and dependent. The ownership of the province was not in his hands, but in the hands of the companies of London merchants who had supplied the sinews of war for the English armies, or in the hands of the greedy aristocrats and legal cormorants who had schemed and intrigued while he had fought. The end of the Cromwellian settlement then found the "commonality", to use a good old word, dispossessed and defrauded of all hold upon the soil of Ireland—the Catholic dispossessed by force, the Protestant centering round the succession to the throne.[8]

Following the Restoration of the Stuart monarchy little change was made in Ireland. The landowners and manufacturers began to expand and, in particular, the woollen manufacturers in Ulster grew to such proportions that Irish woollens acquired a good reputation throughout Europe. English capitalists grew jealous at the colonists' success and the English Parliament passed an Act in 1663 forbidding Irish ships to carry goods to any part of the English Empire. In 1666 Parliament forbade Irish cattle being imported into England thus bringing about the ruin of the cattle industry, the mainstay of the Irish economy.

However, the religious question in Ireland seemed to be improving. The Catholics were free to practise their religious beliefs while Charles II showed himself well disposed towards the Presbyterian colonists. In 1672 he granted their ministers a royal bounty known as the Regium Donum. When James II succeeded his brother in 1685 he was not renowned for his diplomacy. He Forces of Ireland. Talbot was an ardent Catholic who began his appointed Richard Talbot, Lord Tyrconnell, General of the

administration by dismissing Protestants from key offices and fill-
ing them with Catholics. There was some disquiet among the
Protestant section of the community for Tyrconnell was known
to have stated he wanted to rid Ireland of the colonist ghettoes.

James was doing his best to bring England back to the
Catholic fold and his religious policies aroused a fierce opposition
in England. In 1688 seven members of the English government
invited William of Orange, husband of James's Protestant
daughter, to invade England and become king. To protect himself against foreign interference, James allied himself with Louis
XIV and succeeded in making England a semi-dependency of
France. Louis XIV was bent on European domination. Lorraine
was turned into a subject state, Genoa was bombarded and the
Catholic Louis marched his army on Rome, humiliating the
Pope. The leaders of Europe were overawed by the strength of
the French imperialists. So worried did they become that in 1686
the Emperor of Germany, King of Spain, William of Orange
and Pope Innocent XI entered into the Treaty of Augsberg to
protect themselves from French encroachments on their respective territories. Therefore a peculiar position arose. When, in
November, 1688, William of Orange landed in England, he was
politically backed by the head of the Catholic Church and the
Catholic kingdom of Spain, in his effort to overthrow the
Catholic king of England.

James fled to Ireland, via France, where Tyrconnell assured
him the country was his, except where the Presbyterian colonists
had barricaded themselves in Derry, Enniskillen and Coleraine.
However, King James's Parliament sitting in Dublin in 1689
passed Acts XIII and XV declaring all religions equal under the
law and that each priest or minister should be supported by his
own congregation only, and that no tithes should be levied upon
any person for support of a church to which he did not belong.
All religious discrimination in Ireland was therefore abolished by
law.

William was soon in Ireland and at the Boyne river on June
30 and July 1, 1690, a rather indecisive battle, but a Williamite
victory nevertheless, was fought. James II fled to France. When
news of William's victory over James II (who is known unaffec-
tionately in Ireland as *Seamus an Chaca*) reached Rome a
Te Deum was sung in celebration in St. Peter's while similar

celebrations were held at the great Catholic capitals of Madrid, Brussells and in the Catholic Cathedral of Vienna.

It is ironic that Protestants in Ulster today are taught that "William of Orange and our immortal forefathers overthrew the Pope and Popery at the Boyne" and, indeed, they hold marches to celebrate the event. It is highly ironic when one considers that part of the arms and equipment of William of Orange's army was paid for by Pope Innocent XI under the Treaty of Augsberg. Another fable taught today is that the Battle of the Boyne marked the beginning of religious liberty of the Protestants. Firstly, the Boyne was not the decisive victory, but the Williamite victory at Aughrim on July 12, 1691, and the end of the second siege of Limerick, marked the end of the war which is known in Irish history as *Cogadh an Dha Ri*—the war of the two kings. More important, however, is the fact that religious liberty was granted by Acts of James II's Dublin Parliament. When the Treaty of Limerick was signed on October 3, 1691, it agreed that Catholics would have the same religious rights as they enjoyed under Charles II. Yet, although William agreed to retain the principles of the Acts of the Dublin Parliament, the Episcopalian Church was established as the only legal church while the Catholic and Presbyterian religion were banned by test which no loyal member of the Scottish church could take.

Not only were the representatives of the Roman Catholics expressly excluded but even the members of the Scottish colony in the North were, for the greater part of the eighteenth century, proscribed and excluded from equal civil rights by the obnoxious test which no royal member of the Scottish church could take.

In 1691 a Presbyterian minister was liable to three months in the common jail for delivering a sermon and a fine of £100 for celebrating the Lord's Supper. Presbyterians were forbidden to be married by their own ministers. At Lisburn and Tullyish, Presbyterians were actually punished after it was discovered that a Presbyterian minister had married them. In 1704 a Test Act was introduced in which all Presbyterians were excluded from offices in Law, Army, Navy, Customs, Excise and Municipal Employment. The Act was enforced all over Ireland.

In 1713 an Act was passed at Westminster making Presbyterian schoolmasters liable to three month's imprisonment for teaching. Intermarriage between Presbyterians and Episcopalians was declared illegal, let alone those between Presbyterians and Catholics. During the same year four Presbyterians were sentenced for holding a prayer meeting on Presbyterian lines. Similar prosecutions followed. As late as 1772 a number of Presbyterians were arrested for attempting to hold a religious meeting in Belturbet. The *History of Irish Presbyterianism* states:

> Presbyterians, having no political power, had to submit to political persecutions. The feudal system which transferred the ownership of the soil from the toiler to the landlord was one of the many evils introduced by the power of England. The Presbyterian farmer was a serf who had to submit to the will of his landlord, and in elections when he had a vote, to support the enemies of his creed, his class and his country.

The "religious liberty" thus won by William of Orange in 1691 caused some 250,000 Protestant Ulstermen to migrate to America between the years 1717 and 1776 alone. The historian Froude states:

> Twenty thousand left Ulster on the destruction of the woollen trade. Many more were driven away by the first passing of the Test Act ... Men of spirit and energy refused to remain in a country where they were held unfit to receive the rights of citizens; and thenceforward, until the spell of tyranny was broken in 1782, annual shiploads of families poured themselves out from Belfast and Londonderry ... Religious bigotry, commercial jealousy, and modern landlordism had combined to do their worst against the Ulster settlement . . . Vexed with suits in ecclesiastical courts, forbidden to educate their children in their own faith, treated as dangerous in a state which but for them would have no existence, and associated with Papists in an Act of Parliament which deprived them of their civil rights, the most earnest of them at length abandoned the unthankful service. They saw at last that the liberties for which their fathers had fought were not to be theirs in Ireland ... During the first half of the eighteenth century Down, Antrim, Armagh and Derry were emptied of their Protestant families who were of more value to Ireland than California gold mines.[9]

The Catholic religion, needless to say, suffered similarly. Every priest was required to take an oath of allegiance to the Protestant succession. No prelate was allowed to reside in Ireland under a penalty of being hanged, drawn and quartered. A scale of rewards for informers was drawn up. No Catholic could serve in the armed forces or possess arms, even a sword, nor ride a horse worth more than £5. They could not vote or be members of parliament or citizens of an incorporated town. They were not allowed to become artisans without paying a special tax. If a Catholic went to school he was brought up as an Anglican Protestant; nor were Catholics allowed to be educated abroad. "The law," wrote a Lord Chancellor, "does not take into account the existence of such a person as an Irish Roman Catholic."

The position of the Presbyterian was alleviated by the Irish Parliament in the 1780s pressured by the armed Irish Volunteers, while Catholics were accorded their civil rights under the Emancipation Act of 1829. The attempt to smash the Catholic and majority Protestant religion (Presbyterians) drove the two people together against their Anglican persecutors. They began to join forces in vast smuggling activities made necessary by the difficulties of living. Chauviré states :

> . . . and thus the conception of a possible community of interests was starting to dawn among the two peoples who up to then had been antagonistic.[10]

Indeed, it was the Presbyterian group who were to throw up some of the great Irish democratic republican nationalist leaders, especially in the 1798 uprising when Presbyterians took the initiative against the English. Presbyterianism embodied a distinctly democratic ideal while Catholicism predisposes its adherents towards the acceptance of authority. Presbyterians were therefore in the vanguard of insurgency activities and their current "loyalism" is very unnatural in this context. During this time in some of the "mixed" areas, such as Tyrone and Fermanagh, the Catholics tried to adopt the Presbyterian usage of electing their own ministers. This was squashed by the Catholic Hierarchy.

In the meantime, culturally at least, the latest wave of colonists who had come to occupy the 1,500,000 acres confiscated by William, were being absorbed into an Irish speaking society. The

author of *A True Way to Render Ireland Happy, 1697,*
wrote :

> We cannot wonder at this when we consider how many there
> are of the children of Oliver's soldiers in Ireland who cannot but
> speak one word of English (which is strange) and the same may
> be said of the children of William's soldiers who came but t'other
> day into the country.

Chapter 4

A CENTURY OF UNREST

THE 18TH CENTURY was one of deep anguish and unrest for the people of Ireland. The Irish were truly a conquered people and the English policy was to treat Ireland as a colonial territory ensuring that the colonists could not compete with the "mother country" in matters of trade and commerce. This shortsighted policy ensured the rise of a powerful colonial nationalism in Ireland concurrent with the rise of colonial nationalism in the American colonies. Rich Catholics and Dissenters managed to survive the Penal Laws for they, at least, were tolerated in society. By 1778, 5 per cent of Irish land was still in Catholic hands and these rich Catholics found themselves taking up the profession of money-lending just as in earlier times the Jews of Christendom had been precluded from the professions of "gentlemen" and had consequently concentrated on trade and usury. The need to ingratiate themselves with their "betters" had tended to the cultivation of suavity, an "oiliness" frequently remarked on by anti-semites. Among the English people this "Irish" characteristic of telling people what it was thought they wished to hear was charitably labelled "Blarney". The similar desire among the Welsh to placate the all-powerful foreigner was more generally ascribed to "natural Welsh deceit". This characteristic is very rarely found among Presbyterian Irish and their co-religionists in Scotland. In 1763 Protestants tried to get greater facilities in order to borrow money from Catholics and a Bill was proposed to that effect. This, however, was defeated.

The general condition of the Irish people in the 18th century was extreme wretchedness and poverty. In the 1740 famine it was estimated that 400,000 people died while famines in 1757, 1765 and 1770 increased their desperate condition. This wretchedness did not emanate from the Penal Laws or directly from the English conquest, although Catholics and Dissenters were placed at a disadvantage in having to pay tithes to the Established Anglican Church. It mattered not to the people of

Ireland whether their landlords were Catholics, Dissenters or Anglicans, Irish or English.

One of the biggest sources of Irish wretchedness was absentee landlordism. This grew steadily throughout the country and, by 1831, it was estimated that there were 1,500 absentee landlords owning 3,200,000 acres living in London and Paris while a further 4,500 absentee landlords, owning 4,200,000 acres, lived in Dublin. O'Neill writes :

> Absenteeism bred a horde of middlemen. The landlords rented their estates to these vultures for a fixed sum, thus ensuring a regular income without taking the slightest interest in their lands. The middlemen then sub-let their farms on the "canting" system. Tenants whose leases had expired were compelled to bid against strangers for their holdings and the insecurity of tenure forced up the rent with each expiration of the lease. The depredations of the middlemen in the first half of the century is so shameful that almost every writer has referred to them.[1]

Arthur Young during his tour in Ireland in 1776 described the middlemen in these words :

> Living upon the spot, surrounded by their little under-tenants, the middlemen prove the most oppressive species of tyrants that ever lent assistance to the destruction of a country. They re-let the land, at short tenure, to the occupiers of small farms, and often give no leases at all. Not satisfied with screwing up the rent to the uttermost farthing, they are rapacious and relentless in the collection of it ... But farther, the dependence of the occupier on the resident middlemen goes to other circumstances; personal services of themselves, their cars and horses, is exacted for lending turf, hay, corn, gravel etc. insomuch that the poor under tenants often lose their own crop and turf from being obliged to obey these calls of their superiors. Nay, I have even heard these jobbers gravely assert that, without under-tenants to furnish cars and teams at half or two thirds the common price of the country, they could carry out no improvements at all; yet taking a merit to themselves for works wrought out of the sweat and ruin of a pack of wretches, assigned to their plunder by the inhumanity of the landlords.[2]

Gill also adds to our picture of the system :

> No tenant, even if he paid rent regularly, and worked his land well, was secure in his holding; for in any year the land might be

offered to a higher bidder, and the tenant would be driven away without compensation. If he would escape eviction he must pay, or at least promise, a higher rent than any competitor. Thus short leases meant rack renting; and rack renting meant that it was never worth while for a tenant to improve his land, because all the benefit would go to the landlord or his agent. The depressing effort of rack renting was all the greater since the peasants were very often tempted to promise more than they could pay. Their rents were always in arrears, and if they made any additional wealth it would simply go to reduce slightly a burden of debt from which they could never wholly escape. Consequently it was to the interest of the peasantry to starve the soil, and to draw from it no more than would keep themselves and their families at subsistence level, with only so much surplus as would satisfy the most urgent claims of the rent agent.[3]

Only in parts of Ulster did tenants have "rights" where compensation for improvements were paid. When Ulster landlords made attempts to invade this tenant right, agrarian warfare split the province. Arthur Young provided a horrifying picture of conditions on estates. Several "landlords of consequence" admitted to Young that they forced the wives and daughters of their tenants to sleep with them. Young comments that the landlords:

> ... assured me that many of their cottiers would think themselves honoured by having their wives and daughters sent for to the bed of their master—a mark of slavery which proves the oppression under which the people must live.

Sigerson comments:

> To visitors from England (now as before) the position of the Irish tenantry seemed one of deplorable slavery. They could compare it to nothing but the condition of the serfs in Russia, or the peasants in France before the Revolution of 1793.

Young's description gives one a terrible picture of a country suffering from the worst phase of feudalism.

> The abominable distinction of religion united with the oppressive conduct of the little country gentlemen, or rather vermin of the kingdom, altogether still bear heavy on the poor people, and subject them to situations more mortifying than we ever beheld

in England. The landlord of an Irish estate, inhabited by Roman Catholics, is a sort of despot who yields obedience, in whatever concerns the poor, to no law but that of his will.

The Irish legislature was representative of an extremely small minority in the country, namely the Established Church. The Penal Laws excluded Catholics, Presbyterians and other Dissenters, although the English parliament had passed an Act of Toleration in 1719 which forced the Anglican Church to make a concession of liberty of conscience to the dissident Presbyterians. As well as this small minority represented, some constituencies (rotten boroughs) had few or no electors and belonged to patrons. Seats in the Dublin legislature could be bought by means of titles, pensions and sinecures. A thriving business was made out of selling such places. However, in this colonial parliament, a nationalist force was springing up which would flower in the 1780's.

In the meantime, under such conditions, the Catholic rich and poor began to diverge in search of their class interests. Between 1703 and 1788 some 5,000 land-owning Catholic families joined the Anglican Church in order to protect their property from confiscation. The Catholic clergy did not speak out against the ruling-class injustice for fear of their own position. Many bishops, such as Doyle of Kildare and Leighlin, denounced peasants for their "crimes" against property owners during the agrarian troubles. Many of the Catholic clergy actually crossed to the Anglican Church, a number denouncing their proscribed hierarchy to the authorities and picking up financial rewards. The population had risen, standards of living had dropped and competition for property had pushed up rents to impossible figures. Trade restrictions, lack of mineral wealth, capitalists investing their money in more favourable enterprises, condemned the Irish people to live on what little they could grow in what land they could obtain. The potato, introduced in Ireland in the 16th century, now became the only source of sustenence for the people, while to own a pig was wealth indeed.

The Irish social system was now dead and the people were sinking into an abyss of ignorance, a poverty of mind as well as body. However, the old concepts died hard and as an example of spontaneous desire among a conquered people for education, an illegal education system grew up known as Hedge Schools. The old Irish educational system, the Bardic schools, represented "a highly developed system providing, up to nearly the middle of the 17th century, the nearest approach to what might be called a university education."[4] During the centuries before the Anglo-Norman conquest, the Irish educational facilities had attracted scholars from all over Europe.

> The Hedge Schools owe their origin to the suppression of all the ordinary legitimate means of education, first during the Cromwellian régime and then under the Penal Code introduced in the reign of William III and operating from that time in increasing measure till 1782.[5]

The peasant people of Ireland, building shelters for their schoolmasters, managed to keep alive fragments of the ancient Irish civilisation, their language and poetry, in spite of an increased cultural imperialism. But because of the complete absence of any status for the Irish language, the majority of Hedge Schoolmasters concentrated their efforts on teaching their pupils English and thus contributing to the gradual erosion of the language.

> Because the law forbade the schoolmaster to teach, he was compelled to give instruction secretly, because the householder was penalised for harbouring the schoolmaster, he had perforce to teach, and that only when the weather permitted, out of doors. He therefore selected, in some remote spot, the sunny side of a hedge or bank which effectively hid him and his pupils from the eye of the chance passer-by, and there he sat upon a stone as he taught his little schools, while his scholars lay stretched upon the green sward about him. One pupil was usually placed at a point of vantage to give warning of the approach of strangers; and if the latter were suspected of being law officers or informers, the class was quickly disbanded for the day—only to meet again on the morrow in some place still more sheltered and remote.
>
> In winter the schoolmaster moved from place to place living upon the hospitality of the people, earning a little perhaps by turning his hand to farm work, or, when he dared, by teaching the children of his hosts.[6]

It seems that quite a high standard of education was taught in these "people's schools". The classics and humanities were also taught and students from Hedge Schools gained a sufficient

degree of education to be able to pass into such universities as
that of Salamanca.

It was Jonathan Swift (1667-1745), dean of St. Patrick's
Cathedral, Dublin, who first raised the voice of bitter protest at
the conditions in Ireland. Swift, the satirist, author of *Gulliver's
Travels* and *A Tale of the Tub*, published in 1729, a vitriolic
attack on society entitled : *A Modest Proposal for Preventing the
Children of the Poor People in Ireland from becoming a Burden
on their Parents or Country, and for making them Beneficial to
the public*. Swift's "modest proposal" was that poor Irish children aged one year old be killed off and made into "a most
delicious, nourishing and wholesome food". He wrote :

> I have already computed the charge if nursing a beggar's child
> (in which list I reckon all cottagers, labourers and four fifths of
> the farmers) to be about two shillings per annum, rags included,
> and I believe no gentleman would refuse to give ten shillings for
> the carcase of a good fat child, which I have said, will make four
> dishes of excellent nutrious meat.

What a comment on the social conditions which made such
irony possible.

It was inevitable that the Irish people would rebel against
their worsening environment. The first flash point was Munster
where a secret peasant organisation known as the Whiteboys (so
called due to the fact they wore white shirts over their clothes
when conducting raids) posted notices in Cork, Waterford,
Limerick and Tipperary in 1762. The notices threatened vengeance on landlords evicting poor peasants. The reasons for the
rise of the Whiteboys were published in a pamphlet *An Inquiry
into the Causes of the Outrages Committed by the Levellers or
Whiteboys, 1762* :

> . . . some landlords let their land to cottiers far above their value;
> and, to highten their burthens, allowed commonage to their ten-
> ants; afterwards, in despite of all equity, contrary to all compacts,
> the landlords enclosed these commons, and precluded their un-
> happy tenants from making their bargain.

In 1762 peasants gathered and levelled these enclosures earning the name "levellers". They were later renamed Whiteboys
and, according to Edmund Burke[7] the movement was organised

by a Protestant lawyer named Fant and many poor Protestants enlisted in the movement alongside their Catholic brothers. The Whiteboys started to resist the excessive exactions of rents and tithes, carrying on a guerrilla warfare, similar to the Tories, riding on horseback considerable distances to the estate they were to attack. Warning notices from the Whiteboys were signed "Sive Oultagh" or "Queen Sive". Sigerson comments:

> Against evictions, exactions, and intolerable oppressions the peasant productive class waged a long fluctuating warfare, and, although with frightful suffering, maintained their ground. Misery made them desperate. They had nothing to lose but their lives ...

Lose their lives they did. The Government showed no mercy to anyone suspected of Whiteboyism. Hangings, shootings, transportations, village raids in the dead of night, were common practices. A reward of £100 for Whiteboy leaders was offered by the Government while the Anglican inhabitants of Cork offered £300 for the leader and £50 for his accomplices. Catholic landowners, not to be outdone, offered £200 for the Whiteboy leader and £40 for his accomplices.

> In spite of admonitions, denunciations and even excommunications by their own clergy, oathbound secret societies continued to exist, and, particularly in times of distress, the people obeyed the local Whiteboy code instead of the law of the land.[8]

The agrarian warfare in Munster continued, causing Henry Flood, one of the emerging colonial nationalists, to criticise the administration in 1763 for not adequately dealing with the "rebellious peasants". Some peasants, in an effort to combat the system by legitimate means, formed themselves into co-operative societies or "knots", based on the ancient Celtic custom, by electing one of their number to bid against a planter when his lease expired. Sigerson points out that "The Protestant landlords, who had helped to forge the Penal Laws, helped as readily to sacrifice Protestantism to its Juggernaut." If the co-operative rented land it was divided amongst the members. Little success was achieved by this method.

On July 1, 1786, there was a mass meeting of Munster

peasants and, following the meeting, a document was drawn up which was subsequently published as a pamphlet in October of the same year. Connolly describes it as a remarkable document. It was a *"Letter Addressed to Munster peasantry"*.

To obviate the bad impression made by the calumnies of our enemies, we beg leave to submit to you our claim for the protection of a humane gentry and humbly solicit yours, if said claim shall appear to you founded in justices and good policy.

In every age, country and religion, the priesthood are allowed to have been artful, usurping, and tenacious of their ill-acquired prerogatives. Often have their jarring interests and opinions deluged with Christian blood this long devoted isle.

Some thirty years ago our unhappy fathers—galled beyond human sufferance—like a captive lion vainly struggling in the toils, strove violently to snap their bonds asunder, but instead riveted them more tight. Exhausted by the bloody struggle, the poor of this province submitted to their oppression, and fattened with their vitals each decimating leech.

The luxurious parson drowned in the riot of his table the bitter groans of those wretches that his proctor fleeced and the poor remnant of the proctor's rapine was sure to be gleaned by the rapacious priest; but it was blasphemy to complain to him; Heaven, we thought, would wing its lightening to blast the wretch who grudged the Holy Father's share. Thus plundered by either clergy, we had reason to wish for our simple Druids again.

At last, however, it pleased pitying Heaven to dispel the murky cloud of bigotry that hovered over us so long. Liberality shot her cheering rays, and enlightened the peasant's hovel as well as the splendid hall. O'Leary told us, plain as friar could, that a God of universal love would not confine His salvation to one sect alone, and that the subject's election was the best title to the crown.

Thus improved in our religion and our politics . . . we resolve to evince on every occasion the change in our sentiments and hope to succeed in our sincere attempts. We examined the double causes of our grievances, and debated long how to get them removed, until at length our resolve terminated in this general peaceful remonstrance.

Humanity, justice and policy enforce our request. Whilst the tithe farmer enjoys the fruit of our labours, agriculture must decrease, and while the griping priest insists on more from the bridegroom than he is worth, population must be retarded.

Let the legislature befriend us now, and we are theirs for ever. Our sincerity in the warmth of our attachment when one professed was never in question, and we are bold to say no such imputations will ever fall on the Munster peasantry.

At a very numerous and peaceable meeting of the delegates of the Munster peasantry, held on Thursday, the 1st day of July, 1786, the following resolutions were unanimously agreed to, viz :

Resolved—That we will continue to oppose our oppressors by the most justifiable means in our power, either until they are glutted with our blood or until humanity raises her angry voice in the councils of the nation to protect the toiling peasant and lighten his burden.

Resolved—That the fickleness of the multitude makes it necessary for all and each of us to swear not to pay voluntarily the priest or parson more than as follows :—

Potatoes, first crop 6s. per acre; do., second crop, 4s.; wheat, 4s.; barley, 4s.; oats, 3s.; meadowing, 2s. 6d.; marriage, 5s.; baptism, 1s. 6d.; each family confession, 2s.; Par. Priest's Sun. Mass, 1s.; any other, 1s.; Extreme Unction, 1s.

Signed by order,

William O'Driscol
General to the Munster Peasantry

It was the province of Ulster, however, that gave the greatest cause of concern to the ruling classes. Once again, it was Ulster that was the hotbed of revolution, both social and national. In the year following the appearance of the Whiteboys, 1763, the Dissenting peasants rose against the ruling and landowning classes. They wore an oak leaf in their hats and were named Hearts of Oak or Oakboys. They first appeared in Armagh, Derry and Fermanagh as a backlash to the oppressive road corvées, the obligation to perform gratuitous labour, in this case maintenance of the roads, for a feudal or sovereign lord (i.e. the landowners). The movement spread to resist exactions, rack rents and oppressive tithes. In 1771 another movement known as the Hearts of Steel swooped down on the landowning classes, maiming cattle and burning crops. These Presbyterian organisations were more formidable than their Catholic counterparts and incurred the wrath of repressive forces. Montgomery points out :

Both the Oakboys and the Hearts of Steel were exclusively Protestant organisations; this is a remarkable proof that the struggle between nation and nation, or creed and creed, was rapidly changing to a class war between landlord and tenant.

Biggar comments:

> They carried on their agitation in the face of all the power
> vested interests of the governing class, and without their vital
> struggle and enormous sacrifice Ulster tenant right and the Ulster
> custom would never have become a reality, and the remnant of a
> strong agricultural class would have dwindled to mere serfs, with-
> out any rights or claims on the houses they built and the lands
> they cultivated.[9]

Throughout the century appeasing noises were made concerning the disabilities placed on Catholics and Presbyterians under
the Penal Laws and, in 1757, the Duke of Bedford promised to
abridge these laws but with no result. It was in 1771 that an act
was passed allowing Catholics to lease fifty acres of thoroughly
unprofitable bog land, with a half acre of land at one mile dis-
tance from a town. If half the bog land had not been reclaimed
within twenty-one years, eviction followed. In 1778 an Act was
passed allowing Catholics to obtain leases for 999 years.

In Ulster now there was growing a strong republican feeling
among the Presbyterians in particular. These were the people
who had relatives in the American colonies of England, who
were now fighting the English for their independence (1775-81).

> Many thousands of Protestants emigrated from these parts of
> Ulster to the American settlements where they appeared in arms
> against the British government and contributed powerfully by
> their zeal and valour to the separation of the American colonies
> from Great Britain.[10]

The sympathy felt for the American colonists was reflected in
the growing colonial, or Protestant, nationalism, led by the Earl
of Charlemont, Henry Flood and Henry Grattan, although the
Irish legislature had given its wholehearted support to the
English Imperial policy. During 1778-9 France and Spain, seizing advantage of England's difficulties in America, entered the
war on America's side. A "Volunteer" fever swept the British
Isles and in Ireland volunteer corps were formed mainly by
Protestant Irishmen in order to protect the country from invasion. The Volunteers provided not only a patriotic outlet but
each corps became a debating society. It was soon evident that
a drastic shift in power had taken place in the Volunteers who

were controlled not by the Establishment but by progressive politically minded people. The Volunteers turned their attention to demands for reforms which the Establishment—weakened by its colonial wars—was not strong enough to resist. The Volunteers became the military wing of the colonial nationalists led by Grattan and Flood. A review of the Volunteer's military strength speeded up the repeal of Poynings' Law. Passed during the parliament of 1494-5, Poynings' Law embodied the right of the English administration to govern Ireland. The second concession was that of Free Trade, enabling the Irish merchants to trade on the same terms as their English rivals. This was the repeal, in 1779, of the acts prohibiting the export of Irish woollen and glass goods, acts against carrying gold and silver into Ireland, and the rising Irish brewing industry was allowed to import foreign hops. However, trade between England and Ireland was still impeded by Customs restrictions.

This was the heyday of "Grattan's Parliament" and Ireland was becoming an independent kingdom sharing a monarch with England. Signs of this independence appeared with the foundation of the Bank of Ireland, an independent post office and the building of the Fourt Courts and Customs House. The Volunteers now started to press further reforms, such as demands for a universal franchise in elections, the removal of the Penal Laws, and while Grattan pressed Bills for the further relief of Catholics in 1782 and 1792 (by which Catholics were admitted to practise law and intermarry with Protestants) the leaders of the Volunteers began to desert them.

The radical Volunteers of Dublin, led by James Napper Tandy, tried to organise a reform convention made up of delegates elected by the people. On October 25, 1784, the meeting was held and a plan of reform discussed but the leadership, Henry Flood and Lord Charlemont (commander-in-chief of the Volunteers) completely deserted the radicals. The leaders had obtained what they sought; they had a fairly independent Ireland, still ruled by the aristocracy, with the capitalist class free from English trade restrictions which had crippled the development of capitalism in Ireland. Henry Flood believed in Protestant democracy and opposed religious freedom. Henry Grattan believed in religious freedom but opposed democracy. He advocated only landowners having the franchise. In these circumstances the Volunteers, which had brought these men to positions of power, were now a hindrance which had to be removed. An "Arms and Gunpowder Bill" was passed requiring the Volunteers to give up their arms. Connolly commented : "The working men fought, the capitalists sold out, and the lawyers bluffed." He described how the three divisions of Dublin Volunteers were disarmed and uses it as an illustration as to how the country at large was disarmed.

In Dublin there were three divisions of Volunteers— corresponding to the three popular divisions of the patriotic forces. There was the Liberty Corps, recruited exclusively from the working class; the Merchants Corps, composed of the capitalist class, and the Lawyers Corps, the members of the legal fraternity. Henry Grattan Jr. telling of the action of the Government after the passage of the "Arms and Gunpowder Bill" requiring the Volunteers to give up their arms to the authorities for safe keeping, says the Government "seized the artillery of the Liberty Corps, made a private arrangement by which it got possession of that belonging to the Merchants Corps; they induced the Lawyers to give up theirs, first making a public procession before they were surrendered."

In other words and plainer language, the Government had to use force to seize the arms of the working men, but the capitalists gave up theirs secretly as the result of a private bargain, the terms of which we are not made acquainted with; and the lawyers took theirs through the streets of Dublin in a public parade to maintain the prestige of the legal fraternity in the eyes of the credulous Dublin workers, and then, whilst their throats still husky from publicly cheering the "guns of the Volunteers", privately handed over those guns to the enemies of the people.

The conduct of "Grattan's Parliament" and especially Grattan's fervent belief in the English connection caused a young Protestant barrister named Theobald Wolfe Tone to write a bitter attack in a pamphlet, *An Argument on behalf of the Catholics of Ireland*, published in September, 1791. Tone commented : "I have said that we have no National Government. Before the year 1782 it was not pretended that we had." He went on :

The Revolution of 1782 was a Revolution which enabled Irishmen to sell at a much higher price their honour, their integrity, and the interests of their country; it was a Revolution

which, while at one blow it doubled the value of every borough
monger in the kingdom, left three fourths of our countrymen
slaves as it found them, and the government of Ireland in the
base and wicked and contemptible hands of those who had spent
their lives degrading and plundering her; nay, some of whom had
given their last vote decidedly, though hopelessly, against this,
our famous Revolution. Who of the veteran enemies of the
country lost his place or his pension? Who was called forth to
station or office from the ranks of the opposition? Not one. The
power remained in the hands of our enemies again to be exerted
for our ruin, with this difference, that formerly we had our
distress, our injuries, and our insults *gratis* at the hands of
England; but now we pay very dearly to receive the same with
aggravation, through the hands of Irishmen—yet this we boast of
and call a Revolution !

During this century the foundations for the eventual partition
of Ireland were being laid. Peadar O'Donnell wrote : "Partition
arises out of this uneven development of capitalism in
Ireland . . ."[11] During the 18th century, Ulster was the industrially backward and revolutionary part of the country while it
was the south that was the centre of industrial capitalism. The
Irish linen industry of the north was basically a peasant industry
and it was not until 1820 that modern industrial techniques were
employed. Gill writes :

> It would seem natural that the southern manufacturer,
> designed for greater efficiency, elimination of waste, and better
> distribution of risk, should be more successful and more perman-
> ent than the ill organised industry of Ulster.[12]

The capitalism of the south, that which supported "Grattan's
Parliament" was a non-professional one; its adventurers were
centralised and heavily subsidised. Above all, they were "gentlemen" and had not clawed their way up from the working
classes. Gill comments "manufacture in the south was too much
the work of amateurs." Moreover, the southern capitalists were
faced with a strong trade union movement and did not know
how to combat it. Chart writes :

> Irish workmen . . . perhaps to a greater degree than those of
> Great Britain, showed themselves hostile to the adoption of

labour saving machinery . . . Even in England there were riots directed against the use of machinery, and the reform was carried by the high hand of the employers. In Ireland this class was weaker and less capable of facing the struggle. Even to this day it is difficult in southern Ireland to introduce labour saving machinery into an existing business.[13]

A Dublin manufacturer named Stephenson complained :

If a manufacturer wants to engage in any new branch of the linen manufacture, there must first be a consultation among the weavers to know if they will allow him to carry it into execution, for in the southern provinces they are to a man sworn into a combination to support a bill of prices they have made.[14]

The basic reason why industrial capitalism started its growth in the north was the difference in the system of land tenure. We have already seen that the bulk of the people outside of the Ulster province were tenants-at-will but in Ulster the "tenant right" existed. The land system made productive investment in the south of the country impossible. The efforts of the southern capitalists in the 18th century to start industry were nullified by the land system. The "tenant right" or "Ulster custom" allowed security of tenure and led to an improvement in the value of the land. At the end of the 18th century the capitalist industries of the south disappeared, except for the Guinness breweries, while the north started along the road to modern capitalist industry. We shall examine this growth later.

At the end of the 18th century also, the seeds of religious disunity, making the grounds for partition that much easier, were also sown. The Catholics and dissenting Presbyterians had long suffered jointly from the Penal Laws and had also joined together to fight the landowning classes. On January 2, 1793, Catholic delegates returned from petitioning the king on the Penal Laws, and Sigerson writes :

It is to be noted as marking the cordial friendship that had grown up amongst the inhabitants holding different religious creeds, that the delegates chose to pass through the north, and that their carriages were drawn through the streets of Belfast by a Presbyterian populace, amid the acclamation of all.

The idea of the Catholics and Presbyterians joining forces against the Establishment horrified the Anglican Archbishop of Armagh, Hugh Boulter, who wrote :

> The worst of this is that it stands to unite Protestant and Papist, and whenever that happens, goodbye to the English interest in Ireland forever.

Lord Grenville wrote to the Lord Lieutenant of Ireland in 1779 :

> I cannot help feeling a very great anxiety that such measures may be taken as may effectually counteract the union between Catholics and Dissenters at which the latter are evidently aiming. There is no evil I would not prophesy if that union takes place.

It is perhaps somewhat significant that in 1784 an extreme Anglican Protestant organisation started raiding Catholic homes, unofficially enforcing the code forbidding Catholics to keep firearms. Swooping at dawn, and thus earning themselves the name Peep o' Day Boys, they attacked or placed warning notices on Catholic homes. The general wording of the notice was :

> To Hell or Connaught immediately, or we, Captain Rakeall and Captain Firebrand, will come and destroy you and send your souls to hell and damnation.[15]

The Catholic population reacted by establishing its own militant group known as The Defenders. To most of these groups there was little point in denominational warfare and they mainly attacked landlords and the clergy of the Established Church. By 1792 a terrorist campaign from both Protestants and Catholics had forced down rents in Meath and Cavan and tithes were becoming increasingly difficult to collect. The alarming growth of these activities caused a reaction in 1793 when Catholic and Protestant landlords organised committees to discover and punish the offenders. The landlords organised bands of retainers to fight the agrarian guerrillas and these bands were to become Orangemen by 1797.

Orangeism, as it stood in September 1795, was a reaction against Defenderism which, itself, has its origins in resistance to Peep O' Day Boy raids. By 1795 Defenderism had become a national movement which in the southern counties was directed against landlords.[16]

In 1795 James Wilson, a Presbyterian farmer of Dian, Co. Tyrone, formed a movement called the Orange Boys, named after William of Orange. Wilson received little support from his fellow co-religionists and when the Orange Order itself was formed, in 1795, "to maintain the laws and peace of the country and the Protestant institutions", it was strictly an Anglican movement and Presbyterians were not admitted into the Order for several years. But the radical democratic-republicanism of the Ulster Presbyterians was being split. Senior comments :

The radical movement which emerged after the Volunteer convention of 1748 drew its main support from the Dissenters of Ulster who had sympathised with the American rebellion and for a long time accepted Whig leadership. This movement, however, included some Catholics and many nominal members of the Established Church. It represented a general middle class as well as Dissenter radicalism. Among its leaders were both convinced revolutionaries and adventurers, but the Irish middle class and the Dissenters in particular, despite their taste for radical literature and oratory, felt they had too much to lose and were thus as little inclined towards revolution as the gentry. When the cause of radicalism became identified with illegal conspiracy and a rising of the Catholic peasantry, the Irish middle class drew back and many of its erstwhile radicals took refuge in the Orange Lodges.[17]

Chapter 5

THE UNITED IRISHMEN

T HE UNITED IRISHMEN was the first major Irish radical and anti-imperialist movement, a movement which was both nationalist and internationalist, working with like movements in Scotland, England and other European countries. When the young Protestant lawyer from Dublin, Theobald Wolfe Tone, published *An Argument on Behalf of the Catholics of Ireland*, in September, 1791, he was invited to Belfast by the city's Presbyterian liberals. After two weeks of discussion the Belfast Society of United Irishmen was born on October 14. Soon, with the aid of the radical James Napper Tandy, a Dublin society also came into being. Connolly, quoting from the minutes of the inauguration meeting of the society, held at the Eagle Inn, Eustace Street, Dublin, on November 9, 1791, illustrates some of the principles of the movement.

> For the attainment then of this great and important object— the removal of absurd and ruinous distinctions—and for promoting a complete coalition of the people, a club has been formed composed of all religious persuasions who have adopted for their name The Society of United Irishmen of Dublin, and have taken as their declaration that of a similar society in Belfast, which is as follows :
>
> In the present great era of reform, when unjust governments are falling in every quarter of Europe, when religious persecution is compelled to abjure her tyranny over conscience; when the Rights of Man are ascertained in Theory, and that Theory substantiated in Practice; when antiquity can no longer defend absurd and oppressive forms against the common sense and common interests of mankind; when all government is acknowledged to originate from the people, and to be so far only obligatory as it protects their rights and promotes their welfare; we think it is our duty as Irishmen to come forward and state what we feel to be our heavy grievance, and what we know to be its effectual remedy.
>
> We have no National Government : we are ruled by

Englishmen and the servants of Englishmen, whose object is the interests of another country; whose instrument is corruption; whose strength is the weakness of Ireland; and these men have the whole of the power and patronage of the country as means to seduce and subdue the honesty and the spirit of her representatives in the legislature. Such an extrinsic power, acting with uniform force in a direction too frequently opposite to the true line of our obvious interests, can be resisted with effect solely by unanimity, decision, and spirit in the people, qualities which may be exerted most legally, constitutionally, and efficaciously by the great measure essential to the prosperity and freedom of Ireland—an equal Representation of all the People in Parliament . . .

We have gone to what we conceive to be the root of the evil; we have stated what we conceive to be the remedy—with a Parliament thus reformed everything is easy; without it nothing can be done.

Connolly writes :

Here we have a plan of campaign indicated on the lines of those afterwards followed so successfully by the Socialists of Europe—a revolutionary party openly declaring their revolutionary sympathies but limiting their first demand to a popular measure such as would enfranchise the masses, upon whose support their ultimate success must rest.

The Dublin society prepared a plan early in 1794 which divided the country into 300 constituencies equal in population with a vote for every man . . . one proposal was made that women should have the vote as well. Soon repressive measures were being taken against the movement and as a natural reaction the United Irishmen became more revolutionary. It must be emphasised that the movement was, at first, entirely constitutional. It became revolutionary as a result of oppressive measures. It is worth noting that it might have been less vulnerable to informers had it been specifically revolutionary from the outset. The United Irishmen became an oathbound secret society based on the middle class reformers, urban working men and peasants (long accustomed to agrarian conspiracy) pledged to obtain national and social emancipation. The organisation was based on innumerable small committees sending representatives to local committees who likewise sent delegates to provincial committees and so on to a national committee. Delegates from the United Irishmen were sent to similar movements in Scotland and England. Simon Butler, A. Hamilton Rowan and Dr. Drennan attended meetings held by the Friends of the People movement in Edinburgh. The Establishment brought the Scottish radicals to heel first by a series of trials in 1793-4. The first blow was struck when the young Scottish advocate Thomas Muir was sentenced to fourteen years transportation after a "fixed" trial. Muir, who had been made an honorary member of the United Irishmen, escaped and lived in exile in France, where he died in 1799 of a wound suffered during a fight between a ship he was travelling on and an English "man o' war" in Cadiz Bay. Muir was named president of the "Provisional Government of the Scottish Republic" when a new Scottish radical movement, named the United Scotsmen, made an abortive attempt at a rising in 1797.[1]

An agreement was drawn up between the United Irishmen, United Scotsmen and the United Englishmen movements, that each "British nation" would form a "distinct republick". While the Irish and Scots had a definite "national liberation" programme, all three movements shared each other's social liberation programme.

The social programme of the United Irishmen movement can be summed up in the phrase "the greatest happiness of the greatest number". The founding philosophy of the movement was expressed in a "Secret Manifesto to the Friends of Freedom in Ireland", circulated throughout the country in June, 1791. The manifesto was written by Wolfe Tone in collaboration with Samuel Nielson and others and passages from it were quoted by Connolly "to show the democratic view of its (United Irishmen) founders".

> This society is likely to be a means the most powerful for the promotion of a great end. What end? The Rights of Man in Ireland. The greatest happiness of the greatest number in this island, the inherent and indefeasible claim of every free nation to rest in their nation—the will and the power to be happy to pursue the common weal as an individual pursues his private welfare, and to stand in insulated independence, an imperatorial people.
>
> The greatest happiness of the greatest number.—On the rock of this principle let this society rest; by this let it judge and

determine every political question, and whatever is necessary for
this end let it not be accounted hazardous, but rather our interest, our duty, our glory and our common religion. The Rights of
Man are the Rights of God, and to vindicate the one is to
maintain the other. We must be free in order to serve Him
whose service is perfect freedom.

The external business of this society will be—first, publication,
in order to propagate their second principles and effectuate
their ends. Second, communication with the different towns and
to be assiduously kept up and every exertion used to accomplish
a National Convention of the People of Ireland, who may profit
by past errors and by many unexpected circumstances which
have happened since this last meeting. Third, communications
with similar societies abroad—as the Jacobin Club of Paris, the
Revolutionary Society in England, the Committee for Reform in
Scotland. Let the nations go abreast. Let the interchange of sen-
tinels among mankind concerning the Rights of Man be as immediate as possible.

When the aristocracy come forward, the people fall backward, when the people come forward, the aristocracy, fearful of
being left behind, insinuate themselves into our ranks and rise
into timid leaders or treacherous auxiliaries. They mean to
make us their instrument; let us rather make them our instruments. One of the two must happen. The people must serve the
party, or the party must emerge in the mightiness of the people,
and Hercules will then lean upon his club. On the 14th of July,
the day which shall ever commemorate the French Revolution,
let this society pour out their first libation to European liberty,
eventually the liberty of the world, and, their eyes raised to
Heaven in His presence who breathed into them an ever living
soul, let them swear to maintain the rights and prerogatives of
their nature as men, and the right and prerogative of Ireland as
an independent people.

Connolly comments:

It would be hard to find in modern Socialist literature anything more broadly International in its scope and aims, more
definitely of a class character in its methods, or more avowedly
democratic in its nature than this manifesto . . .

Indeed, the manifesto clearly shows that Tone placed his
beliefs in revolution on the people rather than the landowning

classes. In his second best known quotation, Tone sums up this belief clearly :

> Our freedom must be had at all hazards. If the men of property will not help us, they must fall; we will free ourselves by the aid of that large and respectable class of the community—the men of no property.

But it must be emphasised that Tone's policies were developed on a basis of the interest of the Dissenting middle class which developed from the Plantations that encompassed the newly emerging Catholic middle class, then the mass of the peasantry, forging a revolutionary alliance to create a national democratic revolution which would have created a modern bourgeois nation, which had happened in France. The most clear picture of the social programme of the United Irishmen comes from Tone's famous *An Address to the People of Ireland*, Belfast, 1796. The *Address* was written for distribution on the landing of the proposed 1796 expeditionary force from France and was brought again with the 1798 expedition; copies were seized by an English squadron under Admiral Warren, from a French warship off Tory Island in October that year.

The *Address* speaks of the "new order of things commencing in Europe"; of the establishment of the French Republic "on the broad firm basis of equal rights, liberties and laws"; that "the doctrine of Republicanism will finally subvert that of Monarchy, and establish a system of justice and rational liberty, on the ruins of the Thrones of the Despots of Europe". Tone put his case bluntly :

> The alternative which is now submitted to your choice, with regard to England is, in one word, Union or Separation! You must determine, and that instantly, between slavery and independence, there is no third way.

Having briefly given a historical sketch of Ireland and given a critical appraisal of the position of the country, Tone visualises the Irish Republic that the United Irishmen would create :

> The aristocracy of Ireland, which exists only by our slavery, and is maintained in its pomp and splendour by the sale of our

lives, liberties and properties, will tumble in the dust; the People will be no longer mocked with a vain appearance of a Parliament, over which they have neither influence or control. Instead of a King, representing himself, a House of Lords representing themselves, we shall have a wise and honest Legislature, chosen by the People, whom they will indeed represent, and whose interest, even for their own sakes, they will strenuously support. Our commerce will be free, our arts encouraged, our manufactures protected, for our enemies will no longer be our law-makers. The benches of our Legislature will no longer groan under the load of placemen and pensioners, the hirelings of a foreign power, and the betrayers of our country; we shall have upright Judges to administer the laws, for the road to the judgement seat will no longer be through the mire of Parliamentary corruption; we shall have honest Juries to determine on our liberties, properties and lives, for the Crown will no longer nominate our Sheriffs, on the recommendation of this or that grandee; the host of useless offices, multiplied without end for the purpose of corruption, will be annihilated, and men will be made hereafter for places and not places for men; the burdens of the people will be lightened, for it will be no longer the custom to buy majorities in Parliament; the taxes, which will be hereafter levied will be honestly applied to the exigencies of the State, the regulation of commerce, the formation of a Navy, the making of roads, the cutting of canals, the opening of mines, the deepening of our harbours, and calling into activity the native energy of the land. Instead of the state of daily suicide wherein Ireland now exists, her resources will at length be actively employed for her interest and her glory. Admission to the Legislature will no longer be purchased with money, and the execrable system of jobbing, so long our disgrace and ruin, will be forever destroyed, the trade of Parliament will fail, and your borough mongers become bankrupts. Your peasantry will be no longer seen in rags and misery, their complaints will be examined, and their suffering removed; instead of the barbarous policy which has so long kept them in want and ignorance, it will be the interest as well as duty of National Government to redress their grievances and enlighten their minds. The unnatural union between Church and State, which has degraded Religion into an engine of policy, will be dissolved, tithes, the pet of agriculture, will be abolished, the memory of religious dissensions will be lost when no sect shall have a right to govern their fellow citizens, each sect will maintain their own Clergy, and no citizen shall be disfranchised for worshipping God according to his conscience. To say all in one

word, IRELAND SHALL BE INDEPENDENT. We shall be a Nation
and not a Province; Citizens not Slaves. Every man shall rank in
the State according to his merits and talents. Our commerce
shall extend to the four quarters of the globe, our flag shall be
seen on the ocean, our name shall be known among the nations,
and we shall at length assume that station for which God and
nature have designed us.

The United Irishmen grew to a considerable strength, arming, drilling, with Tone beginning to draw up plans for an
uprising to establish his radical Irish Republic. In the spring of
1794, a United Irish emissary to France, Rev. William Jackson,
a Church of Ireland (Anglican) clergyman, was captured with a
paper outlining the position in Ireland for a republican uprising. Charged with high treason, Jackson committed suicide in
the dock on April 30, 1795. The paper he carried declared that
the Presbyterians were "the most enlightened body of the
Nation".

"The Dissenters are enemies to the English Power from
reason and reflection, the Catholics from a hatred of the
English name."

Elaborating on the position of the Dissenters the paper comments :

> They are steady Republicans, devoted to liberty and through
> all the stages of the French Revolution have been enthusiastically
> attached to it. The Catholics, the great body of the people, are in
> the lowest degree of ignorance and want, ready for any change
> because no change can make them worse, the whole peasantry of
> Ireland, the most oppressed and wretched in Europe, may be said
> to be Catholic.[2]

As Thompson points out :

> In the years before and after '98, the Dissenters of Ulster, the
> most industrialised province, were not the most loyal, but
> the most "Jacobinical" of the Irish; while it was only after
> the repression of the rebellion that the antagonism between the
> "Orangemen" and "Papists" was deliberately fostered by the
> Castle, as a means of maintaining power.[3]

Tone affirmed the Dissenter attitude in his *Autobiography*,
when he wrote:

The Dissenters of the north, and more especially of the town of Belfast, are, from the genius of their religion, and from the superior diffusion of political information among them, sincere and enlightened republicans. They had even been foremost in the pursuit of Parliamentary reform, and I have already mentioned the early wisdom of the town of Belfast in proposing the emancipation of the Catholics as far back as the year 1783. The French revolution awakened all parties in the nation from the stupor in which they lay plunged . . . and the citizens of Belfast were first to raise their heads from the abyss, and to look the situations of their country steadily in the face.[4]

Jackson had received his report directly from Tone who, on Jackson's capture, was immediately compromised but, due to influential friends, was allowed to emigrate to America which he used as a stepping stone to reach France, arriving there in 1796. Here he met the Scottish revolutionary Muir (whom he disliked), Tom Paine (author of *The Rights of Man*) and other great social revolutionaries of the day. He began to petition the French to organise an invasion of Ireland to aid the Irish overthrow of the administration. Tone appealed for military aid to France not only because France was at war with England but because she was then regarded to stand at the head of the forces of world liberation. The French Republic was thought to be the embodiment and representative of the principles of freedom and of the international solidarity of a liberated world. He appealed as a democratic-republican to his fellow republican-democrats. At the same time the Scots were trying to induce the French to aid them establish a Scottish Republic. Representatives were sent to Scotland to observe the situation and Citoyen Menguad reported that he found the Scots much disposed to revolution and "this feeling had existed since the Union of England and Scotland". The Irish pointed out, however, that if the French secured control of the Irish ports it was clear that English trade would be seriously injured and so, in December, one of the most brilliant of the French revolutionary generals, Hoche, and a French fleet with 14,000 troops on board, set out for Ireland. Winter storms scattered the fleet and while units did reach Bantry Bay, they failed to make a landing.

Alarmed, the administration took vigorous counter measures

and a systematic raiding for arms in Ulster ("long the heart of the United Irish movement") was conducted by General Gerard Lake. This seriously weakened the movement in the province. The major asset of the Establishment was its intelligence system, its ability to bribe and corrupt the weak in order to obtain information. One such informer was Thomas Reynolds of Kildare, who, being a member of the Leinster provincial committee (Leinster Directory), betrayed the plans of his movement. On his advice, in March, 1798, the Leinster Directory was arrested. In May, 1798, the United Irishmen could wait no longer for French aid and the great insurrection began.

The radicals in England wholeheartedly supported the Irish uprising. *An Address to the Irish Nation*, dated January 30, 1798, from the revolutionary London Corresponding Society, signed by R. T. Crossfield, president, and Thomas Evans, secretary, was sent to the insurgents.

> Generous, Gallant Nation.
> May the present Address convince you how truly we sympathise in all your sufferings ... May Nations learn that "existing circumstances" have been the Watchword of Despotism in all Ages and in all Countries; and that when a People once permits Government to violate all the genuine Principles of Liberty, Encroachment will be grafted upon Encroachment; Evil will grow upon Evil; Violation will follow Violation, and Power will engender Power, till the liberties of ALL will be held at despotic command ...

Thompson comments:

> It is a moving address, which redeems the English from the charge of total complicity in the Irish repression, and which included an appeal to English soldiers in Ireland to refuse to act as "Agents of enslaving Ireland!"[5]

The English radical movements were suffering great repression at this time. In 1797 the London poor had stoned the carriage of George III shouting "Peace! Bread! No War! No King!" That year 50,000 seamen at Spithead and Nore took over their ships, expelled their officers, set up their own delegate committees and ran up the red flag. While Connolly, probably believing Tone's statement that of the sailors of the Fleet "two-thirds of them are

Irishmen", was convinced it was the activities of former United Irishmen, impressed into the English Navy, which led to this great mutiny, Dugan points out ". . . it was not until they saw the surprising effectiveness of the mutinies that the United Irishmen began pouring agitators into the King's Navy. They went aboard on quota lists to build up revolutionary cells of fellow countrymen."[6] The main responsibility of the mutiny was due to the English radicals and the revolutionary United Englishmen movement.

The United Irishmen uprising was, from a practical viewpoint, a series of badly co-ordinated and isolated peasant struggles. The vast majority of the middle class leadership quietly vanished from all protestations of revolution. The big lesson of the uprising was bitterly expressed by Henry Joy McCracken in a letter to his sister in 1798 : "The Rich always betray the Poor." Waterford and Wexford were secured by the insurgents who tried to drive west and north but were halted at New Ross and Arklow. The military engaged the insurgent troops at Enniscorthy (Vinegar Hill) on June 21, where, after a fierce battle, the insurgents were dispersed. Although the insurgents were led by Father John Murphy (who was afterwards hanged) it must be stressed that the Catholic priests were effective in sabotaging the rising, urging their parishioners to hand in their arms. The overall effect of the priests' influence was to deprive the insurrection of the element of surprise. The risings in Antrim and Down were quickly suppressed while only skirmishes occurred elsewhere. In August a small French army under Humbert landed at Killas, Co. Mayo, where they were joined by the local United Irishmen, and the Irish Republic was proclaimed. This group met with initial success but, having made its way almost halfway across the country to Co. Longford, the force was surrounded by a larger one, led by Viceroy Cornwallis, and compelled to surrender at Ballinamuck on September 23.

News of Humbert's initial success had created excitement in France, especially among the expatriate Irish and Scots. Another expeditionary force was organised, comprising one sail of the line and eight small frigates commanded by Commodore Bompart. On board were 5,000 men led by General Hardy. With them went Tone, determined to reach Ireland and take command, declaring that if the Government sent only a corporal's guard, he felt it his duty to go along with them. On October 11 they reached Lough Swilly where an English squadron was waiting. Bompart urged Tone to remove himself to a lighter ship which might escape from the English. Tone answered: "Shall it be said that I fled while the French were fighting the battles of my country?" The French were defeated, Tone was captured and brought to trial on November 10, 1798. Condemned to death Tone wounded himself in his cell on the evening of November 11 and died on November 19.

The failure of the United Irishmen uprising was due to three basic reasons. One, the lack of co-ordination. Connolly makes this extremely clear in his analysis:

> The people were wretchedly armed, totally undrilled, and compelled to act without any systematic plan of campaign, because of the sudden arrest and imprisonment of their leaders. Yet they fought and defeated the British troops on a score of battlefields, despite the fact that the latter were thoroughly disciplined, splendidly armed, and directed like a huge machine, from one common centre. To suppress the insurrection in the counties of Wicklow and Wexford alone required the efforts of 30,000 soldiers; had the plan of the United Irishmen for a concerted uprising all over the island on a given date not failed, the task of coping with the Republican forces would have been too great for the Government to achieve. As it was, the lack of means of communication prevalent in those days made it possible for the insurrection in any one district to be almost fought and lost before news of its course had penetrated into other parts of the country.

The second reason was the administration's intelligence network, its large number of spies and informers which had penetrated the organisation and betrayed practically every move the revolutionaries made.

The third reason was the expert use of the time honoured *divide et impera* policy. The administration was well aware of the growing union between Protestant and Catholic in the unifying United Irishmen movement. Archbishop Boulter had warned "whenever that happens, goodbye to the English interest in Ireland forever." Therefore great propaganda was made of the fact that the majority, should the republicans succeed in their democratic state, would be Catholic. Senior comments:

Fear of the consequences of a Catholic dominated revolution, combined with General Lake's repressive measures in Ulster, had, by the eve of the rebellion of 1798, driven many erstwhile republicans into the Orange Order.[7]

The administration painted the 1798 uprising as a religious war whereby the Catholics were uniting to throw out the Protestants. This, despite the fact that the leadership of the United Irishmen were—in the main—Protestants appealing to the mass of the people on a non sectarian basis. Castlereagh wrote to Wickham on June 12, 1798 :

... Priests led the rebels to battles; on their march they kneel down and pray, and show the most desperate resolution in their attack. They put such Protestants as are reported to be Orange-men to death, saving others on condition of their embracing the Catholic faith ...[8]

Yet one eyewitness of the events describes a Catholic priest calling down damnation on his flock if they lifted a finger against "their lawful rulers" while a Presbyterian minister was seen, gun in hand, leading his parishioners in an attack against the English soldiers. Senior says :

Most of the northern rebels who took up arms were Protestants. The largely Catholic Monaghan Militia was, in fact, one of the mainstays of the Government forces in the north.

But the Establishment succeeded only too well in their propaganda exercise. Senior adds :

News of the United Irish (religious) outrages in the south, in combination with the defeat of the feeble revolt in the north, accelerated the flow of repentant radicals into the (Orange) Lodges.

A movement riddled with spies, lack of co-ordination and planning, susceptibility to Establishment propaganda, these were the faults of the United Irishmen. But of all the lessons learnt, it is the voice of McCracken that seems to echo down the years into modern Irish history : "The Rich always betray the Poor."

Chapter 6

PIONEERS OF SOCIALISM

F OLLOWING THE SUPPRESSION of the 1798 uprising, the complete take-over of the Irish legislature by the English Government was inevitable. William Pitt, England's Prime Minister, decided upon the idea in 1798 and argued that the union would ensure a co-ordination of activity in an emergency, such as another insurrection, and that the union would also encourage English capitalists to invest in Ireland, thus raising the country's standard of living. After a heated debate, the Irish parliament rejected the idea in 1799 but an amendment from W. B. Ponsonby to prevent such a proposal coming before the Irish legislature again was rejected by 106 votes to 105 votes. The Establishment then resorted to the tactics which had been successfully used to obtain the union with Scotland in 1707. Out of the 300 members of the Irish legislature, pressure was brought to bear on 72 members who held positions controlled by the English administration; 84 "rotten borough" members were paid-off and 28 other members were given peerages, thus securing a majority (158 for and 115 against the Act of Union, which was finally passed on June 7, 1800). It cost the Establishment just over one million pounds and, in January, 1801, Ireland became part of the United Kingdom represented by 100 common members and 28 peers. The English attitude was summarised by Under Secretary Edward Cooke, writing to Pitt in 1799:

> By giving the Irish a hundred members in an Assembly of six hundred and fifty they will be impotent to operate upon that Assembly, but it will be invested with Irish assent to its authority.

On June 28, 1886, in Liverpool, Premier Gladstone was to declare: "There is no blacker or fouler transaction in the history of man." Strangely enough, in view of modern history, the most vociferous anti-Unionists were the Orange Order. Gill states:

"Yet most Orangemen were among the violent anti-Unionists ... To avoid splitting their organisation and provoking an open clash with government, Orange leaders adopted a policy of discouraging the discussion of the union at meetings." The Orangemen, the combination of the Volunteers of "1782" and the United Irishmen, caused great concern to the authorities but, by carefully fence sitting, the Government Orangemen avoided the mobilisation of the Orange Order against the Union and soon afterwards, with Establishment prodding, the Order became the biggest tool of Unionist philosophy. Strangely again, while the Orange Order were anti-Unionists, the Catholic Hierarchy were for the union and saw rule from Westminster as a way of achieving status for the Church in Ireland. They had already been given the sop of the establishment of a Catholic seminary at Maynooth, in 1795, in which to train and educate their priests. This had been given them by the Government because it was felt that priests, trained in revolutionary Europe, were bringing radical ideas into Ireland. The Catholic orator, Richard Lalor Shiel, was more than forthright when addressing the House of Commons on the occasion of the Maynooth Grant of 1845:

> You are taking a step in the right direction. You must not take the Catholic Clergy into your pay, but you can take the Catholic Clergy under your care ... Are not lectures at Maynooth cheaper than State prosecutions? Are not professors less costly than Crown solicitors? Is not a large standing army and a great constabulary force more expensive than the moral police with which by the priesthood of Ireland you can be thirstily and efficaciously supplied?

Following the union, the remnants of the United Irishmen, led by Robert Emmet, brother of Thomas Addis Emmet, one of the '98 leaders, started to prepare plans for a further rising. This conspiracy, says Connolly, "was more of a working class character than its predecessors." In 1802 Emmet was in France and had an interview with Napoleon, then First Consul of the Republic. Although the Treaty of Amiens (March 27, 1802) had stopped the war between England and France, Napoleon was of the opinion that the war would soon be renewed—it was in May, 1803. He promised Emmet aid. An alliance had also continued with the revolutionary United

Englishmen. According to the Castlereagh papers Emmet was in contact with the movement via a United Irishman named William Dowdall of Dublin. The man Emmet was reportedly in contact with was Colonel Edmund Marcus Despard. Despard (1751-1803) came of a family who owned land in Ireland. According to E. P. Thompson ". . . Despard was also an Irishman, and by 1796 or 1797 he had become so deeply committed to the cause of Irish independence that he was serving both on the committees of the London Corresponding Society and in the more shadowy circles of the United Irishmen and United Englishmen in London."[1] According to a spy's report, Despard and Emmet were organising a simultaneous uprising. However, on November 13, 1802, Despard and nineteen others were arrested and charged with high treason. One of the witnesses for the defence was the famous English sailor, Horatio Nelson, who had great praise for Despard's military career. "We have measured the height of the enemies' walls together," he told the court. Despite Nelson's pleading, Despard was executed in January, 1803.[2] Thompson says of the Despard affair: "It linked the struggle of the Irish nationalists . . . with the grievances of London labourers and of croppers and weavers in the north of England." Emmet, however, realised that there was now no likelihood of a joint rising by the Irish and English working classes.

In 1802 there were sporadic armed risings in Waterford, Tipperary and Limerick due "to the dearness of the potatoes" and "the right of the old tenantry to retain possession of their farms."[3] Realising he could wait no longer, Emmet devised an elaborate plan to attack and hold Dublin Castle as the main spark of the insurrection. A proclamation was drawn up in the name of the "provisional Government of Ireland" leaving one in no doubt about the politics of Emmet's revolution. Article One confiscates the whole of church property and nationalises it. Articles Two and Three forbid and declare void the transfer of all landed property, bonds, debentures and public securities until a national government, elected by universal suffrage, is established and the national will on such transactions declared.[4] Connolly states:

Two things are thus established—viz. that Emmet believed the "national will" was superior to property rights, and could abolish them at will; and also that he realised that the producing classes could not be expected to rally to the revolution unless given to understand that it meant their freedom from social as well as political bondage.

The plans for the rising, however, miscarried badly and only 100 insurgents gathered for the attack on the Castle. The authorities turned out in strength. One of the members of the Lawyers' Yeomanry Corps of Dublin, a young Catholic lawyer, who turned out to hunt for Emmet's insurgents, was Daniel O'Connell, ironically known to Irish history as "The Liberator".[5] Emmet went "on the run" but was caught on August 25 and brought to trial on September 19. His speech from the dock has long been a rallying call of national liberation movements all over the world: "When my country takes her place among the nations of the earth," declared twenty-five-year-old Emmet, "then, and not till then, let my epitaph be written." He was executed the next day.

Now Ireland was at the mercy of the Establishment, without leaders or a sense of destiny. The population was increasing and with it starvation, illness and crime. The basic problem was, of course, land; high rents and insecurity of tenure contributed to the worsening situation. There was no provision made, by the small oligarchies who controlled local government, for the relief of the destitute. Irish industry declined rapidly, unable to compete with English industries. Large numbers of Irish workers, especially from the nine Ulster counties, began a migration to sell their labour in Glasgow, Lanark, Manchester, Lancashire and Yorkshire. The decay of the Irish textile industry, a direct result of the union, increased migration. This migration caused the loss of many remarkable figures to the Irish working class movement. But Ireland's loss was the gain of the American and English workers' movements. One such loss was John Doherty of Buncrana, Co. Donegal, who arrived in Manchester in 1817, becoming a leader of a cotton spinners' union based on the organisation of the United Irishmen. The working class leaders thrown up by the emigration of the Irish, Scots and Welsh caused the English writer, H. S. Foxwell, to observe: "Socialist propagandism has been mainly carried on by men of Celtic and Semitic blood."[6] The activities of Irish emigrants in the struggle for the emancipation of the working classes in England does not, however, fall within the scope of this work.

The position in Ireland worsened at the end of the Napoleonic wars when thousands of disbanded soldiers and sailors arrived home to an Ireland with a high unemployment figure in urban areas and "in rural areas the landlords engaged in a war of extermination with their tenantry." The commercial crisis intensified bitterness between the working classes and the capitalists. Secret terrorist organisations, such as the Whiteboys, were revived and agrarian warfare became the order of the day. According to Connolly:

> ...at this time Irish trade unionism, although secret and illegal, attained to its maximum of strength and compact organisation. In 1824 the chief constable of Dublin, testifying before a committee of the House of Commons, declared that the trades of Dublin were perfectly organised, and many of the employers were already beginning to complain of the "tyranny of the Irish trade unions".

The situation in Ireland was reflected, though to a lesser extent, in England and among the other nations of Europe. Among these nations philosophers sprang up with ideas for an improvement of the existing social order by improving the workers' lot and abolishing poverty. Basic philosophies were Jeremy Bentham's Utilitarianism or "the greatest happiness of the greatest number", reflected in the United Irishmen philosophy, and that of Owenism or co-operation which relied on the paternalism of the ruling classes.

Ireland produced William Thompson of Clonkeen, Roscarbery, Co. Cork, who demands recognition as the formulator of the economic theories usually associated with Karl Marx. Thompson was the anticipator of many of the basic Marxian theories and thus could be described as a founding father of Scientific Socialism. Harold J. Laski, in introducing the Communist Manifesto, says Thompson "laid the foundations" which Marx and Engels "brought so remarkably to completion". Marx was, unfortunately, less than generous in his acknowledgements to Thompson. Only slight references to this "First Irish Socialist", as Connolly describes him, are made in *Poverty of Philosophy*, 1847; *Critique of Political Economy*, 1859; and *Das Kapital*, 1867.

William Thompson was born in Cork City in 1775, one of
the Protestant Ascendancy class who had acquired land in
Ireland in 1682-6. His father was Alderman John Thompson,
a rich Cork merchant, sometime mayor of the city and High
Sheriff of the county. Thompson was thirty-nine years old
when he inherited his father's estates—1,400 acres and a trading fleet—in 1814. But he was not a businessman. A member
of the Cork Institution and the Philosophical, Scientific and
Literary Society, he was widely travelled, had studied works of
Simon de Sismondi and others of the then modernist school
of French political economy. On inheriting his father's estate
he was confronted with the Irish land question, immediately
ceasing to be an absentee landlord and giving his tenants
leases on such generous terms that he brought the wrath of the
Establishment about his head. "I am not," he wrote, "what is
usually called a labourer. Under equitable social arrangements,
possessed of health and strength, I ought to blush making this
declaration." He became obsessed with a sense of guilt for
living on rents, "the produce of the efforts of others."

During the years 1812-26 he supported Christopher Hely-
Hutchinson, an advocate of Catholic Emancipation and his
first essay into public affairs was in 1818 when he advocated
popular education and educational reforms in a series of letters
to the *Cork Southern Reporter*. These letters were subsequently published in pamphlet form as *Practical Education
for the South of Ireland*. Thompson became interested in
Bentham's doctrine of Utilitarianism and then studied the
economic theories of David Ricardo who argued that the
value of a commodity was equal to the value of the labour
that produced it. Unlike Ricardo, however, Thompson felt
that the labourer was entitled to the full value of the labour.
Under capitalism the labourer was paid the lowest wage that
market competition for labour determined. The rest of the
produce went to the capitalist in profit and interest. Few explained this as clearly as Thompson, certainly no one worked
out the economic significance more clearly and it is this that
made Thompson the founding figure of Scientific Socialism.
The concept of surplus value is the fundamental principle of
Marxist Socialism.

In 1824 Thompson published his 276,000-word work: *An
Inquiry into the principles of distribution of wealth most*

conducive to human happiness; applied to the new proposed system of voluntary equality of wealth. In this work Thompson became the first writer to explain the evolution towards Socialism and that the rich, as a class, would oppose the advance of the majority towards an egalitarian society. "A few individuals," he added, "may rise above the impulses of their class . . ." but these would be exceptions. In this statement, Thompson came into conflict with the ideas of his fellow Celt, the Welshman, Robert Owen, who believed that appeals to the rich and aristocratic patronage would move society towards co-operative communities. Thompson's philosophy was that the workers could only improve their lot through their own exertions.

Thompson's work had an electrifying effect on the workers' movements growing up in Europe. John Minter Morgan acclaimed the work as a masterpiece and subsequently wrote:

> Neglected Thompson, whose attainment towers
> Beyond the reach of critic's feeble powers
> And vain attempts his reasoning to refute,
> Has taught them wisdom—for behold them mute.
> But when this weaker generation's past
> And struggling truths, unfetter'd, rise at last,
> Then shall his work transcendant be confess'd
> And distant nations by his genius bless'd.[7]

Owen was impressed by Thompson and distributed his work at his own expense from Messrs. Wheatley and Alard in the Strand, London. When he set out to establish his commune at New Harmony, Indiana, U.S.A., Owen took a large number of copies with him.

Thompson was also an avowed feminist, a ceaseless advocate of woman's emancipation. He was a close friend of Anna Wheeler, born in 1785, the youngest daughter of an Irish Protestant Archbishop. Anna was prominent in the Co-operative Movement in which Thompson was now a leading figure. She wrote to Robert Owen: "Shall man be free and woman a slave . . . never say I!" In 1825 Thompson published *An appeal of one half of the human race, women, against the pretensions of the other half, men, to retain them in political and thence in civil and domestic slavery.* The work, he wrote, was a "joint property" with Anna Wheeler and part of the work was the exclusive product of "her mind and pen". Both Thompson and Anna were bitter opponents to marriage with its unbreakable bonds, disabilities imposed on women, unequal moral standards and the false odour of sanctity. Pankhurst writes:

> The *Appeal* was a landmark in history. The book gave a more concrete view of the legal and social disabilities of women, it adopted an altogether bolder and more challenging approach than had yet been attempted and gave point and impetus to latent yearnings. From its time onward publications advocating the emancipation of women became more frequent, bolder, and more definitely applied to remedy the evils of the law.[8]

The year of the *Appeal's* publication Thompson took part in the historic debates of the Co-operators at Chancery Lane and Red Lion Square, London, when it is believed that the term "Socialism" was first coined.[9] In 1827 Thompson published *Labour Rewarded. The Claims of Labour and Capital conciliated by one of the Idle Classes.* This went further to enhance his position as one of the leaders of the Co-operative in the United Kingdom. In Thompson's day the discussion among pioneer Socialists was not that of the Marxian era—i.e. whether Socialism could be achieved in one country surrounded by the capitalist world. The discussion was whether Socialism, or communes, could succeed in one district.

Thompson was no mere theoretician and he had long urged the establishment of communes. In the *Co-operative Magazine* in 1826 Thompson argued that communities should be formed "not by agriculturalists alone to produce food, but by labourers and tradesmen of every description to supply each other with all the comforts as well as the necessities of life." His *Address to the Industrious Classes of Great Britain*, in 1826, embodies his ideas on communes. In 1827 the *Co-operative Magazine* published "A prospectus of the Cork Co-operative Community".[10] In this Thompson proposed a community of 2,000 people, each having one acre of land. The constitution provided complete freedom of thought and expression; religion was a private thing, women were eligible for advancement to any office to which their talent might lead them. Idlers and "persons with vicious tendencies would, if deemed irreclaimable by mild treatment", be exiled from the commune. However, it does not appear that

Thompson's plans for a commune advanced beyond the stage of resolutions and paper constitutions.

In July, 1830, Thompson's most important work was published: *Practical directions for the speedy and economic establishment of communities, on the principle of mutual co-operation, united possessions, equality of exertions and the means of enjoyment*. This work placed Thompson rather than Owen in the forefront of the Co-operative movement and, because of Thompson's more radical, revolutionary, Socialist outlook, Owen grew increasingly bitter. Following the publication of this work, Owen wrote to Thompson and expressed their basic difference.

> While you are boldly operating on the whole mass, I am endeavouring to arrange a little part of the social machine, not forgetting its connection with the whole.[11]

Thompson was a delegate of the Cork Co-operative Society, which had its offices at 14 The Parade, Cork, to the Second Co-operative Congress in 1831. He pressed his ideas for establishing communes but received no aid from Owen who saw Thompson as a threat to his own position in the movement. Thompson suffered from a chest ailment which grew steadily worse and on March 28, 1833, he died aged fifty-eight. He left his money and property to the Co-operative Movement and his body to science. Relatives contested the will on the grounds that Thompson was insane. The case dragged on for twenty-five years and it was the lawyers, with their exhorbitant fees, who became the chief beneficiaries.

Despite the fact that Thompson's works were still in print in the 1880's, he remains a largely unknown and overlooked figure to all but a few students of Socialist history, despite the fact that William Lovett's Chartist Movement drew their inspiration from *Labour Rewarded*. During the early part of this century his works were still read and studied in Europe, particularly in Germany. Connolly comments:

> Fervent Celtic enthusiasts are fond of claiming, and the researches of our day seem to bear out the claim, that Irish missionaries were the first to rekindle the lamp of learning in Europe, and dispel the intellectual darkness following the downfall of the Roman Empire; may we not also take pride in the fact that an Irishman was the first to pierce the worse than Egyptian darkness of capitalist barbarism, and to point out to the toiler the

conditions of their enslavement, and the essential pre-requisites of their emancipation?

Thompson had failed in his efforts to establish a commune. Owen's 30,000-acre commune in Indiana, U.S.A., known as New Harmony, which he established in 1825 had lasted only two years. Similarly, a commune at Orbiston in Scotland, lasted only to 1827. But during the last years of Thompson's life a commune was established at Ralahine, in Co. Clare, which was so successful that it became "a Mecca for social reformers." Like most rural parts of Ireland at the time, Co. Clare was a hotbed of agrarian unrest, insurrection and crime. On May 10, 1830, the whole county was declared to be in a state of disturbance, the Peace Preservation Act was brought into force and troops flooded the area. The cause was the Whiteboys who were organising the people against paying rents, taxes, or tithes and, similarly, a group calling itself the Lady Clare Boys (because they disguised themselves in women's shawls) were also carrying out agitation. Edward Thomas Craig describes the situation thus :

> Here was a melancholy picture of a rich soil only partially cultivated and a willing people unemployed. Condemned to remain ignorant, they had become brutal in their revenge for social injustice and driven to wild and demoniacal deeds of desperate violence through lack of food, work and useful employment. Goaded to resistance by centuries of wrong and bad government, they were aroused to fury by famine, and now showed "the dragon's teeth" with a vengeance. The only measures that were popular as remedies were military and police "repression", legal penalties and religious influence. To preserve property it was sagely deemed necessary to shoot and destroy the creators of wealth. Fear and suspicion seized upon all hearts, all classes seemed paralysed and utterly powerless and incapable of suggesting, let alone adopting, a remedy.
> It was at this time the spirit of vengeance reached Ralahine, and the family of the proprietor was obliged to leave their mansion in the charge of an armed police force and seek safety in the city of Limerick. This circumstance prompted the proprietor John Scott Vandeleur, Esq., then late High Sheriff of the county of Clare, to carry into action a desire he had long cherished of establishing a co-operative farm at his property at Ralahine. The condition of the peasantry urged him to make the change sooner than he had intended.[12]

Vandeleur had been converted to the idea of Owenite co-operatism by Owen himself when on a visit to Dublin he had expounded the principles of his philosophy. Not being sure of the best methods to employ in the establishment of a co-operative farm, Vandeleur sought the aid of Edward Thomas Craig, the editor of the *Lancashire Co-operator*. Craig, who had been born in Manchester in 1804, was grandson of a Scottish clansman who had fought for the Jacobite cause in 1745 and had himself been present at the Peterloo Massacre. Vandeleur invited Craig to manage the commune. "I was doubtful of success," wrote Craig, "among a people in a state of insurrection..." Nevertheless, Craig took up the challenge and arrived at the 618-acre estate at Ralahine. The former estate manager an evil individual who had made his workers labour without water or rest, had been shot after the workers had drawn lots as to which one of them should rid the world of him.

Craig's arrival was treated with deep suspicion and the fact that he could speak no Irish created difficulties in putting his ideas across. He settled himself to master the language, though not without some horseplay by the still suspicious Irish. Craig writes that the man teaching him the language taught him to say "Tharah ma dhoel" [sic] when greeting anyone. Only when an infuriated Irishman was about to beat him up did Craig learn the phrase meant "Go to the devil!"

A meeting of the estate workers was held on November 7, 1831, at which the estate was turned over to the commune bearing the title "The Ralahine Agricultural and Manufacturing Co-operative Association". The objects of the association were:

1. The acquisition of a common capital.
2. The mutual assurance of its members against the evils of poverty, sickness, infirmity and old age.
3. The attainment of a greater share of the comforts of life than the working classes now possess.
4. The mental and moral improvement of its adult members and
5. The education of their children.

The Commune was to be governed "by a committee of nine members, to be chosen half yearly, by ballot, by all the adult male and female members, the ballot lists to contain at least four of the last committee." A lengthy constitution was drawn up and adopted covering production, distribution and domestic economy, education and formation of character, government etc. An agreement was then signed on November 10, 1831, between Vandeleur and representatives of the commune emphasising that the estate and all property belonged to Vandeleur "until the Society accumulates sufficient to pay for them; they then become the joint property of the Society."

Ralahine became a tremendous success. Even the London *Times* devoted an article to the commune and a young London law clerk walked to Liverpool, shipped to Dublin, and walked across Ireland to join the community. The agrarian outrages in the area suddenly ceased. Connolly comments:

> In the most crime ridden county in Ireland this partial experiment in Socialism abolished crime; where the fiercest fight for religious domination had been fought it brought the mildest tolerance; where drunkenness had fed fuel to the darkest passions it established sobriety and gentleness; where poverty and destitution had engendered brutality, midnight marauding and a contempt for all social bonds, it enthroned security, peace and reverence for justice, and it did this solely by virtue of the influence of the new social conception attendant upon the institution of common property bringing a common interests to all.

An English visitor, Mr. Finch, wrote concerning the educational attitudes of the commune:

> The only religion taught by the society was the unceasing practice of promoting the happiness of every man, woman, and child to the utmost extent of their power. Hence the Bible was not used as a school book; no sectarian opinions were taught in schools; no public dispute about religious dogmas or party political questions took place; nor were members allowed to ridicule each other's religions; nor were there any attempts at proselytism. Perfect freedom in the performance of all religious duties and religious exercises was guaranteed to all. The teaching of religion was left to ministers of religion and to the parents; but no priest or minister received anything from the funds of the society. Nevertheless, both Protestant and Catholic priests were friendly to the system as soon as they understood it, and one reason was that they found these sober, industrious persons had now a little to give them out of their earnings, whereas formerly they had been beggars.

The workers did not receive ordinary currency as payment but a "Labour Note" was adopted which they were able to exchange in the common store for any of the necessities of life. There was little need for money, however, as members of the commune could take as much of the common produce of the estate as they wished and there was no worry about the children's education expenses for this was provided for by a common fund.

Ralahine was the "model commune" and when Craig wrote his *History of Ralahine* it was immediately translated into French, German and Italian. M. Godin, who translated the book into French, used the blueprint of Ralahine to set up his own community, Familistere at Guise. On August 21, 1833, Craig wrote an address "to the agricultural labourers of County Clare" in which he said ". . . if the working classes would cordially and peacefully unite to adopt our system, no power or party could prevent their success."

Unfortunately, an unlooked for power brought about the destruction of Ralahine. John Scott Vandeleur was overfond of gambling with the Dublin aristocracy. He lost all his money and fled the country in disgrace and deeply in debt. The land laws refused to recognise the right of a community to hold a lease or act as tenants and the estate was taken over to pay off Vandeleur's debts. Craig recalls how the people on the estate set up a *Caoinan* (*Caointeachán*), an act of lamentation or wail for the dead, when they heard the news. "Ochón! Ochón! Seán Vandeleur! Why did you go from us! Ochón! Vandeleur! Why did you leave us! Why have you left your own people at Ralahine!"[13] On November 23, 1833, the workers of Ralahine signed a declaration:

> We, the undersigned members of the Ralahine Agricultural and Manufacturing Co-operative Association, have experienced for the last two years contentment, peace and happiness . . .

Within a few years of leaving Ralahine, agrarian unrest was again rampant in Co. Clare, murders were being committed, estates burnt down and the county was again under martial law. Connolly writes:

> So Ralahine ended. But in the rejuvenated Ireland of the future the achievement of those simple peasants will be dwelt upon with admiration as a great and important landmark in the march of the human race towards its complete social emancipation. Ralahine was an Irish point of interrogation erected amidst the

wilderness of capitalist thought and feudal practice, challenging both in vain for an answer.

Although Ralahine was the most successful commune to be established in Ireland, it was not by any means the only such experiment. *A Memoir of E. T. Craig* tells us:

> The system of sharing profits with the labourers was imitated with success on one hundred acres of County Galway upon the system adopted by Mr Craig at Ralahine.[14]

This community was established on the estate of Lord Wallscourt. Connolly mentions the fact that the Quakers of Dublin established a Co-operative Woollen Factory while the Quarterly Magazine of November, 1819, refers to a community, nine miles outside of Dublin, which held thirty acres, supported a priest, a school of 300 children and comprised butchers, carpenters and wheelwrights who made and sold jaunting cars.

The importance of these early Irish Socialist pioneers is immense. Thompson, with his revolutionary Scientific Socialism, provided a new philosophy which developed into Marxism. Ralahine provided a practical example that communism, or, rather, community-ism was a workable concept.

Chapter 7

O'CONNELL—THE ENEMY WITHIN

THE UNION BETWEEN Ireland and England brought no
improvement to conditions of the ordinary Irish people. They
continued to suffer, as they had in the 18th century, in unspeak-
able misery and as little more than serfs to the landowning
classes. The war between England and France had raised the
cost of living and of rents; evictions of peasant farmers unable to
meet the high prices were increasing. As so often happens during
periods of extreme poverty in a country, the population increased
dramatically. Between 1800 and 1847 it nearly doubled.
Chauviré comments that the peasantry "preserved in its deepest
self the memory of its ancestors and a pride in what they had
been, combined with a profound bitterness at the wrong which
was being done to them." The administrations, bearing in mind
the lessons of 1789, when a union between the Presbyterians and
Catholics came near to throwing out the imperialist interest in
Ireland, decided to grant a Regium Donum to Presbyterian
clergy raised to £14,000 which was shared between 186 congregations—working out at £75 per minister. The Crown
retained the power to refuse this sum to any Presbyterian minister whom it considered to be of seditious and disloyal principles.
The terms seem to have been gladly accepted by the
Presbyterians and, by March 30, 1805, Dr. Black was able to
write to the Government reporting that there were only two disloyal ministers in the Presbyterian Assembly. Presbyterian ministers henceforth became advocates and a bulwark of Unionism
and when, in 1834, the Anglican Orange Order opened its ranks
to all non-Catholics, the Presbyterians literally swamped the
Order. The former anti-Unionists were now the most strongly
Unionist element in the country, the non-conformist radicalism
of the United Irishmen being perverted to the meso-Fascism of
the Orange Order.

At the same time industry, such as it was, was failing to compete against its stronger English rival. By 1829 the Irish cotton

and woollen trade was on the verge of extinction. The Ulster linen trade was saved by entrepreneurs changing the system to power spinning and weaving and centralising the industry on modern capitalist lines. While such a development allowed Ulster industry to corner a portion of the market in England, the majority of Irish industry became extinct except on the Irish home market. Davitt says:

> High freights and heavy customs dues militated very much against external trade in those days and kept the home market for the native producer.[1]

Against these conditions the Irish people conducted a continuing agrarian warfare as they had done during the preceding century. Davitt writes:

> The Catholic Church, however, became more and more the opponent to Whiteboyism, and of its various offshoots in Connaught and Leinster, as the deferred promise of (Catholic) emancipation loomed within the domain of possibility. Thrashers and Steelboys arose in all the western counties, and made no distinction among enemies, whether clergy or landlords or their adherents. The law and its agents were defied, outrages were made to follow evictions or grabbings, in regular and certain punishment, while altar denunciation failed to frighten the leaders, who could command the loyalty of the peasants who knew that their homes were secure only through terrorism which the doubly banned associations created. Insurrection acts and the older Whiteboy laws were enforced to put the agrarian bands down with the usual crop of hangings and transportations. There was, however, no regular police force to deal with these lawless societies, the military being the only available power to put the law in operation, and full advantage was taken of this state of things by the various "Captains" who were the peasant leaders. An irregular insurrection was kept up in midnight raids, threatening letters and violence in all forms, in the West and in some of the Southern Counties, until after 1825 the attention of the country was diverted from these doings to the great and absorbing issue of Catholic Emancipation.[2]

Of the peasant agrarian warfare, Davitt comments:

> The varied forms in which Whiteboyism manifested itself in

the South and West, in the earlier period of O'Connell's time, indicated little or no change in purpose or methods. Districts or counties gave names of their own to a branch of the same movement. The "Whitefeet" and "Blackfeet", the "Terry Alts", "Rockites", "The Lady Clares" and the rest, were all peasant bands leagued irregularly against the common enemy— landlordism, and the law, government, class or interests on which its relief for the power to rack rent the land and to harass the lives of the labouring poor. In the South the evil of turning tillage land into grazing farms to the injury of the labourers and of the interests of general industry engaged the attention of the Whiteboys, and showed on their part an intelligent appreciation of sound political economy.

The peasant warfare was such a thorn in the side of the administration that between 1800 and 1833 no less than 114 parliamentary commissions and sixty select committees were established to investigate conditions provoking this agitation. Sir George Cornewall Lewis, in his *Local Disturbances in Ireland*, 1836, wrote : "The Whiteboy Associations may be considered as a vast trades union for the protection of the Irish peasantry." Addressing a special commission grand jury in Limerick in 1831, Mr. Justice Webb commented that Whiteboyism was :

. . . a war of the peasantry against the proprietors and occupiers of the land. The object of this warfare is to deprive the proprietors and occupiers of land of the power of disposing of their property as they think fit, to dictate to them the terms on which their estates and property shall be dealt out to the peasantry and to punish by all means that can be resorted to such as disobey those dictates which the people think proper to issue.[3]

Lord Wellesley, the Lord Lieutenant of Ireland, wrote to Lord Melbourne on April 5, 1834, that the Whiteboys had

. . . a complete system of legislation, with the most prompt, vigorous and severe executive power, sworn, equipped and armed for all purposes of savage punishment, is established in every district.[4]

In the north, a society called the Ribbonmen had grown out of the old Defender movement of Ulster. "It absorbed almost all the existing agrarian bodies after 1830," wrote Davitt, "Whitboyism being largely transformed into the better organised and more widely spread Ribbon combination." This soon became an oath-bound secret society, laying the foundations for the Young Ireland and Fenian movements. Such were the conditions of the ordinary Irish people. Despite this, for the first twenty-nine years of the Union with England, no measure for the protection of the Irish tenant was even introduced into the Westminster Parliament by any minister or member.

In spite of the excellent conditions that prevailed in Ireland during 1800-29 for a successful agrarian-based revolution, the terrible conditions of the land system were completely over-shadowed by the fight to win religious freedom in the form of Catholic Emancipation. Most of the Penal Laws had been repealed in the 1780's and 1790's by the Irish legislature. Catholics could maintain schools, join professions and vote at parliamentary elections according to their status as regards the then very restricted franchise. They could not, however, sit in parliament, be ministers in government, hold any office except the most junior in the civil service, be judges or colonels in the army or officers in the navy. Naturally these restrictions only affected the Irish Catholic middle and upper classes. To the mass of the people the most serious life and death problem was that of land tenure. Ominous warnings on this problem had been shown in a famine of 1817 and a greater famine in 1821-2. The famines had occurred not because there was shortage of food in the country. Indeed, during 1822, one million quarters of grain were exported to England while the Irish people starved to death. The English Radical, William Cobbett, made the most telling comment following a debate on the famine in the House of Commons in 1822.

> Money, it seems, is wanted in Ireland. Now people do not eat money. No; but the money will buy them something to eat! What! The food is *there*, then pray observe this, reader, pray observe this, and let the parties get out of the concern if they can. The food is there, but those who have it in their possession will not give it without the money. And we know the food is there; for since the famine has been declared in Parliament thousands of quarters of corn have been exported every week from Ireland to England.[5]

It is surely a peculiar tribute to the leaders of the movement for "Catholic Emancipation" that they managed to turn the mass of the Irish people from their life and death struggle to a subject of interest to bourgeois place-seekers only. The man who led the movement for emancipation was Daniel O'Connell, a Dublin lawyer and landowner. O'Connell had turned out in 1803 to fight against the United Irishmen. Like his fellow Irishman, Edmund Burke, he was an anti-revolutionary. When he spoke about liberty he had in mind the mid-19th century English middle class conception. He was an ardent monarchist and cherished a romantic attachment for his "darling little Queen" (Victoria). Brought up in Derrynane, Co. Kerry, he was a fluent speaker of the Irish language but became the greatest enemy of the language.

In O'Connell's day some 4,000,000 spoke the language which the proletariat had managed to keep alive, despite the Hedge Schools which, although they used Irish as a medium of instruction, concentrated on reading in English with Latin and some Greek, thus sabotaging the overall position of the language and anticipating the National Education system. The bourgeoisie had, of course, long abandoned the language to ape their imperial masters. The United Irishmen movement had seen the importance of the linguistic struggle as part of the anti-imperialist struggle of the Irish nation and, at a meeting in Dublin, decided "that the English language should be abolished, setting themselves to the study of the Irish tongue."[6] This is a fitting rejoinder to those who claim that Tone and the United Irishmen were advocates of an English-speaking Ireland. Robert Emmet was also a keen student of the language. The opportunist O'Connell, however, "could witness without a sigh, the gradual disuse of Irish." O'Connell, a speaker of the language, even insisted on holding his meetings in English when in Irish-speaking areas." "I am sufficiently utilitarian not to regret its abandonment." The effect of O'Connell's support for English cultural imperialism is still seen in Ireland today. The language was alive as the speech of the peasants and workers and it was these people whom O'Connell had managed to seduce to his cause and win their worship. Keep the language from the children, was the lesson he taught them and this they did in the years to come with devastating effect for the position of the language in the country.

The myth of O'Connellism was even accepted by Davitt who

was lavish in his praise of him, though pointing out that O'Connell "was not, in any sense, an active land reformer . . ." Indeed, O'Connell, the landlord, was actively against the peasants' agrarian warfare and, together with Dr. Doyle, Bishop of Ossory, made fierce attacks on the peasants "anxious to disassociate the Catholic cause from the violence and raiding of the insurgent peasants."[7] O'Connell and the Catholic Church united in their denunciation of the landless Irish peasants. Even O'Connell's admirer, Davitt, was forced to admit :

> The Church was making itself too much the slave of an abominable law, and was tacitly upholding landlordism by not denouncing the glaring injustices which drove the tenants to outrage as the only protection against a condoned and tolerated oppression of the poor.

During the first twenty years of the union Catholic agitation was carried on by landlords, merchants and professional men. In 1823 O'Connell formed the Catholic Association which aimed at mass support. He called in the aid of the Catholic clergy, who had not as yet played a part in the movement. These clergy were well placed to lead local agitation. A campaign fund was started and everyone was asked to give 1d per month to the Catholic Association's "war chest". The poor people were enlisted by the activity of the clergy. Chart writes :

> The priests threw themselves whole-heartedly into the collection of this tribute, sometimes using methods which were not far short of intimidation.[8]

There was a general election in the summer of 1826. Catholics who were classed as 40s freeholders were allowed to vote but they usually voted for the landlord's nominees (otherwise evictions followed). In 1826 in Cos. Waterford, Westmeath, Louth and Monaghan, Protestants (the only denomination who could sit in parliament) were returned pledged to Catholic Emancipation supported by the Association. In 1828 there was an election in Co. Clare and O'Connell himself announced his intention of standing, although, as a Catholic, he would not be able to take his seat. He was elected by 2,057 votes against 982 votes for his rival. Prime Minister Wellington and his Home Secretary, Sir

Robert Peel, recognising the dangers of the situation, introduced the Catholic Emancipation Bill which became law on April 13, 1829. O'Connell was now the hero of the Irish masses, leading a small band of Irish members in the House of Commons. O'Connell had won the support of the Catholic Irish working classes because they had, unfortunately, believed him when he told them that the decay of Irish industry, trade and the appalling living conditions they were suffering, was purely due to the union with England. They also did not really believe in his avowed monarchism and pacifism.

The attitude of the trade unions to Catholic Emancipation did not emerge until after their conflict with O'Connell in 1837-8. In an "Open letter of the trades' committee to Daniel O'Connell", published in *Freeman's Journal,* January 18, 1838, they asked:

> ... what advantage is it to the tradesmen of Ireland that thirteen hundred situations have been thrown open by emancipation? ... Has it given a loaf of bread to any of the thousand starving families of the poor operatives of this city?

In 1831 a primary education system was instituted, giving birth to the National School system of Ireland. Daniel Corkery writes:

> The new Board of National Education simplified their own special problem by presuming that the Irish language did not exist. As a matter of fact, there were probably more people speaking Irish in 1831, when this scheme appeared, than ever before.[9]

Pearse aptly described the so called "National Education" system as "The Murder Machine". However, O'Connell's influence had taken hold over the people and they were trying to discard their language and culture.

Also in 1831 O'Connell turned his powers to the subject of tithes. At this time the clergy of the Anglican Church ("the Church as by law established" were entitled to demand taxes from the people of each district, irrespective of religion, for the upkeep of their church and its ministers. As Connolly points out "the fact that this was in conformity with the practice of the Catholic Church in countries where it was dominant did not, of course, make this any more palatable to the Catholic peasantry of Ireland, who continually saw a part of their crops seized and sold to maintain a clergy whose ministrations they never attended, and whose religion they detested." Escorted by soldiers the Anglican clergy seized the produce of the peasants and workers while they were left near starvation. While O'Connell moved for the abolition of tithes, at the same time he continued to condemn the peasantry who were taking a more active line by carrying off crops and cattle and terrorising auctioneers and buyers. The ensuing "Tithe War" assumed all the appearances of a full scale civil war with clashes between the peasantry and military. It was thanks to the pressure of the peasantry, rather than the opportunist politics of O'Connell, that the Tithe Commutation Act of 1838 was passed.

From 1830 the various trades unions in Ireland began to agitate for the return of an Irish Parliament, the Repeal of the Union with England. They sought not a political objective but a socio-economic one, i.e. they thought that with the return of an independent Irish legislature, Ireland would return to an economic paradise which they believed it had been prior to 1800. By August, 1831, thirty-nine separate trades had held meetings which passed resolutions calling for the Repeal. O'Connell had expressed himself in support of the Repeal but feared that the workers might grow into a violent revolutionary force. In November, 1830, trade unionist Peter Martin, speaking at a working carpenters' repeal meeting, explained O'Connell's insistence on legal methods of agitation and promised O'Connell that they would follow "his instructions to observe peace and good order."[10]

On August 19, 1831, a Dublin Trades' Political Union was formed in which radical politicians and trade unionists began to agitate for Repeal independently of O'Connell. It caused considerable embarrassment to O'Connell but, by 1832, it had lost its working-class dynamism by opening its ranks to farmers and clergymen who fell in with O'Connell's ideology. It held its last public meeting on March 19, 1848.[11]

After the spring of 1833 there was a noticeable increase in the "outrages" by workmen's trade combinations. One hundred and twenty employers and "respectable citizens" signed a petition on December 3, 1833, calling on the Lord Mayor of Dublin to preside at a public meeting on the situation, in order to take into consideration the most effectual means of bringing to justice those persons who committed, and also those who were concerned in the barbarous and violent outrages recently committed in our city, arising out of combination, and also to take into consideration the propriety of petitioning parliament to enact such laws as may prevent a further recurrence of those outrages.

A secret meeting of workers was held at the carpenters headquarters in Summerhill, Dublin, on the night of December 6 at which it was resolved to "upset the proposed public meeting" by a mass attendance of workers. The workers also sent delegates to O'Connell to ask him to attend the meeting on their side. O'Connell refused. The meeting was held and duly overwhelmed by the workmen.

There had been a comparative peace in labour relations between 1830 and 1833 when the working classes were caught up in the prospect of Repeal generated by O'Connell. During the early months of 1834 O'Connell had promised a Repeal discussion by the second week of Easter but, after the resounding defeat of a repeal motion on April 29, he began to delay the question in order to avoid the coercive measures which he felt would be the inevitable consequence of a renewed Repeal Campaign. The uneasy alliance between the working class movements and O'Connell was shattered.

As O'Connell furthered his career he attracted himself to the ruling classes and became a necessary extension of their policies. Connolly points out: "he ceased to play for the favour of organised labour" (which he had done during the Emancipation and Tithe years) "and gradually developed into the most bitter and unscrupulous enemy of trade unionism Ireland has yet produced, singling the trades of Dublin always out for his most venomous attack."

Apart from attacks on trade unions in 1826, 1831, and in August, 1836, O'Connell had never done anything which might identify himself with the employer class in opposition to the workers. His political reliance on the masses led him to a contrary position. In 1835, however, O'Connell took his seat as a supporter of the Whig Government in the House of Commons and threw all his support against social reform. In May, 1838, he voted against a proposal to shorten the hours of child labour in factories.

1837 was the most violent year in 19th century Dublin labour history; workers were beaten up for refusing to join unions and for working under the prices asked by unions. To this situation was added bread riots during the summer. Workers armed with pitchforks attacked wagons loaded with bread destined for the English soldiers in Richmond barracks. These attacks reached a peak in July and died off in August. However, trade union "outrages" still continued. Fergus A. D'Arcy writes:

Were these assaults committed by artisans in the pursuit of trade union aims, or by unskilled men as a result of personal feuds? It is a necessary question for it would be an easy error to identify as labour crimes such outrages as then occurred simply because those involved were porters, carpenters or dock labourers.

Of the forty-four cases of 1836 in which informations were forthcoming, details of those involved and the reasons for the assaults are extant. Sixty-four per cent were the direct result of the pursuit of trade union objectives. Only twelve per cent of the forty-four cases were of the semi-personal, semi-political type arising from the activities of men like the Dublin coal porters. As for the year 1837, informations were taken in no less than ninety-seven cases arising from combination assaults. Details are extant for only twenty-four of these. Of the twenty-four cases, seventy-one per cent were committed in the pursuit of trade union objectives and twenty-nine per cent were of the semi-personal type arising from feuds. A very high proportion of assaults were committed, therefore, in the name of trade unionism in these two violent years. This is not to say that individual trade union committees actually sanctioned a policy of violence, for which there is no evidence; but even if committed by men acting on individual initiative, the general body of artisans were to suffer the inevitable ill-repute.

These labour outrages arose from the attempt of organised workers to enforce three things: the limitation of apprentices, the compulsory membership of unions and the enforcement of a minimum wage. Repeated outrages over a period were bound to lead to a confrontation between the employing class and terrorised citizenry on the one hand and the trade unionists on the other, unless the violence died down.[12]

Daniel O'Connell made his first major attack on the trade unions on November 6, 1837: "Those associations which I denounce are freed from political bias of any kind and have objects connected with the regulation of trade which they assume control and management of." He condemned trade unionists for seeking the limitation of apprentices, a compulsory membership of unions and a minimum wage. Replies to O'Connell's speech came quickly from prominent trade union leaders such as Thomas Daly, secretary of the printers' union, who, in an extremely restrained address pointed out that the facts cited by O'Connell were entirely erroneous. In December O'Connell, for the first time, systematically denounced the major tenets of trade unionism. He raised a storm of protest which took the form of meetings held by unionists who replied point by point to O'Connell's denunciations. The conflict reached a climax when O'Connell met trade unionists in open debate at the Old Chapel, Ringsend, on January 8, 1838. O'Connell spoke for a marathon three and a half hours in which he made personal attacks on trade union leaders. Finally, he threatened them with religion by saying "do you think your clergy will be able to administer sacraments to you while you continue to deny the children their just right?" This was a reference to apprentice-limitation by which, O'Connell claimed, many children were being prevented from helping their families by their labour.

Patrick O'Brien, president of the carpenters' union, said that unionists had "followed and aided Mr. O'Connell as long as he did not seek to oppress us, but when he seeks to take the bread out of our mouths it is time for us to defend the moral combination by which we support our children." Feelings were bitter and O'Connell was in actual physical danger from the angry workmen. The meeting was finally adjourned in utter chaos.[13]

On January 8 trade unionists met and issued a reply to O'Connell deprecating his attempt at religious and sectarian blackmail. O'Connell replied by making a speech in the House of Commons on February 13, 1838:

There was no tyranny equal to that which was exercised by the trade unionists in Dublin over their fellow labourers. One rule of the workmen prescribed a minimum rate of wages so that the best workman received no more than the worst. Another part of their system was directed towards depriving the masters of all freedom in their selecting workmen, the name of the workmen being inscribed in a book, and the employer compelled to take the first on the list.

O'Connell managed to persuade the Whig Government to set up a Special Committee to inquire into the acts of the Irish trade unions. He opposed the introduction of a "Bill to more effectually regulate Factory Works" introduced by Lord Ashley on June 23, 1838. The bill sought to stop capitalists using children under nine years of age from working long hours down mines and other such activities. O'Connell commented that "their ridiculous humanity ... would end by converting their manufacturers into beggars." This, then, was the man who is known to Irish history as "The Liberator"; historians have, so far, not made clear what was "liberated" by him.

Neither James Connolly nor William P. Ryan (*Irish Labour Movement*) doubted that O'Connell was inherently opposed to the Irish working classes while Clarkson (*Labour and Nationalism*) observed: "to describe O'Connell as the friend of labour would be absurd." In O'Connell's own view, he was not consciously opposed to the workers.

He did not care for being called the enemy of the working classes whilst he felt satisfied in his own mind that he was acting as their best friend. He had not yielded to the taunts of the aristocracy when he thought he was in the right, and he should certainly not now give way to the working classes upon a point in which he considered they were considerably in error.[14]

According to D'Arcy:

But his own brand of political economy, summarily expressed in his declaration that the workers "were not entitled to wages out of capital; they were only entitled to them out of profits, and if their employers made no profits the wages must decrease", made him an even more dangerous, if unwitting, enemy, than the worst of their employers.[15]

In 1840 O'Connell, sensing the growing nationalism of the Irish people in their demand for a repeal of the Act of Union, came out in favour of the re-establishment of the Irish legislature. In July he formed the Loyal National Repeal Association. Again O'Connell received massive support from the Irish people and soon found himself Lord Mayor of Dublin (November, 1841-2). But his almost exclusive Catholic pre-occupation, his equation of Catholicism and Nationalism, strongly helped the estrangement of the Presbyterians. Without this equating of Catholicism and Nationalism, the official bribery of the radical Presbyterians would have been only partly successful.[16] It was on October 15, 1842, that Thomas Davis, John Dillon and Charles Gavan Duffy founded a newspaper called *The Nation* which was to become the voice of a more radical Irish movement.

In the meantime O'Connell was once more in his element, proclaiming 1843 as "Repeal Year", started a series of monster meetings, beginning at Tuam on June 11, demanding the re-establishment of the Irish parliament. On August 15 some half million people gathered at Tara to hear him. In 1843 O'Connell announced that the greatest meeting of all would take place on Sunday, October 8, at Clontarf. The Government, convinced a rising would follow, prohibited the meeting. Tens of thousands of people began massing, the great majority with arms, convinced O'Connell would "give the word". The Irish people were not alone in this belief that O'Connell would seize independence. Friedrich Engels, the son of a wealthy German textile manufacturer, had arrived in England in 1842, aged twenty-two, to manage his father's factory in Manchester. He was already working towards his socio-political philosophy, though his first meeting, leading to his friendship and collaboration, with Karl Marx was not to take place until August, 1844. In 1842 Engels wrote of O'Connell's movement :

What people ! They haven't a penny to lose, more than half of them have not a shirt to their back, they are real proletarians and *sans culottes*, and Irish besides—wild, ungovernable, fanatical Gaels. Nobody knows what the Irish are like unless he has seen them. If I had two hundred thousand Irish I could overthrow the whole British monarchy.[17]

A year later, when Engels had examined the movement more carefully, he dismissed O'Connell's leadership. Writing three months before the Clontarf fiasco, he said :

If O'Connell were really a popular leader, if he had sufficient
courage and he was himself not afraid of the people, i.e. if he
were not a double faced Whig but a straight, consistent democrat, then long ago there would not have been one English soldier
in Ireland, not one Protestant (Anglican) parasitic minister in
purely Catholic districts... Give the people freedom for one
second and they will do with O'Connell and his financial aristocracy what the latter want to do with the Tories.[18]

In this assessment Engels was supported by John Mitchel[18], a
Young Ireland leader, who said of O'Connell, "next to the
British Government, he was the greatest enemy Ireland ever
had."[19] Engels' interest in Ireland was more than passing. He had
been brought face to face with the terrible result of Irish emigration to England in Manchester. In his work *The Conditions
of the Working Class in England,* which he wrote between
September, 1844, and March, 1845, there is a section entitled
"Irish Immigration" in which Engels paints an appalling picture
of Irish conditions in Manchester. He became extremely interested in Irish problems and mentions that he often heard Irish
spoken in the City. It was a language he was later to learn. In
1845 he developed a personal reason for his interest. He married
Mary Burns, an Irishwoman, who was to die of a heart attack
on January 3, 1863. Mary, as Marx wrote to Engels, gave Engels
"a home, completely free and far from all filth of humanity,
as often as you needed it." Engels turned for solace to Mary's
sister Elizabeth, who was a staunch Fenian and aided Engels in
mastering the language. Although Engels was enthusiastic about
Irish independence he saw at once, in *Conditions,* that

> ... Irish distress cannot be removed by an Act of Repeal. Such
> an Act would, however, at once lay bare the fact that the cause
> of Irish misery, which now seems to come from abroad, is really
> to be found at home.

O'Connell, having brought the people to a point where a confrontation at Clontarf was possible, ordered them to go home for
"human blood is no cement for the temple of liberty." Davitt
comments :

> O'Connell's chief weakness ... was his political abhorrence of
> revolutionary media. His constant declaration on this head and

his truly ridiculous contention that liberty was not worth the shedding of human blood, injured the political force of his movement enormously with English rulers.

O'Connell's attitude cannot be explained away by a pacifist creed for he had turned out in 1803 to fight Emmet's insurgents. More recently he had encouraged his son in recruiting for Irish volunteers to defend the Papal state against invasion from the Piedmontese. Pacifism was not part of O'Connell's creed, opportunism was. A week after the Clontarf affair O'Connell was arrested and sentenced to one year's imprisonment for conspiracy at Richmond Bridewell on March 30 but he was released on September 24. O'Connell's star was in the decline and, having been betrayed, the people of Ireland gradually fell away from his movement.

At this time, however, Irish Chartist Associations were springing up throughout the country. An article in the *United Irishman* in 1848 says that they had grown so strong and hostile to O'Connellism that negotiations were being undertaken to organise a public debate between O'Connell and their representatives. The English Chartists were, at this time, led by Fergus O'Connor, who had been elected as a Repeal member of parliament for Co. Cork in 1832. He had tried to work with O'Connell but found his anti-working-class policies obnoxious and broke with him in 1836. In 1837 he published a pamphlet *A series of letters from Fergus O'Connor to Daniel O'Connell. In* this pamphlet he pleaded for a united agitation of Irish peasants and English industrial workers to right the wrongs of both. O'Connell's influence kept Irish nationalists and English radicals apart and it was not until after his death that the two forces began to join together as they had done in 1798 and 1803. Another leader of the English Chartist movement at the time was J. Bronterre O'Brien, a Dublin lawyer. Likewise John Doherty, founder of the National Association for the Protection of Labour, was another working class leader in England. The links were there to achieve a union of purpose. Thompson comments:

> If O'Connor had been able to carry Ireland with him as he carried the north of England, then the Chartist and Young Ireland movements might have come to a common insurrectionary flashpoint. The reservation of the 'moral force' Chartists on

the one hand, and the influence of O'Connell and the priesthood
on the other, together with the terrible demoralisation of the
"Great Hunger" prevented this from happening.[20]

The suffering of the peasantry continued and Westminster had
forced an Irish Poor Law to come into being on July 31, 1838,
against opposition from the O'Connell faction. In February,
1845, the Devon Commission had made its report on a study "to
inquire into the law and practice with regard to the occupation
of land in Ireland." It was estimated that £7,000,000 was pouring out of the country annually to absentee landlords. In 1845 a
blight hit the Irish potato crops, the basic food of the peasants
and workers. The years of the "Great Hunger" had begun and
were to last until 1849. In 1841 the population of Ireland was
8,175,124 and, according to the Census Committee's estimates, it
should have reached over 9 millions in 1851 by natural increases.
Instead there was a loss of $2\frac{1}{2}$ million; 1 million having emigrated while $1\frac{1}{2}$ million had perished of starvation and disease.
Again, as Cobbett had pointed out in the 1822 famine, there was
no need for people to starve ... the food was there. The House of
Commons was told that during the first three months of the
famine, up to February 5, 1846, some 258,000 quarters of grain,
701,000 hundredweights of barley, and one million quarters of
oats and oatmeal were exported out of Ireland to England while
over 1,000 people died of starvation. After that date exports continued at the same rate to make money for the landlords. John
Mitchel pointed out:

> During all the famine years, Ireland was producing sufficient
> food, wool and flax to feed and clothe not nine but nineteen mil-
> lions of people.[21]

He asserted that a charity relief ship bearing a cargo of grain
sailing into an Irish port was "sure to meet six ships sailing out
with a similar cargo". The peasants were forced to sell their
produce to pay their rents to the landlords. Woodham Smith
comments:

> ... It would be a desperate man who ate up his rent, with the
> certainty before him of eviction and "death by slow torture".
> Therefore the Irish peasant sold his little produce, even when his

children were crying with hunger, to save them from a worse
fate.[22]

. The power of the landlords to prevent the Irish peasants from
benefiting from the home grown food created a burning sense of
injustice and the landowning classes were forced to provide
military guards for the produce leaving the Irish ports for shipment to England. O'Connell's son, John O'Connell, M.P., gave
the most bizarre comment on the state of the peasantry when
reading a letter from a West Cork bishop in Conciliation Hall,
Dublin, 1847. The bishop had written:

> The famine is spreading with fearful rapidity, and scores of
> persons are dying of starvation and fever, but the tenants are
> bravely paying their rents.

"I thank God," said John O'Connell, "I live among a people
who would rather die of hunger than defraud their landlords of
rent!"

John Mitchel stormed, in despair:

> ...immense herds of cattle, sheep and hogs... floating off on
> every tide, out of every one of our thirteen seaports, bound for
> England; and the landlords were receiving their rents and going
> to England to spend them; and many hundreds of poor people
> had laid down and died on the roadsides for want of food.[23]

Even the London *Times* was moved to declare:

> They are suffering a real though artificial famine. Nature does
> her duty; the land is fruitful enough, nor can it be fairly said that
> man is wanting. The Irishman is disposed to work, in fact man
> and nature together do produce abundantly. The island is full
> and overflowing with human food. But something ever intervenes
> between the hungry mouth and the ample banquet.[24]

Against this background of suffering the Young Ireland move-
ment was born, leading to the 1848 uprising. In July, 1846,
O'Connell was an exhausted old man of seventy and his son,
John O'Connell, had gained control of the Repeal Association.
He succeeded in "uniting a stealthy ambition to a narrow intel-
lect." That month the group which ran *The Nation* newspaper

walked out of a Repeal meeting in Conciliation Hall, Dublin, and formed the Young Ireland movement. They were led by William Smith O'Brien, a Protestant landlord, who for fifteen years had been a repeal member of parliament. With him were Charles Gavan Duffy, son of a Catholic grocer from Monaghan, and editor of *The Nation;* Thomas Francis Meagher, son of the Catholic mayor of Waterford, and John Mitchel, son of a Unitarian minister in Ulster. Of this group, Mitchel was the most outstanding as a radical and revolutionist.

On January 13, 1847, Young Ireland decided to found a new militant organisation to compel the government to concede repeal immediately. They did not succeed. The masses were too destitute to worry about parliamentary reform while the middle classes continued to side with O'Connell and were therefore hostile to the new radical movement. During this year the Italian revolutionary Giuseppe Mazzini was in London where he had formed the Peoples' International League to "disseminate the principles of national freedom ... to embody and manifest an efficient public opinion in favour of the right of every people to self-government and the maintenance of its own nationality." A list of "nations of the future" was drawn up but Ireland's name was omitted. The Young Ireland movement, who had taken their name and inspiration from Mazzini's Young Italy, wrote to the People's International League. Mazzini replied. Bolton King writes:

His argument was addressed to Separatists but it would apply almost equally to Home Rulers; it proves how radically he misunderstood the Irish movement, and he seems to have felt himself on unsafe ground. He regarded the Irish demand as at bottom one for better government only; and he had every sympathy with their "just consciousness of human dignity claiming its long violated rights", their "wish to have rulers, educators, not masters", their protests against "legislation grounded on distrust and hostility". But he believed that the nationalist movement was not likely to be permanent, and he refused to see any elements of true nationality in it, on the grounds that the Irish did not "plead for any distinct principle of life or system of legislation derived from native peculiarities, and contrasting radically with English wants and wishes" nor claimed for their country any "high special function" to discharge in the interests of humanity.[25]

In fairness to Mazzini it can be conceded that O'Connell's Emancipation and Repeal movements, which were the only yardsticks by which Mazzini could judge the situation, were little more than a claim for Catholic rule in what he fully accepted to be part of the English world. Mazzini also wanted to steer clear of friction between himself and his English patrons. He wrote to Giuseppe Giglioli in March, 1847 : "We have no Irish in the council (People's International League) because that would bring up the question of Repeal which would be fatal to us."

Daniel O'Connell died in Genoa in March, 1847, and his son John took complete control of the Repeal Association, but it had become almost extinct. At this time of deep depression a new and revolutionary force appeared in Irish politics. This was the forty-year-old hunchbacked James Fintan Lalor, son of a former repeal member of parliament from Tenakill, near Abbeyleix. Peadar Macken, writing in the *Irish Nation* in 1910, comments :

> Lalor, not a Socialist in the modern sense, was at least con-
> vinced of the truth of the Socialist doctrine in so far as it related
> to a country, mainly, if not entirely, agricultural.

Lalor had come under the influence of an agrarian reformer named William Conner, from Queen's County, who proposed fixity of tenure for tenant farmers and a scheme of arbitration for rents. He was later expelled from O'Connell's Repeal Association for daring to suggest that repealers should not pay rent or any other charges arising from land and property. Lalor wrote to *The Nation* in January, 1847, that there was "a new social order to be arranged".

> When the independent families who form the natural popu-
> lation of a country compose and organise into a regular commun-
> ity, the imperfect compact or agreement by which each man
> holds his land must necessarily assume the more perfect shape of
> a positive and precise grant from the people ... That grant must
> necessarily assume and establish the general and common right of
> all people as joint and co-equal proprietors of all the land.[26]

Lalor called for an agrarian revolution and not just a Repeal of the Act of Union but the establishment of an Irish Republic. Lalor found an immediate comrade in John Mitchel who adopted Lalor's theories and plans and, with a vision of the Irish peasantry rising, set about "a deliberate study of the theory and practice of guerilla war". According to Davitt: "There was no real Irish revolutionary mind in the '48 period except Lalor's." He comments:

> But it was only in the head and heart of a little, deformed gentleman farmer's son—a descendant of an outlawed Tory of the early confiscations—that the spirit and fire and purpose of a true Celtic revolutionist were found. Lalor's plan was suited to the race, the time, and the calamity, it was intended to cope with. It was exactly what the occasion demanded. It combined the national sentiment with the agrarian interest and passion, and would have rallied the aggressive Whiteboy and Ribbon spirit, and entire peasant feeling of the country, behind a movement that would have given Lord Clarendon a social insurrection, as well as a revolutionary nationalist uprising, to deal with before that year of 1848.

During the summer of 1847 Lalor tried to get *The Nation* to allow him to expand his policies but Smith O'Brien, Gavan Duffy and other leading Young Irelanders, with the exception of Mitchel, hung back, scared of provoking a peasant uprising. In disgust Mitchel broke away and formed a group dedicated to armed insurrection on the basis of Lalor's political and social programme. Lalor had, during the summer of 1847, founded a Tenant Right League in Tipperary with the aid of Michael Doheny but found it impossible to bring about a strike of tenants against the payment of rents. On February 12, 1848, Mitchel began the publication of the *United Irishmen* newspaper "to prepare the country for rebellion". Mitchel's newspaper was sold by English Chartists as if it were one of their own publications.
On February 22, 1848, the French Government, which had, under King Louis Philippe, consistently refused reforms, was overthrown and a republic declared. Duffy and Smith O'Brien decided that the "moderate" Young Ireland movement should now prepare for an armed insurrection. Mitchel, whose *United Irishmen* was printing articles on street fighting in Dublin, how to erect barricades, make bombs from empty soda water bottles, was welcomed back into the council of the Young Ireland movement. All over the European continent during the spring of 1848 oppressed peoples were rising and governments and kings were

falling. Alarmed by events in Ireland, Lord Russell, the English premier, sent Lord Minto, Lord Privy Seal, to the Vatican on a private mission to the Pope.[27] On February 5, a Papal Rescript from Pope Pius I admonished the Irish priesthood for their political activities; and priests, such as Father Kenyon of Templederry, Co. Tipperary, a Young Irelander, were suspended by the Irish Hierarchy.

Now troops began to pour into Ireland and on March 21 Smith O'Brien, Meagher and Mitchel were arrested and charged with sedition. Later they were released on bail and Smith O'Brien and Meagher went immediately to Paris to make contact with the French republicans. There was little forthcoming from the French except that Acting President, Alphonse de Lamartine, presented Smith O'Brien with a tricolour modelled on the French flag (to Meagher's design) of Green, White and Orange, symbolising an eventual unity between the Orangemen and Catholics. This was to be the flag of the Irish Republic. In England, on April 10, 1848, a great Chartist meeting took place at Kennington Common, near London, when the Chartists' "Charter" was drawn up, of which one article was for the re-establishment of the Irish parliament. Mitchel chaired a meeting in Princess Theatre, Dublin, attended by 300 delegates, in order to establish an alliance with the English Chartists.

Smith O'Brien came to trial on Monday, May 15, and was defended by a young lawyer named Isaac Butt, later to lead the "Home Rule" Party. Because of one dissenting juror, he was freed. A similar thing happened at Meagher's trial. Mitchel, however, was convicted by a packed jury and transported to Bermuda, then to Van Diemen's Land, but escaped to the United States of America in 1853. Mitchel showed his acceptance of Lalor's policies in an article in which he states:

> Dynasties and thrones are not half so important as workshops, farms and factories. Rather we may say that dynasties and thrones, and even provisional governments, are good for anything exactly in proportion as they secure fair play, justice, and freedom to those who labour.

He referred to the "true and old principles of protection of labour and the right and duty of combination among workmen."

With Mitchel gone, two newspapers sprang up to take the

place of the *United Irishmen* —*The Irish Felon*, run by John Martin, Mitchel's brother-in-law, and the *Irish Tribune*, which stood for "the moral right of insurrection". Fintan Lalor and Thomas Devin Reilly became the chief writers for *The Irish Felon*. Reilly, from Co. Monaghan, had long been involved with the working class movements. *The Nation* had published a series of his articles on Louis Blanc, the French Socialist. In *The Irish Felon* Reilly stated that "the social system in which a man willing to work is compelled to starve, is a blasphemy, an anarchy and no system." He continued :

But for all that, the rights of labour are not conquered, and will not and cannot be conquered. Again and again the labourer will rise up against the idler—the working men will meet this bourgeoisie and grapple and war with them till their equality is established, not in word, but in fact.

In exile in the U.S.A. Reilly became editor of the *Protective Union* a newspaper which advocated co-operative principles and the rights of labour—he was one of the first pioneers of Socialist journalism in the U.S.A. As for Fintan Lalor, he continued to expound his social theories in a series of articles. Writing in *The Irish Felon* on June 21, 1848, he stated :

The principle I state, and mean to stand upon, is this, that the entire ownership of Ireland, moral and material, up to the sun and down to the centre, is vested of right in the people of Ireland; that they, and none but they, are the landowners and lawmakers of this island; that all laws are null and void not made by them; and that this full right of ownership may and ought to be asserted and enforced by any means which God has put in the power of man. In other, if not plainer, words, I hold and maintain that the entire soil of a country belongs of right to the people of that country, and is the rightful property, not of any one class, but the nation at large, in full effective possession, to be let to who they will, on whatever tenures, terms, rents, services, and conditions they will, one condition being, however, unavoidable and essential, the condition that the tenant shall bear full, true, and undirected fealty and allegiance to the nation, and the laws of the nation, whose lands he holds, and owns no allegiance, whatsoever, to any other prince, power, or people, or any obligation of obedience or respect to their will, orders or laws. I hold further, and firmly believe, that the enjoyment by the people of this right of first ownership in the soil is essential to the vigour and vitality of all other rights, to their vitality, efficacy, and value; to their secure possession and safe exercise. For let no people deceive themselves or be deceived by the words and colours and phrases and forms of a mock freedom, by constitutions and charters and articles and franchises. These things are paper and parchment, waste and worthless. Let laws and institutions say what they will, this fact will be stronger than all laws, and prevail against them, the fact that those who own your lands will make your laws and command your liberties and lives. But this is tyranny and slavery; tyranny in its wildest scope and worst shape; slavery of the body and soul, from the cradle to the coffin; slavery with all its horrors and with none of its physical comforts and security; even as it is in Ireland, when the whole community is made up of tyrants, slaves and slave drivers. A people whose lands and lives are thus in the keeping of others instead of their own are not in a position of common safety. The Irish famine of '46 is example and proof. The corn crops were sufficient to feed the island. But the landlords would have their rent in spite of famine and defiance of fever. They took the whole harvest and left hunger to those who raised it. Had the people of Ireland been landlords of Ireland not a human creature would have died of hunger, nor the failure of the potato crop been considered a matter of any consequence.

Fintan Lalor moved to Dublin to help edit *The Irish Felon*. Still suspecting the intentions of Smith O'Brien's Young Ireland movement, he tried to form Felon Clubs. Such a club was even started in Staleybridge, England, by the Chartist B. T. Treanor. The Scottish movement, nearing the staging of an uprising itself, came out in strong support of a revolution in Ireland. John Martin, editor of *The Irish Felon*, was arrested in early July, and Fintan Lalor decided the time for the uprising or the annihilation of the movement was at hand. On July 8, 1848, he published an article called "The Faith of a Felon", which he thought would be his last work. In it Lalor explained his differences with Smith O'Brien's Young Irelanders:

They wanted an alliance with the landowners. They chose to consider them as Irishmen, and imagined they would induce them to hoist the green flag. They wished to preserve an aristocracy. They desired, not a democratic, but merely a national revolution. Had the Confederation, in the May or June of '47, thrown heart and mind and means into the movement, I pointed out they would have made it successful, and settled at once and forever all questions between us and England. The opinions I then stated, and which I yet stand firm to, are these :

1. That in order to save their own lives, the occupying tenants of the soil of Ireland ought, next autumn, to refuse all rent and arrears of rent then due, beyond and except the value of the overplus of harvest produce remaining in their hands, after having dedicated and reserved a due and full provision for their own subsistence during the next ensuing twelve months.

2. That they ought to refuse and resist being made beggars, landless and homeless, under the English law of ejection.

3 That they ought further, on principle, to refuse all rent to the present usurping proprietors, until the people, the true proprietors (or lords paramount, in legal parlance) have, in national congress or convention, decided what rents they are to pay, and to whom they are to pay them.

4. And that the people, on grounds of policy and economy, ought to decide (as a general rule admitting of reservations) that these rents shall be paid to themselves, the people, for public purposes, and for behoof and benefit of them, the entire general of the people.

It has been said to me that such a war, on the principles I propose would be looked on with detestation by Europe. I assert the contrary; I say such a war would propagate itself throughout Europe. Mark the words of this prophecy—the principle I propound goes to the foundations of Europe, and sooner or later will cause Europe to outrise. Mankind will yet be masters of the earth. The right of the people to make the laws—this produced the first great modern earthquake, whose latent shocks, even now, are heaving in the heart of the world. The right of the people to own the land—this will produce the next. Train your hands, and your sons' hands, gentlemen of the earth, for you and they will yet have to use them.

In July, 1848, with the Government moving to arrest them, with troops pouring into the country, William Smith O'Brien decided to try and raise the country. But Young Ireland had no organisation, no central authority, military command, no specific plan of insurrection, or no munitions, or military information. Smith O'Brien met with scant success. In Mullinahone, Co. Tipperary, it is said 6,000 men did turn out, barricades

were put up and pikes made at the local smithy, on
Wednesday, July 28. Within a few days the number had
dwindled to a few hundred. D'Arcy McGee, another Young
Irelander, managed to raise 400 volunteers in Glasgow and
Greenock and, back in Ireland, he contacted the agrarian terrorist movement, the Molly Maguires, who promised to help
only if the insurrection was actually begun by the Young
Irelanders. All attempts to raise the country by Smith O'Brien
were doomed to failure.

Fintan Lalor along with other more radical elements were arrested and the Young Ireland movement ended with a skirmish
at Ballingarry. During this skirmish, Smith O'Brien's aide-de-
camp, twenty-four-year-old James Stephens, a civil engineer with
the Waterford-Limerick railway, was wounded but managed to
escape to France. Stephens, who was later to learn his Socialism
in revolutionary France, was to become leader of the Fenian
movement. With the fiasco at Ballingarry, the Young Ireland insurrection came to an end. Mitchel blames the priesthood for the
part they played in persuading the people not to fight.

> When the final scene was gathering itself to crush us, the clergy
> as a body were found on the side of the enemy. They hoped for
> their Church in a union with monarchical and aristocratic
> England than in an Ireland revolutionised and republicanised;
> and having taken their part, they certainly did the enemy's work
> well.

Most of the Young Ireland leaders, like Smith O'Brien, were
transported. Fintan Lalor spent several months in Newgate
prison but was released in November, 1848, due to ill health. He
immediately contacted former comrades, John O'Leary, Thomas
Clark Luby and Charles Kickham, later to become Fenian
leaders, and tried to re-establish a new social-based national
movement. The movement achieved some success in Tipperary
and Limerick. A fringe group of Lalor's movement evolved plans
to kidnap Queen Victoria on her state visit to Ireland in August,
1849. The main body of the movement tried to organise a rising
on Sunday, September 16, in Cork, Limerick, Clare, Kilkenny,
Tipperary and Waterford. At Capoquin alone did an attack on
the police barracks take place. Lalor tried to lead an attack on

Cashel police barracks but could not raise enough men. His health declined seriously and he died on December 17, 1849.

O'Neill writes :

> His influence remained. The young men who had acted with him in his last year were to carry into the next generation the plan of organisation which was the basis of Fenianism.[28]

Chapter 8

MARX, ENGELS AND THE FENIANS

IN 1849 THE Government passed an Encumbered Estates
Act which reduced the number of colonialist landowners and
established a large native landlord class out of the former
"middlemen" land agents. Davitt comments:

> In 1849 the humane rulers of Ireland passed an Encumbered
> Estates Act to enable the impecunious Irish landlords to break
> the legal bonds of the English law of primogeniture and to sell
> their estates. A large number of them disposed of their properties
> and removed from the country, to make way for a new class who
> were induced to invest capital in Irish land as a purely profit
> making enterprise, and for the social distinction which the owner-
> ship of estates offers to members of English society. The tenants
> were virtually bought with the land, under the operation of this
> act—that is, their improvements and occupancy rights were.[1]

Of the 3,000 estates sold immediately following the act, however, there were 80,000 purchasers and 90 per cent of these were
native Irish. The native Irish land-owning class was strengthened
in its property rights from the Irish merchant or money-lending
classes who had no ties of sentiment or interest with the peasantry. The hated middleman became the landlord. Karl Marx,
who had arrived in England during that year of 1849, pointed
out that the Act had started a revolution in Irish land relations.
Writing in *Neue Oder Zeitung*, 1855, he commented:

> This revolution consists in the Irish agrarian system yielding to
> the English, the system of small tenantry is being replaced by big
> tenantry—just as the old landlords are being replaced by new
> capitalists. The chief stages making way for this change are—the
> famine of 1847 which killed about one million Irish; emigration
> to America and Australia, which has already torn another million
> souls out of Ireland and which continues to uproot fresh millions;
> the unsuccessful revolt of 1848, breaking Ireland's last faith in

itself; finally the Act of Parliament which condemned to auction
the property of the indebted Irish nobility and drove the nobility
off the land just as starvation drove off the farmers, tenants and
cottagers.

Marx went more deeply into the situation in a letter to Engels
written on November 30, 1867.

What the English do not understand is that since 1846 the
economic grip, and consequently also the political aim of the
English rule in Ireland, has entered upon an entirely new phase,
and that, for this reason, Fenianism is characterised by a socialist
tendency (in a negative sense as directed against the appro-
priation of the land) and has become a "lower orders" movement.
What can be more absurd than to lump the barbarities of
Elizabeth and Cromwell who wanted to supplant the Irish by
English colonists (in the Roman sense) with the present system?
The system in force from 1801 to 1846 (eviction during this period
being only exceptional, principally in Leinster where the land is
particularly good for raising cattle) with its rack rents and middlemen, fell to pieces in 1846. The repeal of the Corn Laws which
was partly the result of, and in any case, accelerated by, the Irish
Famine, took from Ireland the monopoly of providing England
with corn in average seasons. Wool and meat was the watchword,
and so the conversion of tillage into pasture. Out of this there
developed the systematic consolidation of farms. The Encumbered
Estates Act, which turned a mass of former middlemen, who had
feathered their nests, into landlords, accelerated the process. The
clearing of estates in Ireland is now the only thought of English
rule in Ireland. The stupid English Government in London naturally understands nothing of this immense change since 1846. But
the Irish know it. From Meagher's proclamation (1848) up to the
Election Address of Hennessy (1866), the Tory and Urquhartite,
the Irish have expressed their consciousness of this fact in the
clearest and most forcible manner.

Now comes the question, what are we to advise the English
workers to do? In my opinion they must include as a clause in
their platform the Repeal of the Union (in short the joke of 1783,
only democratised and brought up to date). It is the only legal
and so only possible form of Irish emancipation which can be accepted as part of the programme of an English party. Experience
must show later whether the merely personal union between these
two countries can continue to exist. I half believe it can if it were
to take place at once.

What the Irish people want is (1) self government and independence from England; (2) Agrarian Revolution. With the best will in the world, the English cannot do that for them but they can give them the legal means to do it for themselves; (3) protective tariffs against England.

From 1783 to 1801 all branches of Irish industry were in a flourishing condition. The union, by breaking down the protective tariff wall, which the Irish parliament had erected, destroyed all industrial life in Ireland. The very small linen industry in nowise compensates for this. The Union of 1801 had the same effects on the whole of Irish industry as the measures for the suppression of the Irish woollen industry etc. passed by the English Parliaments under Anne, George etc.

As soon as the Irish are independent, necessity will force them to become Protectionists, like Canada, Australia, etc.[2]

Marx considered that it was the change in land ownership which gave stimulus to Fenianism becoming a mass movement with an agrarian Socialist tendency directed against land monopoly. When *Das Kapital* (Capital), Marx's great economic treatise, was published on September 14, 1867, he devoted some time to making an analysis of the years 1861-5.[3] In these years the area under cereal crops decreased by 428,041 acres; green crops by 107,084 acres, while grass and clover lands increased by 82,834 acres and the area under flax by 122,750 acres. There was a decrease in the total cultivated land of 330,860 acres. In this period some 500,000 emigrated and the absolute number of people sank by more than one third of a million. The tremendous decrease in population, consolidation of farms, turning tillage into pasture, meant that Ireland was becoming a land of capitalist agriculture of a colonial type in which the masses of the peasantry and labourers, far from getting any benefit from the population decrease suffered as much as before. In Ireland tillage became grazing or lay idle and the waste land and turf bogs, formerly unused, were now made to serve for cattle breeding. One by one the small farmers were destroyed. In normal capitalist countries (such as England) the expropriated peasantry were absorbed in industry, but Ireland had no industry except her limited linen manufacture. Marx comments:

England, a country with fully developed capitalist production, and pre-eminently industrial, would have bled to death with such a drain as Ireland had suffered. But Ireland is at present only an agricultural district of England, marked off by a wide channel from the country to which it yields corn, wool, cattle, industrial and military recruits.

Marx prophesied that under this system the Irish were doomed to emigrate from Ireland "that thus she may fulfil her true destiny, that of an English sheep walk and cattle pasture." In the third volume of *Das Kapital*, Marx writes:

> The tenant there (Ireland) is generally a small farmer. What he pays to the landlord in the form of rent frequently absorbs not merely a part of his profit, that is, his own surplus labour (to which he is entitled as possessor of his own instruments of labour) but also a part of his normal wage, which he would otherwise receive for the same amount of labour. Besides, the landlord, who does nothing at all for the improvement of the land, also expatriates his small capital, which the tenant for the most part incorporates in the land through his own labour. This is precisely what a usurer would do under similar circumstances, with just the difference that the usurer would at least risk his own capital in the operation. This continual plunder is the core of the dispute over the Irish Tenancy Rights Bill. The main purpose of the Bill is to compel the landlord when ordering his tenant off the land to indemnify the latter for his improvements on the land, or for his capital incorporated in the land. Palmerston used to wave their demand aside with the cynical answer "The House of Commons is a house of landed proprietors".

With the passing of the Encumbered Estates Act and the rise of an even more unsympathetic landowning class, there was an increase of agrarian unrest and activity among the peasant secret societies, especially in Connaught and Munster. Marx comments:

> The landlords of Ireland are confederated for a fiendish war of extermination against the cotiers; or, as they call it, they combine for the economical experiment of clearing the land of useless mouths. The small native tenants are to be disposed of with no more ado than vermin by the housemaid. The despairing wretches, on their part, attempt a feeble resistance by the formation of secret societies, scattered over the land, and powerless for effecting anything beyond demonstrations of individual vengeance.[4]

That same year of 1849, two Catholic curates, Father Thomas O'Shea and Father Matthew Keefe, started the Cullen Tenant Right Society which had, for its slogan, "Fair Rents, Tenant Right and Employment". Charles Gavan Duffy, the only Young Irelander leader left at liberty in the country, took over this small association and began to build it into the more substantial Tenant Right League of North and South. Gavan Duffy's organisational ability made the League a strong force on the Irish political scene. It was supported by two publications—*The Tablet*, run from Dublin by an Englishman named Lucas, and *The Banner of Ulster*, edited by a Presbyterian minister, Dr. McKnight. The country was united in a demand for a Tenant's Charter. The Rev. T. W. Croke, curate of Charleville, Co. Cork (later Archbishop of Cashel and a Land League supporter) established a programme for the League:

Let there be established in each parish a Tenant Society including, if possible, every tenant farmer in the parish, whose members would take a pledge in these terms; "We promise God, our country and each other, never to bid for any farm or land from which any industrious farmer in this district has been ejected." Should any persons violate this pledge, his name must be struck off the registry as unworthy to associate with honest men. To sustain the tenantry, there would be established, at the same time in the chief town of every district, a tenant protection society, consisting of shop keepers, professional men, and artisans which would collect a fund for the sustenance of the tenants unjustly evicted. If any member bid for land from which a tenant farmer had been ejected he must forfeit his membership, and at the same time "the call and patronage of his townsfolk and district."[5]

In actual fact this programme was more or less that of the Whiteboys though placed, unlike Whiteboyism, on a non violent basis. The philosophy united both Catholics and Protestants as had Tone's ideology that gave effect to the rising of 1798. In 1853 the *New York Tribune* carried a closely reasoned article on Tenant Right by Karl Marx. In his articles both in German and American newspapers, Marx was making known the plight of Ireland to the world. Expounding the cause of Tenant Right, Marx pointed out that the process by which landlords increased rents after the tenant had made an improvement to their farm amounted to the tenant paying interest on his own money. The London *Times* had commented that the only thing wrong in Ireland was the absence of "normal social conditions". To this Marx replied :

> England has destroyed the conditions of Irish society. First of all, she has confiscated the lands of the Irish, then by "Parliamentary decrees" she has suppressed Irish industry; finally, by armed force she has broken the activity and energy of the Irish people. In this way England has created the "social conditions" which allow a small caste of robber landlords to dictate to the Irish people the conditions in which they are allowed to hold the land and live on it. Still too weak to overthrow "the social conditions" by revolutionary methods, the people turn to Parliament, demanding at least the alleviation or regulation of these conditions.[6]

Marx argued that only the expropriation of the landlords by nationalisation of the land would solve the Irish agrarian question.

The Tenant Right League was only too successful in uniting the country under its banner. Davitt comments :

> English rulers, watchful over ascendancy interests in Ireland, were not slow to see the danger to their hold on the country in a unity between the Protestant North and the Catholic South. National unity would stand for strength and political progress, and it has ever been the purpose of English rule in Ireland, and in India, to divide people to keep them down.[7]

The downfall of the League, as with so many mass Irish movements, was religion. After the Pope returned from his exile of 1848, a new ecclesiastical map was drawn up so that Catholic Sees in England, Wales and Scotland corresponded more with the new post-industrial revolution demographic pattern. The Whig Premier, Lord John Russell, immediately raised the cry of "No Popery!" bringing forward the debate as to whether a Protestant country should tolerate a Catholic Hierarchy. In 1851 he put through an Ecclesiastical Titles Act which made it illegal for Catholic bishops to assume titles of new sees created by the Pope. Immediately a Catholic Defence Association sprang up in Ireland. The leaders were William Keogh and John Sadlier who had expressed themselves in strong support of the Tenant Right League. Keogh and Sadlier started a campaign concerning the position of the Catholic clergy and their right to titles and this began to alienate Protestant supporters of Tenant Right, earning the title of "The Pope's Brass Band" for the Keogh and Sadlier faction. In July, 1852, some forty members of the League were returned to the House of Commons having agreed to form an independent party in the English Parliament resolved to establishing Tenant Rights. Each member pledged not to accept any office offered them by the Government. Keogh and Sadlier immediately betrayed the League and accepted posts as Irish Solicitor General and Junior Lord of the Treasury respectively. They took with them nineteen "Tenant Leaguers". The "divide and rule" policy had worked and the League began to collapse.

The League, of course, also had powerful enemies in Ireland such as the Catholic Archbishop of Dublin, Dr. Paul Cullen, who had lived some years in Italy and had returned with a paranoiac fear of the Carbonari. Cullen grew increasingly reactionary during his years of office and opposed every popular movement with monotonous consistency. He condemned the League in 1854. Gavan Duffy, as well as leader of the League represented New Ross as M.P., wrote bitterly ". . . every defeat of the League at the hustings was directly attributable to the influence of some Whig bishop."

The League finally collapsed in 1856 and Gavan Duffy left in disgust for Australia where he became Minister of Victoria Province, receiving the K.C.M.G. from a grateful queen in 1873. He died in Nice in 1903. Sadlier, one of the men whose ardent Catholic activities brought about the downfall of the League, committed suicide in 1856 realising his forgeries and sharp practices as a banker would soon be discovered. Keogh followed Sadlier's example later in a Belgian hotel.

In the year 1856 Jeremiah O'Donovan Rossa established a Phoenix National and Literary Society in Skibbereen, Co. Cork, a purely national movement which was later to merge with the Fenians. That same year Joseph Denieffe arrived from America to study the Irish situation on behalf of a group of revolutionary exiles, to estimate whether the time was ripe for a new national movement. In the same year also, Friedrich Engels, with his Irish wife Mary Burns, arrived in Ireland to tour the country. Returning to England he wrote to Marx on May 23 :

In our tour of Ireland we went from Dublin to Galway, on the west coast, then twenty miles inland, then to Limerick, down the Shannon to Tarbert, Tralee and Killarney and back to Dublin. In all, about 450-500 English miles through the country, so we've seen about two thirds of the whole country. With the exception of Dublin—which is to London what Dusseldorf is to Berlin, and whose character is completely that of a small one-time capital, and which is entirely English built—the country, and especially the towns, make one feel as if one were in the south of France or Northern Italy. Gendarmes, priests, lawyers, bureaucrats, squires in pleasing profusion, and a total absence of any and every industry, so that it would be hard to understand what these parasitic growths live on if the misery of the peasants didn't supply the other half of the picture. Strong measures are evident throughout the length and breadth of the country and the government meddles in everything; there is no trace of so-called self government. Ireland can be regarded as the first English colony, and as one which, because of its proximity, is still ruled directly in the old way. Here it can be clearly seen that the so-called liberty of the English citizens is based on the oppression of the colonies. In no other country have I seen so many gendarmes, and Schnapps-expression of the Prussian gendarme is developed to the highest perfection here among the constabulary, who are armed with carbines, bayonets and handcuffs.

Characteristic of the country are its ruins, the oldest dating from the 5th and 6th centuries, the latest from the 19th, and covering the whole intervening period. The oldest are all churches, after 1100 churches and castles; and, after 1800, peasants' houses. The whole of the West, and the neighbourhood of Galway in particular, is covered with these ruined peasant houses, most of which have only been abandoned since 1846. I never thought a famine could have such a tangible reality. Whole villages are devastated, and in between them are the splendid parks of the smaller landlords (mostly lawyers), almost the only people who still live there. Famine, emigration and clearance together have brought this about. There are not even cattle in the fields. The land is an utter desert which nobody wants. It is a little better in Co. Clare, south of Galway, where at least there are some cattle. The hills towards Limerick are very well cultivated, mostly by Scottish farmers, the ruins have been cleared and the country has a bourgeois appearance. There is a lot of mountain and bog land in the South West, but some wonderfully rich forest growth as well. Beyond that there are fine pastures, especially in Tipperary. And towards Dublin one can see that the land is being taken over by the big farmers.

The country has been completely ruined by the English wars of conquest from 1100 to 1850 (for in reality the wars and the state of siege lasted that long). It is a fact that most of the ruins were produced by destruction during the wars. This gave the people their singular character; and in spite of all their Irish nationalist fanaticism they feel they're not at home any more in their own country. Ireland for the Saxon! This is now being realised with every advantage. Emigration will go on until the almost exclusively Celtic character of the people is gone to the devil. How often have the Irish made the attempt to come to something, only to be crushed politically and industrially again and again? They have been artificially forced by consistent oppression to become a lumpenised nation; and now it is notorious that they fulfil the function of providing England, America, Australia etc. with other lumpen. This lumpen characteristic is found in the aristocracy as well. The estate owners, who everywhere else have taken on bourgeois qualities, have become lumpenised here. Their country seats are surrounded by enormous, wonderfully beautiful parks, but all around them is desert. Where the money comes from is not easy to see. These fellows ought to be shot dead. Of mixed blood, mostly tall, strong, handsome fellows, they all wear enormous moustaches under colossal Roman noses, give themselves the sham military airs of retired colonels, travel around the country after all sorts of pleasures, and, if one makes an enquiry, they haven't a penny, are laden with debts, and live in dread of the Encumbered Estates Court . . .[8]

Joseph Denieffe, who had arrived in Ireland that year of 1856, to survey the country from the point of view of establishing a new national movement, was an emissary of the embryo Fenian movement. The name deriving from the Fianna, the mythical warriors of Fionn Mac Cumhal. The Fenians, or rather the Irish Republican Brotherhood, came into being on March 17, 1858, at a meeting in Dublin. It was a secret oathbound revolutionary movement dedicated to overthrowing English rule in Ireland by force and establishing an Irish Republic. The leader of the movement was James Stephens, the former Young Irelander who had been Smith O'Brien's aide-de-camp at the skirmish of Ballingarry where he had been wounded. Davitt comments:

In his wanderings abroad Stephens had come into contact with Socialist theories, he assimilated a little of them, and he rubbed his experiences of 1848 and the current state of the national movement against what he had learned.[9]

According to another famous Fenian leader, John Devoy, Stephens "claimed that he was an enrolled member of the Communist Party."[10] Whether or not this is true, for in the 1870's Stephens repudiated that his policies consisted of the "Utopian Socialism" of the European revolutionists, Stephens was a member of the International Working Men's Association (the First International) along with other prominent Fenians.[11] According to Desmond Ryan, writing about Stephens and his colleague, John O'Mahoney, after the two had fled following the abortive 1848 uprising :

> These two men settled down for a while into the Bohemian and revolutionary circles of Paris, and came into touch with the leading European revolutionaries and the secret societies and their chiefs. As they had not given up hope of a future blow in Ireland, they joined the most powerful of these societies. There was a strong current of sympathy among many of the Young Ireland refugees with the Republican and semi-Socialistic ideas of these societies and O'Mahoney and Stephens, leaning much more to the ideals of Mitchel and Fintan Lalor than those of Smith O'Brien and Gavan Duffy on landlordism and the rights of property, found their principles after their hearts and the practice useful.[12]

Stephens himself claimed to share the social ideas of Louis Blanc and August Blanqui. In fact Stephens had approached General Gustave-Paul Cluseret, who won fame as the defender of the Paris Commune of 1870-1, to act as commander-in-chief of the Fenian forces.[13] Cluseret did not accept the office but did take part in the Fenian attack on Chester Castle in 1867 and was subsequently condemned to death *in absentia* by the English.[14] Stephens is said to have fought on the barricades of Paris against the coup d'état of Louis Napoleon. It is also claimed that he had knowledge of sixteen languages; whatever the truth in this, he certainly had fluency in French and Italian for, while in Paris, he translated Charles Dickens's *Martin Chuzzlewit* and *David Copperfield* into French but their publication brought him little fortune.

It was with his friend John O'Mahoney that Stephens first

formed his ideas for the Fenian movement. O'Leary, another Fenian leader, described O'Mahoney as "an advanced democrat or even a Socialist"[15] and, indeed, O'Mahoney was a member of the First International with Stephens. He was also a first class language scholar. Ryan comments:

> O'Mahoney's enthusiasm for the Irish language was shared by the Fenians in general since Irish was still a living language in the south, west and parts of Ulster, although there was no organised movement to preserve and advance it. In his speeches O'Mahoney often prophesied that movement on the lines that the Gaelic League afterwards followed, must come with independence. O'Donovan Rossa, like O'Mahoney, also had a deep literary knowledge of Irish and was a close friend of John O'Donovan, the Irish scholar, whose four sons were ardent Fenians.[16]

In 1853 O'Mahoney had left Stephens in Paris to go to America where he joined Michael Doheny, who had helped Fintan Lalor in an attempt to establish a Tenant Right League in Tipperary. The two men started to organise the Irish exiles. Following the foundation of the Irish Republican Brotherhood, Stephens took an extensive tour in Ireland during 1858-9 which showed his remarkable powers of organisation. He became known as *An Seabhac Siúlach* (The Wandering Hawk). To the peasants *An Seabhac Siúlach* was a shadowy omnipotent figure who would emerge with invincible armies to free Ireland. Everywhere the phrase was being whispered: *"Tá an lá ag teacht . . . !"* ("The day is coming . . . !") There arose a complexed, highly organised secret society in Ireland, and wherever Irishmen were found abroad Fenianism grew. Even soldiers serving in the armed forces took the Fenian oath to the Irish Republic "virtually established". Davitt was critical of the movement and blames Fenian leadership for not marrying agrarian agitation to the national question.

> Fintan Lalor's policy still held. It was useless "to keep up a feeble and ineffectual fire from a foolish distance upon the English Government", it was necessary "to wheel their batteries round and bend them on the English garrison of landlords". Had Stephens flung the whole weight of the Fenians into the

battle against the landlords the transition from the mass agrarian struggle in the national revolution would have provided
the Castle (English administration) with more than a few
isolated skirmishes to subdue. The revolutionists failed to see
the importance of the agrarian movement and it was left to
the parliamentary reformists to realise its value to them if can-
alised with sufficient skill.[17]

It is true that Stephens remarked that he did not try to
push his political thinking on the Fenian movement, but the
philosophy of the Fenian leadership, with their membership of
the First International, did marry the agrarian and national
revolt, causing Marx to observe "the Fenian movement, in that
it aimed at smashing the power of the landlords and exalted
that of the common people, had a Socialist tendency."[18] The
Fenian programme was internationalist in that the IRB
declared its support "for all struggling nationalities in the
British Empire and elsewhere." The following quotations from
The Irish People during 1865 give an idea of the radical attitude of Fenian aims.

Twenty years ago Thomas Davis appealed to the aristocracy to
save the people with their own hands. We make no appeal to the
aristocracy ... they are the willing tools of the alien government
whose policy it is to slay the people, or drive them like noxious
vermin from the soil. The people must save themselves.

Something more even than a successful insurrection is
demanded. And what is that? An entire revolution which will
restore the country to its rightful owners. And who are these? The
people.

Every man has one simple object to accomplish. It is to rid the
land of robbers, and render every cultivator of the soil his own
landlord, the proprietor in fee simple of the house and land of his
fathers which will be an inheritance worth a free man's while to
bequeath to his children, and worth the children's while to enjoy a
nation which bows to no power under heaven.

We saw that the people must be taught to distinguish between
the priest as a minister of religion and the priest as a politician
before they could advance one step on the road to emancipation ... Our only hope is revolution, but most bishops and many
of the clergy are opposed to revolution ... When priests turn the
altar into a platform, when it is pronounced a "mortal sin" to read
the *Irish People*, a "mortal sin" to even wish Ireland should be
free, when priests call upon the people to turn informers ... When,

in a word, bishops and priests are doing the work of the enemy, we believe it is our duty to tell the people that bishops and priests may be bad politicians and worse Irishmen.

Emancipation was a measure calculated almost exclusively to benefit the upper and middle classes of the Catholics. Emancipation separate from the cause of independence has turned out to be simply a means of bribing or corrupting wealthy or educated Catholics of seducing them from the National rank.

To the leadership of the Fenian movement had come Thomas Clarke Luby, who attacked the social order in *The Irish People*, and stated he stood for "an Irish Republic in which the people of Ireland would own the wealth of Ireland and administer it for the benefit of the entire community and not one class." To the leadership had come John O'Leary and Charles Kickham, both followers of Fintan Lalor; Colonel Thomas Kelly, a Galway man, who later took over the leadership of the movement, had been a prominent trade unionist in the New York Printers' Union; John Devoy, who became a member of the First International's executive after its transference to New York in 1870;[19] and came Michael Davitt, sentenced to 15 years' penal servitude on July 18, 1870 as a Fenian organiser, he was later to lead the Irish in the Land War years. These were the type of men who led the Fenians. Of Stephens, Ryan somewhat erroneously remarks:

> ... (he was the first Irish leader to grasp and to act upon the idea that it was only from the masses of the Irish people in Ireland and everywhere that power could be drawn that would frighten or force England either to mend her government in Ireland or clear out of it with her rule.[20]

The philosophies expressed by the Fenian leadership brought down the wrath of the Catholic Church and the clergy accused them, fairly accurately for once, of being communists. But communism to the Irish peasantry was represented as something evil, associated with irreligion and anti-Christianity. Sir Shane Leslie comments: "No one cursed the Fenians more heartily than Cardinal Cullen."[21] The Catholic Church also won praise from the London *Times*: "It is gratifying to record the consistent firmness with which our Roman Catholic clergymen at least have discounted all sympathy with Fenianism."[22]

The agrarian unrest continued, heightened by Deasy's Land Act of 1840, which gave landlords *carte blanche* to plunder tenants' improvements of their property without compensation. Between 1829 and 1879 some fifty Land Bills proposing improvements in conditions for tenants were rejected or rendered useless by the House of Commons, Between 1849 and 1882 some 100,000 families were evicted from their homes. Under such conditions the Fenian philosophy was falling on ground fertile for revolution. It was thought that Stephen's big mistake was the launching of the newspaper *The Irish People*, to act as the mouthpiece and propaganda sheet for the Fenian organisation. The journal was launched on November 28, 1863, and almost at once the Fenian movement began to be infiltrated by Government spies and informers. In London, on September 28, 1864, the International Working Men's Association had been formed and prominent in this movement was Karl Marx. "Since the days of the Chartists, Marx had associated himself with the demand for Irish independence."[23] Jackson writes:

> Marx, the leading spirit in the newly formed IWMA, seems early to have seen the revolutionary significance of the Fenian movement. Naturally, the Fenians (officially the Irish Republican Brotherhood) being a secret society, no correspondence is extant to establish any direct connection, but there are clear indications that from as early as 1864 the Fenians in London, Manchester and elsewhere found the IWMA a convenient camouflage and recruiting ground, and that conversely they aided the establishment of the International in Dublin and Cork, as well as in Pendleton, Manchester.[24]

The Fenians certainly welcomed the moral support of the English working classes via the International and other bodies. The history of Irish nationalism and English radicalism is extremely closely entwined. Thompson explains:

> ... there were many reasons why English Radicalism or Chartism and Irish Nationalism should make common cause, although the alliance was never free from tensions. Antagonism could scarcely take racialist forms in the Army, Navy, or in the northern mill-towns, in all of which the Irish fought or worked side by side with English fellow victims. From the days of the United

Irishmen—and the time when the Irish with their shillelaghs had helped in the defence of Thomas Hardy's house—a conscious political alliance had been maintained. English reformers generally supported the cause of Catholic Emancipation; for years, Sir Francis Burdett was its foremost parliamentary champion, while Cobbett furthered the cause ... London Irish formed an Association for Civil and Political Liberty, which had Hunt's and Cobbett's support, which co-operated closely with advanced English Radicals, and which was one of the precursors of the National Union of the Working Classes (1830)—itself a forerunner of the Chartist Working Men's Association (1836). There is thus a clear consecutive alliance between Irish Nationalism and English Radicalism between 1790 and 1850 ...[25]

The war between the American States was looked to with interest by the Fenian leadership. Serving in both armies were entire regiments of Irish-Americans (a whole brigade with the northerners), not just Irishmen but many sworn Fenians as well. Stephens decided that 1865 would be the year of the Fenian uprising but the Government were becoming increasingly alarmed and concerned at the strength of the movement that their spies were uncovering. The offices of *The Irish People* were regarded as the headquarters of the movement and, without warning, a swoop was made on this office on September 15, 1865, by a strong force of military and police. The coup was so sudden and effective that by November 11, John O'Leary, Thomas Clarke Luby, Jeremiah O'Donovan Rossa, Charles J. Kickham, Hugh Brophy, Edward Duffy and James Stephens himself were behind bars along with many other rank and file Fenians. Sentences of twenty years' penal servitude were given and a systematic round-up of Fenians with a series of trials began. With Habeas Corpus suspended, the remaining Fenian leaders could not decide whether to take action or not. While they dithered, John Devoy was arrested.

The war between the States was now at a close and the former Young Irelander, John Mitchel, voiced the thoughts of the Irish-Americans. "Here in America we have a force of soldiery trained in the Confederate and Federal Armies, strong enough to free Ireland." With the Fenian movement in Ireland appearing on the verge of collapse, a group of Fenian officers met in New York on December 20, 1865, under the chairmanship of Godfrey

Massey, a former Confederate officer. Massey proposed that the
Fenians in America should invade Canada.

In March, 1866, the English Government received a shock
when Col. Thomas Kelly, an Irish-American officer, succeeded in
rescuing James Stephens from prison. On March 12 the Fenian
leader landed safely in France and made his way to America,
arriving there in May. He found the movement split. John
O'Mahoney had been deposed but had taken his followers with
him, while the main body adhered to a wealthy Irish merchant
named William R. Roberts. Stephens condemned both sides and
urged them to reunite under his supreme leadership. Both sides
rejected Stephens' pleas. The Roberts' faction supported Massey's
plan to invade Canada while Stephens vainly tried to plead that
any uprising must occur in Ireland.

On the night of May 31/June 1, 1866, a Fenian army of 600
men crossed the Niagara River, near Buffalo, led by Colonel
John O'Neill. At 4 a.m. the Irish tricolour was raised for the first
time on English territory by Colonel Starr, who commanded the
first two boatloads of men to cross. The Irish then positioned
themselves at Limeston Ridge, near Fort Erie. At 7 a.m. the
Toronto "Queen's Own" regiment of volunteers, under Colonel
Booker, attacked the Irish troops but were beaten off with losses
of twelve dead, thirty wounded and twenty prisoners. On June 2
a stronger British column were advancing against the Fenian
positions and O'Neill, who had not been reinforced according to
plan, decided to recross into the United States. The Fenian attack in Canada was another shock to the government.

Stephens, however, was angry. In Ireland, Fenianism was losing its effectiveness, prestige and organisation with the loss of its
leaders. Under Stephens' directions Fenian Irish-Americans made
their way to Ireland and began to prepare for the rising by in-
structing and drilling the people in the use of arms. Among them
was Col. Thomas Kelly, Stephens' rescuer, who with General
Cluseret and General Vifquain planned an attack on Chester
Castle as part of a series of diversionary raids which were to have
been made on English garrisons all over England on February
11, 1867, to coincide with the Irish uprising. The raid was
betrayed and the attackers narrowly escaped capture. On
Wednesday, February 13, Fenians at Cahirciveen, Co. Kerry,
not having received a countermanding order which put back the
rising to March 5, marched with their weapons. They learnt of

the cancellation some time later but the English administration, pre-warned, immediately suspended Habeas Corpus and began a systematic round-up of all suspected Fenians, particularly an internment of Irishmen returning from America. Finally, on March 5, 1867, the Fenians went into action in Dublin, Louth, Tipperary, Cork, Waterford, Limerick, and Clare. The rising was a disaster. Confronted by well-armed and disciplined troops, the peasants of Ireland were ill-armed; the March weather was a mid-winter hail and snow and the Fenian ranks were full of spies and informers. Within a few days the rising was at an end. Engels was later to write to Eduard Bernstein, the German Socialist leader, that the Irish had no hope against England with her naval fleets, her army, her police and spy system. He also pointed out that England had agreed to pay the U.S.A. a sum of money after the Civil War in order to buy off American intervention on Ireland's behalf.

The Fenian movement was not broken, however. In August, 1867, the remaining leaders of the Irish Republican Brotherhood met in Manchester and appointed Colonel Thomas Kelly as successor to Stephens. The following month Kelly and his aide, Captain Timothy Deasy of Co. Cork, were arrested in the city. The local Fenians decided on a rescue attempt to free the leaders. They ambushed the prison van taking Kelly and Deasy to Bellevue Gaol, Manchester, and succeeded in freeing the two men. But, in the ambush, a police sergeant named Brett was shot and the police succeeded in capturing some of the rescuers, as well as others who had taken no part in the affair at all. Kelly and Deasy eventually made their way to the U.S.A. Wilhelm Liebnecht, the famous German philologist and Socialist and father of Karl Liebnecht, declared that one of the escaped Manchester prisoners was sheltered by Engels and his second wife, Lizzie Burns, a staunch Fenian. While Engels makes no reference to it, perhaps because he was far too good a revolutionary to talk about such matters, Liebnecht was his close friend and confidant, and therefore knowledgeable in this field. Certainly Engels was involved with the Fenians and helped them financially and it is no surprise that the defence counsel employed for the Manchester prisoners was the leading Chartist, Ernest Jones, a Welshman who took no fee for the defence. After a far from fair trial, seven men were sentenced to penal servitude while William Philip Allen, Michael Larkin, Michael O'Brien,

Thomas Maguire and O'Meagher Condon were condemned to death.

Immediately the English working classes mobilised in favour of the Fenians. A meeting of the International Working Men's Association on Tuesday, November 19, expressed strong support for the Fenians. John Weston commented: "The crime of starving the Irish was far greater than the accidental killing of one man in trying to rescue Fenian prisoners." The meeting was reported in the London *Times* of November 21 and *Reynolds News* of November 24. Eugène Dupont, secretary for France, described Fenianism as "the vindication by an oppressed people of its right to social and political existence . . . the English working class who blame the Fenians commit more than a fault. . . . they have the same enemy to defeat—the territorial aristocracy and the capitalists." There was a public meeting on November 20 at Cambridge Hall, Newman Street, London, when Rev. M. Solly, organiser of the Working Men's Club and Institute Union, addressed his members pleading for the lives of the Fenians. Charles Bradlaugh, the implacable radical and atheist, called the Government cowardly to execute the Fenians. Some 20,000 to 25,000 working men met on Clerkenwell Green, London, on November 21, to petition the Queen for mercy. The Manchester radical member of parliament, John Bright, wrote in his diary on the same day:

> Home Office talk with Mr. Hardy in favour of Fenian convicts at Manchester; without avail, I fear Tories know little mercy; terror is their only specific.

The defence lawyers put forward a legal plea that was rejected on November 21 and that day in the House of Commons a Mr. Maguire initiated an adjournment debate pleading to the Government "in the name of all that was just . . . not to perpetrate a legal murder." The English radical working class newspaper, *The Beehive*, of October 19, 1867, had commented:

> There is, however, no doubt of one thing, that the gross injustice inflicted on Ireland for so many years by the British Government and Legislature, has created a deep rooted hatred of English rule in the hearts of all true Irishmen and that the perpetrators and abettors of this unjust Irish policy are now reaping the fruits of their own bad legislation.

There were two reprieves—O'Meagher Condon and Maguire. But Allen, Larkin and O'Brien were hanged at Salford Prison, Manchester, on November 23. Making notes for a speech on November 26, Marx wrote :

> Since our last meeting the object of our discussion, Fenianism, has entered a new phase. It has been baptised in blood by the English Government. The political executions at Manchester remind us of the fate of John Brown at Harper's Ferry. They open a new period in the struggle between Ireland and England . . .

Writing to Engels on November 28 Marx adds :

> . . . Jenny (Marx's eldest daughter) goes in black since the Manchester executions and wears her Polish Cross (commemorating the Polish insurrection) on a green ribbon.

On December 13, 1867, an attempt was made by a group of Fenians to free two other prisoners, Burke and Casey, from Clerkenwell Prison, London. The bomb, by which the attackers hoped to blow a hole in the prison wall, was misplaced causing a loss of innocent life. A wave of resentment went through England and the administration lost no time in using it to stir up a hatred of the Irish. On December 14 Marx wrote to Engels :

> This last escapade of the Fenians is very stupid . . . It is not to be expected that the mass of the Londoners who have shown much sympathy with Ireland will allow themselves to be blown up for the greater honour and glory of the emissaries of the Fenians . . .

Michael Barrett, who was hanged for his part in the explosion, on May 26, 1868, became the last person to be publicly hanged in England. Three days after the explosion, on December 16, when the Londoners were still thirsty for the blood of Fenians, Karl Marx delivered a lecture on Ireland to the London Workers' Educational Association still supporting Fenianism.[26] The English working class, generally, continued to support Fenianism and the London *Times* of November 23, 1868, reported :

Yesterday, Hyde Park was again disgraced by a field day of the London "roughs" who assembled there in the name of the murderers who were executed this day last year for the murder of police sergeant Brett. These murderers are called "martyrs" . . .

An inflammatory handbill was distributed among the dwellers in the courts about the worst parts of Bethnal Green, Whitechapel, Southwark, Greenwich, Deptford, Ratcliffe-highway, Grays Inn Lane, Holborn, and other places in the metropolis. The bill was printed in green with a deep mourning border and headed by a funeral rose . . .

In December, 1868, Gladstone and his Liberals formed their first cabinet. His first act to pacify Ireland, in 1869, was the disestablishment of the Anglican Church of Ireland . . . now the Irish people did not have to pay tithes to a church they did not support. At the same time, following agitation by Mrs. O'Donovan Rossa and Mrs. Clarke Luby, an Irish Amnesty Association for the Fenian prisoners was formed, pressing for the release of the prisoners. The International Working Men's Association immediately expressed its wholehearted support for the movement and the English working class newspaper, *The Workman's Advocate*, on January 6, 1869, gave publicity to the movement. Mrs. O'Donovan Rossa became secretary of the International's Relief Fund Committee in Dublin and collecting sheets were sent out to all trade unions.

In September, 1869, Engels made his second and last tour of Ireland. On September 17 he wrote to Marx :

The country itself looks absolutely depopulated, and the thought immediately occurs that there are too few people here. The state of war strikes one everywhere. Bands of the Royal Irish Constabulary are to be seen everywhere, with cutlasses, and sometimes revolvers at their sides and their police truncheons held openly in their hands. In Dublin a battery of field artillery drove right down the middle of the city, something I've never seen in England. There are soldiers everywhere, everywhere.

The worst thing about the Irish is that they become corruptible as soon as they stop being peasants and become bourgeois. Admittedly this is the case with all peasant nations. But it is especially bad in Ireland. For this reason the press is shockingly lousy . . .

On his return to England, Engels decided to write a history of

Ireland, to unmask the system and methods of English colonial rule and to expose its serious effects on the historical fate of both the oppressed and oppressor nation. In a letter to Marx of October 24 he observed : "Irish history shows how disastrous it is for a nation to have subjugated another nation." His letters to Marx over this period are full of comment and queries. He had learnt the Irish language ("It doesn't seem all that difficult"—he wrote to Marx on January 19, 1870) but he sought to improve his knowledge in order to read the ancient Irish laws which were "infinitely more civilised than the present English laws."[27] He asked Marx to find him an Irish grammar in London for the one he had was "atrocious" and "I would be horribly vexed to have quoted a Celtic word wrong—perhaps in the genitive or nominative plural instead of the nominative singular." By May, 1870, Engels had made a plan for his history and filled some fifteen notebooks but he had written only one chapter and half of a second one (the book was to be divided into four such chapters, broken down into numerous sections) when events such as the Paris Commune, the fight against the Bakuninists and work in the International prevented him from completing the work. A Russian translation of the unfinished history became available in the 1940's and this was translated into English, part of which appeared in the *Irish Democrat* between 1950 and 1953. The original German version was published in 1962 in Volume 16 of the *Works of Marx and Engels* and a translation of this, by Angela Clifford, was published in 1965 by the Irish Communist Organisation. The German editor wrote :

> Marx supported Engels throughout his studies for the history and placed great significance on the projected work.

In this history, had it been more widely known, Engels would have made an impact as a "traditional historian" apart from his Marxist interpretation. Engels mentions the battle of Clontarf, until then decried by English historians as an Irish fabrication. Engels, however, mentions that the Icelandic sagas verify the Irish accounts. At this time the Icelandic sagas were largely unknown to English and Irish scholars.

Marx and Engels worked hard to publicise the Irish Amnesty movement. At a meeting of the Central Committee of the International on Tuesday, November 12, 1869, Marx again raised the question of the amnesty and proposed the following resolution which was adopted :

> That in his reply to the Irish demands for the release of the imprisoned Irish patriots—a reply contained in his letter to Mr. O'Shea and etc.—Mr. Gladstone deliberately insulted the Irish nation.
> That he clogs political amnesty with conditions alike degrading to the victims of misgovernment and the people they belong to.
> That having, in the teeth of his responsible position, publicly and enthusiastically cheered on the American shareholders' rebellion, he now steps in to preach to the Irish people the doctrine of passive obedience.
> That his whole proceedings with reference to the Irish Amnesty question are the true and genuine offspring of that "political conquest" by the fiery denunciation of which Mr. Gladstone ousted his Tory rivals from office.
> That the General Council of the International Working Men's Association express their admiration of the spirited, firm and high souled manner in which the Irish people carry on their amnesty movement.
> That these resolutions be communicated to all branches of, and working men's bodies connected with, the International Working Men's Association in Europe and America.

The next Sunday, November 17, the Reform League, which was connected with the International, held a great meeting in Hyde Park to demand an amnesty for the prisoners. It was the first historic public demonstration of English and Irish workers for Irish independence. Karl Marx opened the meeting, reproposing his resolution, damning Gladstone and expressing his belief in the eventual liberation of Ireland. Only three men opposed Marx, Odgers, Applegarth and Mottershead, three leading English trade unionists who believed in the co-operation of labour and capital and not the overthrow of capital. Mottershead commented : "Ireland cannot be independent... I regret that Englishmen applauded the statements of Dr. Marx..." The debate was reported on the front page of *Reynolds News*. On November 19, Engels wrote to Marx :

> Lizzie passed you a vote of thanks for the resolution (carried) and is annoyed she cannot be there on Tuesday.

That November the people of Tipperary voted the prisoner O'Donovan Rossa as their member of parliament. The first O'Donovan Rossa heard of it was when he was taken before the governor and told: "I am instructed to inform you by the Secretary of State that the county of Tipperary has elected you a member of Parliament; but I am also desired by him to tell you that it in no way changes your prison treatment." O'Donovan remarked wryly :

> ...if I were taken before the House, I think I would be found talking Irish to them and if they would not understand me—why, let them get an interpreter... I was an Irishman, representing an Irish county, and had a right to be heard in the language of my country.[28]

On November 26 Marx wrote to Engels: "Three cheers for O'Donovan Rossa!" Rossa was, of course, immediately disqualified from sitting but the Fenian, Charles J. Kickham, who had been released from prison earlier in 1869, completely broken in health, was immediately elected in Rossa's place. Writing to Dr. Kugelman, the distinguished Hamburg gynaecologist and student of Marx in the Communist League, on November 19, Marx comments:

> The Irish have played the British Government a splendid trick by the election of the convict-felon O'Donovan Rossa as a member of parliament. The Government newspapers immediately threatened another suspension of the Habeas Corpus Act, "a renewed reign of terror" etc. As a matter of fact, England has never ruled Ireland in any other way and cannot rule it any other way so long as the present Union persists, except by the most hideous reign of terror and the most revolting corruption.

Marx was increasingly angry that the *Irishman*, mouthpiece of the Irish Amnesty movement, took no notice of the activities of the International, nor even bothered to report Marx's resolution in favour of the Amnesty. He wrote to Engels on December 4 :

> Up to today there is intentionally not a word about it (the resolution). The ass (editor of the *Irishman*) was similarly mis-

leading during our debates and petition for the Manchester people. The Irish question must be treated as something apart and unconnected with the rest of the world, and especially dead silence must be observed about the fact that the English workers sympathise with the Irish! What sort of a herd can be got from one cow!

Marx told Engels that he was sending a copy of his resolution to Isaac Butt, whom he refers to as president of the Irish Working Men's Association. By this time Marx and Engels had come to seven basic conclusions on the Irish question.

1. The Fenian movement as the struggle of a subjugated people against both the fact and the causes of their subjection, is essentially revolutionary alike in its methods and objectives.

2. The relative backwardness of Irish economic development is a reflex co-relative of the advance of British economic development.

3. The political separation of Ireland from Britain is indispensable as much in the interests of the British workers as in that of the Irish workers and working farmers.

4. Such a separation is an indispensable preliminary to any future federal union of the two peoples as equals. The British workers should take the initiative in forcing their separation.

5. An independent Irish Republic would, pending the development of a Socialist world economy, have to defend its economic reconstruction by means of protective tariffs.

6. The Fenian movement in that it aimed at smashing the power of the landlords and exalted that of the common people had a certain Socialist tendency.

7. The success of an agrarian revolution in Ireland would have a vital and far reaching importance for the settlement of the Social question of the world.[29]

In a letter to Engels dated December 10, 1869, Marx comes to the following conclusion:

... it is to the direct and absolute interest of the English working class to get rid of their present connection with Ireland. And this is my deepest conviction, and on grounds which, in part, I cannot communicate to the British workers themselves, I did believe for a long time that it was possible to overthrow the Irish regime by English working class ascendancy. I have constantly put forward this point of view in the *New York Tribune*. Deeper study has now led me to the opposite conclusion. The English working class will never do anything before it has got rid of Ireland. The wedge must be driven in in Ireland. That is why the Irish question is of such importance for the Socialist movement generally.

It is in this letter that Marx makes an analysis of the Irish revolutionary movement of Wolfe Tone and observes:

First of all, in 1798-99 are repeated (in a stronger form, perhaps) the atrocities of the English in 1588-89. Secondly, in the Irish movement itself a movement of classes can easily be shown. Thirdly, the vile policy of Pitt. Fourthly—what is very annoying to the English—the Irish failed because from a revolutionary standpoint, they were too advanced for the English church and king mob, and, on the other hand, English reaction in England itself, as in Cromwell's time, was operating on the enslavement of Ireland.

On January 1, 1870, a special session of the General Council of the International was held at which Marx pressed that another resolution on Ireland should be passed. The resolution, written by Marx and showing his attitude to the Irish question, was accepted by the International:

If England is the fortress of European landlordism and capitalism, then the only point from which a strong blow can be struck at official England is Ireland.

Above all, Ireland is the fortress of English landlordism. If it falls in Ireland then it will inevitably fall in England also. In Ireland this operation is a hundred times easier because the economic struggle is concentrated there exclusively around landed property, this struggle is also a national one and the people of Ireland are more revolutionary and embittered than in England. Landlordism in Ireland is only supported by the English army. The moment an end is put to the compulsory union of these two countries, a social revolution will break out in Ireland, although in old fashioned forms.

Marx goes on to discuss the agrarian democratic character of the revolutionary movements of Ireland, and continues:

English landlordism will lose not only a big source of its wealth, but also its most important source of moral strength as the representative of the rule of England over Ireland. On the other hand, the English proletariat will make its landlords invulnerable in England so long as their power remains inviolate in Ireland.

On the other hand, the English bourgeoisie has not only exploited Irish poverty in order to worsen the conditions of the working class in England, by the forced transplantation of poor Irish peasants, but it has moreover divided the proletariat into hostile camps. The revolutionary fire of the Celtic workers does not harmonise with the restrained force but slowness of the Anglo-Saxons. In all the big industrial centres of England a deep antagonism exists between the English and Irish workers. The average English worker hates the Irish as a competitor who lowers his wages and level of living. He feels national and religious antagonism towards him. He appears to him in much the same light as the black slaves appeared to the poor whites in the Southern States of North America. This antagonism between the proletarians of England is artificially cultivated and maintained by the bourgeoisie. It knows that in this antagonism lies the real secret of maintaining its power.

This antagonism also appears on the other side of the Atlantic. Turned off their native land by bullocks and sheep, the Irish emigrate to the U.S.A., where they are an important and growing part of the population. Their sole thought, their sole passion, is hatred to the English. The English and the American Government—that is, the classes which represent them—cultivated the hatred so as to perpetuate international contradictions, which are a brake on every serious and honest union between the working class of both countries and a brake on their common liberation.

Ireland is the only excuse of the English Government for maintaining a big standing army, which in case of need they send against the English workers, as has happened after the army became turned into praetorians in Ireland. Finally, England is at present what Ancient Rome was, in even greater degree. A people which enslaves another people forges its own chains.

In this way the viewpoint of the International Working Men's Association on the Irish question is very clear. Its first task is the speeding of the social revolution in England. For this end the decisive blow must be struck in Ireland.

The resolutions of the General Council on the Irish amnesty must be the forerunner of other resolutions. In the latter it will be shown that, without mentioning international justice, the essential preliminary condition of the emancipation of the English working class is the turning of the present compulsory union, that is slavery, of Ireland with England, into an equal and free union, if that is possible, or into full separation if this is inevitable.

Marx continued to work unsparingly for the Fenian prisoners and published another article entitled "The English Government and the Fenian Prisoners" in *L'Internationale* (no. 59) on February 27, 1870. At the same time a similar article of his appeared in the Belgian newspaper *L'Egalité*. This exposed the facts of ill treatment of the prisoners. Twenty of them were either dead or had been driven insane by the brutal prison conditions. Marx brands Gladstone's Land Bill of 1870, which was the first land act to allow the Irish tenant any compensation for improvement or right of occupancy or safeguard against arbitrary eviction, as a manoeuvre to cover his refusal of an amnesty. Gladstone himself admitted the Bill was a concession to "the intensity of Fenianism". The article was widely reproduced and Gladstone's own newspaper, the *Daily News,* had to publish a refutation, asking French liberals not to confuse the case of O'Donovan Rossa with that of Rochefort, a French liberal imprisoned by Napoleon III. Pressure was building up in Ireland and that year the Ulster Protestant lawyer, Isaac Butt, who had defended at the trials of Young Irelanders and Fenians, launched a constitutional Home Rule movement calling for federal self-government within a United Kingdom framework. Butt had become a member of parliament in 1852 and was member for Limerick at his death in 1879. In 1873 he made Tenant Right part of his party's platform. The French Radical newspaper, *Le Marseillaise,* now printed a series of articles on ill-treatment of Fenian prisoners and the author of these articles was Jenny Marx, Marx's eldest daughter, writing under the pseudonym of J. Williams. These articles were reproduced not only in the working-class press of Europe but in a number of major newspapers.

Gladstone was forced by public opinion to set up a commission of inquiry headed by Lord Devon and a report was published on September 20, 1870. As a result of this and continuing pressure, Gladstone wrote from Downing Street on December 16, 1870, extending royal clemency to Fenian prisoners "so far as it is compatible with the assured maintenance of tranquillity and order in the country . . ." He adds : "They (the prisoners) will, therefore, be discharged upon the condition of not remaining in, nor returning to, the United Kingdom." Some prisoners refused to abide by this clause and preferred to remain in jail. Many of the prisoners went into exile in the United States. Stekloff writes :

A warm welcome was given by the Central Committee (of the International) to the Fenian leader O'Donovan Rossa upon his arrival in New York. This reception made a very good impression upon the Irish, and won their sympathies for the cause of the International. A number of fresh sections sprang into being and sent their affiliation to the Central Committee.[30]

One of the New York sections, No. 7, sent a letter to Marx dated March 2, 1871, which was presented to the General Council meeting of March 14, which states that John Devoy was the delegate of this section to the New York Committee. "We hope (wrote released Fenian prisoners) we shall ever continue as we have begun, meriting by our actions the co-operation and support of the great International Working Men's Association and of all lovers of Freedom by whatsoever name they may be known." Jenny Marx wrote to Dr. Kugelman on December 21, 1871 :

The Irish in London are entering the ranks of the International. Irish sections are being formed in various parts of the East End.

The Irish branch of the International now grew stronger and those sections at Dublin and Cork were particularly large. In Cork several trade unionists joined with many of "the oldest and most respected advocates of Irish independence" from the city in the International. J. De Morgan, a language teacher, popular among Cork workers, was elected secretary while the secretary for all Ireland was J. P. McDonnell. In the Manifesto of the Irish Section of the International, the Irish workers wrote :

The national antagonism between English and Irish working men in England has hitherto been one of the main impediments in the way of every attempted movement for the emancipation of the working class, and therefore one of the main stays of class domination in England as well as in Ireland. The spread of the

International in Ireland and the formation of Irish branches in England threatened to put an end to this state of things.[31]

Police immediately took an interest in their activities : two constables watched De Morgan's house day and night. A strike of coachmakers in Cork for a minimum fifty-four-hour week was the cue the authorities had been waiting for in order to break up the International, who supported the Cork men. A local priest named Father Maguire denounced De Morgan from the pulpit. De Morgan pressed ahead, however, and branches of the International sent relief funds to the strikers. The Catholic Church then denounced the Internationalists as murderers and atheists, claiming that Internationalists had murdered priests during the Paris Commune of 1870-1. A meeting of the International in Cork was attacked by a crowd inflamed by such statements but the workers managed to defend themselves.

Two forces, however, were destroying the International; the activities of opportunist trade union leaders in England and the opposition of the ultra-left followers of the Russian Mikhail Bakunin. The Bakuninists were strongly critical of Marx's support for Irish independence. Rather than let the International fall into the hands of these people, Marx proposed the transfer of the General Council to New York :

> ... the documents of the International would be kept in greater safety where so many working class men from so many countries were living that it would be possible to find sincere and dedicated men ready to carry on the work. Here at last it would be possible to avoid the party frictions which endangered the movement in London. Marx was adamant. It was New York or nothing; he refused to consider any alternatives. He demanded an immediate vote. There were 26 votes in favour of New York, 23 against, and nine abstentions. Many who had voted against Marx were his faithful supporters. They realised that by moving to New York, the General Council would have no further influence on the working class movement in Europe, that Marx himself would retire from the scene and that the International had received its death blow.[32]

The Irish branches, however, were unanimous in supporting Marx in this move and by 1872 they had disappeared.

In 1875 John Mitchel stood as a parliamentary candidate for

Tipperary. He urged "universal tenant right" and the "sovereign independence of Ireland", and also declared that, if elected, he would conduct an abstentionist policy, refusing to go to Westminster. He was elected on February 16 but his election was immediately declared invalid. He was re-elected on March 11 but died through ill health on March 20. That April Charles Stewart Parnell was elected Home Rule M.P. for Meath and within two years he had become president of the Home Rule Confederation of Great Britain in place of Isaac Butt (August 27, 1877). The Confederation had been formed in February, 1873, to demand self-government for the Celtic countries of Ireland, Scotland and Wales.

In the meantime the Irish Republican Brotherhood were still active in America. They had decided to withdraw their support from the parliamentary movement for home rule, still placing their faith in revolution. Davitt, the former Fenian organiser who, at the age of nineteen had taken part in the attack on Chester Castle, was released from prison on December 19, 1877, on the condition he remain abroad for two years. Davitt, with his passion for social justice, went to America to contact John Devoy and urged him to support a common front of independence and the land question. Devoy supported the idea, but the Supreme Council of the Irish Republican Brotherhood, meeting in Paris in January, 1879, were not in favour, although Devoy managed to prevent them condemning the idea. Bitterly disappointed, Davitt returned to Ireland; to an Ireland suffering from an economic crisis, to the aftermath of the severe winter of 1878-9, which threatened people with a disaster comparable to the great famine. Falling prices, crop failure, bad weather, evictions and exorbitant rents were causing a multitude of small farmers to face starvation. Davitt immediately began to organise the peasantry and workers for what was to become known as the Land War.

Chapter 9

THE PEOPLE'S WAR 1879-82

THE PERIOD OF the Land War, or the Land League, takes its place in Irish History as "The People's War" because, for the first time, the tremendous energy of the continuing agrarian warfare was organised into a united national movement with specific aims. Unfortunately the aims of the Land League were not achieved because the opportunist politicians who led the movement sold out to the Government. Conditions in Ireland in 1879 were extremely bad. The deterioration in agriculture, the basis of the Irish economy, was due to a fall in world prices for agricultural produce and large scale agricultural improvements in the U.S.A. aided by the expansion of marine transport. Between 1875 and 1879 prices fell rapidly ... the Irish potato crop, worth £12,500,000 in 1876 was worth only £3,300,000 by 1878. The landowning classes of Ireland, however, expected their tenants to continue to pay rents in accordance with previous production figures. When the tenants could not meet the demands, evictions, which had fallen to an all-time low during the Fenian period, began again. In 1877 some 980 families were turned out of their homes, increasing to 2,100 families in 1880. In all, between 1878 and 1886 some 130,000 families were evicted. The land in Ireland at this time was owned by 20,000 landlords of whom 750 owned half of the country.[1] Under such conditions agrarian unrest was increasing and assassinations were occurring. On April 2, 1878, one of Ireland's biggest landowners, the Earl of Leitrim, was killed while out riding. He had estates in Cos. Donegal, Leitrim (he owned 77,000 acres in these two counties alone), Derry and Sligo. Leitrim had systematically evicted and consolidated his estates into pasture lands. Significantly the assassination took place near the mud hut where he had recently evicted a poor widow. The poor harvests and increasing prices were creating another great famine situation. Liberal-minded people took it upon themselves to organise charities and appeals were made in many countries to render aid to Ireland. The Duchess of

Marlborough, a leading figure in the charity movement, wrote to the London *Times,* January 23, 1880, "it cannot be doubted that the want throughout the land, if not promptly responded to by the voice of charity, will culminate in a famine."

Early in 1879, at Quinltagh, near Irishtown, Co. Mayo, the local parish priest, Geoffrey Burke, inherited his brother's property. Because of the general situation in the country, the tenants on these lands were well in arrears with their rent. Father Burke immediately issued eviction notices against the tenants. Michael Davitt with such men as Thomas Brennan, a prominent Fenian, and J. O'Connor Power, the local Home Rule member of parliament, organised a meeting on Sunday, April 20, "to protest against the action of Canon Burke, to demand a reduction of rents, and to denounce the whole landlord system." An estimated 7,000 people attended the meeting. Thomas Brennan went straight to the heart of the matter :

> ... you may get a Federal Parliament, perhaps the Repeal of the Union—nay more, you may establish an Irish Republic, but as long as tillers of the soil are forced to support a useless and indolent aristocracy, your Federal Parliament would be a bauble and your Irish Republic a fraud.[2]

The Irish Land League was born not only to obtain fair rents and fixity of tenure : it developed a philosophy to overthrow landlordism in Ireland. Davitt toured the country, organising and addressing meetings. He approached Charles Stewart Parnell to ask him to consider becoming president of the League. Parnell was now leader of the Irish Home Rule party, the majority Irish party at Westminster. Under the leadership of Isaac Butt the Irish Home Rule League had won sixty seats in 1874. Butt's idea, however, was to achieve a domestic self-government as a reform of the Empire and to this end he bent over backwards to win the respect and confidence of the English members of parliament, trying not to offend them in any way. Parnell, however, was more radical. With Joseph Gillis Biggar, M.P. for Cavan, an Ulster Protestant who, unknown to his comrades, was also a member of the Supreme Council of the Irish Republican Brotherhood, Parnell developed the technique of obstruction or "the art of parliamentary procrastination". It was Biggar who first scandalised the House of Commons when the Prince of

Wales took a seat in the gallery to listen to a debate. Biggar announced that he "espied strangers". Under the rules of the House Mr. Speaker had no option but to order the Prince of Wales to leave. Every rule and parliamentary device was used by Biggar, Parnell and their followers to interrupt, delay and generally embarrass the House of Commons. When English M.P.s tried to drown Parnell by coughing, whistling, groaning and loud conversation Biggar would move an adjournment "until the House was ready to listen". This became a regular technique. The Irish Parliamentary Party therefore become the first disciplined political parliamentary party in the United Kingdom. The present House of Commons procedure results very much from the filibustering tactics of Parnell. At the time Butt was still *de jure* leader of the Irish and was called upon to use his influence to prevent Parnellism in the House. He lectured the Parnellites severely and lost the respect of the movement.

Butt died in 1879 and Parnell had to oust William Shaw who had been nominated Butt's successor. This he succeeded in doing without difficulty for he had become popular not only for his activities but because he refused to describe the Fenians as murderers, whereas Butt and his faction were only too ready to use this terminology to appease the Government. Having settled himself as leader of the party he greeted Davitt's idea coldly: the party itself consisted of landlords and, indeed, Parnell himself was a landlord and a magistrate. Moreover, Parnell feared that the religious sects in Ireland would condemn any such movement to the party's detriment if they were officially supporting it. But Parnell was a shrewd politician. Charles Kickham had once remarked that the people "would go to the gates of hell" for the land and Parnell, realising this fact, saw the opportunity of placing his land-owning party at the head of a popular movement. He therefore threw in his lot with Davitt.

On June 8, 1879, Davitt invited Parnell to address a meeting at Westport, Co. Meath. On June 5, Dr. John MacHale, Archbishop of Tuam, published a letter denouncing the meeting. Nevertheless, some 10,000 arrived to listen to Parnell who now flung himself into the movement.

A fair rent is a rent the tenant can reasonably pay according to the times, but in bad times a tenant cannot be expected to pay as much as he did in good times, three or four years ago. If such rents are insisted upon a repetition of the scenes of 1847 and 1848 will be witnessed. Now what must we do to induce the landlords to see the position? You must show them that you intend to hold a firm grip of your homesteads and lands. You must not allow yourselves to be dispossessed as your fathers were dispossessed in 1847. You must not allow your small holdings to be conso- lidated ... You must help yourselves and the public opinion of the world will stand by and support you in your struggle to defend your homesteads.[3]

Reaction to Parnell's speech from the Establishment was a fore- gone conclusion. The *Evening Mail,* Dublin, of June 10, carried an editorial denouncing "Communism in Connaught". The *Evening Mail* became a "front line" landlord mouthpiece denouncing the Land League as radical, dangerous and wholly bad.[4] It was part of a "gigantic revolutionary scheme" to unite with "extreme radicals" in England and labour movements in the U.S.A. under the banner of revolution. It was "a form of Continental Communism" dashed with "Irish-American treason". It was a social war by the "Have-Nots" against the "Haves" and, as such, it should be crushed without mercy. Ireland should beware less the virus of class war spread. The *Daily Express* observed that the language of the League was the outcome of "doctrines of a Socialist tendency which for some years have promulgated through the West". The *Evening Mail, New York Herald, New York World,* and *New York Evening Post* unanimously condemned the new movement as "subver- sive and communistic".

By September, 1879, the Irish National League, with Parnell as its president, with branches throughout Ireland, was an estab- lished fact. Reacting to the establishment of this organisation landlords, gentry and clergy began to organise and, in November, 1879, they held their first meeting to deliberate on the state of the country. The same month they established an Irish Land Committee to counteract the claims of the peasants about their conditions made to a Royal Commission on Agriculture which was being held. This committee issued eleven pamphlets between November, 1880, and April, 1881, propagat- ing the idea how benevolent landlords were to their tenants. These pamphlets were distributed widely at low cost, subsidised by the landlords. Landowners, led by the Earl of Donoughmore, tried to establish a combination to counteract the League. The *Evening Mail* of September 27, 1880, explained: "Abandoned by Government, owners of property must protect themselves." One of the biggest forces of reaction was the Orange Order, led against the League by an appeal to religious bigotry. However, Michael Davitt had addressed a number of Orange Lodges and succeeded in winning support from many Orangemen. Like its predecessor, the Tenant Right League, the Land League managed to unite a large section of Protestants and Catholics in its non-sectarian ambitions.

The Government did not remain idle while the Land League organised itself. Davitt had been released from prison in 1877 not having completed his full fifteen-year sentence. The Government decided to suspend his "ticket of leave" and, on November 19, he was arrested. The basic object was to frighten the leaders of the movement. Three days later, Parnell headed a big demonstration at Balla, Co. Mayo, where a threatened eviction was about to take place. The Government took action against this defiance by prosecuting Davitt and other prominent League members. During the first week of the preliminary hearing, the League took the opportunity to hold numerous demonstrations and the newspapers complained to the Government that they were playing into the League's hands. The prosecutions were stopped. Nevertheless, landlords raised their voices against the League, denouncing Parnell as an arch-Communist. The main body of the Catholic Church united for the landlords led by the Archbishop of Dublin. Only two Catholic prelates supported the League, William Croke, Archbishop of Cashel, and Dr. Nulty, Bishop of Meath, who wrote an *Essay on the Land Question*, in which he stated: "The land of every country is the common property of the people of that country . . ." But Croke and Nulty were exceptions, and Croke was eventually to disown the League when it issued its "No Rents Manifesto".

The League was now a most formidable force and its philosophy was summed up in a popular song of the time:

> To be landlord of a few dirty acres of ground
>   is the cure for all evils you see
> And before very long in this land will be found
>   a peasant proprietaree.[5]

The people were no longer meekly submitting to eviction orders. In January, 1880, at Carraroe, Connemara, sixty armed police were protecting two bailiffs serving eviction orders when a crowd of peasants started to throw stones and jeer them. Several people were wounded by police bayonets but the bailiffs only managed to serve four of the 120 eviction orders. Attacks on bailiffs and land agents continued. The *Evening Mail* comments:

> There are signs that the wild waves of democracy are surging round the shores of Ireland. It is time for all respectable classes to stand shoulder to shoulder and stem the tide of revolutionary feelings.[6]

The Land League continued to grow in strength and perfect its organisation. Parnell, in an attempt to win constitutionalist nationalists and revolutionaries to his leadership, stated his belief that "a true revolutionary movement in Ireland should partake both of a constitutional and illegal character."[7] The Irish revolutionaries in America, however, were dubious about Parnell's motives. In September, 1878, in New York they had declared that:

> ... the abolition of the foreign landlord system and substitution of one by which the tiller of the soil will be fixed permanently upon it, and holding directly from the State, is the only true solution of the Irish land question, which an Irish Republic can alone effect.[8]

There inevitably came a clash with the Home Rule Party, with its landlord membership. Land Leaguers issued a manifesto calling upon the people not to vote for landlords. The General Election of 1880, which swept Gladstone and his Liberals into their second ministry, saw a change in the composition of the Home Rule Party. A number of landlord M.P.s were replaced by non-landowning professional men, thus turning the Home Rulers from a landowning party into a bourgeois party. An illustration of the unity of the Irish people is shown by the fact that an Ulster Presbyterian minister, Rev. Isaac Nelson, was elected on the Land League ticket for Mayo, perhaps the most doggedly Catholic county of Ireland.

During the summer of 1880 Parnell presented a Bill in the House of Commons which would have given all tenants

compensation when thrown out by the landlords. The Bill was rejected on July 26 and had the effect of strengthening support for
the League. Riots at evictions and assaults on landgrabbers were
commonplace. A group of Fenians captured an English gunboat
in Cork Harbour and made off with forty cases of rifles and ammunition. On September 19, 1880, Parnell addressed a meeting
at Ennis, at which he presented the Irish people with an alternative policy to violence. Parnell had reached a point in his
speech when he asked what should be done with a man who bids
for a farm from which people have been evicted. Someone cried
"Shoot him!" Parnell paused, then continued:

> I think I heard somebody say "Shoot him!"—(loud cries of
> "quite right too" with renewed applause) but I wish to point out
> to you a very much better way—a more Christian, and a more
> charitable way, which will give the lost sinner an opportunity of
> repenting. When a man takes a farm from which another has
> been evicted, you must show him on the roadside, when you meet
> him, you must show him in the streets of the town, you must
> show him in the fair and the market place, and even in the place
> of worship, by leaving him *severely alone*—putting him into a
> kind of moral Coventry, isolating him from his kind like the leper
> of old—you must show him your detestation of the crime he has
> committed. And you may depend upon it, that there is no man so
> full of avarice, so lost to shame, as to dare the public opinion of
> all right thinking men, and to transgress your unwritten code of
> laws.

In these words Parnell gave a modern application to the Greek
word "ostracism". The idea fired not only Ireland but was accepted by the English trade union movement. The idea of
"ostracism" as a weapon had been fermenting among the leaders
of the Land League for some time. Davitt first referred to it in a
speech at Knockaroo, Queen's County, on January 22, 1880.
Three days after Parnell's Ennis speech the Irish gave their
own word for "ostracism" to the English language—the word
"boycott".

Captain Charles S. Boycott, a petty landowner himself, was
the land agent of the Earl of Erne, managing his large estate on
the eastern shore of Lough Mask, Co. Mayo. Lord Erne lived on
a 31,000-acre estate in Fermanagh and had not been to Mayo
for ten years, leaving the running of his estate to Boycott. On

September 22, Boycott sent his bailiff, guarded by police, to deliver eviction notices to his tenants. The angry tenants attacked the bailiff and drove him to seek shelter in Lough Mask House. The Land League decided that here was their first confrontation. The Local Land League of Ballinrobe, led by Father John O'Malley, decided on an "ostracism" campaign aimed against Boycott. On September 24, all Captain Boycott's servants left with all the estate's farm labourers. In Ballinrobe all shopkeepers, the laundress, blacksmith etc. refused to serve Boycott. In desperation Boycott wrote an appeal to the London *Times* asking for help to save his crops. On November 11, fifty Orangemen, volunteers from Ulster, arrived to work for Boycott, led by six Ulster landowners with ten servants in attendance. They arrived at Claremorris by rail guarded by 200 troops of the 76th regiment; 400 troops of the 84th regiment; 200 troops of the 19th Hussars, two companies of the army service corps, ammunition wagons, ambulances etc. They had to march the fifteen miles to Ballinrobe in drenching rain, ignored by everyone, much to the consternation of the soldiery who were expecting a pitched battle. On November 26 they left, still shunned by the people, having saved Boycott's crop worth £300 . . . at a cost of £3,000. The people had won and Boycott left for England within a few days. He was to return to Lough Mask, however, after the suppression of the Land League.

"Boycott is gone," wrote Thomas Brennan in the *Irish World* on December 11, 1880, "but Boycotting remains." A new word had been born. The application of the technique of a boycott was repeated in scores of similar cases during 1881 and become a major Land League weapon. The Land League had strengthened its position in rural Ireland so much that to all intents and purposes it could be regarded as *de facto* government. Land League courts were held to decide the punishment of transgressors and many local newspapers supported them. Practically the whole of rural Ireland, with the exception of the major parts of Ulster, came under the rule of the League which grew to be the most powerful class-based association Ireland had even known. Connolly commented :

> During Land League days in Ireland, when a tenant was evicted from a farm not only his fellow tenants but practically the whole country united to help him in his fight. When the

evicted farm was rented by another tenant, a land grabber or "scab", every person in the countryside shunned him as a leper, and, still better, fought him as a traitor . . . At the command of the Land League every servant and labourer quit the service of the landlord . . . When the landlord had declared war upon the tenant by evicting him, the labourers responded by war upon the landlord.[9]

On November 2 the Government decided to start proceedings against Parnell, Davitt and Land League leaders for "seditious conspiracy". The trials began in Dublin on January 5, 1881, and lasted twenty days . . . the jury failed to agree and the prisoners were discharged. That month a Central Land League of the Ladies of Ireland was formed. The Government now renewed their attack on the League and, on February 3, Davitt was again arrested and his "ticket of leave" suspended. Soon other Land League leaders were following him into jail as Parliament passed Coercion Acts to suppress the organisation. The *Evening Mail* was confident of the League's collapse in its editorial of February 4, 1881 :

> Under Davitt the Land League became a power, without him it will sink into insignificance. There can be no possibility of replacing him. With his return there may be expected to return to Ireland a season of peace and prosperity.

There returned to Ireland an increasingly bitter period of agrarian warfare. On April 2, police fired on a crowd at Ballaghadereen, Co. Sligo, killing two men; at Clonmel, thirty peasants were killed or wounded while two policemen were killed. Ireland was tottering on the verge of revolution. Guerilla warfare did break out in Cork in June when the West Cork police barracks was attacked and destroyed, telegraph wires were cut, all communications stopped, miles of road torn up, and the country armed. The London *Times* of June 7 admitted : "anarchy reigns in many districts". The *Irish World* of June 18 commented :

> Every day, Ireland is pushed nearer the brink of revolution . . . every farm from which a tenant is evicted is becoming a battlefield.

A strong leader could have turned the situation to a tactical advantage. Unfortunately, the only man of foresight, Davitt, was in prison. In an effort to decrease the growing intensity of the Irish problem, Gladstone introduced a new Land Act, on Thursday, April 7, which incorporated recommendations made by Bessborough and Carlingford who had conducted commissions of inquiry on the situation. Bessborough, in fact, made an interesting comment in his report on the philosophy of the Irish peasant.

> There has in general survived to him (the Irish tenant) through all vicissitudes, despite of the seeming or real veto of the law, in apparent defiance of political economy, a living tradition of possessory right such as belonged in the more primitive ages of society to the status of men who tilled the soil.[10]

Palmer commented :

> The Irish peasants, in short, believed that the land they tilled, like the air they breathed, belonged of right to no man or group of men, but to the people as a whole.[11]

Gladstone's Act established the "three F's", i.e. fair rent, fixity of tenure, and freedom of sale. Tribunals were to be set up to fix rents for a period of fifteen years and during this time the tenants could not be evicted. The conditions, which already existed in the north (the Ulster Custom) were now made legally binding on the rest of Ireland. The Tories denounced the Act as "a gross interference with the rights of property". A supplement Arrears Bill was also presented which intended to wipe out arrears in 130,000 cases at a state cost of £800,000. There were fifty-eight sittings on the Bill and 800 amendments before it finally became law on August 22. The Land League rejected the Bill. T. P. O'Connor, making a speech in Kansas in 1882, commented :

> Gladstone's policy was to fix a relation between landlord and tenants; the policy of the League was to abolish the relation and trample landlordism beneath its heels.

Apart from the different philosophies, however, the Bill was too full of complications and legal loopholes to be really effective, and only alleviated the peasant suffering slightly. According to Elinor Burns :

> By offering some measure of security, the British Government immediately succeeded in winning large numbers of the peasants away from revolutionary action, and in this policy the former leaders of the land war became the Government's most effective allies.[12]

But the big betrayal was yet to come. On September 15, 1881, some 1,300 delegates attended the National Convention of the Land League in Dublin. With Parnell in the chair, the Convention decided :

> ... no settlement of the Land Question can be satisfactorily effective or practicable which does not abolish landlordism root and branch and make the tiller the owner of the soil.

When the Convention ended on September 17 delegates resolved that the League be called the Irish National Land League and the Labour and Industrial Movement. Thus the movement united not only the peasants but the urban workers. The League's recommendation to reject the new Land Act was totally condemned by the Catholic Church. On October 12 the Government reacted by arresting Parnell and other prominent League members. The League now issued their No Rent Manifesto, endorsed by the League's executive on Tuesday, October 18.

> Fellow countrymen :—the hour to try your souls and to redeem your pledges has arrived. The executive of the National Land League, forced to abandon the policy of testing the Land Act, feels bound to advise the tenant farmers of Ireland from this (day) forth to pay no rents under any circumstances to their landlords until the Government relinquishes the existing system of terrorism and restores the constitutional rights of the people.
> Do not be daunted by the removal of your leaders. Your fathers abolished tithes by the same methods without any leaders at all and with scarcely a shadow of the magnificent organisation that covers every portion of Ireland today. Do not suffer yourselves to be intimidated by threats of military violence. It is as lawful to refuse to pay rents as it is to receive them. Against the passive resistance of an entire population, military power has no

weapons. Do not be wheedled into compromise of any sort by the dread of eviction. If you only act together in the spirit to which, within the last two years, you have countless times solemnly pledged your vows, they can no more evict a whole nation than they can imprison them.

On October 20, W. E. Forster, Secretary for Ireland, prohibited the Land League, making it an illegal society. Before Parnell had been taken to prison he had been asked who would deputise for him in his absence. "Ah," Parnell replied, "Captain Moonlight will take my place." Captain Moonlight, the name by which certain agrarian revolutionary leaders became known, did take over. Agrarian crime mounted beyond all previous heights. The country was again on the verge of war. Not one of the Land League leadership recognised that the direct consequence of the land war, the No Rent campaign, must be an actual seizure of land leading to a struggle for power against the English ruling classes arising out of agrarian revolution. They were not prepared to go through to the final issue.

The Ladies' Land League tried to alleviate suffering on a charity level and were immediately denounced by the Archbishop of Dublin. Archbishop Croke won passing admiration by publicly rebuking his fellow prelate. The Government, realising something must be done to bring the situation under control and that Coercion would of itself not correct matters, entered into secret negotiations with Parnell. On May 2, 1882, Parnell reached an agreement with the Government for an armistice. His conditions were : 1, cessation of Coercion and the release of Land League prisoners; 2, state aid to wipe off arrears which prevented tenants taking advantage of the 1881 Act; 3, in return the Land League would suppress agrarian crime; and 4, the Irish Home Rule Party would co-operate in promotion of legislation in line with "liberal" principles in the House of Commons. Davitt commented dryly : "It was the vital turning point in Mr. Parnell's career and he unfortunately turned the wrong way."[13]

In fairness to Parnell it must be said that his "backing down" from the logical conclusion of agrarian revolution was not a betrayal according to his philosophy. He was, after all, a landowning, Protestant aristocrat, who, superficially, had every reason to support the status quo. The line he took, in attacking the Establishment, led him to financial impoverishment. Again, if

Parnell had allowed a revolution to start, it is doubtful it would have been successful. The Orangemen, seduced from their original radical republicanism, would have sided with the English administration turning the revolution into civil war. On the other hand, had Parnell successfully won Home Rule, under his leadership as a Protestant there would have been a good possibility of winning the Orangemen back to their proper social and national loyalty.

With the release of the Land League leaders, including Davitt, the Viceroy Earl Cowper and Chief Secretary Forster resigned in disgust. On May 6, the very day of Davitt's release the new Viceroy, Lord Frederick Cavendish, and Under Secretary Burke were assassinated in the grounds of the Viceregal Lodge by a group of men armed with knives. They escaped. The group was later identified as the "Invincibles", a group of breakaway Fenians who made their appearance following the collapse of the Land League along with O'Donovan Rossa's breakaway dynamiters. Jackson comments:

> Each was closely analogous to the terrorist-anarchist manifestations which evidence the break-up and degeneration of the Bakuninists' sections of the First International, after the fall of the (Paris) Commune in 1871—which manifestation supplied these quasi-Fenian degenerations with their mutual aspiration.[14]

Parnell immediately went to see Gladstone and offered to resign from public office to show the English how "ashamed" the Irish leadership was of the political assassinations. Gladstone, having "tamed" Parnell, did not want to be confronted with a new leader and so persuaded Parnell to continue. Coercion continued and privately Gladstone repudiated his "Kilmainham Pact" with Parnell, while still allowing the Land League leaders their freedom. Neither side could, of course, admit such a pact existed—Gladstone for fear of his "right wing" and Parnell for fear of his "left wing".

The remnants of the Land League now pushed forward into agitation for local-self-government and gradual land reform by the foundation on October 17, 1882, of the Irish National League.

The National League was formed

...To attain for the Irish people the following objects (1) national self government; (2) land law reforms; (3) local self government; (4) extension of the parliamentary and municipal franchise and (5) the development and encouragement of the labour and industrial interests of Ireland.

But with the agrarian revolution successfully checked a new class of small proprietors had been brought into existence. The Act of 1881 was followed by four other measures which provided against eviction, against raising rents after tenants' improvements and establishing peasant "ownership" by state loans. The Land Purchase Acts of 1885, 1891, 1896 and 1902 authorised Land Commissioners to advance sums to tenants to purchase their holdings. The sums advanced were raised by means of public loans on which the landowner paid a fixed annual sum (annuity) in interest and repayment of the principal. In the thirty-six years following the first Land Purchase Act over 400,000 holdings with a total of more than thirteen million acres were sold at aggregate purchase price of £124,000,000. Elinor Burns comments:

The transfer of rent from the landholder to the loanholder made little difference in the actual condition of the poor peasants. On the whole, the change tended to help the capitalist farmer to extend his farm, but left the position of the "uneconomic" holder and of the agricultural labourer untouched. By means of other measures, including the Agricultural Labourers' Acts of 1883 to 1906 and the establishment of the Congested Districts Board in 1891, attempts were made to satisfy the land hunger of both these groups. The Congested Districts Board was designed to deal with the overcrowded areas of the south-west, where, according to an official report, the people "were in a chronic state of famine and their standard of living was at the lowest point."[15]

The Irish Land League, however, gave inspiration to Ireland's sister Celtic nation, Scotland. In 1883 a Highland Land League, *Commun An Fhearain,* was launched, "that Scotland may become again an independent nation, and that all lands, mines and fisheries be restored to the Scottish commonwealth." It was active between the years 1883 and 1895 and then lay moribund until the turn of the century when it was revived and continued in force until the 1920's. A leading figure was Dr. Gavin Brown

Clark (1840-1925) who had been associated with the First International, was elected to Westminster, and was involved with presenting numerous Self-Government for Scotland Bills. *Commun An Fhearain* was recognised by the Scottish Labour Party (then pledged to Scottish self-government) as is its equivalent in the still Scottish Gaelic speaking areas of Scotland.[16]

Chapter 10

THE RISE OF ORGANISED LABOUR

O N O C T O B E R 1 7 , 1 8 8 2 , an Irish National League was formed "to attain for the Irish people the following objectives: (1) national self-government; (2) land law reforms; (3) local self-government; (4) extension of the parliamentary and municipal franchise; (5) the development and encouragement of the labour and industrial resources of Ireland." But the 1881 Land Act had taken the steam out of the agrarian movement, although as late as 1895 some 45 per cent of Ireland's agricultural produce still went as tax compared to England's 10 per cent. Landlords continued to demand rent arrears from the peasantry and although Davitt, now a member of Parnell's constitutional Nationalist Party, tried to reiterate the principles of land nationalisation, the farmers favoured the bourgeois leadership of John Dillon and William O'Brien who sought piecemeal reform. Dillon and O'Brien had led a "Plan of Campaign" against rent arrears but abandoned it when agitation in 1898 threatened the bourgeois domination of the political scene. The 1891 Land Act of Balfour set up a Congested Districts Board to relieve local problems and the policy of transforming tenantry into proprietors climaxed with Wyndham's Land Act of 1903. By 1909, 270,000 of the remaining 500,000 tenants had bought their holdings.

William O'Brien had initiated a revival of the Land League and enlisted the aid of Davitt in the establishment of a United Ireland League which produced a social programme of ending rural leaseholds, division of western grazing estates, more smallholdings for the peasantry, more power for the local authorities, restoration of the excess Irish taxes, an end to urban ground rents and terminal leases, a separate Irish Catholic University and the "preservation" of the Irish language. Campaigning by O'Brien resulted in the 1903 Land Act which established preconditions for complete tenant land purchase.

Since 1881, however, the smaller Irish Catholic capitalist had grown influential and, while O'Brien tried to compromise with them, they eventually dominated his United Ireland League. O'Brien resigned and the secretaryship passed to Joseph Devlin, a Catholic who was Nationalist M.P. for West Belfast. In 1904 Devlin became the first national president of the Ancient Order of Hibernians, a Catholic charitable body which became the representative organisation of Irish petty capitalism. The Order was the Catholic equivalent of the Orange Order, maintaining that it traced its ancestry back to the Defender societies of 1775. By giving its support to the National Party, and thereby a sectarian basis to nationalism, the party lost support from the Protestant sections of the community, although, out of the eighty-five Nationalist M.P.s, twelve were Protestants. In 1909 O'Brien and T. M. Healy formed an anti-Hibernian All For Ireland League to offset the damage by trying to present a nonsectarian basis.

The election of 1885 had achieved a unique position for Parnell's party in that the Irish now held the balance of power between the parties in the House of Commons. One wonders whether this influenced Gladstone's "conversion" to Irish Home Rule later that year. The next year, with Irish support, Gladstone formed his third administration and introduced his Home Rule for Ireland Bill in the House of Commons on April 8. The Bill drove most of the mainly Ulster based Irish liberals into the Unionist Party. Lord Randolph Churchill wrote: "I decided some time ago that if the G.O.M. (Gladstone) went for Home Rule, the Orange card would be the one to play. Please God it may turn out the ace of trumps and not the two." The Unionists aroused the Orange Order and using religious scare tactics (i.e. "Home Rule is Rome Rule") provoked a series of sectarian riots against the Bill. The Bill was defeated by thirty votes on June 7. The Orange card worked and in a general election held in July the Gladstone government were swept from office.

The London *Times* had begun a series of articles under the general heading "Parnellism and Crime" aimed at influencing the elections and justifying Coercion in Ireland by implicating Parnell with agrarian outrages. The final article reproduced a letter purported to be written by Parnell condoning the Phoenix Park murders. This last article appeared, significantly enough, on the morning of the day fixed for the second reading of yet another of the Government's Coercion Acts. The articles plus an unsuccessful action for libel brought against *The Times* by

F. Hugh O'Donnell, ex-member of the Parnell Party, led to the institution of a Special Commission to inquire into the newspaper's allegations. Representing the newspaper were the Attorney General and Solicitor General, in their "private capacity". It was soon proved that the Phoenix Park letter was forged and a scapegoat was found in Richard Pigott, who had a reputation in Dublin as a pedlar of forged Fenian documents. Pigott, after two days in the witness box, fled the country leaving behind a full confession. Pursued by the police, he blew out his brains in Madrid.

Winston Churchill wrote that the Government were now out "to recover in the Divorce Court the credit lost before the Special Commission". Captain W. H. O'Shea, an Irish M.P., was persuaded to sue his wife for divorce naming Parnell as co-respondent. On November 17, 1890, the verdict was given for Captain O'Shea as neither Mrs. Katherine O'Shea or Parnell contested the claim. Kitty O'Shea had met Parnell in 1880 after living separately from O'Shea for some time. In the period between 1880-90 Captain O'Shea had had seventeen known affairs.

The first reaction of the Irish people was to support Parnell against this "hit below the belt" by the Establishment but, by playing on religion and morality, the unity of both the Irish people and their party began to crack. The final push was given by the Catholic hierarchy who issued a manifesto on December 3 condemning Parnell. From November 15 to December 6, 1890, the Irish Party argued the situation in Committee Room 15 at Westminster. Finally forty-five members walked out with Justin MacCarthy, a right-wing religious bigot, while only twenty-six declared for Parnell. By October 6, 1891, Parnell was dead at the age of forty-five and the Irish Party was split. In December 1891, the conservative John Redmond was elected leader of the Parnellite section of the party. Under Parnell the party had appealed to the working people; split now by two conservative leaders, there was little hope of a strong, popular and united party. Gladstone was again returned to power in the July, 1892, election. On February 13, 1893, he introduced his second Home Rule for Ireland Bill which passed the Commons on September 1 but was defeated by the Lords on September 8.

When in 1898, local councils were established in Ireland, many labour representatives were elected. Young radicals were joining the still functioning Irish Republican Brotherhood while others joined various national literary societies many of which acted as front organisations for the revolutionary movement. Support began to fall away from the Irish Party to new political group-ings. In February, 1900, however, Redmond became leader of a united Irish Party but its existence was tenuous. The party's only hope was the achievement of its political aims and this looked hopeful with the return of the Liberals in 1906. But the Liberals offered only a form of devolution and so increased militancy among Irish radicals. The party was put at a further disadvan-tage by the activities of Joseph Devlin whose Board of Erin, a breakaway group from the Ancient Order of Hibernians, dominated the party on a sectarian basis. Padraic Pearse wrote : "The narrowing of nationalism to the members of one creed is the most hateful thing that has occurred in Ireland since the days of the Pope's Brass Band." James Connolly dismissed the Board as "the foulest brood that ever came into Ireland".

During this period, as in common with many small European nations almost destroyed by imperialism, a National Awakening was taking place. In 1879 Standish James O'Grady, a member of the Protestant Ascendancy class, published his *History of Ireland—Heroic Period* which was a fantasia based on ancient Irish mythology, a work of literature rather than a history, revealing a wealth of Irish literature unknown to the generations of English-speaking Irish people. In writing this book O'Grady helped to inspire poets and literary men who, like Yeats, Synge, George Russell ("AE"), James Stephens etc., turned to the Irish mythology and folklore for their inspiration. From 1888 the Irish Literary Revival gave a new hope and impetus to the Irish lan-guage and culture which had been dying under the crushing weight of Anglicisation. Having interpreted the ideas of the an-cient Irish, O'Grady became intrigued by the concept of Celtic communism. George Russell comments :

> He preached a new communism, and at one stage sketched in arresting detail a possible, and, he maintained, a practicable com-mune, a series of communes, for weary clerks and others who would go back to the land.[1]

O'Grady's ideas on communes were published in his work *The Pope's Green Island*. He tried to establish a commune on his farm but it seems his plans did not work out. He later wrote a letter "to the landlords of Ireland", more in sorrow than in anger, reluctantly expressing the belief that the landlords would never lead the Irish to national and social independence.

Activity was also taking place to try to save the language of the people and in 1876 the Society for the Preservation of the Irish Language had been formed. It was replaced in 1879 by the Gaelic Union, but these societies were more scholarly groups than popular linguistic movements. However, on July 31, 1893, *Conradh na Gaeilge* (The Gaelic League) was formed with the aim of saving the Irish language from destruction in the areas of Ireland where it was still the first language. The formation of this popular movement was part of the establishment of similar movements throughout the Gaelic-speaking world during that decade . . . i.e. *An Comunn Gaidhealach* in Scotland in 1891 and *Yn Cheshaght Ghailckagh* in the Isle of Man in 1899. Led by Dr. Douglas Hyde, the League put forward a policy of de-Anglicisation and the aim of completely restoring the language to all the people of Ireland. The League, in this respect, was in line with other language movements throughout Europe. Other countries such as Lithuania, Latvia, Estonia, Slovenia, Armenia, Faroes, Albania, Rumania, Finland and many more had found themselves in a similar position to Ireland and undertook the task of language restoration. They have, in the past century, achieved complete success. Ireland is, today, the only exception of a country having formed a native government pledged to restore the native language and culture which has failed in this aim. *Conradh na Gaeilge* sparked off a tremendous enthusiasm for Irish culture and in 1899 the first issue of *An Cliadheamh Solais* ("The Sword of Light"—one of the four treasures of the *Tuatha de Danaan* of Irish mythology) was launched as the official organ of the language movement. Publications of the movement sold a quarter of a million per year. The advent of *Conradh na Gaeilge* opened the way for great activity in the fields of literature, drama, art and history in Ireland. On a practical level the movement secured the teaching of Irish in schools during normal school hours in 1906; Irish qualifications as a necessity for teachers going to teach in Irish-speaking areas (*Gaeltacht*) and Irish as a matriculation subject in the new National University 1910-13. It might be commented here that the commission established to enquire about the worth of Irish as a university subject demonstrated the essential insularity of English academics by their deprecatory remarks on the language which were brought into high relief by the testimonials of such continental Celtic scholars as the German Kuno Meyer.

In the 1880's co-operative societies began to make headway in Ireland mainly as a result of the introduction of the mechanical cream separator which gave a chance to petty capitalists to strengthen their position at the cost of the small farmer. Co-operative creameries soon found a backer in the Unionist Horace Plunkett. By April, 1894, a national body— the Irish Agricultural Organisation Society was established. This was backed in 1898 by the Irish Wholesale Society which gave a fair deal to small farmers in the agricultural supplies trade. The following year Plunkett became the first secretary of the newly created Government Department of Agriculture and initiated a state subsidy for the IAOS and the establishment of Co-operative Credit Unions. By 1899, 477 such co-operative societies were in existence. At this time Ireland was setting something of a lead in co-operatives and Plunkett lectured on the subject throughout Europe, including Scandinavia where his ideas were well received. Now, the Scandinavian countries with largely co-operative economies, are immeasurably ahead in this field. While Plunkett's ideas on co-operatism were purely a way to "better business", George Russell ("AE"), who edited the movement's journal, *The Irish Homestead*, envisaged a new society in Ireland based upon rural communes. He took his inspiration from Ralahine and this brought him into close connection with James Connolly, the revolutionary Socialist.[2] They both felt strongly about female emancipation and helped found the United Irishwomen (later the Irish Countrywomen's Association) in 1910. In 1904 Plunkett offended the Catholic hierarchy in his book *Ireland in the New Century* and gradually pressure was brought to bear on the movement. The new Liberal Government of 1906 was prevailed upon to get rid of Plunkett and stop the grant to the IAOS. This all but destroyed co-operatism except in places where there arose an organiser of strong determination such as Paddy ("the Cope") Gallagher of Co. Donegal.[3] The Co-operative credit banks were closed, and the remnants of the movement were subsidised from American appeals until the grant was restored in 1913. The year of 1913, however, was a

fateful year for Irish Labour and it was in that year that
George Russell discovered the Labour movement and realised
the possibilities of linking rural co-operatism with urban
labour.

In 1896 twenty-six-year-old James Connolly had founded
the Irish Socialist Republican Party in Dublin. Connolly had
been born of Co. Monaghan parents and raised in Edinburgh,
Scotland, where he was forced to work at a very early age. He
became an avowed Marxist and was also influenced by his
uncle, John Leslie, a Fenian who was also a propagandist for
the Marxist Social Democratic Federation. Leslie had written
The Present Condition of the Irish Question which summed
up the Land League struggle from a Socialist viewpoint and
is still a valid assessment. Connolly was considering emigration
to Chile, having found himself victimised in Edinburgh due to
his Socialist belief (he had stood as a Socialist candidate in an
Edinburgh municipal election). It was Leslie who persuaded
the young Connolly to establish a Socialist party in Ireland.

Working as a navvy and then as a proof reader on a
Sunday newspaper in Dublin, Connolly became the organiser
of the Dublin Socialist Society. He started to preach that
Socialism and national liberation were complementary to each
other, that national and social freedom were not two separate
issues but were two sides of one great democratic principle,
each being incomplete without the other. In *Shan Van Vocht*
(*An tSean bhean bhocht*) he wrote "Can Irish Republicans be
Politicians?" urging the use of constitutional and unconstitutional methods in the national struggle. In 1897 he published
his first pamphlet entitled *Erin's Hope* which gave a very un-
compromising statement of the Socialist case beginning by in-
voking the common ownership of the land which characterised
the Irish clan system—an embryo which he later developed in
his *Labour in Irish History*.

Connolly's Irish Socialist Republican Party sought to
achieve a Worker's Republic in Ireland and, compared with all
previous movements, showed a tremendous advance in social
theory. The manifesto of the party included a programme of
nationalisation of banks, transport, popular control of schools,
free education to higher university level, pensions for the aged,
infirmed, widows, orphans, free maintenance for children,
graduated income tax, universal suffrage and a standard forty-

five hour working week. It was, avows O'Connor Lysaght, "too advanced for its time."[4] The basic aim of the party was clear :

> The establishment of an Irish Socialist Republic based upon the public ownership by the people of Ireland of the land and instruments of production, distribution and exchange. Agriculture to be administered as a public function, under boards of management elected by the agricultural population and responsible to them and to the nation at large. All other forms of labour necessary to the well being of the community to be conducted on the same principle.

The first man outside Ireland to join the ISRP was Dr. Edward Aveling, son of a London Congregational minister, scientist, playwright, author, actor, critic and brilliant scientific speaker. His mistress, Eleanor Marx, daughter of Karl, wrote in her *History of the Working Class Movements in England,* "It is certain that the hope of Ireland a Nation lies not in her middle class O'Connells but in her generous, devoted, heroic working men and women."

In 1898 Connolly started a newspaper called *Workers' Republic,* which, launched on August 12, went to eleven issues during that year. The Scottish Independent Labour Party leader Keir Hardie gave £50 for the venture for Connolly was a frequent contributor to Hardie's *Labour Leader.* In May, 1899, it became a ½d weekly and appeared on and off as funds allowed until May, 1903. The party busied themselves printing such works as Lalor's *Rights of Ireland* and *Faith of a Felon.* In 1898 Connolly joined a committee preparing a commemoration for the 1798 uprising and his *'98 Readings* became famous. In 1901 he published another pamphlet, *The New Evangel,* in which he rebuked leaders of religion for condemning Socialism as anti-religion.

> Socialism, as a party, bases itself upon the knowledge of facts of economic truths, and leaves the building up of religious ideals or faiths to the outside public, or to its individual members if they so will. It is neither Freethinker, nor Christian, Turk nor Jew, Buddhist nor Idolator, Mahommedan nor Parsee—it is only HUMAN.

In 1898 the establishment of county councils allowed the ISRP to fight municipal elections. In 1899 and 1900 E. W. Stewart, manager of the *Workers' Republic* stood for the North Dock Ward of Dublin and in 1901 W. McLoughlin, treasurer of the Tailor's Society, was a candidate. Connolly himself stood for the Wood Quay Ward, Dublin, in 1902 and 1903, endorsed by the Dublin Trades Council on which he represented the United Labourers. In 1900 Connolly had secured the right of the ISRP delegates to the International Socialist Congress in Paris to sit as delegates from the Irish nation and not as part of the United Kingdom delegation. The party, however, could not achieve popular support, was split internally by quarrels, and Connolly, faced with the prospect of bringing up a large family, decided to emigrate to the United States of America in 1903. He later wrote that it was the greatest mistake of his life.

With the departure of Connolly, Socialism had only a precarious toe-hold in Ireland. There were Fabian societies and branches of the Independent Labour Party in Belfast and Dublin. In 1893 the British Trade Union Congress had met in Belfast leaving behind them a branch of the ILP. In 1898 William Walker, who was president of the Irish Trade Union Congress from 1894 to 1907, won a seat on the Belfast corporation with six other colleagues. Walker edited a newspaper called *Labour Chronicle*. He was a full time official of the Amalgamated Society of Carpenters and Joiners. In 1905 he stood as an ILP candidate for North Belfast with Ramsay MacDonald as his election agent. He took up a completely sectarian attitude, however, expressing open support for the Union declaring that Catholics should not be allowed to hold office. "Protestantism," he said, "means protesting against superstition, hence true Protestantism is synonomous with labour." Walker was defeated. He twice contested the seat again, within a year, but was twice defeated. In 1908 he published a pamphlet on *The Irish Question* in which he opposed the establishment of an Irish Parliament. In his attitude Walker seemed to go against the philosophy of the founding father of the ILP, the Scottish Socialist Keir Hardie, who stood for Irish, Welsh and Scottish self government. As a prospective parliamentary candidate for Merthyr Tydfil, Wales, in 1898, Hardie said : "When the men elected to make laws are but a small part of a foreign parliament, that is when all healthy national feeling dies ... I have always been a zealous supporter of self government." Perhaps it was with Walker in mind that Hardie was later to reflect : "I often wonder why it is that some men oppose Home Rule for the land of their birth." Ramsay MacDonald, Walker's agent, was—until shortly before he became Prime Minister of the U.K. in 1923—a zealous campaigner of Scottish self-government. Some years later Walker and James Connolly were to clash in a bitter conflict of basic ideology.

In 1900 some twenty national literary societies had merged into a movement called *Cumman na nGaedhael* whose first president was the ageing Fenian John O'Leary, but its moving spirits were William Rooney and Arthur Griffith, who became the body's main ideologist. In 1904 Griffith produced *Resurrection of Hungary,* describing how the Hungarians had won their independence from Austria in 1867, a parallel was drawn with Ireland. The Hungarian representatives in the Austrian *diet* had withdrawn and established their own parliament. They recognised the Emperor of Austria only in so far as he was King of Hungary. Griffith was essentially a monarchist and would recognise the King of England in so far as he was King of Ireland. He also envisaged an Anglo-Irish Empire on the lines of the Austro-Hungarian Empire. In November 1905 *Cumann na nGaedhael* merged with other bodies to form a new political party known as *Sinn Féin,* translated as "ourselves" the name really implies "self help" in the collective national sense.

At the first meeting of *Sinn Féin* Griffith outlined an economic programme which included Irish control of banking tariffs, a subsidised mercantile marine, recall of all possible Irish capital, re-forestation, revival of fisheries, more tillage, a national system of insurance, reform of poor laws and control of retail prices. The economic programme appealed to the petty bourgeois classes and reflected their ideas of an independent Ireland in the Grattan tradition. However, the *Sinn Féin* movement included people like P. T. Daly, a former ISRP man, on the left wing, to Griffith, the monarchist, on the right wing. The Irish Nationalist Party M.P.s for Kilkenny and North Leitrim resigned from their party to join *Sinn Féin* but lost their seats at elections in 1907.

A new force began to take its place on the Irish scene . . . that of organised labour. As in England, combinations of workers had been illegal from the 16th century. Nevertheless, trade unionism in Ireland existed from an early period. A Carpenters' Society was in existence in 1764 and had thirty-two rules, the salient ones being support of the sick, burying the dead, providing for the widows, educating apprentices, regulation of wages and fund raising when the society was in litigation with employers. There were many other such societies in existence about this time as revealed to a Select Committee of the House of Commons in 1824. The year of 1780 stands out as the year when the Master Corporation of Hosiers actually struck work until a Bill of Wages was agreed to. The strike ended successfully. In 1824 Richard Smyth, Lord Mayor of Dublin, told the Select Committee : "the state of society among the working classes in Dublin is truly alarming". A Dublin solicitor named William Hall estimated that there were twenty-five or twenty-six distinctive unions with branches in the capital who had administered oaths and that one trade union would take up the cause of another. In 1812 the Builders' and Plasterers' Guild made a report on their trade before and since the union—it urged that the English working classes should not be blamed for the misery brought about by English rule.

In 1834 an Ulster trade unionist named George Kerr published *Exposition of Legislative Tyranny and Defence of the Trade Union* in Belfast, which gave an expressive account of the ordeals of early Irish trade unionists. Kerr, who suffered imprisonment, wrote : "We have the woeful example before us of the harsh and inhuman treatment of the trade unionists that are everywhere taking place." A strike of telegraphists in Dublin and Belfast in 1871, due to workers being penalised for attempting to start a union, shocked society.

In 1863 the Dublin United Trades Association had been formed and in 1868 it had joined the British Trade Union Congress. Belfast did not develop its Trade Union Council until 1881. By the end of the 1880's most Irish towns had their own Trade Union Councils, but the London based TUC found it had no time to give to Irish problems. It was decided to establish an Irish Trade Union Congress. W. P. Ryan[5] estimated that at the time there were ninety-three trade unions in Ireland with a total membership of 17,476. The first meeting of the Irish TUC, with John Simmons acting as secretary, took place in 1895 and was attended by 119 delegates. The British TUC took no notice of the Irish departure. However, on July 17, 1900, the British TUC invited the Irish TUC to recorporate itself, an invitation which was refused.

By 1906 employers in England, Wales and Scotland had been forced to concede the right of combination to the men employed in the transport trade. Ireland, however, despite her early start in trade union organisation, was still twenty years behind England. As a rule the employers totally ignored trade unions and actually condemned them. The basic right of combination for the workers had to be fought out in Ireland town by town : Belfast in 1907; Dublin, 1908 and Cork in 1909. At the time the workers were members of English-based trade unions, despite the autonomy of the Irish TUC, and these trade unions failed to realise that the Irish employers' attitude was a primitive one by English standards. They also failed to grasp the different national situation in Ireland. This, then, was the situation when in late January, 1907, thirty-one-year-old James Larkin arrived in Belfast to organise dockers for the National Dock Labourers' Union. Larkin, a Liverpudlian, was the son of Irish emigrants who was deeply conscious of the Irish national struggle for independence and republican in sympathy. As well as being a staunch trade unionist he became a Marxist early in life, joining the Social Democratic Federation which drew its inspiration from Marx.

On the afternoon of Monday, May 6, a number of dockers struck at the York Dock of the Belfast Steamship Company because they objected to working with two non-union men. Larkin urged the men to return to work but, when they did so, they found their places had been filled by fifty English dockers imported through the Shipping Federation. The cause of the minor dispute did not concern the Belfast Steamship Company; they were merely using the incident as a lever by which to smash the union and evidence for this was obtained in the form of correspondence between the company and the secretary of the Shipping Federation written nearly a week before the incident.[6] In the meantime a hundred more "blackleg" workers were sent to Ireland despite an attempt by the Lord Mayor of Belfast to arbitrate. Larkin was willing to discuss the matter but Thomas Gallagher, chairman of the Belfast Steamship Company, who also owned large tobacco and rope factories in the country, refused to negotiate.

The "lock out" was entering its third week when Larkin was arrested on May 31 for assaulting one of the "blacklegs" who had arrived on the SS *Caloric*. The man, Richard Bamber, had, in fact, attacked Larkin with a knife and Larkin had felled him with a stone, but only after Bamber had stabbed three other men. The hearing was a farce and was finally suspended until early in 1908 when Larkin was found "not guilty".[7] The arrest of Larkin caused tension to mount and the "lock out" and sympathetic strike now affected 1,000 men. Military and police cordoned off the quays from the men's pickets. Carters who carried goods from the docks struck work in sympathy with Larkin's union, many of them left the tame Carters' Association to join Larkin.

The fact that Larkin was a Catholic was used for propaganda purposes by the employers, relying once again on the "Orange card". Larkin offered to resign and let a non-Catholic lead the men.[8] But Alexandar Boyd, a Belfast Socialist, trade unionist and Protestant, said that the Establishment's attempt to divide the men on this religious issue "would not be successful because men of all creeds were determined to stand together in fighting the common enemy, the employer who denied the right of the workers to a fair wage."[9] Larkin now returned to the attack by threatening a general strike. The Master Carriers' Association retaliated by locking out their men, issuing an ultimatum signed by eighteen firms striking at the trade unions' right of combination and avowing non-recognition of unions.[10] The result was that 1,000 coalmen were added to the 1,000 carters and 500 dockers. The Orange card failed and the strike was supported by members of the Independent Orange Order.

There now came a dramatic event... the Royal Irish Constabulary mutinied. They had for some time been dissatisfied with their wages and working conditions. Only six months previously a Royal Commission had heard evidence of their grievances but the report had been shelved. Larkin in a speech on July 18, supported the police in their right to improve their conditions. Led by Constable Barrett, the police presented their demands; the authorities tried to arrest Barrett and on July 24, the police mutinied. Thousands of troops were poured into the city and by August 6 the mutiny was suppressed. With the exception of the leaders, who were prosecuted, the Belfast policemen were transferred to outlying country districts in Ireland.

The struggle continued and on August 11 the Strike Committee called a monster rally at which Larkin, and R. Lindsay

Crawford, leader of the Independent Orange Order, were speakers. Also speaking was Joseph Devlin, hopping on to the bandwagon and explaining his previous indifference by the fact that he "did not want to give the capitalist press the opportunity for raising sectarian differences among the workers."[11] The army had been drafted into areas such as the Falls Road, a Catholic working-class area which, significantly enough, was away from areas where the strike pickets were. The area was a nationalist one and the stationing of troops there was obviously provocative. Inevitably clashes were reported and on Tuesday, August 12, during five hours of rioting the army fired on the people killing a young man and a girl and wounding several others.[12] Religious and political rioting could have swept away the Belfast workers' united stand. Larkin issued a handbill:

> Not as Catholics or Protestants, as Nationalists or Unionists, but as Belfast men and workers, stand together and don't be misled by the employers' game of dividing Catholic and Protestant.

The Board of Trade now intervened and sent George Askwith (later Lord Askwith) to arbitrate. On August 15 the 1,000 dockers agreed to return to work and on August 28 a new wage scale was agreed for the coal workers. The dockers fared badly, however, for they were allowed to return to work only if they agreed to give an undertaking to "behave themselves". By November 1 all the workers had returned, although, two weeks later, 500 coal workers were out again claiming the employers had broken their agreement. The strike did not last long.

The Belfast dispute was of tremendous significance. The workers had organised and, despite the Establishment's efforts to play off Protestant against Catholic, they had held together. Emmet Larkin wrote:

> What happened in Belfast can, of course, be conceived in the most grandiose terms. It could include the destruction of political and religious bigotry, organising the workers for the revolutionary act and contributing to the dignity and integrity of the working classes. The rub is that Larkin did achieve all these things, but only to a limited extent. He did blend, for example, Orange and Green on a Labour canvas, but the pigment proved soluble in the religious wash.[13]

In 1908, the following year, the Irish TUC met in Belfast, where an ILP member, John Murphy of the Belfast Trades Council, made the first presidential speech endorsing "the alliance between trade unions and Socialists."

> The Socialist has analysed the human misery and connected it with our industrial conditions, and has proposed a remedy. Until a better plan is suggested we may reasonably refuse to be drawn aside from the pursuit of a scheme which, while not perfect, is at least comprehensive, and appeals to all that is best in our hearts and minds...I am not advocating anything in the nature of contentment among Irish trade unionists. We have no reason to be contented...No doctrine which backs up the present conditions of society—where the drones revel in luxury and the bees perish for want—will stand the fire of present day criticism.[14]

Larkin now concentrated his energies in Dublin. He had made his first trip to Dublin to raise funds for the Belfast workers and also to launch a branch of the National Union of Dock Labourers. By September, 1907, he had some 2,000 men in the Dublin branch. Early in July, 1908, the branch had grown to 2,700 and the employers began to see Larkin's activities as a growing menace. That same month the Dublin Coal Masters' Association decided to break up the union by locking their men out. This affected 400 men. On July 30 an agreement was made with the English headquarters of the union above Larkin's head. Larkin was discouraged by his union's high-handed attitude and lack of knowledge of Irish conditions. He continued organising and in August, 1908, he sent James Fearon, secretary of the Dundalk and Newry branches of the union, to organise a branch in Cork. By November there were 800 workers in the Cork branch and Fearon considered it was strong enough to approach the employers concerning an improvement in wages and conditions. Dockers in Cork had not received a wage increase for twenty years.[15] The employers ignored the dockers' letters and so on Monday, November 9, 150 men ceased work on the docks of the City of Cork Steam Packet Company. The strike quickly spread to other docks and the next day the employers filled the places of 700 strikers with English "blacklegs", again imported by the Shipping Federation. Larkin arrived in Cork on Wednesday, November 11, and by the next day a truce was arranged. Under arbitration, in December, the dockers had found they had won a very substantial victory over the employers for, with only minor modifications, their claims were met.

In the meantime Larkin was agitating for an increase in the wages of the Dublin carters but despite numerous letters the employers refused to recognise his union. On November 16 carters in four firms struck work. The next day a visitor "could not be blamed if he thought the city was in what is termed a state of siege."[16] Mounted police patrolled the streets. On November 19 a Board of Trade representative tried to arbitrate and Larkin emphasised there would be no settlement unless the employers recognised the right of men to combine. The men returned to work pending negotiations but on November 26 the Grand Canal Company and the Master Carriers' Association broke off negotiations. Once again over 2,000 workers were on strike. Larkin was defiant: They would crush the Carters' Association or be crushed by it . . . Let them now get the British army out as they did in Belfast. He hoped the day would arrive when these men would have to face a citizen army.[17] A few days later the Lord Mayor and Archbishops of Dublin (Catholic and Protestant) succeeded in getting arbitration under way again but, on December 11, the Master Carriers' Association again broke off negotiations. The *Freeman's Journal* commented:

> It is extremely unlikely that the attitude adopted by the Master Carriers' Association will find many defenders among the general public.[18]

Now the maltmen came out on strike making the total number 2,500. The Union executive in London had informed Larkin he was on his own as regards funds and the position was desperate. But a week later the employers gave way in the face of hostile press, pulpit and public opinion. On December 21 the dispute went back to arbitration and the results were published in February, 1909. They were not to Larkin's liking.

The internal conflict between Larkin and James Sexton, the General Secretary of the National Union of Dock Labourers and his executive, due to their lack of contact with the Irish situation, drew to a head. Larkin was fed up with his union's apathy towards Irish events and wrote to Sexton: "There was a movement on foot for organising the whole of unskilled labour in Ireland" He was in favour of the international federation of labour but it was a question whether the first step was not to organise the Irish workers as Irishmen, separately and then to federate. He was seriously considering whether he should take up this project.[19] Sexton wrote on December 7 suspending Larkin from office.

Larkin's answer to his suspension was to form the Irish Transport and General Workers' Union. In the Union Rule Book[20] Larkin announced an end to the "policy of grafting ourselves on the English Trade Union Movement". The Irish Labour Movement was born with Larkin summing up its philosophy in one phrase : "The land of Ireland for the people of Ireland."

Chapter 11

THE DUBLIN LOCK-OUT

WHEN LARKIN FORMED the Irish Transport and General Workers' Union in Dublin, the city had a population of 305,000 people. It was a commercial, distributive and shipping centre rather than an industrial city. Thousands of families had to exist on less than 15s a week and there were many cases of families' total earnings being as low as 10s and less. The highest wage cited for a labourer was 20s and the minimum hours worked were twelve a day. The highest paid labourers were the dockers who earned 24s for a seventy-hour week. Conditions were terrible. In 1911 Dublin's death rate was 27·6 per cent per 1,000 people per annum compared with Calcutta, a city infested with plague and cholera, whose death rate was 27 per cent. Even Moscow, groaning under Tsarist tyranny, had a lower death rate of 26 per cent. In Dublin 41·9 per cent of all deaths occurred in pauper workhouses as against 22 per cent in England. Death for the working classes of Dublin was, at least, the end of a frightful existence. The number of families who lived in only one room was as high as 20,000 while those who had two rooms numbered 5,000. Of the 5,000 tenements, at least 1,500 were actually condemned and, on September 2, 1913, two four-storey tenement buildings collapsed killing seven and injuring many more. In 1910 the infant mortality rate was 142 per 1,000, considerably more than any city in England. In such circumstances prostitution flourished and O'Connell and Grafton Streets were crowded with unfortunate women who flocked there nightly from working class districts to better their standard of living. Women were allowed to board ships while in dock to sleep with the crew. Larkin refused to allow his dockers to work a ship where such a state of affairs existed.[1] Streets were also crowded with children who had no permanent home or parents and who begged and hawked for a living from passers-by. This, then, was the city in which Larkin launched his new union.

The first attack, however, occurred in Cork. The Cork em-

ployers decided to counteract the growing militancy of labour by
forming a Federation of Employers in late May, 1909. In June,
however, 140 members of the Transport Union struck work at
docks owned by the Cork Steam Packet Company because they
objected to working with members of a notorious "scab" union.
They were summarily suspended. On the following day 1,000
railway workers came out in sympathy. The inevitable supply of
"blacklegs" were shipped into Ireland by the Shipping
Federation to break the strike. Now carters struck work and the
Cork employers issued an ultimatum from the Cork Employers
Federation Ltd. :

> That we, the employers of Cork, hereby bind ourselves and the
> firms we represent as follows :
> 1) To immediately dismiss any employee who shall wilfully
> disobey any lawful order out of sympathy with any strike or trade
> dispute.
> 2) That the vacancy so caused shall be filled forthwith by local
> labour if procurable, failing this the vacancy shall be filled from
> any available source.
> 3) That any such employee discharged shall not be employed
> by any member of the Federation.[2]

The strike was a tactical blunder for the Cork, Dublin and
Belfast Trades Councils had no resources. What little the
ITGWU had was soon exhausted. By the end of June 6,000 men
were on strike and the recruiting sergeants were busy on behalf of
the army. On July 14 the carters, after holding out for one
month without strike pay, were forced to return and the strike
was broken. What was worse for the Cork labour movement, the
union was in shambles. The ITGWU's branch ceased to function
and was not resurrected for nearly four years. Larkin was arrested on August 18, 1909, and charged with "conspiracy to
defraud" with James Fearon and two members of the Cork
branch. The Cork branch had sent some £147 to the Dublin carters to aid them in their strike of 1908 and the Crown maintained that the money had been used by Larkin for personal
reasons. Fearon received six months' hard labour and those arrested with him received one to four months. After some delay,
in June, 1910, Larkin received a year's hard labour. He was
released, however, after serving only three months, due to
petitions and demonstrations.

While Larkin was in prison, in July, 1910, James Connolly arrived back in Ireland. He had written to his friend William O'Brien in May of the previous year : "I may confess to you that I regard my emigration to America as the great mistake of my life, and I have never ceased to regret it." Despite his regrets, Connolly had thrown himself into the American labour movement, becoming organiser of the Socialist Party of America. He formed the Irish Socialist Federation in 1907 among expatriates and started the publication of *The Harp* the following year. In January, 1910, he transferred the publication of the journal to Ireland. Connolly also became organiser of the syndicalist Industrial Workers of the World. His ideology had developed a great deal and the publication of *Socialism Made Easy* in Chicago in 1909 showed a development towards syndicalism. He pioneered the idea of workers' control not only in Ireland but in England and the U.S.A.[3]

William O'Brien, a tailor who had been a member of Connolly's Irish Socialist Republican Party, had established *Cummannacht na hÉireann* (Socialist Party of Ireland) in 1909. O'Brien formed a committee of its members and arranged for Connolly's return and appointment as national organiser of the party. Also, immediately on Connolly's return to Ireland, two of his best known works were published. These were *Labour in Irish History*, which presented the first Marxist view of Irish history, and *Labour, Nationality and Religion*, a devastating reply to Father Robert Kane, SJ, who had made an almost hysterical attack on Socialism during the course of Lenten Discourses in Gardiner Street Church, Dublin. These two works did much to establish Connolly 's reputation.

In the spring of 1911 Connolly took up residence in Belfast. When a seamen's strike involved the Irish ports in July that year, Connolly was appointed Belfast secretary of the ITGWU. Connolly had joined Larkin's union "having in mind that its mission is not to make slavery tolerable but to overthrow it, and to replace it by a free and independent Workers' Republic."[4] Connolly soon showed his powers as an organiser and had 600 men on the low docks out in sympathy with the seamen with also specific demands for the men on shore. The Belfast members managed to raise the general wage from 5s a day to 6s and reduce the discharging output to 100 tons against the previous standard of 150 to 200 tons. Later that year Belfast members compelled the abolition of the old irregular system by which stevedores paid men when they liked, where they liked, how they liked and whom they liked. For many years Belfast remained the only area in the north of Ireland in which the ITGWU could operate effectively. The ITGWU was able to unite Catholics and Protestants in its branches and the impoverished band, formed during the dispute, was made up of instruments borrowed impartially from Catholic and Orange societies to which the men belonged.

In June, 1911, Larkin made his debut as editor of *The Irish Worker and People's Advocate*. Emmet Larkin writes:

> Nothing like it has ever been seen since it was suppressed by the British Government in the early months of the First World War. This novel production was and remains unique in the history of working class journalism.[5]

The idea for a competent labour newspaper had been on Larkin's mind as early as 1907. Journals had been brought out by the Cork Trades Council and Dublin Trades Council. The first had a protectionist slant and the latter, a mediocre effort, collapsed in September, 1909. The *Irish Worker* was a fantastic success. In June, 1911, 26,000 copies were sold; in July, 64,000 copies; in August, 74,750 copies and in September, 94,994 copies. This is a large figure for an Irish weekly journal, compared, say, with *Sinn Féin's* 2,000 copies per week. The *Irish Worker* pulled no punches, it named names and listed the indiscretions of employers, racketeers and landowners. Those who tried to sue for libel usually came the worse off.

A great wave of industrial unrest was sweeping England, Wales, Scotland and Ireland in the summer of 1911. The shipping strike which brought Connolly into the ITGWU as Belfast secretary and Ulster organiser ended in victory. In August a second great strike, this time of railwaymen, starting in England, soon spread to Ireland where most railwaymen were members of the English-based Amalgamated Society of Railway Servants. A truce was eventually arranged but timber merchants locked out 500 of their employees due to the disruption. These were members of the ITGWU. Members of the railway union struck in sympathy and J. E. Williams, general secretary of the ASRS was sent to Dublin to negotiate a settlement. The employers refused to recognise the ASRS and Williams called for a national strike in Ireland on September 21. To the disgust of the Irish, who had originally struck in sympathy with their English brothers, the English, Welsh and Scottish branches of the union did not support them. They felt betrayed and ITGWU membership began to increase.

The first significant struggle of the ITGWU began in August that year, when two Wexford ironmasters decided to close their works, locking out 550 employees simply because they were members of the ITGWU. They had made no demands on the employers nor created any trouble.[6] P. T. Daly, who had organised the Wexford branch of the ITGWU, raised no objection to the men joining any other union if they wished so long as the management recognised the right of the men to join the ITGWU. The employers refused to discuss the matter and by September 8 some 250 extra police had been drafted into the town. Other employers, including the Mayor of Waterford, joined their colleagues in closing down their factories where the men were members of the ITGWU. It was an all-out attempt to smash the union in the town. The police used their batons liberally on demonstrating workers, a worker died and many others were injured in incidents. Daly did magnificent work in keeping the men together, so magnificent, in fact, that in January, 1912, Daly was arrested and forcibly moved to Waterford. Connolly was then sent to take charge of the situation and proposed that the men organise an Irish Foundry Worker's Union which would be affiliated to the ITGWU. The employers compromised in February and the Irish Foundry Workers' Union was formed but, for all practical purposes, it was a branch of the ITGWU and did, in 1914, merge as an official branch. It was a significant victory for the union. It had survived an attempt to destroy it.

Larkin maintained that he did not believe in strikes.[7] As early as 1909 he was advocating Compulsory Arbitration Courts and later Compulsory Wages and Arbitration Boards. On April 26, 1913, in an "Open Letter to the People on How to Stop Strikes" (*Irish Worker*) he reiterated his belief in arbitration and added that "the ultimate solution is the ownership and control of the means of life by the whole people." At this time the idea of syndicalism was challenging the old Marxist concept that parliamentary democracy was the way to implement the Socialist state. The syndicate or trade union was to be the tool by which to educate the workers and a weapon by which to seize control of power. Connolly supported syndicalism as it was exactly in line with the "One Big Union" syndicalism of the Industrial Workers of the World. Connolly observed that syndicalism was "simply the discovery that the workers are strongest at the point of production, that they have no force available except economic force, and by linking the revolutionary movement with the daily fight of the workshop, mill, shipyard and factory, the necessary economic force can be organised. Also that the revolutionary organisation necessary for that purpose provides the framework of the Socialist Republic."[8] Connolly is now regarded as a pioneer of workers' control. This did not mean he totally rejected the parliamentary path.

Since the general election of 1910, which resulted in a return to Westminster of 314 Liberal/Labour M.P.s and 271 Tories with 84 Irish Nationalists holding the crucial balance of power, it seemed certain that Ireland would now get her long awaited Home Rule. Connolly, realising that "some form of self government seems practically certain of realisation", saw the necessity of a united Socialist party being ready to enter the Irish Parliament when established. In the labour journal, *Forward*, May 27, 1911, Connolly wrote a plea for "Socialist Unity in Ireland". All the Socialist factions should unite into one Irish Socialist Party. On June 3 William Walker of Belfast replied reiterating his belief in union with England and in Protestantism in an article entitled "Rebel Ireland and its Protestant Leaders". Dismissing Irish nationalism, Walker ended "My place of birth was accidental but my duty to my class is world wide, hence my internationalism." Connolly's reply was so damning in its facts and logic that Walker, in another reply, descended to personal abuse. The Connolly-Walker controversy continued until the editor in desperation ended it by announcing "unless this correspondence can be raised to the discussion of principles it had better cease." Connolly, in fact, reopened the controversy in 1913 engaging in the subject with others. Walker, however, in 1912 departed from the Labour Movement accepting a Government position under the New National Insurance Act introduced by Lloyd George. By pressing the point Connolly managed to get majority support for an Independent Irish Labour Party from the Irish TUC meeting at Clonmel in May, 1912. Connolly stressed the need for "an Irish Labour Party, independent of all other parties in the country, in order that organised workers might be able to enter the proposed Irish Parliament in an organised Labour Party in the political field." Larkin was the first to support Connolly.

In the meantime Larkin had been a founder member of the Dublin Labour Party which had adopted its rules and constitution on April 3, 1911. In January, 1912, some twenty of the eighty seats on Dublin Corporation were open for nominations. On January 16, election day, seven labour candidates— including Larkin—stood for Dublin constituencies. Every means was taken to discredit the new party especially by William M. Murphy's Irish Independent Group of newspapers. Atrocious things were printed about Socialism but, despite this, five of the candidates were returned including Larkin who polled 1,200 votes to 500 for his opponent. A by-election occurred three weeks later bringing Labour's strength to six councillors. Larkin, however, was sued for his seat on the grounds that he was a convicted criminal who was not legally entitled to sit on the council. A court debarred him from sitting for five years. A by-election took place and Labour's candidate was Peadar Macken, a painter and avowed Socialist who had been a member of *Cumannacht na hÉireann*. He was elected in Larkin's place and by 1913 Labour's Labour's representation increased to eight members.

In Belfast, in January, 1913, Connolly was also trying his luck at the polls contesting Dock Ward for the Belfast Corporation. He gained 900 votes.

Both men were increasingly active with their union work. On September 5, 1911, an Irish Women Workers' Union had been formed and by the spring of 1912 it was strong enough to apply for affiliation to the ITUC with 1,000 members. Connolly had founded an Irish Textile Workers' Union in Belfast with Mrs. Thomas Johnson and had helped to organise female workers in the linen industry with much success. He was prominent in the suffragist movement.

The activities of Larkin and Connolly incurred the wrath not only of the Unionists but of the Nationalists as well. Griffith, speaking officially for *Sinn Féin*, was vehement in his attack on the Irish Labour Movement and, in particular, on Larkin ("the English Trade Unionist") as well as Connolly. So bitter and damning were his attacks that Eamonn Ceannt, a member of the left wing of *Sinn Féin*, wrote attacking Griffith and supporting the working classes. He wrote :

Permit me as an individual Sinn Féiner to dissociate myself from the general tone of your recent pronouncements on the Wexford labour troubles, and most emphatically from the humbug written by some anonymous hero calling himself Boyesen of Kollund dealing with the railway strike. You appear to see Larkin at the bottom of all trouble. You do not condescend to analyse any of the principles for which Larkin professes to stand. Sufficient for you is that Larkin is the agitator causing troubles between employer and employed. In similar manner the English Tory and his Irish allies described Irish politicians as vile agitators who caused trouble between the good kind landlords and their willing slaves, the tenant farmers of Ireland. It is an open secret that Parnell, who was an aristocrat, had no desire to tack on a land agitation to his political programme, but Davitt and Kettle induced him to do so. Would it not be wise to take a leaf out of Parnell's book if you will not take it out of Larkin's book as gravely suggested by Padraic Mac Piarais (Pearse) to the Gaelic League on Language Sunday?[9]

In the next issue Griffith hit back at Ceannt :

Some of the strike orators have tried to draw a parallel between the fight of the farmers for security of tenure and fair rents and the strike of industrial workers for higher wages. The fight of the Irish people for the land was the fight of a nation for reconquest of a soil that had been theirs and had been confiscated. The landlord did not make the soil—the industrialists made the industry.

In the same issue Griffith wrote an editorial :

In Dublin the wives of some men that Larkin has led out on strike are begging in the streets. The consequences of Larkinism are workless fathers, mourning mothers, hungry children and broken homes. Not the capitalist but the policy of Larkin has raised the price of food until the poorest in Dublin are in a state of semi-famine—the curses of women are being poured on this man's head—Mr. Larkin's career of destruction is coming to a close, but when it has closed it will have established his name in the memory of Dublin as the man who did the maximum of injury to trade unionism and the industrial revival.

Larkin and Connolly were staunch republicans and, by definition in supporting national liberation for Ireland, were nationalists. But Connolly's nationalism was clearcut :

> We cannot conceive of a free Ireland with a subject working
> class; we cannot conceive of a subject Ireland with a free work-
> ing class.[10]

He later wrote :

> We are out for Ireland for the Irish. But who are the Irish?
> Not the rack-renting, slum owning landlord; not the sweating,
> profit-grinding capitalist; not the sleek and oily lawyer; not the
> prostitute pressmen—the hired liars of the enemy. Not these are
> the Irish upon whom the future depends. Not these, but the Irish
> working class, the only secure foundation upon which a free
> nation can be reared.[11]

Both Larkin and Connolly supported the struggle against cultural imperialism. Connolly realised that the destruction of the
Irish language and culture resulted from imperialism and capitalism, echoing the words of Marx : 'Capitalism creates a world
after its own image." Writing in *The Harp*, Connolly said :

> ... it is well to remember that nations which submit to conquest
> or races which abandon their language in favour of that of an
> oppressor do so, not because of the altruistic motives, or because
> of a love of brotherhood of man, but from a slavish and cringing
> spirit. From a spirit which cannot exist side by side with the
> revolutionary idea.

He added :

> I cannot conceive of a Socialist hesitating in his choice between
> a policy resulting in such self-abasement and a policy of defiant
> self reliance and confident trust in a people's own power of self
> emancipation by a people.[12]

In the *Workers' Republic* he wrote :

> ... those who drop Irish in favour of English are generally
> actuated by the meanest of motives, and are lick spittles desirous
> of aping the gentry, whereas the rank and file of the Gaelic

movement are for the most part thoroughly democratic in sentiment and spirit.[13]

Ryan states :

Larkin was quick to see the importance of the Gaelic idea, and
supported it strongly, taking the practical step of having his boys
educated in the most distinctive Irish school of our time, Sgoil
Eanna. Connolly, as we have seen, set the fact of the Gaelic basis
and inspiration at the very heart of his programme.[14]

In this, both men were part of a general pattern throughout
Europe. Many Socialists in countries like Armenia, Lithuania
and Slovenia etc. supported the movement for language restoration as part of the struggle for national liberation.

Sgoil Eanna, to which Larkin sent his sons, had been established by Padraic Pearse, a former barrister turned schoolmaster,
Irish language scholar, poet, playwright and short story writer,
who edited the journal of *Conradh na Gaeilge*. *Sgoil Eanna* was
founded for boys in Rathmines, near Dublin, while *Sgoil Ite*, for
girls, was founded a few miles away at Rathfarnham. *Sgoil Ite*
was forced to close after a few years but *Sgoil Eanna* lasted until
after the 1916 uprising. The professed policy of the school was
bilingualism but it was more accurate to describe it as a serious
educational attempt at instruction through the medium of Irish.
Pearse's pamphlet, *The Murder Machine*, published in 1912,
gives a damning attack on English education in Ireland which
was destroying the country's language and culture. Extracts from
the school journals written by Pearse, later published under *The
Story of a Success,* shows just how well Pearse adapted the old
Irish concepts of education (i.e. *aiteachas*—fosterage) to fit in his
schools.

The Irish Labour Movement was now heading towards the
biggest confrontation between workers and employers that
Europe had ever seen. On June 30, 1911, the Dublin Employers'
Federation Ltd. had been established for the "mutual protection
and indemnity of all employers of labour in Dublin". Dublin had
followed the Cork employers' lead of 1909. Among the founders
of the Dublin Employers' Federation was William Martin
Murphy whose big business interests included the Dublin United
Tramways Company and the Irish Independent Group of

Newspapers. By August, 1913, the employers, led by Murphy, decided to smash the ITGWU once and for all and, on August 15, Murphy took the initiative by calling a meeting of the dispatch department his newspaper company. He told workers that all members of the ITGWU must resign from the union or accept dismissal notices. Similar orders were given to drivers and conductors of the trams. Employees were also asked to sign a declaration as to their loyalty and an assurance they would not strike. The ITGWU retaliated by declaring Murphy's newspapers "black" and Murphy answered this by locking out all members of his newspapers' dispatch department who were union members.

At 9.40 a.m. on Tuesday, August 26, 700 employees of the tramways company walked off their trams leaving them wherever they happened to be. Murphy immediately called a meeting of the Employers' Federation Ltd. and by September 3, 400 employers had agreed to lock out their employees. By September 22, some 25,000 Dublin workers were affected. Some twenty-seven unions were now locked out and it was obvious that the objective of the employers was the emasculation of the whole trade union movement. Even a later Government Court of Inquiry reported "whatever may have been the intention of the employers, this document (swearing that the workers would not join a union and if a member, resign forthwith) imposes upon the signatories conditions which are contrary to individual liberty, and which no workman or body of workmen could reasonably be expected to accept."

Murphy summed up the employers' tactics when he said they would starve the employees into submission. Kier Hardie, the Scottish Socialist, addressing a meeting in Dublin, commented: "Most of you have served too long an apprenticeship to starvation, to be very much afraid of that."[15] On August 27, the day after the tramways strike, a warrant was issued for Larkin's arrest with other trade union leaders on a charge of "seditious conspiracy". The next day E. G. Swifte, a police magistrate, issued a proclamation prohibiting a meeting fixed for Sunday, August 31, by the strikers in O'Connell Street as being seditious. At a meeting in Beresford Place, before 10,000 people, Larkin burnt this proclamation declaring: "People make kings and people can unmake them." By Saturday another warrant had been issued for

Larkin's arrest and he went into hiding in the house of Countess Markievicz in Rathmines.

Constance, Countess Markievicz was something of an enigma. Born of the Anglo-Irish aristocracy, the Gore-Booth family, and married to a Polish count, she became interested in politics in 1900 being drawn towards Griffith's *Sinn Féin*. She had gone to Irish classes, joining *Conradh na Gaeilge*, and then had joined with Maud Gonne (the famous Irish beauty with whom W. B. Yeats fell in love) in *Inghinidhe na hÉireann* (Daughters of Ireland) and helping to launch *Bean na hÉireann* (Irish Woman) in 1903 to which she contributed. By 1908 she was a declared *Sinn Féin* member and the following year was on its executive. That year she founded the *Fianna Éireann*, the Irish boy scouts. She was also an ardent suffragette. In the spring of 1909 she read Craig's *History of Ralahine* and decided to establish a similar commune. She eventually rented Raheny, a big house six miles north of Dublin, but her attempt lasted only a few months, the commune collapsing in April, 1911. On discovering Larkin and Connolly, the "Red" Countess, as she became known, flung herself into the labour movement.

Having spent Saturday night with Count and Countess Markievicz, Larkin went to the proscribed O'Connell Street meeting heavily disguised. Crowds were in the street, surrounded by police, wondering if Larkin would show up. Larkin, dressed as an old man, went to the Imperial Hotel, ironically the property of William Murphy. Once inside the hotel he went to the first floor, stepped on to a balcony and began to address the cheering crowd. Immediately the police entered and dragged Larkin off to jail. The police then attempted to seize Countess Markievicz, in her carriage outside the hotel. There was a scuffle. The police panicked and fell upon the people with their batons. Many of the people were nothing to do with the demonstration but merely returning from mass in the pro-Cathedral in Marlborough Street. The police batoned indiscriminately. A section of the panic-stricken crowd fled up Prince's Street straight into the arms of another squad of police who had orders to allow no one to pass. They fell on the fleeing people unmercifully. V. I. Lenin, writing on what was to be known as Bloody Sunday, commented:

The police have positively gone wild; drunken policemen assault peaceful workers, break into houses, torment the aged, women and children. Hundreds of workers (over 400) have been injured and two killed ... such are the casualties of this war. All prominent leaders of the workers have been arrested. People are thrown into prison for making the most peaceful speeches. The city is like an armed camp.[16]

Dublin was in uproar. A committee was appointed to inquire into the actions of the police; its findings, when published five months later, completely whitewashed them. The action of the employers and the police created a sensation all over Europe. The British TUC, holding their annual congress in Manchester on the following day, denounced the actions of the police and sent a deputation to Dublin. Later it helped to organise cargoes of food supplies for a kitchen set up in Liberty Hall, the ITGWU headquarters, by Countess Markievicz and Mrs. Hanna Sheehy-Skeffington, wife of Francis Sheehy-Skeffington, well known as an advocate of women's suffrage and pacifism and Dublin corre-spondent of Lansbury's *Daily Herald*.

The general lock-out had developed into a mass resistance to the employers' onslaught on trade unionism and personal liberty and throughout the world Dublin and Liberty Hall had become the symbol and the standard bearer of trade unionism in battle for its very existence.[17]

Connolly had hastened from Belfast to help organise the Dublin workers but was arrested. He refused to recognise the court and denied the right of English government in Ireland. Sentenced to three months in Mountjoy he was released after an eight-day hunger strike. On September 12 Larkin was released on bail. He left for England, speaking and raising funds, but was back in Dublin a few days later. He was taking a tough line. "I am out for revolution." As for the employers: "they can only kill me and there are thousands to come after me." The British TUC responded by raising £93,637 for the locked-out men. William O'Brien, secretary of the Dublin Lock-Out Committee was able to report funds of £150,000. There were sympathetic strikes in Liverpool, Manchester and Birmingham but the English trade union leaders refused to exert more pressure to alleviate the suffering of the Dublin men.

Ireland's leading intellectuals were outspoken in favour of the workers' resistance. These included Padraic Pearse, W. B. Yeats,

James Stephens, Padraic Colum, Seumas O'Sullivan, Joseph Plunkett, Thomas MacDonagh, Susan Mitchell and George Russell. In one of a series of articles "From a Hermitage", Pearse explained the conditions of the Irish workers and asked "Can you wonder that protest at last is made?" Arthur Griffith, however, attacked the workers, commenting that he would like to see every last one of them bayoneted. Leading intellectuals established a Dublin Peace Committee and a Civic League to try to act as intermediaries but met with no response from employers.

The Government finally intervened on September 26 when Sir George Askwith of the Board of Trade announced a Court of Inquiry which opened three days later. T. M. Healy K.C., a Nationalist M.P., represented the employers, many of whom, like Murphy, were ardent supporters of the Irish Nationalist Party. The report of the inquiry pointed out that the onus for a settlement was on the employers, but Murphy and his colleagues refused to accept the report as a basis for negotiation and backed out of the inquiry. On October 7, the *Irish Times* printed an "Open Letter to the Masters of Dublin" from the poet, playwright and co-operatist, George Russell ("AE"):

Sirs—I address this warning to you, the aristocracy of industry in this city : like all aristocracies, you tend to grow blind in long authority, and to be unaware that you and your class and its every action are being considered and judged day by day by those who have power to shake or overturn the whole Social order, and whose restlessness in poverty today is making our industrial civilisation stir like a quaking log. You do not seem to realise that your assumption that you are answerable to yourselves alone for your actions in the industries you control is one that becomes less and less tolerable in a world so crowded with necessitous life. Some of you have helped Irish farmers to upset a landed aristocracy in this island, an aristocracy richer and more powerful in its sphere than you are in yours, with its roots deep in history. They, too, as a class, though not all of them, were scornful or neglectful of the workers in the industry by which they profited; and to many who knew them in their pride of place and thought them all powerful they are already becoming a memory, the good disappearing together with the bad. If they had done their duty by those from whose labour came their wealth they might have continued unquestioned in power and *prestige* for centuries to come. The relation of landlord and tenant is not an ideal one, but any relations in a social order will endure if there is infused into them some of the spirit of human sympathy which qualified for immortality. Despotisms endure while they are benevolent, and aristocracies while *noblesse oblige* is not a phrase to be referred to with a cynical smile. Even an oligarchy might be permanent if the spirit of human kindness, which harmonises all things otherwise incompatible, is present.

You do not seem to read history so as to learn its lesson. That you are an uncultivated class was obvious from recent utterances of some of you upon art. That you are incompetent men in the sphere in which you arrogate imperial powers is certain, because for many years, long before the present uprising of labour, your enterprises have been dwindling in the regard of investors, and this while you have carried them on in the cheapest labour market in these islands, with a labour reserve always hungry and ready to accept any pittance. You are bad citizens, for we rarely, if ever, hear of the wealthy among you endowing your city with the munificent gifts which it is the pride of merchant princes in other cities to offer, and Irishmen not of your city who offer to supply the wants left by your lack of generosity are met with derision and abuse. Those who have economic power have civic power also, yet you have not used the power that was yours to right what was wrong in the evil administration of this city. You have allowed the poor to be herded together so that one thinks of certain places in Dublin as a pestilence. There are twenty thousand rooms, in each of which live entire families, and sometimes more, where no functions of the body can be concealed, and delicacy and modesty are creatures that are stifled ere they are born. The obvious duty of you in regard to these things you might have left undone, and it be imputed to ignorance or forgetfulness; but your collective and conscious action as a class in the present labour dispute have revealed you to the world in so malign an aspect that the mirror must be held up to you so that you may see yourselves as every humane person sees you.

The conceptions of yourselves as altogether virtuous and wronged is, I assure you, not at all the one which onlookers hold of you. No doubt, you have rights on your side. No doubt, some of you suffered without just cause. But nothing which has been done to you cries aloud to Heaven for condemnation as your own actions. Let me show you how it seems to those who have followed critically the dispute, trying to weigh in a balance the rights and wrongs. You were within the rights society allows you when you locked out your men and insisted on the fixing of some principle to adjust your future relations with labour when the policy of labour made it impossible for some of you to carry on

your enterprises. Labour desired the fixing of some such principle
as much as you did. But, having once decided on such a step,
knowing how many thousands of men, women and children,
nearly one third of the population of this city, would be affected,
you should not have let one day have passed without unremitting
endeavours to find a solution of the problem.

What did you do? The representatives of labour unions in
Great Britain met you, and you made of them a preposterous, an
impossible demand, and because they would not accede to it you
closed the Conference; you refused to meet them further; you assumed that no other guarantees than those you asked were possible, and you determined deliberately, in cold anger, to starve
out one third of the population of this city, to break the manhood
of the men by the sight of the sufferings of their wives and the
hunger of their children. We read in the Dark Ages of the rack
and thumb screw. But these iniquities were hidden and concealed
from the knowledge of men in dungeons and torture chambers.
Even in Dark Ages humanity could not endure the sight of such
suffering, and it learnt of such misuse of power by slow degrees,
through rumour, and when it was certain it razed its Bastilles to
their foundations. It remained for the twentieth century and the
capital city of Ireland to see an oligarchy of four hundred masters deciding openly upon starving one hundred thousand people,
and refusing to consider any solution except that fixed by their
pride. You, masters, asked men to do that which masters of labour in any other city in these islands had not dared to do. You
insolently demanded of those men who were members of a trade
union that they should resign from that union; and from those
who were not members you insisted on a vow that they would
never join it.

Your insolence and ignorance of the rights conceded to workers
universally in the modern world were incredible, and as great as
your inhumanity. If you had between you collectively a portion
of human soul as large as a threepenny bit, you would have sat
night and day with the representatives of labour, trying this or
that solution of the trouble, mindful of the women and children,
who at least were innocent of wrong against you. But no! You
reminded labour you could always have your three square meals
a day while it went hungry. You went into conference again with
representatives of the State, because dull as you are, you knew
public opinion would not stand your holding out. You chose as
your spokesman the bitterest tongue that ever wagged in this
island, and then, when an award was made by men who have an
experience in industrial matters a thousand times transcending

yours, who have settled disputes in industries so great that the sum of your petty enterprises would not equal them, you withdrew again, and will not agree to accept their solution, and fall back again on your devilish policy of starvation. Cry aloud to Heaven for new souls! The souls you have got cast upon the screen of publicity appear like the horrid writhing creatures enlarged from the insect world, and revealed to us by the cinematograph.

You may succeed in your policy and ensure your own damnation by your victory. The men whose manhood you have broken will loathe you, and will always be brooding and scheming to strike a fresh blow. The children will be taught to curse you. The infant being moulded in the womb will have breathed into its starved body the vitality of hate. It is not they—it is you who are blind Samsons pulling down the pillars of the social order. You are sounding the death knell of autocracy in industry. There was autocracy in political life, and it was superseded by democracy. So surely will democratic power wrest from you the control of industry. The fate of you, the aristocracy of industry, will be as the fate of the aristocracy of the land if you do not show that you have some humanity still among you. Humanity abhors, above all things, a vacuum in itself, and your class will be cut off from humanity as the surgeon cuts the cancer and alien growth from the body. Be warned ere it is too late. Yours etc. "AE"

Even an editorial in the London *Times* of the following day commented that it was about time the Dublin employers learnt their lesson.

On Monday, October 27, Larkin was brought to trial and sentenced to seven months in Mountjoy. James Connolly took over the leadership and the following Sunday was speaking at a gigantic meeting in London's Albert Hall with George Bernard Shaw, Delia Larkin, Ben Tillet and George Lansbury, to protest at Larkin's jailing. Connolly demanded that everyone should work and vote against the Liberal Government until Larkin was set free. On November 9 a Tory won a by-election in Reading while a Liberal majority at Linlithgow was severely decreased in another by-election. Lloyd George commented: "There are explanations, the most prominent of which is, probably, Jim Larkin."[18] Larkin was released on November 14 having served only seventeen days.

The workers were putting up a strong resistance. The

Redmondite Nationalist newspaper, *Freeman's Journal,* now dropped its neutrality and sided with the employers. Stephen Gwynn, a Nationalist M.P. for Galway, immediately disassociated himself from the journal. The employers were trying to import "blacklegs" and Connolly ordered mass picketing on the Dublin quays, finally closing the port entirely. Larkin and Connolly issued a manifesto to workers in England, Scotland and Wales urging them to keep the port closed and so support the Irish workers. A plea was made to the British TUC to prevent the importation of non-union labour in Dublin. The English trade unionists were beginning to denounce Larkin and the methods of the ITGWU and Larkin retaliated by attacking the leaders of English labour. On December 9 the first ever special meeting of the British TUC met in Farringdon Hall, London, to discuss the situation. Connolly presented the Irish case for holding out. To everyone's amazement, Ben Tillet, then considered the most militant trade unionist and Socialist, whose speeches on the Dublin Lock-Out had been described by Lenin as "outstanding"[19] moved a resolution deploring and condemning the Irish Labour leaders' tactics. Larkin, called upon to reply, created a near riot in his condemnation of English union leaders. The British TUC rejected further support for the Irish and it seemed evident that it was only a matter of time before the situation deteriorated. The Irish had no more funds to carry on the struggle.

In September of that year Captain Jack R. White, D.S.O., a Protestant Ulsterman, addressed the Civic League in Dublin on his idea of a workers' defence force to protect the workers from police attack. The Aungier Street branch of the ITGWU had formed a band with instruments bought on hire purchase. They had annoyed the police by playing "The Peeler and the Goat" and the police threatened to smash their instruments. The workers promptly formed a guard for their band armed with hurley sticks and the idea of a workers' defence force soon caught on. By October, the Irish Citizen Army, which has been described as the world's first Red Guard, was formed with Captain White as its drill instructor. Connolly wrote :

An armed organisation of the Irish working class is a phenomenon in Ireland. Hitherto the workers of Ireland have fought as parts of the armies led by their masters, never as a member of any army officered, trained and inspired by men of their own class. Now, with arms in their hands, they propose to steer their own course, to carve their own future.

Neither Home Rule, nor lack of Home Rule, will make them lay down their arms . . .

We cannot be swerved from our course by honeyed words, lulled into carelessness by freedom to parade and strut in uniforms, nor betrayed by high sounding phrases.

The Irish Citizen Army will only co-operate in a forward movement. The moment that forward movement ceases it reserves to itself the right to step out of alignment, and advance by itself if needs be, in an effort to plant the banner of freedom one reach further towards its goal.[20]

But the death knell for the struggle was being sounded. On February 1, 1914, the 3,000 strong Builders' Labourers' Union agreed to go back to work on condition "that none of its members remain or become in the future a member of the Irish Transport Workers' Union. Its members will take no part in or support any form of sympathetic strike; they will handle all materials, and carry out all instructions, given them in the course of their employment. Further, they will work amicably with all employees, whether they be unionists or non-unionists."[21] By February 11 the Dublin Relief Fund was exhausted and Connolly wrote :

And so we Irish workers must again go down into Hell, bow our backs to the last of the slave drivers, let our hearts be seared by the iron of his hatred and instead of the sacramental wafer of brotherhood and common sacrifice, eat the dust of defeat and betrayal. Dublin is isolated.[22]

Larkin wrote that the lock-out was lost because the Trade Unionists in England, Wales and Scotland refused to continue to support the Dublin men. They refused sympathetic strikes and to commit themselves to an industrial war over a "purely Irish" matter. In 1913 there were two paths confronting the workers of the United Kingdom—Reform or Revolution. The Irish chose revolution—the English, Scots and Welsh chose reform. Summing up the lock-out struggle in November, 1914, Connolly wrote :

The battle was a drawn battle. The employers, despite their Napoleonic plan of campaign, and their more than Napoleonic ruthlessness and unscrupulous use of foul means, were unable to enforce their document, unable to carry on their business without men and women who remained loyal to their unions. The workers were unable to force the employers to a formal recognition of the union and to give preference to organised labour.

From the facts of this drawn battle both sides are still bearing heavy scars. How deep those scars are none will ever reveal.

But the working class has lost none of its aggressiveness, none of its confidence, none of its hope in the ultimate triumph. No traitor among the ranks of that class has permanently gained, even materially, by his or her treachery. The flag of the Irish Transport and General Workers' Union still flies proudly and defiantly at the head of the gathering hosts who stand for a regenerated nation, resting upon a people industrially free.

Storm clouds were now gathering over Ireland from other directions. The election of 1910 had placed the Irish Nationalist Party in a superb strategic position, holding the balance of power between parties, to press for Home Rule. The first reading of a Home Rule for Ireland Bill passed the House of Commons in 1912. There was an immediate protest from the Irish industrial capitalists, who were chiefly concentrated in the north-east of Ulster. Since the Union of 1801 the capitalist industries of the north had been developed for the English imperial markets and so industrial capitalism had thrown its weight behind the union with England. The mainly southern petty capitalist, however, relied on the home market and needed to seal off the Irish market behind strong protective barriers in order to bring about a flourishing native manufacturing capitalism in Ireland. They therefore championed self-government which would have spelt destruction for the northern industrialists.

In its natural growth capitalism has two stages, national and imperialist. In its national stage it has to protect itself behind national barriers in order to gather strength. In this period it develops on the basis of the home market. But then it reaches a point where, in order to develop further, it must go beyond the home market and find an international market. It has to find colonies in which it can get cheap raw material and sell its manufactured goods, and to which it can export capital. (In 1880, at the Berlin Congress, the entire world was divided into spheres of influence by the existing capitalist powers.) Ireland has had probably the most distorted development of any country on earth. In 1912 monopoly capitalism, which was dependent on the imperialist market and which could not have survived protection, existed side by side with an ambitious middle class which could not develop without protection.[23]

This conflict of diametrically opposed interests, resulting from the differing stages of the development of capitalism, north and south, was the foundation on which Ireland was to be eventually partitioned. To keep a considerable weight of opinion behind the northern capitalist interests great play was made on the fact that a section of the northern counties of Ulster were Protestant in religion. The "Orange Card" (as Randolph Churchill put it) was an inevitable one to play. A series of Protestant demonstrations against Home Rule, carefully fostered by the industrialists, resulted in attacks on the Catholics and, on July 12, 1912, 2,000 Catholic workers were driven from Belfast shipyards.

The leader of the Irish Unionists was Sir Edward Henry Carson, later to become Lord Carson. He was a Dublin lawyer and landowner, a one time Solicitor General who had taken an almost sadistic delight in prosecuting Land Leaguers and republicans. He was also Tory M.P. for Dublin University and a member of the Privy Council. Carson, with Captain James Craig, launched a campaign on September 23, 1911, supported by the wealthy industrialists against Home Rule. Members of the Orange Order were persuaded to declare a "Holy War" against the Catholics. Ulster Protestants were told that to fight Home Rule was to defend the purity of Protestantism against the imposition of Catholicism. By 1912 a Solemn League and Covenant was subscribed to in Ulster. 218,000 pledged themselves to use "all means necessary to defeat Home Rule". By 1913 an army called the Ulster Volunteers had been formed and armed by gun running from Germany to defend the Protestant minority in Ireland from becoming part of the proposed Irish state. The Volunteers were commanded by a notable soldier, General Sir George Richardson, while many other famous English generals promised their services to the Ulster Protestants who were described as "loyalists".

To the average Ulster Orangeman, he was simply defending

his religion and being loyal to the Crown of England. But, since it was absolutely necessary for the industrial capitalists to have access to an imperial market, they sought for another imperialistic power with which to ally themselves should Ireland receive Home Rule. In 1910 the Ulster Unionist Council had warned : "If we are to be deserted by Great Britain we would rather be governed by Germany." In 1911 Craig had emphasised "Germany and the German Emperor would be preferred to the rule of John Redmond." In the middle of August, 1913, therefore, Sir Edward Carson lunched with the German Kaiser at Hamburg where tentative discussions on German aid to Ulster were discussed. The Protestant *Irish Churchman* declared :

> We have the offer of aid from a powerful continental monarch, who if Home Rule is forced on the Protestants of Ireland, is prepared to send an army sufficient to release England of any further trouble in Ireland by attaching it to his dominion ... And should our King sign the Home Rule Bill, the Protestants of Ireland will welcome this continental deliverer as their forefathers under similar circumstances did once before.[24]

Lenin, observing the situation, reiterated Marx's philosophy that Ireland must be independent "because the English workers could not become free so long as they helped (or even allowed) the keeping of another nation in slavery." He went on :

> ... the British Conservatives, led by that Black Hundred landlord, Purishkevich—that is to say Carson, have raised a frightful howl against Irish autonomy. That means, they say, subjecting Ulsterites to alien people of alien faith ! Lord Carson has threatened rebellion, and has organised armed Black Hundred gangs for this purpose.
>
> This is an empty threat, of course. There can be no question of a rebellion by a handful of hooligans. Nor could there be any question of an Irish Parliament (whose power is determined by British law) "oppressing Protestants".
>
> The point is simply that the Black Hundred landlords are trying to frighten the Liberals.
>
> And the Liberals are quaking, bowing to the Black Hundreds, making concessions to them, offering to take a referendum in Ulster and to postpone the application of the reform to Ulster for six years.
>
> The haggling between the Liberals and the Black Hundreds

continues. The reform can wait; the Irish have waited half a century, they can wait a little longer, after all one mustn't offend the
landlords.

Of course, if the Liberals appealed to the people of Britain, to
the proletariat, Carson's Black Hundred gangs would melt away
and disappear. The peaceful and full achievement of freedom by
Ireland would be guaranteed.

But is it conceivable that the Liberal bourgeoisie will turn to
the proletariat for aid against the landlords? Why, the Liberals in
Britain are also lackeys of the money bags, capable only of cring-
ing to the Carsons.[25]

With the Ulster Volunteers now threatening the achievement
of Home Rule, Eoin MacNeill, leading figure in *Conradh na
Gaeilge* and a professor of Irish, wrote in *An Claidheamh Solais*
a proposal for the formation of the Irish Volunteers to defend
Home Rule. Members of the Irish Republican Brotherhood
seized the opportunity to set up a military front organisation
which could be turned into a revolutionary force. The Irish
Volunteers came into being on November 25, 1913, when 4,000
men enrolled. By the end of 1914 the Irish Volunteers numbered
180,000. They were initially controlled by a council of twenty-
five men, a number of whom were prominent IRB members. At
the same time as the Irish Volunteers were formed, *Cumann na
mBan,* a women's nursing auxiliary, was established. The Ulster
Volunteers had armed themselves by running guns from
Germany and it was obvious that the Irish Volunteers would
undertake similar methods. On December 5, however, a Royal
Proclamation prohibited the use of arms in Ireland. Nevertheless,
the Ulster Volunteers continued in their arming and by April,
1914, it was estimated that 100,000 Ulstermen were armed.
Their biggest coup took place on April 24 when 35,000 rifles and
2,500,000 rounds of ammunition were landed in Bangor,
Donaghadee and Larne from Germany.

The English were now in a quandary and Winston Churchill
drafted a plan for a raid on Craigavon, headquarters of the
Ulster Volunteers, in order to arrest their leaders and safeguard
army property in Ulster. Orders to this effect were sent to Sir
Arthur Paget, General Officer Commanding in Ireland on
March 20. He telegraphed the Government that his officers, led
by Brigadier General Sir Hubert Gough, commanding the 3rd
Cavalry Brigade at the Curragh Camp, had refused to serve

against the Ulster Volunteers and that many men were resigning their commissions. Ministerial conferences took place and the army officer corps were given written assurances that the Crown Forces would not be used against the Unionists. Fox observed :

> With the Curragh mutiny, the fiction that the army is above or beneath politics vanished. This has always been one of the English democratic fictions. Now, however, it was perceived that army officers were armed men with opinions—or, at least, prejudices. In Ireland—where the veneer of constitutionalism is fairly thin—the lesson was not lost upon the young men who looked for their inspiration to the Fenians, to Robert Emmet and to Wolfe Tone.[26]

Lenin also observed :

> March 21, 1914, will be an epoch making turning point, the day when the noble landlords of Britain smashed the British Constitution and British law to bits and gave an excellent lesson in class struggle.
>
> This lesson was a result of the impossibility of blunting the acuteness of the antagonism between the British proletariat and bourgeoisie by means of the half hearted, hypocritical, sham reformist policy of the Liberals. The lesson will not be lost upon the British labour movement; the working class will now quickly proceed to shake off its philistine faith in the scrap of paper which the British aristocrats called the British law and constitution.[27]

It was Lloyd George who now invented a compromise to appease the northern capitalists : a plan which excluded the province of Ulster from the operation of Home Rule for a period of six years. Premier Asquith seized upon the idea of a sop to the Unionists and introduced an Amending Bill to this effect.

In March, 1914, Larkin and Connolly reconstituted the Irish Citizen Army which, after the struggle of 1913, had lost many members. The new constitution agreed :

1) That the first and last principle of the Irish Citizen Army is the avowal that the ownership of Ireland, moral and material, is vested of right in the people of Ireland.
2) That its principal objects shall be
   a. to arm and train all Irishmen capable of bearing arms

to enforce and defend its first principle.

b. to sink all differences of birth, privilege and creed under the common names of the Irish people.

3) That the Citizen Army shall stand for absolute unity of Irish Nationhood and recognition of the rights and liberties of the world's democracies.

4) That the Citizen Army shall be opened to all who are prepared to accept the principle of equal rights and opportunities for the People of Ireland and to work in harmony with organised Labour towards that end.

5) Every enrolled member must be, if possible, a member of a Trades Union recognised by the Irish Trades Union Congress.[28]

Countess Markievicz was the treasurer and Sean Ó Cathasaigh, later became known as Sean O'Casey the playwright, was secretary. O'Casey, or Ó Cathasaigh, as he then used his Irish name, had joined *Conradh na Gaeilge* in 1903 and became a member of the IRB. Ernest Blythe, in his book *Trasna na Boinne*, relates how O'Casey brought him into the movement. O'Casey, in *Feathers from the Green Crow*, 1962, says he realised "the real struggle was not between the English Imperialist and the Irish Republican, but between international capitalism and the workers of the world." He tried to get the republican movement to harness the energy of the working classes to the national struggle. But many of O'Casey's articles seem to contradict his professed Socialism. In 1913 he wrote :

The delivery of Ireland is not in the Labour Manifesto, good and salutary as it may be, but in the strength, beauty, nobility and imagination of the Gaelic ideal.[29]

A few days later in *Irish Freedom* he stated :

But woe unto us if we hand over our ideals to be squared and shaped and glossed by those who would write in our skies that Socialism is Ireland's hope, and hang around our necks the green ribbons of *Cumannacht na hÉireann.*

On becoming secretary of the ICA O'Casey started writing a militant column called Citizen Army notes in the *Irish Worker,* urging revolution.

In Europe the massive race for imperial gains, colonies and possessions was arriving at its logical conclusion. War was on the horizon. The Ulster "loyalists" showed no inclination to remain "loyal" to England in the coming crisis despite strong support from English Tories. On July 8 the Amending Bill was so transformed in the House of Lords to provide for the permanent exclusion of the whole of the nine counties of Ulster. This would have meant, taking the purely religious excuse of the Unionists, that Protestants, who were a minority in Ulster, would rule the Catholic majority. The percentages for the whole of the nine counties of Ulster, in the 1911 Census, were :

		Catholic p.c.	Protestant p.c.
Antrim		20.5	79.5
Armagh	Protestant majority	45.3	54.7
Down	(Unionist)	31.6	68.4
Derry		45.8	54.2
Fermanagh		56.2	43.8
Tyrone		55.4	44.6
Cavan	Catholic majority	81.5	18.5
Monaghan	(Nationalist)	74.7	25.3
Donegal		78.9	21.1

Therefore, only four counties out of the nine counties of the province of Ulster had Protestant ("loyalist") majorities. Had democracy been the criterion for the establishment of the "Ulster" statelet, such a statelet would not have been brought into existence on the Ulster vote alone, regardless of the fact that Ulster was only one of four provinces of a country which had over-whelmingly voted for Home Rule again and again.

The drift towards the European war made a settlement an urgent problem. King George V intervened and a peace conference was held at Buckingham Palace from July 21 to 24, but no agreement could be found. A week later Premier Asquith announced an agreement with Carson and Bonar Law, the Tory leader. Home Rule would be postponed pending a settlement of the European problem. On August 3 Sir Edward Grey announced the Government's decision to declare war on Germany. Carson pledged his Ulster Volunteers to fight and John Redmond rose and assured the English Government that they could withdraw all their troops from Ireland as the Irish

Volunteers would co-operate with the Ulster Volunteers in guarding Ireland from German invasion. Redmond's action was backed by the majority of bourgeois nationalists in the belief that they had Home Rule now and that war booms would be created in agriculture and industry. In fact, during 1914-18 Irish capitalists had a favourable trade balance for the first time since 1904. Irish joint-stock bank deposits rose from £62,000,000 in 1910 to £200,000,000. The army's separation allowance also pacified a great number of the working-class families for it gave regular income to many homes that had not known one. Connolly commented in the *Workers' Republic* :

> Full steam ahead John Redmond said
> that everything was well chum;
> Home Rule will come when we are dead
> and buried out in Belgium.[30]

Larkin also condemned Ireland's involvement in the war. "Oh Irishmen, dear countrymen, take heed of what we say, for if you do England's dirty work, you will surely rue the day."[31] But by October, 1914, Larkin had set off for the U.S.A., tired and exhausted, but with the aim of collecting funds for Irish labour and organising co-operation with the Irish Americans. He was not to return to Ireland until 1923. In his absence James Connolly became acting general secretary of the ITGWU, commander of the Irish Citizen Army and editor of the *Irish Worker*.

Chapter 12

"THE RISEN PEOPLE"

J AMES CONNOLLY WAS horrified at the disintegration of
the European Socialist movement at the outbreak of the First
World War. Extremely few Socialists held back and refused to
fling themselves into the imperialist holocaust. Lenin, Connolly
and John Maclean of Scotland were among the few. Writing just
after the outbreak of the war, Connolly asks:

What then becomes of all our resolutions; all our protests of
fraternisation; all our threats of general strikes; all our carefully
built machinery of internationalism; all our hopes for the future?
Were they all as sound and fury signifying nothing? When the
German artillery-man, a Socialist serving in the German army of
invasion, sends a shell into the ranks of the French army, blowing
off their heads, tearing out their bowels, and mangling the limbs
of dozens of Socialist comrades in that force, will the fact that
he, before leaving for the front, "demonstrated" against the war,
be of any value to the widows and orphans made by the shell he
sent on its mission of murder? Or, when the French rifleman
pours his murderous rifle into the ranks of the German line of
attack, will he be able to derive any comfort from the probability
that his bullets are murdering or maiming comrades who last
year joined in thundering "hochs" and cheers of greeting to the
eloquent Jaures, when in Berlin he pleaded for international solidarity? When the Socialist pressed into the army of the Austrian
Kaiser sticks a long, cruel bayonet knife into the stomach of the
Socialist conscript in the army of the Russian Czar, and gives it a
twist so that when pulled out it will pull the entrails out along
with it, will the terrible act lose any of its fiendish cruelty by the
fact of their common theoretical adhesion to an anti-war propaganda in time of peace? When the Socialist soldier from the
Baltic provinces of Russia is sent forward into Prussian Poland, to
bombard towns and villages until a red trail of blood and fire
covers the homes of the unwilling Polish subjects of Prussia, as he
gazes upon the corpses of those he has slaughtered and the homes
he has destroyed, will he in his turn be comforted by the thought

that the Czar, whom he serves, sent over soldiers a few years ago to carry the same devastations and murder into his own home by the Baltic Sea?[1]

In vain did Connolly point out: "A great continental uprising of the working class would stop the war; a universal protest at public meetings would not save a single life from being wantonly slaughtered." Ironically it was those very same Socialists who had denounced Connolly's demands for national liberation as "chauvinism", who were now flocking to provide cannon fodder for the imperialist banners. Connolly was a "chauvinist" because he advocated the breaking up of empires by the national struggle of subject peoples, as opposed to their support of the war efforts of their respective empires, and working for reforms in those empires whose rivalries had erupted into war. The war was only a few days old when Connolly decided what course the Irish working classes should take. In the *Irish Worker* on August 8, 1914, he wrote an article entitled "Our Duty in This Crisis" in which he pointed out: "Should a German army land in Ireland tomorrow we should be perfectly justified in joining it if by doing so we could rid this country once and for all from its connections with the Brigand Empire that drags us unwillingly into this war." Connolly again stressed: "Should the working class of Europe, rather than slaughter each other for the benefit of kings and financiers, proceed tomorrow to erect barricades all over Europe, to break up bridges and destroy transport services that war might be abolished, we should be perfectly happy in following such a glorious example and contributing our aid to the final dethronement of the vulture class that rule and rob the world. But pending either of these consummations it is our manifest duty to take all possible action to save the poor from the horrors this war has in store." Connolly's idea was that an uprising should be organised to gain national liberation, to disown the imperialist war in Europe and, by so doing, "set the torch to a European conflagration that will not burn out until the last throne and the last capitalist bond and debenture will be shrivelled in the funeral pyre of the last war lord."

Connolly was not so doctrinaire in his beliefs that he visualised a purely working-class uprising. He relised that the only hope of success lay in allying himself to the bourgeois nationalists, or rather, the most progressive section of them.

As early as August 1914 the American Clan na Gael had presented the idea of an Irish insurrection to the German Ambassador in the U.S.A. with the idea of obtaining arms and ammunition. The Supreme Council of the IRB, of which Padraic Pearse was now a member, met during the first months of the war and agreed, though for different reasons, as Connolly—that an uprising must be organised. Pearse, at this time, was somewhat distrusted by the revolutionaries because of his support for the Irish Councils Bill of 1907 and his willingness to accept Home Rule as an instalment to freedom. However, Pearse, working closely with Tom Clarke and Seán MacDiarmada, became Director of Organisation of the IRB by December, 1914.

It had been pointed out by Maureen Wall, in her important study "The Background to the Rising from 1914 until the Countermanding Order on Easter Saturday 1916"[2], that those who favoured an uprising were a small minority even in the IRB itself. She adds that the preparations which the revolutionaries started to make were in total disregard of the IRB constitution which said that the IRB would "await the decision of the Irish nation as expressed by a majority of the Irish people, as to the fit hour for inaugurating a war against England". She states that Clarke and MacDiarmada exercised unlimited authority without the constitutional sanction of the IRB. While this is, of course, true, to condemn the revolutionaries of 1916 on this basis shows a naïve view of what a revolution is about and how it is organised. Miss Wall states that while the 1916 revolutionaries acted in the name of the IRB, at no time did they really have the constitutional authority of the IRB and that the establishment in May/June, 1915, of a revolutionary Military Council, was not an act of the IRB for the act was against the IRB constitution. The Council was set up by the revolutionaries, who constituted the IRB executive, to give IRB authority to the rising.

The revolutionaries had agreed that a rising should take place if the Germans invaded Ireland, if England attempted to enforce conscription or if the war were coming to an end. In the last circumstance, Ireland would declare war on England and claim to be represented as a belligerent nation at the ensuing peace conference. Under IRB auspices a meeting of nationalist groupings was sounded out on their views on an uprising. Arthur Griffith of *Sinn Féin* opposed a rising and broke with the IRB and the

Volunteers. One person at this meeting who sided with the idea was William O'Brien, the founder of *Cumannacht na hÉireann* (Socialist Party of Ireland) who was a close friend and follower of Connolly. It was through O'Brien that Connolly got in touch with Eamonn Ceannt and a conference arranged on September 9, 1914, in the library of *Conradh na Gaeilge*. The meeting included Pearse, Tom Clarke, Joseph Plunkett, John MacBride, Seán T. Ó Ceallaigh, Thomas MacDonagh, Éamonn Ceannt and Seán MacDiarmada. Connolly put forward his proposal that preparations should be made for a rising and that aid, in the form of arms and ammunition, be sought from Germany. T. A. Jackson believes:

> The Gaelic Republicans of whom Padraic Pearse was the best representative were very sceptical of German help. They saw— what traditionalists failed to see—that Tone appealed for military aid to France in 1796, not merely, or even mainly, because it was at war with England, but because it stood, then, *at the head of the forces of World Liberation*. The French Republic to which Tone appealed was the embodiment and representative of the principles of popular freedom and of international solidarity of a liberated world. He appealed as a democratic republican to his fellow republican-democrats. And nobody in 1914 could envisage the Kaiser of the Kaiser's Reich as anything of the kind. Pearse's doctrine, which, at times, he expressed in mystical terms, which obscured its realistic essence, was that Ireland must herself develop the force that achieves freedom. His doctrine of the magical efficacy of a "blood sacrifice" boils down, in practice, to the elementary truth.[3]

But while Connolly had even less faith in German aid than Pearse had, he pointed out that the Irish could do worse than seek German aid.

> The German Empire is a homogeneous Empire of self governing peoples; the British Empire is a heterogeneous collection in which a very small number of self governing communities connive at the subjugation by force of a vast number of despotically ruled subject populations.
> We do not wish to be ruled by either empire, but we certainly believe that the first named contains in germ more of the possibilities of freedom and civilisation than the latter.[4]

It must also be remembered that Pearse and Connolly were also practical revolutionaries and the maxim that "England's difficulty is Ireland's opportunity" was a valid one. The outcome of this conference was that two committees were set up; one would endeavour to form contact with Germany, while the other would be an open organisation to be used for propaganda. This latter became the Irish Neutrality League with Connolly as its president. A manifesto issued on October 5, 1914, states the League was formed :

> . . . for the purpose of defining Ireland's present attitude towards the Anglo-German war as one of neutrality, watching Ireland's interests at every phase of the war, preventing employers from coercing men to enlist, inculcating the view that true patriotism requires Irishmen to remain at home, and taking steps to preserve the food supplies of Ireland for the people of Ireland . . .

The Irish Neutrality League was short lived but, during its existence, did some useful work. On September 25, 1914, Premier Asquith and John Redmond were to address a meeting in Mansion House, Dublin, for the purpose of recruiting for the army, A plan was put forward that Mansion House should be seized and held for twenty-four hours, to prevent the meeting by armed force. Some forty Citizen Army men and eighty Irish Volunteers were organised—among the volunteers was the Pacifist-Socialist, Francis Sheehy-Skeffington. The men were ready to make the attempt when it was learnt that British troops had taken over the Mansion House and the project was called off.

In the meantime, Sean O'Casey had resigned as secretary of the Irish Citizen Army because of its new policy in forming a liaison with the Irish Volunteers. His resignation was a complete reversal of the policy he had once advocated . . . that republicans and labour join together to achieve the national revolution. From preaching national independence he had swung round halfway to a William Walker concept. Tom Clarke, writing to John Devoy, on March 14, 1914, had commented :

> Larkin's people for some time have been making war on the Irish Volunteers. I think this is largely inspired by a disgruntled fellow named O'Casey.

O'Casey never forgave Connolly for leading the workers in the struggle for national independence in 1916. He bitterly reproaches him in his *Story of the Irish Citizen Army*. How much of his bitterness may have been sparked off by feelings of guilt, because for years O'Casey preached national and social revolution but when it came in 1916 he remained aloof, is a matter of conjecture.

On September 24, 1914, the day Asquith and Redmond addressed their recruiting meeting in the Mansion House, the executive of the Irish Volunteers met and repudiated his call to arms for the Empire. Redmond had gained control of the Irish Volunteers by insisting that he appoint twenty-five nominees to the executive council, otherwise he would form his own volunteer force. These nominees were now ejected from the Volunteer executive and a National Convention was held in the Abbey Theatre, Dublin, on October 25, to affirm the determination of the Irish Volunteers to maintain a defence force in Ireland, resisting conscription and defending the unity of the nation and its right to self government. Only 12,000 of the 200,000 Volunteers supported the Convention and these retained the name of the Irish Volunteers. Those who supported Redmond were renamed the National Volunteers. Redmond called the breakaway movement, derisively, "The *Sinn Féin* Volunteers" and the name stuck, creating endless confusion and giving much free publicity to the *Sinn Féin* movement. The Irish Volunteers reached a maximum number of 18,000 while the Citizen Army could only arm and equip 200 men. They would have mustered about 2,000,[5] but, because of the lack of arms, many were encouraged to enlist in the Volunteers. The National Volunteers were now flocking to the British Army. It is estimated that upwards of 250,000 Irishmen, not including those living outside Ireland, enlisted. Of this number, it is further estimated that 40,000 were killed, excluding officers. The Catholic Irish that did volunteer were treated quite insolently by the English Government. It was practically impossible for Catholic Irishmen to get commissions; the National University was not allowed to organise a training corps while the "Protestant" Trinity College was. Irish regiments were to march under the Union Jack only and the wearing of Irish insignia was forbidden. Offers made by Col. Moore, the former Volunteer leader, to form an Irish Brigade to fight in France, were turned down. In contrast, Carson's Ulster Volunteers were enrolled as a separate unit, mainly the 36th

(Ulster) Division, with their own colours, their own officers and a strict ban on Catholics.

On Friday, December 4, a force of military and police smashed the presses of the *Irish Worker* and suppressed the newspaper. Many other revolutionary and nationalist newspapers, such as *Sinn Féin* and *Irish Freedom,* also suffered. Connolly managed to get out a successor called *The Worker* which was printed by the Socialist Labour Press in Glasgow, Scotland. With the sixth issue in February, 1915, this was also suppressed. A printing plant was then established in Liberty Hall where Connolly launched *The Worker's Republic.*

In May, 1915, MacDiarmada told P. S. O'Hegarty that the rising would take place in September, 1915. As early as March 13, 1915, four Dublin Brigade commandants of the Volunteers had attended a meeting at the Volunteer headquarters. Pearse was in the chair and the general plan of the uprising, the same one as that subsequently used in 1916, was outlined. Connolly, although he was not a member of the IRB, was to command the Dublin area. During this time Connolly gave several lectures to the Volunteers on street fighting. During the course of these lectures, according to de Valera, Connolly stated his belief that the government would never permit the army to destroy capitalist owned property in the main streets of Dublin.

The rumour of conscription being forced on Ireland caused an anti-conscription committee to be formed during the summer of 1915. Connolly commented :

> We will not be asked to accept conscription by the British Government unless the British ruling class has made up its mind that only conscription can save the Empire. If it does make up its mind to that measure it will enforce conscription though every river in Ireland runs red with blood.[6]

The Dublin Trades Council, in October, passed a resolution proposed by the Socialist Peadar Macken, who was also a member of the Irish Volunteers' executive :

> That the Dublin Trades Council, while not disposed to obstruct in any way those persons who, through zeal for the British Empire, might be inclined to volunteer for active service abroad, at the same time calls upon the organised workers to join

either the Citizen Army or the Irish Volunteers, as being the best means to avert conscription.

The Volunteer leadership sought co-operation with the Dublin Trades Council to resist the action of employers who were forcing their workers into the army. Several discussions took place between MacNeill, Pearse, MacDiarmada and Seamus O'Connor for the Volunteers and Connolly, O'Brien and Thomas Foran for the Trades Council. Connolly wanted the Volunteers to support the workers militarily for any action that they might have to take against the employers. MacNeill, in particular, would not agree to this.

Tension was growing among the nationalists. On May 19, 1915, the Liberal Cabinet was suspended and a new Coalition Cabinet was formed which included eight Unionists. Sir Edward Carson was appointed Attorney General and F. E. Smith, later Lord Birkenhead, was given the post of Solicitor General. Even moderate Home Rulers saw the chance of such a Cabinet agreeing to the implementation of Home Rule as highly remote. In America, the Fenian, O'Donovan Rossa, died and was brought back to Ireland for burial. Contingents of Volunteers and the Citizen Army accompanied his body to Glasnevin where Pearse gave the funeral oration which has served to inspire Irish people ever since.

> Defenders of this Realm have worked well in secret and in the open. They think that they have pacified Ireland. They think that they have purchased half of us and intimidated the other half. They think that they have foreseen everything, think that they have provided against everything; but the fools, the fools, the fools!—they have left us our Fenian dead, and while Ireland holds these graves, Ireland unfree shall never be at peace.[7]

The insurrection did not materialise in September, 1915. The Volunteers were not ready. This reason did not satisfy Connolly, who had long been suspicious of the bourgeois forces that he was allying himself with. He came out with strong criticism of the failure to launch the rising in 1915.

> Revolutionists who shrink from giving blow for blow until the great day has arrived and they have every shoe-string in its place and every man has got his gun, and the enemy has kindly con-

sented to postpone action in order not to needlessly hurry the revolutionists nor disarrange their plans—such revolutionists exist only in two places—the comic opera stage, and the stage of Irish national politics.[8]

Against this background, the overtures to Germany, seeking arms and support, continued. Jackson comments that the Germans were little interested in the Irish overtures.

> They had banked on Carson's rebellion tying the hands of the British sufficiently to keep them out of the war until France was smashed. As Carson failed them, the Germans had no confidence in the rest of Ireland. They sent the shipload of arms—all paid for at top prices in spot cash—but they did that more to please their American Ambassador (who thought an Irish rebellion would keep America out of the war) than from any hope of military gain.[9]

The IRB envoy to Germany, Roger Casement, however, succeeded in getting the German State Secretary von Zimmermann to sign an undertaking, endorsed by the German Chancellor, to aid the Irish, equip an Irish Brigade and give public recognition, support and goodwill to an independent Irish Government. However, towards the end of 1915 Connolly was beginning to grow uneasy at the seeming inactivity of the Volunteer leaders. The war was drifting on; in January, 1916, conscription was made law in England, Wales and Scotland. Connolly determined that if the Irish Volunteers did not rise, he and his Citizen Army would at least make a gesture. To this end he continued advocating insurrectionary activity. He saw each member of the Citizen Army individually and explained the position, asking the man his opinion—he did not want any member to remain in the Citizen Army who was not willing and prepared to fight. From November to early January, 1916, Connolly intensified his campaign for immediate armed revolution, severely criticising the procrastinating Volunteer leadership as "would-be Wolfe Tones, who were legally seditious and peacefully revolutionary." During 1915 he also published a series of articles, now published as *Revolutionary Warfare*, which classes Connolly as a proficient military scientist. Connolly was no militarist, there is no glorifying or glamourising of war in his writings. Indeed, when Padraic Pearse wrote an essay glorifying war he wrote that anyone who held such views must be a "blithering idiot":

> ... there is no such thing as humane or civilised war. War may be forced upon a subject race or subject class to put an end to subjection of race, or class, or sex. When so waged it must be waged thoroughly and relentlessly, but with no delusion as to its elevating nature, or civilising methods.[10]

Connolly, the realist, therefore made a study of revolutionary warfare, drawing conclusions on guerilla tactics, street warfare and other methods of insurgency fighting. Of all the 1916 leaders, Connolly showed himself to be the most prepared and practical as regards organising resistance. *Revolutionary Warfare* places Connolly as a revolutionary soldier whose concepts and methods have been proved in countless anti-imperialist battlefields in all parts of the world.

While Connolly fumed at the Volunteers' procrastination, the Supreme Council of the IRB decided, at a meeting early in January, that the uprising was to begin on April 22, that year. Connolly was immediately informed. He disappeared from January 19 to January 22 in secret conclave with the IRB leaders. He was made a member of the IRB and co-opted to its Military Council, joining Tom Clarke, Eamonn Ceannt, Seán MacDiarmada, Padraic Pearse and Joseph Plunkett. Thomas MacDonagh was to be co-opted later. Although the three days' disappearance of Connolly remains to some extent a mystery, it is thought that the exact details of the rising were worked out during this period. The plans were detailed and precise and relied on the entire Volunteer movement taking part. Dublin Volunteers were to seize key positions in the city while Volunteers in the provinces were to surround garrisons and prevent troops and police advancing into the city. Those people who opposed a rising, Griffith, Eoin MacNeill, the *de jure* head of the Volunteers, were not told of the plans. Orders were issued to the Volunteers to take part in "three days of manoeuvres" over the Easter Week period. At the same time a message was sent to John Devoy and the Clan na Gael in the U.S.A.

> Unanimous opinion that action cannot be postponed much longer. Delays are disadvantageous to us. Our enemies cannot allow us much more time. Initiative on our part is necessary. The

Irish regiments which are in sympathy with us are being gradually replaced with English regiments.

We have therefore decided to begin action on Easter Saturday. Unless entirely new circumstances arise we must have your arms and munitions in Limerick between Good Friday and Easter Saturday. We expect German help immediately after beginning action. We might be compelled to begin earlier.[11]

Connolly now gave a clear warning of the intended rising in *The Workers' Republic* :

Our notes this week will be short. The issue is clear and we have done our part to clear it. Nothing we can now say can add point to the arguments we have put before our readers in the past few months; nor shall we continue to labour the point.

In solemn acceptance of our duty and the great responsibilities attached hereto, we have planted the seed in the hope and belief that ere many of us are much older it will ripen and blossom into action. For the moment and hour of that ripening, that fruitful and blessed day of days, we are ready.

Will it find you ready?[12]

Eoin MacNeill maintained that no one was ready for an insurrection in 1916 and that no revolutionary situation existed in the country to justify it. In February, 1916, he wrote :

I do not know at this moment whether the time and circumstances will yet justify distinct revolutionary action, but of this I am certain, that the only possible basis for successful revolutionary action is deep and widespread popular discontent. We have only to look around us in the streets to realise that no such conditions exist in Ireland. A few of us, a small proportion, who think about the evils of English government in Ireland, are always discontented. We should be downright fools if we were to measure others by this standard of our own thoughts.

Maureen Wall maintains that MacNeill's attitude and subsequent actions were right.

At first glance it would seem that that in many ways the climate for rebellion had never been so favourable—in spite of all the martial fervour and treasonable activities, a revolutionary situation did not, however, exist in Ireland in the years immediately preceeding 1916. Dublin had been a centre of intense social conflict during the terrible Lock-Out of 1913, but at no time was there any serious danger of a Paris style revolution, with a rush to the barricades. Like the Citizen Army, the Volunteers were formed for defensive not offensive action. Land Reform and land purchase measures and other social and economic benefits as well as the steady stream of emigration from the countryside, had gone far to eradicate the atmosphere of smothered war which had existed in rural Ireland since the mid-eighteenth century. The great bulk of the Irish population supported Redmond and his Home Rule policy, believing, despite or even because of the already grown threat of partition, that the party leaders were best equipped to assess the political situation, and that their policy of supporting the British war effort was the best in the circumstances; that the "loyalist nationalist card" was the best reply to the "Orange Card" if Home Rule for all Ireland was to be obtained.[13]

While one cannot disagree with the facts presented by Maureen Wall, it depends on what one regards as a "revolutionary situation". Very few revolutionaries have been presented with the ideal revolutionary situation; the majority of times they have had to make it for themselves. In modern history perhaps the greatest example is the Cuban Revolution. On November 25, 1956, the small yacht *Granma* set off for Cuba with eighty-three men commanded by Castro with the objective to liberate Cuba from the Fascist military dictatorship of Fulgencio Batista. Batista's army was waiting for them at Algría de Pío. Of the eighty-three men only fifteen survived. With these fifteen men, forty-five days later, Castro started the revolution. Looking at the situation logically, one can hardly describe Algría de Pío as a "revolutionary situation", and yet the revolution succeeded. Revolutionaries do not wait for "revolutionary situations" but create them themselves; a fact clearly demonstrated in Hannah Arendt's book *On Revolution*. Therefore, while MacNeill was correct in saying no revolutionary situation existed, the revolutionaries were equally right, according to revolutionary principles, in seeking to create that situation.

In March the Workers' Dramatic Company performed Connolly's three act play, *Under Which Flag?* at Liberty Hall. The play, set in the Fenian days, was very favourably reviewed for the *Workers' Republic* by Francis Sheehy-Skeffington. On

March 24 the military raided *The Gael* newspaper and entered a newspaper shop, owned by the ITGWU, seeking copies of it. Connolly entered the shop as police were searching through papers and demanded to see their search warrant. On being told they had no warrant he pulled out a revolver and said, "Drop those papers, or I'll drop you." The police withdrew reluctantly and Connolly issued an order mobilising the Citizen Army to protect Liberty Hall from raids by the authorities. From that day until the rising, two sentries, uniformed and fully armed, guarded the entrance.

The time for the uprising was drawing close. It was decided to form a revolutionary military provisional government and a civil provisional government. The military government consisted of Tom Clarke, Seán MacDiarmada, Thomas MacDonagh, Joseph Plunkett, Eamonn Ceannt, James Connolly and Padraic Pearse as president of the government. Thirty-six-year-old Pearse was the son of an Englishman who, having emigrated to Ireland, took up its cause for self-government. The civil government was to look after food supplies, transport and "civilian problems" and consisted of William O'Brien, Mrs. H. Sheehy-Skeffington, Seán T. Ó Ceallaigh, Alderman Tom Kelly and Arthur Griffith.

A mythology has arisen concerning what has been described as the radical differences of the political opinions of Pearse and Connolly. Just how far did these two revolutionary leaders differ in their political thinking? That Pearse was representative of progressive republicanism there is no doubt. O'Connor Lysaght writes:

> The left wing (of the Irish Volunteers) included Pearse, MacDonagh and Ceannt, supported by Thomas Clarke; they were less narrowly bourgeois, of them was Pearse was developing towards the end of his life a theory that challenged the concept of private property.[14]

Pearse was no Socialist in Connolly's interpretation of the word and his writings show no familiarity with Socialist theory. Nevertheless, he was moving, perhaps instinctively, towards Socialism. Pearse wrote in 1913:

> My instinct is with the landless man against the lord of lands, and with the breadless man against the master of millions. I may

be wrong, but I do hold it a most terrible sin that there be landless men in this island of waste yet fertile valleys, and that there should be breadless men in this city where great fortunes are made and enjoyed.[15]

According to Clarkson :

Larkin he admired from afar; with Connolly he became more intimate. In *The Sovereign People* he accepted much of the latter's teachings; the doctrine that the undeniable social evils existent in Ireland were the fruit of foreign domination permitted Pearse, as it had permitted a few of the Young Irelanders, to come very close to a Socialist point of view. Thus came about that junction of forces between militant labour and the Republican idealists.[16]

Proinsias Mac Aonghusa and Liam Ó Réagáin state :

The influence of Connolly's thought is marked in the last pamphlet with its emphasis on giving to "all men and women of the nation ... effective possession of the physical conditions necessary to the reality of this freedom".

The picture of Pearse as a "visionary", a mystic devoted to blood sacrifice, has almost completely eradicated Pearse's real character as a practical political thinker and organiser. In his pamphlet *The Sovereign People*, March 31, 1916, Pearse sums up his political ideology, clearly and concisely. Connolly had written "only the Irish working class remain as the incorruptible inheritors of the fight for freedom in Ireland." Pearse comes to exactly the same conclusion.

Tone had appealed to that numerous and respectable class, the "men of no property", and in that gallant and characteristic phrase he had revealed his perception of a great historic truth, namely, that in Ireland "the gentry" (as they affect to call themselves) have uniformly been corrupted by England, and the merchants and middle class capitalists have, when not corrupted, been uniformly intimidated, whereas the common people have, for the most part, remained unbought and unterrified.

Backing that conclusion Pearse, the practical politician, decided that "in substance that separation from England would be valueless unless it put the people—the actual people and not merely certain rich men— of Ireland in effectual ownership and possession of the soil of Ireland." Pearse felt that "that right to the control of the material resources of a nation does not reside in any individual or in any class of individuals; it resides in the whole people and can be lawfully exercised only by those to whom it is delegated by the whole people, and in the manner in which the people ordains." He points out :

> . . . a nation may, for instance, determine, as the free Irish nation determined and enforced for many centuries, that private owner-ship shall not exist in land; that the whole of a nation's soil is the public property of the nation. A nation may determine, as many modern nations have determined, that all the means of transport within a nation, all its railways and waterways, are the public property of the nation to be administered for the general benefit. A nation may go further and determine that all sources of wealth whatsoever are the property of the nation, and each individual shall give his service for the nation's good, and shall be ade-quately provided for by the nation, and that all surplus wealth shall go to the national treasury, to be expended on national purposes, rather than be accumulated by private persons.

Pearse adds "I do not disallow the right to private property but I insist that all property is held subject to the national sanc-tion." This form of proposed society advocated by Pearse was not too far removed from the Socialist society advocated by James Connolly. Therefore the political gulf between Pearse and Connolly was extremely narrow when they signed the 1916 Proclamation of the Irish Republic declaring "the right of the people of Ireland to the ownership of Ireland and to the unfet-tered control of Irish destinies to be sovereign and indefeasible." The Proclamation, from the stylistic evidence, seems very much the work of Pearse.

On April 8 Connolly announced :

> The Council of the Irish Citizen Army have resolved after grave and earnest deliberation, to hoist the green flag of Ireland over Liberty Hall, as over a fortress held for Ireland by the arms of Irishmen.[17]

The flag was to be hoisted on Palm Sunday, April 16.

8—TIWC * *

Where better could that flag fly than over the unconquered citadel of the Irish Working Class, Liberty Hall, the fortress of the militant Working Class of Ireland.

The cause of labour is the cause of Ireland, the cause of Ireland is the cause of labour. They cannot be dissevered. Ireland seeks freedom. Labour seeks that an Ireland free should be the sole mistress of her own destiny, supreme owner of all material things within and upon her soil . . .

Therefore on Sunday, April 16, the Green Flag of Ireland will be solemnly hoisted over Liberty Hall as the symbol of our faith in freedom and as a token to all the world that the working class of Dublin stands for the cause of Ireland and the cause of Ireland is the cause of a separate and distinct nationality.

A committee meeting of the ITGWU severely criticised Connolly. The majority of the committee favoured a motion by William Fairtlough, an old and influential member, to demand a meeting of members to censure Connolly. Thomas Foran, the union's president, suggested the meeting adjourn to enable Connolly to give an explanation. Connolly said he felt no explanation was needed. He had not thought the union would object to the Irish flag being unfurled over its premises and if the day ever came when they did he would resign from office. The majority of the committee were opposed to Connolly and he requested permission to speak in private to John Farrell, one of those in strongest opposition to him. He told Farrell about the insurrection and that the unfurling of the flag was part of the plan. Farrell withdrew his opposition and swayed the meeting in support of Connolly.

On the evening of Palm Sunday, after the flag had been duly unfurled, Connolly delivered his last lecture to the men of the Citizen Army on guerilla warfare : "I'm going to fight the way I want, not the way the enemy wants. It'll be a new way, one the soldiers haven't been trained to deal with." It was at this lecture that Connolly reminded his men : "The odds against are a thousand to one. But if we should win, hold on to your rifles because the Volunteers may have a different goal. Remember we're out not only for political liberty but for economic liberty as well. So hold on to your rifles."[18]

Communications had been made with the Germans and a ship named the *Aud* sailed from Lubeck on April 9, commanded by Captain Karl Spindler, and carrying arms and ammunition for the insurgents. It reached Tralee Bay on April 20 but already plans had gone wrong. American secret service men had raided the flat of the German attache Wolf von Igel in New York and discovered John Devoy's code book and messages. Some twenty-nine English warships were waiting to pounce on the *Aud*. She was caught and escorted to Queenstown (Cobh) where Spindler scuttled her. On the same day, April 20, Casement and two colleagues landed from a German submarine at Banna Strand. Casement was arrested almost immediately.

On Good Friday Eoin MacNeill, the head of the Irish Volunteers, discovered that the orders for "manouevres" were, in reality, orders for an insurrection. Pearse and the Military Council tried to persuade him to accept a *fait accompli* but the news of the scuttling of the *Aud* and arrest of Casement made MacNeill try to countermand the orders. Messengers were sent to the country to prevent the Volunteers from rising while a statement in the *Sunday Independent* called off the parades and manouevres.

Pearse and Connolly realised that it was a "now or never" situation. The English authorities were already warned. In fact, Lord Wimborne, the Lord Lieutenant, had already arranged for over a hundred leaders of the various revolutionary groupings to be arrested on Easter Monday. The insurrectionists would have to move or be crushed for another generation. At 10 a.m. on Easter Monday, April 24, 1916, only 1,500 men of the Dublin Volunteer Brigade and of the Citizen Army answered the call to parade. MacNeill's countermanding orders had been obeyed by the majority of Volunteers. Only in a few areas did Volunteers march out and fight. In North County Dublin a Volunteer force from Co. Louth broke the Belfast-Dublin railway line and carried out a series of "flying column" attacks. In Co. Wexford, 600 men under Commandant Robert Brennan occupied Enniscorthy until outnumbered when they retreated to Vinegar Hill before finally surrendering. In Galway, Liam Mellowes, a left wing Volunteer leader, led the local Volunteers, almost 1,000 strong, in destroying bridges, cutting telegraph wires and attacking barracks. They captured Athenry but were encircled at Moyvore by troops. Mellows decided to stand and fight but priests persuaded his men to disperse and surrender. Mellowes took to the hills. By the time provincial Volunteer units heard the rising was on, and disregarded MacNeill's orders, the police and military were already on the offensive, arresting and interning suspects.

With Connolly's appointment as commander of the republican forces in Dublin, Michael Mallin, secretary of the Silk Weavers' Union and formerly chief of staff of the Citizen Army was appointed Commandant. Dr. Kathleen Lynn was medical officer of the army. Miss Helena Molony, secretary of the Irish Women Workers' Union, headed a women's section of the army, which was to act as a nursing auxiliary, while Walter Carpenter led a boys' section which was to be a messenger corps. Of the women, Countess Markievicz was the only woman to fight as a combatant with the rank of lieutenant during the rising. The exact number of the Citizen Army was 220 of which thirty-eight men and one woman, Miss Winifred Carney, Connolly's secretary, were in the insurgent GHQ at the General Post Office.

The Irish Volunteers consisted of members of the four battalions of the Dublin Brigade; supported by the nursing auxiliary of *Cumann na mBan* and the *Fianna Éireann* (Boy Scouts) who were to act as messengers.

"From the moment that the first shot is fired there will be no longer Volunteers or Citizen Army," said Connolly, "but only the Army of the Irish Republic."

The insurgent plan was simple. The General Post Office in central Dublin was to be seized by Volunteers and Citizen Army men commanded by Connolly, and the Provisional Government established there. The main road leading from Kingstown (Dun Laoire), by which troops landing from England would have to pass, was covered by Boland's bakery, occupied by the Third Battalion commanded by the Dublin Brigade adjutant, Eamonn de Valera, who had been against the rising but had obeyed the order to turn out. This personal indecision was also reflected during his command of his position. The First Battalion, commanded by Edward Daly, occupied the Fourt Courts buildings. Thomas MacDonagh and the Second Battalion occupied Jacob's Biscuit Factory while Kingsbridge Station, the terminus of the rail-links to the south was controlled by the South Dublin Union, occupied by the Fourth Battalion under Eamonn Ceannt. These were the main insurgent positions. The Citizen Army occupied St. Stephen's Green and Connolly, with a sense of irony, had a Citizen Army flag hoisted over the Imperial Hotel of William Martin

Murphy. Smaller sections of insurgents occupied encircling positions at railway termini and other strategic points. Erroneous statements have been made in histories about the "unsuccessful attempt to take Dublin Castle". Dublin Castle, seat and symbol of English power in Ireland, was not the subject of any attempt to take it. Connolly told William O'Brien that while it would be easy to take the Castle, a collection of straggling buildings commanded at several points by higher buildings, it would be impossible to hold it against enemy attack. Captain Seán Connolly of the Citizen Army, a young Abbey actor, was ordered to take certain buildings commanding the entrance gates but to make no attempt on the Castle itself.

At noon on Easter Monday, Connolly left Liberty Hall to take command of his men. Passing William O'Brien he whispered: "We are going out to be slaughtered." O'Brien asked: "Is there no chance of success?" Connolly replied: "None whatever." A short while later the Proclamation of the Irish Republic was being read to the amazed citizens of Dublin while a transmitter on top of the GPO broadcast the fact in morse to the world.

The rising lasted one week. Pearse and Connolly signed an unconditional surrender document "in order to prevent the further slaughter of Dublin citizens, and in the hope of saving the lives of our followers now surrounded and hopelessly outnumbered" at 3.45 p.m. on April 29. Two more days went by before all the insurgent commands surrendered. Some 1,351 people had been killed or wounded; 179 buildings in central Dublin alone had been utterly destroyed by fire or artillery (disposing of Connolly's belief that a capitalist government would hesitate to destroy capitalist property). Total damage costs were placed initially at £2,500,000 and a third of the population of Dublin demanded public relief. Connolly had been wounded twice during the rising while directing operations but still insisted on supervising matters from a stretcher. Among the casualties of the rising was Francis Sheehy-Skeffington, the pacifist who, while trying to organise a citizen force to prevent looting, was arrested by English soldiers and taken to Portobello Barracks. He and two journalists, unconnected with the national movements, were shot out of hand on the order of Captain Bowen-Colthurst. Sheehy-Skeffington was held in such high esteem that an inquiry was forced and a subsequent court martial found Bowen-Colthurst "of unsound

mind". There were many other cases of questionable conduct by English troops as they advanced on insurgent positions . . . such as the conduct of the 2/6 South Staffs in North King Street, where a number of civilian prisoners were executed. General Sir John Maxwell, sent to command the English troops during the rising, commented :

> Possibly some unfortunate incidents, which we should regret now, may have occurred . . . it is even possible that under the horror of this attack some of them "saw red", that is the inevitable consequence of a rebellion of this kind.[19]

Ninety of the insurgents, including all the leaders, were tried and sentenced to death by secret court martial. The first the public heard was when it was announced that Pearse, MacDonagh and Clarke had been shot on May 3; on May 4, Joseph Plunkett, Edward Daly, Willie Pearse, Padraic's younger brother, and Michael O'Hanrahan, MacDonagh's second-in-command, were shot. On May 5, Major John MacBride was executed and the same day the death sentence on Countess Markievicz was commuted to life imprisonment. On May 8, Eamonn Ceannt, Michael Mallin, Sean Heuston and Con Colbert were shot, while nineteen other death sentences were commuted. On May 9, Tómas Ceannt was executed in Cork for his part in a skirmish there. On May 11 the death sentence on de Valera was commuted. Murphy, the leader of the employers in the Dublin lockout, supported the authorities in his newspapers. With twelve executions already taken place, on May 10 the *Irish Independent* carried a photograph of Connolly and added, significantly, "let the worst of the ringleaders be singled out and dealt with as they deserve." His attitude was echoed by the *Irish Catholic* which, on May 29, described the rising as criminal and insane :

> Pearse was a man of ill balanced mind, if not actually insane . . . selecting him as "chief magistrate" was enough to create serious doubt of the sanity of those who approved . . . crazy and insolent schoolmaster . . . extraordinary combination of rogues and fools.
>
> What was attempted was an act of brigandage pure and simple . . . no reason to lament that its perpetrators have met the fate universally reserved for traitors.

But the blood sacrifice idea was beginning to work with a vengeance. People who had been apathetic or even hostile to the Volunteers and the Citizen Army were shocked, horrified and angered by the executions. The slow deliberateness with which they were carried out, designed to subdue potential rebels, had the opposite effect. Even Irishmen fighting in the British Army in France were reported to be angry at the news from home. The *Manchester Guardian* saw the executions "becoming an atrocity". Even Edward Carson joined in; probably he realised the effect that government's policy was having in Ireland. The Irish Fabian-Socialist George Bernard Shaw wrote :

My own view is that the men who were shot in cold blood, after their capture or surrender, were prisoners of war, and that it was, therefore, entirely incorrect to slaughter them. The relation of Ireland to Dublin Castle is, in this respect, precisely that of the Balkan States to Turkey, or Belgium or the City of Lille to the Kaiser, and of the United States to Great Britain.

Until Dublin Castle is superseded by a National Parliament and Ireland voluntarily incorporated with the British Empire as Canada, Australasia and South Africa have been incorporated, an Irishman resorting to arms to achieve independence of his country is doing only what Englishmen will do, if it be their misfortune to be invaded and conquered by the Germans in the course of the present war. Further, such an Irishman is as much in order morally in accepting assistance from the Germans in his struggle with England, as England is in accepting assistance of Russia in her struggle with Germany. The fact that he knows that his enemies will not respect his rights if they catch him, and that he must, therefore, fight with a rope around his neck, increases his risk, but adds in the same measure to his glory in the eyes of his compatriots and of the disinterested admirers of patriotism throughout the world. It is absolutely impossible to slaughter a man in this position without making him a martyr and a hero, even though the day before the rising he may have been only a minor poet. The shot Irishmen will now take their place beside Emmet and the Manchester Martyrs in Ireland, and beside the heroes of Poland and Serbia and Belgium in Europe; and nothing in Heaven or earth can prevent it . . .

. . . I am bound to contradict any implication that I can regard as a traitor any Irishman taken in a fight for Irish independence against the British Government which was a fair fight in everything except the enormous odds my countrymen had to face.[20]

On May 12 Seán MacDiarmada and James Connolly were shot. These executions, more than the others, set the course the Irish people were to take in the next few years. Connolly had been wounded twice in the leg and was very ill, suffering from infection. On the morning of May 12 he was taken from his bed, placed on a stretcher, carried to the place of execution, tied to a chair and shot. The manner of his death created a wave of revulsion that swept Ireland. It is ironic that the English Socialist Arthur Henderson was a member of the War Cabinet but apparently made no attempt to save his fellow Socialist's life. Perhaps the administration realised the swing in public opinion for all other sentences were now commuted except one. Roger Casement, the IRB envoy to Germany, was hanged in London on August 5. In all some 3,149 men and 72 women had been taken prisoner by the authorities. Of this number 1,104 men and most of the women were released. Some 160 had been convicted by court martial and those who were not executed were sentenced to penal servitude for life, while 27 more had been acquitted. Of the rest, 1,862 men and 5 women were deported to England and confined in special prison camps.

Connolly, just before his execution, remarked : "The Socialists will never understand why I am here." Indeed, the Glasgow *Forward* was extremely perplexed. "A man must either be a nationalist or an internationalist," it observed. In the *Socialist Review* of September, 1916, the journal of the Independent Labour Party, an editorial article stated : "In no degree do we approve of the *Sinn Féin* rebellion. We do not approve of armed rebellion at all, any more than any other form of militarism and war." Lenin commented : "Is there any need to show that these 'anti-militarists', such supporters of disarmament in a country which is a great, and not a small, power, are the worst opportunists?" Ben Tillet, who had publicly wished he was young enough to answer the call to arms to maintain his country's empire, still expressed the jingoistic imperial ideas. He told the British TUC at Derby in 1918 :

We are hoping that, instead of *Sinn Féin* or anything else trying to separate the working classes of Ireland from this country,

the workers of Ireland will try to realise that they are in the same
bondage as ourselves, and that the better wages and conditions
they enjoy today are due to the work of the Trade Unionists in
this country, and that the employers and farmers in Ireland are
even more rapacious than our own employers.

Nevertheless, while Socialists made genuflections to the
memory of Connolly, they neither knew nor understood his
reasons for taking part in the rising, despite his previous teachings. Even Trotsky "wrote off" the real forces behind the 1916
uprising by stating :

> So far as purely military operations against the rebels were
> concerned, the Government emerged as master of the situation
> with comparative ease. An All-Ireland movement such as the
> nationalist dreamers had expected simply failed to materialise.
> The Irish countryside did not stir. The Irish bourgeoisie, and
> likewise the higher and more influential stratum of the Irish intel-
> ligentsia, held aloof. There fought and died only the workers of
> Dublin, together with some revolutionary enthusiasts from the
> petty bourgeois intelligentsia. The basis for a national revolution
> has disappeared even in backward Ireland . . . The young Irish
> working class, coming into existence as it did in an atmosphere
> saturated with the heroic traditions of national revolt and clash-
> ing with the egotistically limited and imperially arrogant union-
> ism of Britain, had naturally wavered between syndicalism and
> nationalism, and is always ready to link these two conceptions
> together in its revolutionary consciousness. It has attracted to
> itself the young intelligentsia and some nationalist enthusiasts,
> who in their turn have ensured the preponderance, in the work-
> ing class movement, of the Green Flag over the Red. Thus
> the "national revolution" in Ireland too has amounted, in prac-
> tice, to a revolt of the workers, and Casement's clearly isolated
> position in the movement merely emphasises this fact more
> sharply . . . The experiment of an Irish national rebellion, in
> which Casement, with undoubted personal courage, represented
> obsolete hopes and out-dated methods, is over. But the historical
> role of the Irish proletariat is only beginning. Already it has
> brought into this revolt, even though under an archaic flag, its
> class indignation against militarism and imperialism. This indig-
> nation will not now subside.[21]

Only Lenin seemed to realise the full significance of the Irish
uprising. An article appeared in *Berner Tagwacht* on May 9,

1916, describing the uprising as nothing more than a "putsch".
A. Kulisher in *Rech*, No. 102, also dubbed the uprising as "the
Dublin putsch". Lenin described this attitude as "monstrously
doctrinaire and pedantic."

The term "putsch" in the scientific sense of the word, may be
employed only when the attempt at insurrection has revealed
nothing but a circle of conspirators or stupid maniacs, and has
aroused no sympathy among the masses. The centuries-old Irish
national movement, having passed through various stages and
combinations of class interests, expressed itself, incidentally in a
mass Irish National Congress in America (*Vorwarts,* March 20,
1916) which called for independence—it expressed itself in street
fighting conducted by a section of the urban petty bourgeoisie
and a section of the workers after a long period of mass agitation,
demonstrations, suppressions of the press etc. Whoever calls such
an uprising a "putsch" is either a hardened reactionary, or a doctrinaire hopelessly incapable of picturing a social revolution as a
living thing.

For to imagine that social revolution is conceivable without
revolts by small nations in the colonies and in Europe without the
revolutionary outbursts of a section of the petty bourgeoisie with
all its prejudices, without a movement of politically non-
conscious proletarian and semi-proletarian masses against landlord, church, monarchical, national and other oppressions—to
imagine that means repudiating social revolution. Very likely one
army will line up in one place and say "we are for Socialism"
while another will do so in another place and say "we are for
imperialism" and that will be the social revolution. Only from
such a ridiculously pedantic angle could one label the Irish rebellion a "putsch".

Whoever expects a "pure" social revolution will never live to
see it. Such a person pays lip service to revolution without under-
standing what revolution really is.

Lenin goes on to say :

... The struggle of the oppressed nations of Europe, a struggle
capable of going to the length of insurrection and street fighting,
of breaking down the iron discipline in the army and martial law,
will sharpen the revolutionary crisis in Europe more than a much
more developed rebellion in a remote colony. A blow delivered
against the British imperialist bourgeois rule by a rebellion in

Ireland is of a hundred times greater political significance than a blow of equal weight in Asia or Africa.

However, Lenin felt:

... The misfortune of the Irish is that they have risen prematurely when the European revolt of the proletariat has not yet matured. Capitalism is not so harmoniously built that the various springs of rebellion can of themselves merge at one effort without reverses and defeats.[22]

In America, Larkin expressed his disappointment that he had not been in Ireland to take part in the rising: "Though fate denied some of us the opportunity of striking a blow for human freedom, we live in hope that we, too, will be given the opportunity."[23]

The 1916 Republic was a "Peoples' Republic": the declaration of the republic guaranteed national independence, equal rights and opportunities to all citizens, religious and civil liberties, the right of the Irish people to the ownership of Ireland and universal suffrage for all citizens, men and women. It has been pointed out that many capitalist republics claim such motivations. The Irish Communist Organisation comments:

But the claim of the 1916 Republic to represent the whole people was something more than a capitalist hypocrisy or a confused use of words. What made it more than that was the presence of Connolly in the leadership of the Republic, and the fact that the armed and class conscious workers were the backbone of the army of the Republic. Connolly and the Citizen Army realised that they were in alliance with property owning classes whose long term interests were different from theirs. They knew that when they spoke of "freedom" these classes did not have the same thing in mind as the working class. For property owners, "freedom" can only mean an increase in private property or a strengthening of the political representation of property. For the workers "freedom" means abolishing private property, and ending the political representation of property. Connolly and the Citizen Army knew this, and knew that, if the Empire was defeated or withdrew, they would probably find themselves in opposition within the Republic to their middle class allies of Easter Monday. They knew this, and they knew that by playing a leading part in the struggle for the independent People's Republic they were gaining a very advantageous position from which to resist the effects of their temporary allies to establish the exclusive rule of the bourgeoisie if independence were won, and from which to wage a struggle for full freedom of the working classes by establishing a Socialist republic.

It is this peculiar disposition of class forces—a strong, organised, armed and class conscious working class joined in alliance with the nationalist property owners against imperialism and in support of the Republic, and represented in the leadership of the movement by a Marxist theorist and organiser—which makes it correct to call the 1916 Republic a People's Republic, and justified its claim to be "representative of the whole people of Ireland".[24]

It must also be remembered that Pearse, MacDonagh, Ceannt and Clarke were to the left of the Volunteer movement, Pearse challenging the concept of private property and accepting many of Connolly's teachings. In the civil provisional government, not brought into force during the rising, was O'Brien, then a Marxist follower of Connolly, Tom Kelly and Mrs. Sheehy-Skeffington, both Socialists. With such representation of the left it would seem that, had 1916 achieved success, a social-democratic system of government would have been the first step in an independent Ireland.

The Irish Labour Movement suffered a hammer blow with the death of Connolly. The military swooped down on the ITGWU, arresting and deporting such officials as P. T. Daly. Thomas Johnson and David Campbell, who had in no way been connected with the rising, disassociating the Labour Movement as a whole from any responsibility, demanded the immediate trial or release of the imprisoned trade unionists and the return of all books and paper seized by the military. From August 7 to August 9 the Irish TUC met in Sligo, chaired by Johnson as head of the national executive.

As a Trade Union Movement we are of varied mind on matters of history and political development, and, consequently, this is not a place to enter into a discussion as to the right or wrong, the wisdom or the folly, of the revolt, but this we may say, that those amongst the rebels who had been associated with us in the past, who have led and inspired some of us with their love of their country and their class, were led to act as they did with no

selfish thought but purely with a passion for freedom and a
hatred of oppression.[25]

The Irish TUC then stood in silent tribute to Irishmen killed
in the rising and in the European war. It was pointed out that
only half of the members of the Citizen Army were, in fact,
members of the ITGWU and this seeming attempt to repudiate
the Citizen Army brought forth strong criticism from a delegate.
Clarkson states :

> Looking at these 1916 Congress proceedings we are compelled
> to the conclusion that Connolly's own view of the role of the
> Citizen Army as the workers' fighting force, received no endorse-
> ment from the Irish Trade Union Congress. Partly this was due
> no doubt, to the feeling that the time was not opportune for any
> defiant declaration. But it must also be remembered that, even in
> Connolly's time, there was strong opposition to the Citizen Army
> using the hall (Liberty Hall) and to the association of the army
> with union activities.[26]

O'Connor Lysaght remarks :

> In this period was being determined the social nature of the
> whole independence struggle. The ITUC (and Labour Party) had
> as a whole failed to understand Connolly's Republicanism. At its
> Sligo Congress in August, 1916, with the Belfast co-operatives'
> organiser, Thomas Johnson, in the chair, it stood in memory both
> of Republicans killed in Dublin and of Volunteers killed in
> France.
> More significant was the ITGWU's withdrawal from the
> national struggle and the simultaneous weakening of the ICA.
> This severed organised Labour's only formal link with the
> Republicans. It also severed the Republicans from much existing
> Irish Socialist thought.
> The ITGWU withdrew from Republicanism for what seemed
> sound ideological reasons. Connolly's successor as acting secre-
> tary, William O'Brien, was a disciple of his teachings. For
> O'Brien syndicalism meant building up a working class organi-
> sation till it could replace the bourgeois state; Republicanism
> meant letting the national issue be clarified so that it would not
> interfere with the establishment of Socialism ... it did mean, in
> the hands of an organisation man such as O'Brien, leaving the
> national struggle to the bourgeois nationalists, as being something
> in which an international Socialist had no interest. The

imaginative activism with which Connolly transcended this ideology was forgotten.[27]

In December, 1916, David Lloyd George became Prime Minister and displayed his "liberalism" by releasing all the interned Irish prisoners, with the exception of those sentenced leaders such as de Valera etc. The IRB Supreme Council was re-constituted and the Volunteers began reorganising and training in secret. On the Supreme Council was Michael Collins who had fought in the GPO as Plunkett's ADC. Collins, writing to his friend Kevin O'Brien, from Frongoch internment camp on October 6, 1916, had said :

...of Pearse and Connolly I admire the latter the most. Connolly was a realist. Pearse the direct opposite. There was an air of earthy directness about Connolly. It impressed me. I would have followed him through hell had such action been necessary.

Collins now became the Director of Organisation for the Volunteers. Griffith, who had been interned, now found himself with the undeserved reputation as "the ideologist of Easter Week". Redmond's remarks about the "*Sinn Féin* Volunteers" had stuck in the minds of the people and 1916 became known as the "*Sinn Féin* Rebellion" despite the fact Griffith had played no part in the rising and condemned it. A good opportunist, however, he seized his new-found glory to push himself and his bourgeois policies forward.

A front organisation, National Aid Association (for participants and dependants who suffered in the rising) was formed by the IRB and *Sinn Féin*. At a Roscommon by-election in February, 1917, the papal count, George Plunkett, father of the executed Joseph, won a seat for the movement and undertook Griffith's abstentionist policy. Immediately the authorities panicked and a number of leaders of national organisations were arrested. Lloyd George offered to implement immediate Home Rule but only for "that part of Ireland that clearly demands it ..." Carson's Ulster would be excluded. On May 6, Joseph McGuiness, a republican prisoner in England, was elected in South Longford. In desperation Lloyd George announced the establishment of a Convention to consider "the Irish question";

the Irish Labour Movement, *Sinn Féin* and other national bodies ignored the Convention and even the London *Times* commented it consisted of "hand picked" government men. A number of Irish Nationalist Party members, with Unionists and Liberals, sat on the Convention for eight months but achieved nothing. On June 17 the remaining one hundred or so republican prisoners, led by Eamonn de Valera, the only surviving senior commandant of the Dublin insurgent forces, arrived in Ireland to a tremendous reception.

On July 11 de Valera was elected for East Clare in another by-election. the people of Ireland were being called upon to democratically re-affirm the Republic of 1916. On October 25, 1917, the *Ard-fheis* of Griffith's *Sinn Féin* took place. Griffith himself was against reaffirming the republic and, indeed, the action of men he had already condemned. He still placed his faith in his dual-monarchy and tried to use the new-found strength of *Sinn Féin* to this end. However, he was forced to concede a new constitution that "*Sinn Féin* aims at securing the international recognition of Ireland as an independent Irish Republic." Griffith then stood down as president of *Sinn Féin* to allow de Valera to be unanimously elected president of the reorganised party. The Irish Volunteers remained independent of *Sinn Féin* but at their *Ard-fheis* on October 27 de Valera was elected president of the Volunteers. The Citizen Army had now reorganised itself with James O'Neill as Commandant.

Throughout 1918 the Volunteers and Citizen Army grew in strength, trained and armed in secret. Attempts to crush them by military drove more and more Irishmen into their ranks. With the threat of conscription hanging over Ireland once more, an All Ireland Labour Committee met at Mansion House on April 20 and it was agreed that a strike be held. On April 25 the working classes, with the exception of the Belfast area, gave a magnificent display of solidarity and the government withdrew any threats of conscription. Clarkson comments:

> Irish Labour, which under Connolly's guidance set a stiff pace for the European Labour Movement, which had been the first to form a Red Guard, was to be the first to carry out, in the midst of war, a general strike against the more vigorous prosecution of that war.

On November 11, 1918, the European war ended and on November 25 parliament was dissolved. The Irish Labour Party announced that it would participate in the election but, in the *Voice of Labour* they announced their withdrawal:

> ...the National Executive has reviewed the position, and has decided to recommend the withdrawal from the election of all labour candidates. They do so in the hope that the democratic demand for self determination, to which the Irish Labour Party and its candidates gives its unqualified adherence, will thereby obtain the greatest chance of expression at the polls. We shall show by this action that while each of the other political parties is prepared to divide the people in their efforts to obtain power, the Irish Labour Party is the only party which is prepared to sacrifice party interests in the interests of the nation in this important crisis in the history of the nation.

Redmond had died some months before and the Irish Nationalist Party was led by John Dillon who declared his intention to fight *Sinn Féin*. *Sinn Féin*'s policy was, if a majority of candidates were elected, to establish their own parliament and re-affirm the Irish Republic. Viewing the situation from the U.S.A. Larkin was worried. He wrote to Thomas Foran of the ITGWU:

> The *Sinn Féin* movement here is anti-Labour and as for the Socialists they think they are anti-Christs. They have tried to impress the American public that the Revolution was a Catholic revolution, in fact they have done the cause incalculable harm. They are the most violent American jingoes always boasting how loyal they are too and how many Irish have fought and died for this Free Republic. Moryah! They make me sick to the soul. They held a meeting in Chicago sometime back and they spent 2,600 dollars on the meeting, 1,700 dollars to erect a special star spangled flag, electrically arrayed which flashed all thru the meeting. They are in a word super fine patriots and the most consummate tricksters of politicians. This applies to all of them without exception and the crowd that have lately come over are no better.[28]

Nora Connolly, eldest daughter of James, and Mrs. Sheehy-

Skeffington were among those who went to the U.S.A. to raise funds for *Sinn Féin*. Larkin commented:

I must call attention to the fact that Mrs. S. is just an apologist for the *Sinn Féin* crowd. She never speaks of the Labour movement nor of the Socialist Party. She leaves the impression that Skeffy (Francis Sheehy-Skeffington) and herself were members of the *Sinn Féin* movement. Nora C. follows the same lines ... they make out that Arthur G (Griffith) is a God-given saint and statesman; that nobody in Ireland did anything but *Sinn Féin*. Connolly and the other boys all recanted Socialism and Labour, and were good *Sinn Féiners*. My God, it is sickening.

Larkin grew increasingly angry when he saw that the Irish Labour movement were ignoring the chance that Connolly had given them to lead the national struggle. "What are O'Brien and the rest doing in allowing the Griffith gang to monopolise all the credit for the effort?" he wrote to Foran in the spring of 1918. "I wish O'Brien and the others would declare themselves. Are they all turned *Sinn Féin*...? Have our section any representatives on the alleged Provisional Government?" Late in 1918, Larkin was pressing the Irish Labour Movement:

Don't be led astray by the ephemeral political movements of a moment. Our work is fundamental. Not only do we want an independent Ireland, but we demand a free Ireland of free men and women. I realise the tortuous paths you and your colleagues must walk. Certain forces in Eire seem to have exploited the struggle for their own ends. Don't be in any way deterred; hew straight to the line, let the chips fall where they may. Be assured we are on the side that must ultimately prevail. Leaders, moryah! and parties rise up and pass away in a night but men live on forever and principles are permanent.

Larkin's activities among the Irish American Socialists drew support for Ireland and a James Connolly Socialist Club was formed in New York. This became the centre of left wing activities among Irish Socialists in the city. Larkin's other activities kept him busy travelling not only in the U.S.A. but to Mexico. Emmet Larkin commented:

Soon after his return from Mexico, then, Larkin sized up the situation among the Irish at home and abroad and decided where he stood. The American Irish must be converted to the movement and the movement in Ireland must not allow itself to be swamped by bourgeois Nationalists.[29]

But the following year Larkin was arrested and sentenced to ten years' imprisonment while in Ireland *Sinn Féin* won a devastating victory at the polls.

Chapter 13

THE NATIONAL STRUGGLE

THE VICTORY OF *Sinn Féin* in the 1918 general election
was overwhelming. Out of 105 seats, *Sinn Féin* won 73 of them
while the Irish Nationalist Party, formerly with 80 seats, won
only 6 seats—they also gained a seat in a Liverpool constituency
making their total 7—and the Unionist Party won 26 seats.
Five of the Irish Nationalists' seats were won in Antrim, Derry,
Down and Armagh—the other 5 Ulster counties returned a
Republican and Nationalist majority, i.e. Tyrone, Fermanagh,
Donegal, Cavan and Monaghan. One of the interesting side-
lights of this election was the fact that Countess Markievicz
became the first woman to be elected to parliament in a United
Kingdom election. The Irish people, therefore, in accordance
with the *Sinn Féin* manifesto had given a clear mandate for the
affirmation of the 1916 Republic ... an affirmation given by
over two-thirds of the people.

On January 21, 1919, at 3.30 p.m. those *Sinn Féin* members
who had been so elected gathered in the Mansion House,
Dublin, and established *Dáil Éireann* (the Irish parliament).
Only thirty *Sinn Féin* deputies answered the roll call, as the
majority of names were read the answer *"Fé ghlas ag Gallaibh"*
(imprisoned by the foreigner) rang out. The Nationalists and
Unionists who had been invited to attend did not do so. Cathal
Brugha presided and a Declaration of Independence was read
out in Irish and English which ratified the 1916 proclamation.
An address to the Free Nations of the World was read in Irish,
French and English, appealing for recognition for the new
republic and aid to get a delegation accepted at the Paris Peace
Conference. Then a Democratic Programme was adopted by the
Dáil.

> We declare in the words of the Irish Republican procla-
> mation the right of the people of Ireland to the ownership of
> Ireland and to the unfettered control of Irish destinies to be

indefeasible; and in the language of our first President Padraic Pearse, we declare that the nation's sovereignty extends not only to all men and women of the nation, but to all its material possessions; the nation's soil and all its resources, all the wealth and all the wealth-producing processes within the nation; and with him we re-affirm that all rights in private property must be subordinate to the public right and welfare.

We declare that we desire our country to be ruled in accordance with the principles of Liberty, Equality, and Justice for all, which alone can secure permanance of governing in the willing adhesion of the people.

We affirm the duty of every man and woman to give allegiance and service to the commonwealth, and declare it as the duty of the nation to assure that every citizen shall have opportunity to spend his or her strength and faculties in the service of the people. In return for willing service, we, in the name of the Republic, declare the right of every citizen to an adequate share of the produce of the nation's labour.

It shall be the first duty of the government of the Republic to make provision for the physical, mental and spiritual well being of the children, to secure that no child shall suffer hunger or cold from lack of food or clothing or shelter, but that all shall be provided with the means and facilities for their proper educating and training as citizens of a free and Gaelic Ireland.

The Irish Republic fully realises the necessity of abolishing the present odious, degrading and foreign poor law system, substituting therefore a sympathetic native scheme for the care of the nation's aged and infirm, who shall no longer be regarded as a burden, but rather entitled to the nation's gratitude and consideration. Likewise it shall be the duty of the Republic to take measures that will safeguard the health of the people and ensure the physical as well as the moral well being of the nation.

It shall be our duty to promote the development of the nation's resources, to increase the productivity of the soil, to exploit its mineral deposits, peat bogs and fisheries, its waterways and harbours, in the interests and for the benefit of the Irish people.

It shall be the duty of the Republic to adopt all measures necessary for the recreation and invigoration of our industries, and to ensure their being developed on the most beneficial and progressive co-operative industrial lines. With the adoption of an extensive Irish consular service, trade with foreign nations shall be revived on terms of mutual advantage and good will; which undertaking the organisation of the nation's trade, import and export, it shall be the duty of the Republic to prevent shipment from Ireland of food and other necessities until the wants of the Irish people are fully satisfied and the future provided for.

It shall devolve upon the national government to seek co-operation of the government of other countries in determining a standard of social and industrial legislation with a view to general and lasting improvements in the conditions under which the working classes live and labour.

This radical document was drawn up by Seán T. Ó Ceallaigh with the advice of Thomas Johnson, secretary of the Labour Party, and William O'Brien, at the request of the *Dáil*.

On February 3, Johnson and Cathal O'Shannon attended the International Labour and Socialist conference at Berne, presenting the conference with a memorandum stating Ireland's case and receiving the support of the conference. The same day de Valera, who had been in Lincoln Gaol, England, escaped and went into hiding. When on March 6, Pierce McCann, a member of the *Dáil* died in Gloucester Gaol, the English government decided to release all Irish political prisoners. On April 1, back in Dublin, de Valera became *Priomh-Aire* (lit. First Minister or President) of the Republic. Seán T. Ó Ceallaigh became *Ceann Comhairle* (Speaker of the *Dáil*) and the government consisted of Arthur Griffith (Home Affairs); Cathal Brugha (Defence); G. N. Plunkett (Industries); Countess Markievicz (Labour); Michael Collins (Finance); Liam Cosgrave (Local Government) with L. Ginnell heading a department of propaganda and R. C. Barton a department of agriculture.

In April de Valera started to make overtures to the Irish workers and trade unions to ensure support for the republic. In fact, *Dáil Eireann* was unanimously recognised as the national government at the Irish TUC and Labour Party congress. On April 8, at the *Ard-fheis* of *Sinn Féin* de Valera commented :

When we wanted the help of Labour against conscription, Labour gave it to us. When we wanted the help of Labour in Berne, Labour gave it to us, and got Ireland recognised as a distinct nation. When we wanted Labour to stand down at the election and not divide us, but that we should stand foursquare

against one enemy, Labour fell in with us. I say Labour
deserves well of the Irish people; the Labour man deserves the
best the country can give.

Previously, at the 1917 *Ard-fheis,* de Valera had said :

Our Labour policy is a policy of the free country, and we ask
Labour to join with us to free the country. We recognise that we
can never free it without Labour. And we say, when Labour frees
this country—helps to free it—Labour can look for its share of
the patrimony.

In a free Ireland with the social conditions that obtained in
Ireland, Labour has a far better chance than it would have in a
capitalist England.

When de Valera went on a mission to the U.S.A. in June,
1919, he addressed a meeting on Connolly.

In the Labour world the Irish Patriot James Connolly . . . was
known as a Socialist. There was nothing inconsistent with his
economic idea to his life and fight and death as an Irish republican . . . His position is very much our position.

The leisured classes were sometimes seduced from their
national allegiance by a seat at the conqueror's table, but Irish
Labour ever stood true to its traditions and to its convictions.
When Irish patriots despaired of winning to its side—the side of
sacrifice—the people of property, they could always count on
that very respectable class, the people of no property, who had no
sacrifice to make but the supreme sacrifice of their lives . . .

The Irish worker, ever true to his Irish national ideals, had
declared himself unmistakably, and finds no clash between his
interests as an Irishman and his class interests as a worker.[1]

De Valera went on to make a Labour Day address in New
York :

It is obvious to everyone that if the privileged classes—the
International financiers and their confreres—can only succeed in
keeping the masses of one nation at the throats of another, they
will retatin the mastery they now possess, and that if the plain
people of the world are ever to be free themselves from their
present economic subjection, it can only be by the closest co-
operation between the working classes of different countries.

The phraseology of Socialism used by the national leaders won support for the Irish Republic . . . the first country to officially recognise the republic being the young Soviet Republic of Russia. O'Brien and Campbell saw the Soviet diplomat, M. M. Litvinov in London who promised Russia's full support for Ireland's claims. Litvinov added that Connolly's works were well known and admired by Lenin and Trotsky as well as among members of the Russian revolutionary movement. Only Arthur Griffith seemed to run true to form; he had not changed at all since those years when, through the pages of *Sinn Féin*, he bade labour repudiate Socialism and resume its rightful place as the humble servant of the nation—occasionally to be petted, perhaps, but never to speak until it was spoken to. The Second International, meeting in Amsterdam, placed its support behind Ireland, demanding :

. . . the principle of free and absolute self determination shall be applied immediately in the case of Ireland.

The International :

. . . affirms the right of the Irish people to political independence; requires that this self government shall rest upon a democratic decision, expressed by the free, equal, adult and secret vote of the people without any military, political or economic pressure from outside or any reservation or restriction imposed by any Government.

The Conference calls upon the Powers and the Peace Conference to make good this rightful claim of the Irish people.[2]

The Irish delegates were prevented from putting their case to the Peace Conference and England began to move to check events in Ireland. On September 11, 1919, *Dáil Éireann* was suppressed as an "illegal assembly" and warrants were sworn out for all members; likewise, all national movements in Ireland were banned. This was a declaration of war. The Irish Volunteers, for whom the *Dáil* had as yet accepted no responsibility, had been building up their strength in numbers and armaments by conducting a series of raids on barracks. The Volunteer policy had more or less presented the *Dáil* with a *fait accompli*. The majority of Irish believed that the situation would not develop into a war one. Before the suppression of the *Dáil* the republican government's policy was that of passive resistance with the hope that a settlement would be reached by Irish admittance to the Peace Conference. But with the rejection of a hearing the republican government realised a conflict was inevitable.

> We sincerely urge if the Peace Conference refuses a hearing to the people of Ireland, in these circumstances, the guilt for the commission of these monstrous crimes and atrocities as well as for the bloody revolution which may follow, must, from this time forward, be shared with Great Britain by the members of the Peace Conference, if not by the peoples which they represent.[3]

Already thousands of English troops were being poured into Ireland, with tanks, armoured cars, motor lorries and other weapons. The Royal Irish Constabulary maintained fortified barracks commanding each town and village; they numbered 9,682 men. The cost of maintaining the army in Ireland amounted to £13,000,000 per year. The running conflict between the Volunteers and the military throughout the early part of 1919 resulted in a number of clashes in which labour played a prominent part. On February 1, the Limerick Trade and Labour Council, representing thirty-five unions, protested at the treatment of political prisoners in Limerick Jail. A prominent member of this Council was Robert J. Byrnes, who was also adjutant of the 2nd Battalion of the Limerick Brigade of Volunteers. He was arrested by the military and went on hunger strike. He was removed to Limerick Union Hospital where the military, hearing that the Volunteers planned a rescue, shot him while he lay weak in bed. On Monday, April 4, a strike of all work was organised to "protest against military tyranny which, because of its dramatic suddenness, its completeness, and the proof it offered that workers' control signifies perfect order, excited world attention."[4] Strike money was printed with a list of food prices, and a citizens' *Bulletin*. Limerick was proclaimed a military area, tanks and armoured cars paraded the streets, everyone had to carry a permit. The strike continued, supported by the Irish Labour Party and Irish TUC who expressed their support at a special meeting on April 18.

Having come to the conclusion that England was not going to give up without a fight, Michael Collins, as Volunteer Director of Organisation and Intelligence, made the immediate object that of obtaining arms and ammunition. The Volunteers now became the army of the Irish Republic, the IRA. The Citizen Army also constituted part of this army and, at a meeting with Cathal Brugha and Collins, O'Neill, the ICA Commandant and Captain R. MacCormack, decided that both military groupings were to retain their separate identity. The Citizen Army organised itself into two battalions, one north of the River Liffey under Captain M. Kelly and one south, under MacCormack, covering the Dublin area.

A clash between IRA men of Cork No. 2 Brigade and the military in Fermoy on September 7 resulted in a soldier being killed. On the following day 200 English regulars descended on Fermoy in an orgy of destruction, sacking and looting shops and wantonly destroying everything they could lay their hands on. The gloves were off and the guerilla war started. Engagements began to take place throughout Ireland developing into a policy of terror and counter-terror.

Against the background of guerilla warfare the *Dáil* continued to carry on governmental work underground. Many wage disputes went to the Labour Department for arbitration. One wage dispute, that in the Rosary Bread factory, is typical of the times. Union members met the employer in a *Dáil* office and were warned that a military raid was expected at a stated hour and that agreement must be reached by then. Countess Markievicz, presiding as Minister for Labour, interrupted the proceedings to remark "twenty minutes", "fifteen minutes", "ten minutes". Finally, the employer lost his nerve, conceded the wage demand and fled.

In the *Dáil* itself Countess Markievicz and Alasdair MacCabe proposed :

That this Assembly pledges itself to a fair and full redistri-
bution of the vacant lands and ranches of Ireland among the
uneconomic holders and landless men.

That no purchase by private individuals of non-residential land
in the Congested Districts, or other land essential for carrying out
of any such scheme of land settlement as the *Dáil* may decide
upon, which has taken place since Easter Monday, 1916, be sanctioned now or subsequently by the Irish Republican Government.
That this resolution be taken as conveying a warning to those
who have recently availed themselves of the crisis in national

affairs to annex large tracts of land against the will and interests of the people.[5]

This radical resolution was withdrawn after discussion and a committee was appointed to consider land policy, consisting of P. Ó Máillíe, J. J. Clancy, Alasdair MacCabe, L. Ginnell, D. Ó Buachalla, P. Moloney, S. Etchingham, E. J. Duggan, J. MacGrath and J. A. Burke. A Land Arbitration Court was eventually established by the *Dáil* in May, 1920. It was flooded with pleas from large landowners, many of them Unionists, to arbitrate in land disputes. In Connaught and Co. Kerry small-holders and landless men seized large estates, mostly owned by absentee landlords, and these were divided up among the workers. The *Dáil* Land Arbitration Court leant over backwards to be "impartial" to Unionist landowners. The majority of their verdicts were for the restoration of land to the landlords and the IRA were sent to ensure the findings were put into practice by the people. It is significant that in areas where the IRA acted as such a counter-revolutionary force, carrying out this outward sign of the *Dáil's* collaboration with the privileged classes, the people were the least active in the national struggle. In such areas where the IRA actually collaborated with the people in the confiscation and division of the ranches and large estates, the people were behind the national struggle to a man. This was especially so in West Cork area. However, the report of the action taken by the *Dáil* Land Courts caused an increasing lack of enthusiasm for the Irish cause by international working-class movements.

Worried by the increasingly deteriorating situation, Premier Lloyd George introduced a Better Government of Ireland Bill in the House of Commons on December 22. It proposed two parliaments, one for the six north-eastern counties of Ulster and one for the other twenty-six counties, with powers to create a council of representatives of both parliaments which would be subservient to Westminster. In fact, it was the old Home Rule idea. Ireland ignored the Bill. Municipal and Urban elections were due in Ireland in January, 1920, and the English Government had introduced a proportional representation system of voting which it hoped, by giving increased representation to the pro-English faction, *Sinn Féin* would be destroyed. Lloyd George was in for a shock. On January 15 of the 206 councils elected

throughout Ireland, 172 fell to *Sinn Féin*. In the nine counties of
Ulster, twenty-three towns fell to *Sinn Féin* and only twenty-two
to the Unionists. The Unionists remained a majority in four
counties alone. The entire government of Ireland, from local to
national level was now in the hands of the republicans. From
January 20, the English policy of military suppression was
intensified.

The guerilla war began to build up and at the end of March,
General Sir Nevil Macready was appointed commander-in-chief
of the English forces in Ireland. At the same time a new force
was recruited in England which became known as the "Black
and Tans". They hold a place in Irish memory in much the same
way as the Nazi Gestapo has a place in European memory. On
April 12, the Irish TUC and Labour Party called a general strike
in support of political prisoners on hunger strike in Mountjoy
prison. They had been on hunger strike for ten days. With the
labour strike three days old the prisoners were all unconditionally
released.

In June that year elections for county councils, rural district
councils and boards of Poor Law Guardians took place. Of the
33 county councils (Tipperary had two), 29 fell to *Sinn Féin* and
only four fell to the Unionists; of the 206 rural district councils,
Sinn Féin won 172 while the Unionists won only 34. Of the 53
rural district councils in Ulster only 19 were controlled by
Unionists while 34 fell to *Sinn Féin*. The elections had shown
that "Unionist" Ulster was overwhelmingly for the Republic.
The northern capitalists began to panic and it was decided that a
series of pogroms should be carried out against Nationalists
(Catholics) in order to achieve a stronger position.

It is common knowledge in Belfast, and had frequently been
admitted by individual Unionists, that plans were matured at
least two months ago to drive all the Home Rule workers in the
shipyards out of their employment.[6]

On July 21 prominent Unionists addressed Protestant workers
in the Belfast shipyards and called for a "Holy War" to drive
out the "Catholic traitors". During the nights and days that followed, armed Orangemen carried out attacks on Catholic areas.
In five days some 200 were injured, seventeen were killed, and
thousands driven from their homes. Men were threatened with

death if they returned to work. The IRA were not strong
enough to aid the people and the military looked on and did
nothing.

The workers were also growing in militancy during this period. During the spring of 1920 some fifty workers struck work
at a creamery in Knocklong owned by Sir Thomas Cleeves, a
prominent Unionist. The creamery was a trading centre for all
the farms of the district and was a distributing centre for the
towns—one of the biggest in Ireland. The dispute was over a
question of wages. In May that year, the strikers, members of
the ITGWU, decided to seize control of the factory under the
slogan: "We make butter, not profits!" and carry on the work
in the factory and mill as the Knocklong Soviet Creamery. The
farmers continued to supply milk to the creamery which continued to process and distribute. In May of the following year
the Arigna coal mines in Co. Leitrim were also taken over by
the workers and a red flag hoisted; in September, the port of
Cork was taken over and run as a soviet; lands were seized by
workers and run as communes or soviets, especially around
Toorahara and Kilfenora, Co. Clare. Unlike their comrades in
the north and midlands, the Munster IRA did not interfere
with the confiscations of ranches and estates. In 1922 soviets
were established in Mallow, Cashel and Ballingarry. The
Labour Movement was highly embarrassed at the workers' radicalism, although Thomas Johnson, reporting to the Dublin
Trades Congress in 1921, said that the establishment of Irish
soviets was:

> ... the most important question that could be raised in the
> Labour Movement or in Social Economy... It is a challenge,
> and let us make no mistake about it, to the rights of property.
> It says: though you happen to have a parchment which allots
> to you the right to use or possess this machine or that particular
> factory, though you have that power under legal enactment,
> henceforth that is not enough. We, as responsible to the workers,
> say these material things shall be continued in use so long as the
> community requires the product. That is the issue raised and it
> is a contention that the Labour Party in Ireland, I hope, will
> continue to espouse and put into operation.

But Labour declined to accept responsibility for the soviets.
The Limerick and Tipperary soviets were destroyed by a boy-

cott of the Irish Farmers' Union, a group of big ranch owners and farmers, while in Clare the soviets were reduced by farmers' units under military directions. The Knocklong Soviet Creamery was destroyed by English troops on August 22 as part of a systematic attack on Irish industrial life and especially co-operative creameries, mills and bacon factories. By April, 1921, English troops had destroyed sixty-one co-operative creameries alone. George Russell, the co-operatist, writing in *Irish Homestead* commented:

In these attacks, creameries and mills have been burned to the ground, their machinery wrecked; agricultural stores have also been burned, property looted, employees have been killed, wounded, beaten, threatened or otherwise ill treated. Why have these economic organisations been specially attacked? Because they have hundreds of members, and if barracks have been burned or police have been killed or wounded in the lamentable strife now being waged in Ireland, and if the armed forces of the Crown cannot capture those guilty of the offences, the policy of reprisals, condoned by the spokesmen of the Government, has led to the wrecking of any enterprise in the neighbourhood, the destruction of which would inflict widespread injury and hurt the interests of the greatest number of people. I say this has been done without regard to the innocence or guilt of the persons whose property is attacked.[7]

The guerilla war continued in increasing ruthlessness. The Citizen Army was prominent in this war. A workers' army, they could rise out of the general body of labour, make swift attacks on vital supplies and installations, and sink back again immediately. As many members of the Citizen Army were dockers, they managed to smuggle arms and ammunition from ships which were destined to supply English troops or for shipment to the U.S.A. One such spectacular coup was achieved when the USS *Defiance* was transporting war munitions back to the States. Citizen Army dockers managed to unload numbers of weapons and quantities of ammunition undetected.

In May, 1920, the ITGWU declared a strike against English military occupation. Macardle writes:

When armed soldiers or Black and Tans boarded a train, the engine driver would refuse to start. By May 22, railwaymen as well as dockers were refusing to handle munitions of war. The strikers were supported by a fund voluntarily subscribed, amounting to a sum of over one hundred and sixteen thousand pounds. Their resistance lasted until the end of the year.[8]

By August, 1920, 1,500 men had been dismissed for so striking. The strike found an ironic parallel in England. The national executive of the National Union of Railwaymen ordered their members to refuse to handle war material intended to aid Poland in her war with Russia. However, it was deemed perfectly in order for English dockers to handle munitions going to Ireland to suppress the Irish people.

In north-east Ulster the pogroms against the Catholics continued. By August 20 that year not a single Catholic out of the 5,000 previously employed in the Belfast shipyards, remained. The death roll was also mounting as men, women and children were attacked, killed or driven southward by frenzied Orange mobs, encouraged with the full propaganda energies of the northern capitalists. The *Daily Mail* commented:

> It seems to me the most outrageous thing which they have ever done in Ireland ... A citizen of Belfast who is "well disposed" to the British government is almost, from the nature of the case, an Orangeman, or, at any rate, a vehement anti-*Sinn Féiner*. These are the very people who have been looting Catholic shops and driving thousands of Catholic women and children from their homes.[9]

The guerilla war's ferocity continued unabated. Villages, such as Balbriggan, were burnt down to try to subdue the republican forces. Even the city of Cork suffered a similar fate at the hands of English troops. On October 25, the *Sinn Féin* Lord Mayor of Cork, Terence MacSwiney—a teacher, poet, dramatist and scholar—died on the seventy-fourth day of a hunger strike while in Brixton Prison, London. A young Vietnamese dishwasher in the Carlton Hotel, London, broke down and cried when he heard the news. "A nation which has such citizens will never surrender." His name was Nguyen Ai Quoc who, in 1941, adopted the name of Ho Chi Minh and took the lessons of the Irish anti-imperialist fight to his own country.[10]

The English Labour Party was now beginning to demand that the Government enter into negotiations with the *Dáil*. On

November 16 the Irish TUC and Labour Party held a National
Conference in Dublin which was attended by a thousand Irish
delegates and declared that it was ready to aid English Labour in
promoting this policy. A Commission of Inquiry was held by
English Labour M.P.s which reported to the Government that
"there did not appear to be any grounds for the belief heard in
certain quarters that *Sinn Féin* was almost ready to surrender
unconditionally."

Lloyd George's Better Government of Ireland Act came into
force on May 3 and it was announced that election of members
to sit on the twenty-six-county parliament would take place on
May 19 while those for the north-east Six Counties' parliament
would be held on May 24. The system of Proportional
Representation had been introduced for the whole of Ireland.
The entire twenty-six counties returned *Sinn Féin* members
unopposed. The republican government announced that it
regarded this election as for the second *Dáil*. In the Six Counties,
Orange mobs and police were employed to openly wreck the
election organisation of *Sinn Féin*, and Catholics who ventured to
the polls were assaulted and beaten up. Of the 52 seats for the
Six Counties' parliament, the Unionists won 40 and the
Nationalists and Republicans won 12. The latter deputies recognised only the *Dáil* in Dublin. On June 15, speaking in
Portmadoc, Lloyd George was forced to admit :

> Two thirds of the population of Ireland demand the setting up
> of an independent Republic in that Ireland. At a recent election
> they re-affirmed that demand. Every effort I have made, publicly
> and otherwise, to secure a modification of that demand has
> failed. They have emphatically stated they will agree to nothing
> else.[11]

In Scotland, the Scottish Socialist leader, John MacLean, was
leading a campaign for a settlement with Ireland. He published
a pamphlet called *The Irish Tragedy—Scotland's Disgrace*.
MacLean had been a friend of Connolly and of Larkin and, like
Connolly, he had stood back from the imperialist holocaust of
the 1914-18 war and was jailed several times for his statements
against the war. MacLean regarded the Irish struggle for
independence as part of the struggle for world Socialism, as
Marx had done fifty years before. He called upon English,

Scottish and Welsh workers to organise a general strike for the withdrawal of troops from Ireland and, in particular, castigated the Scots for allowing Scottish regiments to be used in Ireland. In August, 1920, he published a manifesto entitled *All Hail, the Scottish Worker's Republic!* He was then standing for election in the Gorbals division of Glasgow. He asked "Are we Scots to be used as the bloody tools of the English against our brother Celts of Erin?" Arguing Scotland's case for independence, MacLean said:

> Scotland must again have independence, but not to be ruled by traitor kings and chiefs, lawyers and politicians. The communism of the clans must be re-established on a modern basis. (Bolshevism, to put it roughly, is but the modern expression of the communism of the Mir.) Scotland must therefore work itself into a communism embracing the whole country as a unit. The country must have but one clan, as it were, a united people working in co-operation and co-operatively, using the wealth that is created.
>
> We can safely say, then : Back to Communism and Forward to Communism.

MacLean pointed out :

> Many Irishmen live in Scotland, and, as they are Celts like the Scots, and are out for Irish independence, and as wage-earners have been champion fighters for working class rights, we expect them to ally themselves with us and help us to attain our Scottish Communist Republic, as long as they live in Scotland. Irishmen must remember that Communism prevailed amongst the Irish clans as amongst the Scottish clans, so that, in lining up with Scotsmen, they are but carrying forward the traditions and instincts of the Celtic race.

There was certainly a lot of Celtic co-operation between the Scots and Irish, a co-operation that dated back over a thousand years. Seamus Reader formed a Scottish Brigade of the IRA and a number of Scots, such as Ian Mackenzie Kennedy, fell fighting with the IRA. MacLean went on to establish a Scottish Workers' Republican Party, to fight for the Workers' Republic in Scotland. He died on November 23, 1923, mainly due to the suffering he endured in prison.

On June 24, 1921, Lloyd George opened negotiations with de Valera for a peace settlement. On July 14 a truce was declared between the IRA and English military. In Belfast, however, there was no truce. Orange mobs and newly formed "special police" burnt down 161 Catholic homes, killed fifteen persons and injured sixty-eight. The American White Cross found thousands of Catholic families sheltering in stables and sheds. Initial negotiations showed that England was prepared to give the twenty-six counties dominion status within the British Commonwealth, but partition would remain. Following a bout of negotiations with de Valera, Lloyd George remarked that negotiating with him was "like trying to pick up mercury with a fork". De Valera replied: "Why doesn't he try a spoon?" Eventually a delegation to a peace conference was organised, led by Collins and Griffiths. The conference opened in London on October 11, 1921. Cathal O'Shannon, the vice-president of the Irish Labour Party, announced that the Irish workers were fully behind the bid for recognition of the republic by England.

> *Sinn Féin* cannot compromise. If liberty is not complete liberty it is not liberty at all, and besides the *Dáil* has been specially returned to defend the Republican ideal.[12]

On December 6 at 2.15 p.m. a document known as the Articles of Agreement was signed by the Irish delegation, but without authority from the *Dáil*. It gave twenty-six counties of Ireland dominion status within the British Commonwealth in the form of a Free State (*Saorstát Éireann*) while the six north-eastern counties of Ulster were to remain partitioned and part of the United Kingdom. The agreement had been signed under threat of "an immediate and terrible war" against the Irish people. For the monarchist Griffith the agreement, apart from the partition, was exactly what he wanted all along and he had been the first to succumb to Lloyd George's blustering. For Collins it was merely a stepping stone to a republic. The agreement was brought back to the *Dáil* for ratification and a split began to emerge. Many supported the action of Griffith and Collins while others supported de Valera. Liam Mellowes commented: "That is not the will of the people; that is the fear of the people." He believed that if Ireland rejected the Treaty world opinion would prevent them from renewing the war. Countess Markievicz also held out for the republic.

> ... looking as I do for the prosperity of the many, for the happiness and contentment of the workers, for what I stand, James Connolly's ideal of a Workers' Republic (a deputy—a Soviet Republic !)—a co-operative commonwealth !—these men are to be set up to uphold English interests in Ireland, to uphold the capitalists' interests in Ireland, to block every ideal that the nation may wish to formulate ... My ideal is the Workers' Republic for which Connolly died. And I say this is one of the things that England wishes to prevent. She would sooner give us Home Rule than a democratic republic. It is the capitalist interest in England and Ireland that are pushing this treaty to block the march of the working people in Ireland and England.

On January 7, 64 members of the *Dáil* voted in favour of the Treaty while 57 demanded its rejection and the maintenance of the republic. On January 9 de Valera resigned as president and Griffith was elected by a majority of two votes. The English now began their evacuation of the twenty-six counties but the IRA was beginning to split into Pro-Treaty and Anti-Treaty camps. De Valera's fifty-seven Anti-Treaty deputies now formed a new political group called *Cumann na Poblachta* (Republic Party). Labour decided to launch itself into the political scene :

> With the vote in *Dáil Éireann* approving the treaty between Ireland and England, one more chapter of the still uncompleted story of Ireland's struggle for national freedom has been closed. Tomorrow the struggle for the freedom of Ireland's men and women begins anew. Whatever may be the immediate outcome of the vote of the National Assembly, responsibility for the government of Ireland will rest in future on the Irish people alone.
>
> Henceforward the struggle which you, the workers, must perforce engage in shall be plainly and openly a struggle against capitalism. During the period of crisis in the nation's life we have subordinated our claims and demands to the need for national solidarity.

The Labour Party would now

> ... avail of the machinery of whatever political instruments may be fashioned in pursuance of our objective ... The hour has now

struck for the workers to emerge from the shade ... our opponents are the employers.[13]

By March, 1922, the IRA's nineteen army divisions had split
into eleven divisions for the republic and eight for the *Saorstát*.
The republican groupings formed themselves as an autonomous
body "to maintain the existing Republic." The Citizen Army
Commandant, O'Neill, resigned and the former quartermaster of
the army, J. Hanratty, was elected Commandant and declared
for the republic.

Although the Citizen Army had no part in the negotiations it
was clear at a very early stage that the Treaty would not satisfy
its claim ... the Citizen Army fell back on the Proclamation of the
Republic made in 1916, signed by their leader, along with other
signatories. This document, with its generous democratic spirit,
served as a general statement of aims in the absence of incisive
criticism of the Treaty from their own special standpoint.[14]

Civil war was imminent and clashes were already taking place
between *Saorstát* and Republican supporters. The Irish Labour
Party, at a conference in the Mansion House, in April, tried to
reunite the two sides. It is agreed:

1. That all the legislative, executive and judicial authority is
and shall be derived solely from the Irish people.
2. That *Dáil Éireann* is the supreme governing authority in
Ireland.
3. That the *Dáil* should call into Council representatives of
local authorities and economic organisations from all parts of the
country.
4. That the joint body should act as a Constituent assembly to
prepare a Constitution for submission to the electorate.
5. The *Dàil* to appoint a Council of State or Ministry, not all
of whom need be Ministers of Departments or members of the
Dáil.
6. The Council of State or Ministry to act as Government, and
be responsible to the *Dáil*.
7. Authority to be delegated by the *Dáil* to the Provisional
Government as a committee for the purpose of facilitating the
transfer of the administrative machinery.
8. The activities of the IRA to be confined to preparation for

National defence. No armed parade except by authority from the Council of State.

9. The IRA to be united under common command, and to be responsible to the Civil Authority or the Council of State.

10. A Civil Police Force to be established, and to be under the control of the local Civil Authorities.

Collins and de Valera managed to agree on a Pact whereby a National Coalition be formed for the Third *Dáil* and an election was to take place on June 16 for this *Dáil*. If the Irish people returned a republican majority, Winston Churchill warned them "the resources of civilisation are by no means exhausted." In the *Dáil* 58 *Saorstát* supporters were returned while *Cumman na Poblachta* held only 36 seats; the Labour Party now had 17 seats; the Farmers' Party 7; the Unionists 4 (for Trinity College) and Independents 6. It was a mandate for peace, and the Collins/de Valera coalition. Collins, however, now repudiated the pact.

In the north-east of Ulster the pogroms continued. On May 31 alone over eighty Catholic families were rendered homeless, eight people were killed and again thousands fled south where relief work was hastily organised. Between June 21, 1920, and June 18, 1922, the total casualties were 428 killed, 1,766 wounded, 8,750 Catholics driven from their jobs and 23,000 Catholics rendered homeless. The pogroms were conducted by Ulster B Special Constabulary and Orange mobs. Troops stationed in the Six Counties were ordered not to interfere. The northern statelet was having a painful birth. To protect itself it had organised, in addition to what it termed the Royal Ulster Constabulary, three classes of special police. The A Specials were full time auxiliary policemen; the B specials were part-time; and the C Specials were older men called out in dire emergency. Recruiting was through the Orange Lodges and so the Specials were a Protestant élite.

Churchill now applied pressure in the twenty-six counties. He requested the Irish Government to take steps to suppress the section of the IRA which supported the republic.

The presence in Dublin of a band of men styling themselves the Headquarters of the Republic Executive is a gross breach and defiance of the Treaty. The time has come when it is not unfair, premature or impatient for us to make to this strengthened Irish Government and new Irish Parliament a request in express terms that this sort of thing must come to an end. If it does not come to an end, if through weakness, want of courage, or some other even less creditable reason it is not brought to an end, and a speedy end, then it is my duty to say, on behalf of His Majesty's Government, that we shall regard the Treaty as having been formally violated, that we shall take no steps to carry out or legalise its further stages, and that we shall resume full liberty of action in any direction that may seem proper, to any extent that may be necessary to safeguard the interests and the rights that are entrusted to our care.

Thus, at England's bidding, at 4.7 a.m. on July 28, the newly constituted army of the *Saorstát* opened up with borrowed English field artillery on the Four Courts, headquarters of the republican section of the IRA. Ireland was plunged into civil war. "English propaganda will strive to lay the blame for this war on the Irishmen," commented de Valera before reporting to his old battalion, the 3rd (Dublin Brigade), "but the outside world must not be deceived. England's threat of war, that, and that alone, is responsible for the present situation." When the Four Courts fell, the Citizen Army ceased to function as it was confined to Dublin, now in *Saorstát* hands. Individual members did, however, attach themselves to IRA Flying Columns. One such group of Citizen Army men fought as a separate commando in the Wicklow mountains. The capture of documents, however, led to the round-up in Dublin of all Citizen Army men who were active and their eventual imprisonment in No. 2 Internment camp at the Curragh. The war was swift and bitter. At first the two sides fought in the field. By August 12 Griffith was dead; he had suffered from strain and overwork. Ten days later Collins, who (in his posthumous book *The Path to Freedom*) wanted to negotiate an end to the civil war, was shot in an ambush in Co. Cork. Collins seemed to believe in a hazy form of "co-operatism" and harked back to the Celtic system. His idea, however, was the establishment of a Napoleonic dictatorship "to prevent Communism". O'Connor Lysaght commented: "only he would have had the prestige to impose such a dictatorship."

William Cosgrave now took over as leader of the *Dáil* with Johnson and the Labour Party as opposition. The Labour deputies were active in trying to organise peace talks and during the reading of the Constitution of the *Saorstát Eireann* Bill strove to give it a more democratic character. The Cosgrave government having defeated the republicans in the field now sought to suppress their guerilla activities by a terror campaign. Four republican prisoners in Mountjoy, Liam Mellowes, Rory O'Connor, Joseph McKelvey and Richard Barret were shot without trial on December 8, 1922, as a reprisal for the shooting of a *Saorstát* deputy. Liam Mellowes was the IRA Director of Purchases and a member of the republican *Dáil*. He had been made prisoner after the fall of the Fourt Courts. Between August and September, 1922, he wrote a series of letters from Mountjoy which were used by the *Saorstát* in a "blue paper" called *Correspondence of Eamonn de Valera and others*, dated September 21, 1922. Mellowes' idea was that a Provisional Republican Government be established to unite the forces of Labour and left wing Republicanism. He proposed a measure of state ownership and the establishment of a republic of the workers. He summed up his thoughts in these words: "Free State—Capitalism and Industrialism—Empire. Republic—Workers—Labour." Mellowes believed that without working-class support the republic was lost:

> We should keep Irish Labour for the Republic; it will probably be the biggest factor on our side. Anything that would prevent Irish Labour from becoming Imperialist and respectable will help the Republic ... we are back with Tone—and it is just as well—relying on the men of no property ...

He continues

> ... The unemployment is acute. Starvation is facing thousands of people. The official Labour Movement has deserted the people for the fleshpots of the empire. The Free State Government's attitude towards striking postal workers makes clear what its attitude towards workers generally will be. The situation created by all these must be utilised for the republic. The position must be defined. Free State—Capitalism and Industrialism—Empire. Republic—Workers—Labour.

"Ireland does not want a change of masters," wrote Mellowes. "It would be foolish, surely, to free Ireland from foreign tyranny today, and less than twenty years hence to have to free it from domestic tyranny. Therefore the Irish Republic must have for its foundations the people. It is they who are freeing Ireland; and it is for the people—all the people—that it is being done, not for any section or group."

On December 3, 1922, the *Saorstát* constitution received Royal Assent; the *Saorstát* was now in being. At noon on April 30 the IRA declared a cessation of hostilities towards the *Saorstát* troops. De Valera put forward peace proposals to the *Saorstát* Government and these were rejected. On the day the IRA ceased hostilities, James Larkin landed in Ireland after three years in prison as a victim of Mitchell Palmer's "red scare". On December 10, 1921, Larkin had given his views on the Treaty—"It was born in dishonour and shame. It was drafted and signed by creatures for their own aggrandisement—or because of ambition and due to their lack of courage, signed this unholy compact under duress." His position was simple. "We pledge ourselves now and in the future, to destroy this plan of a nation's destruction. We propose carrying on the fight until we make the land of Erin a land fit for men and women—a Workers' Republic or Death." Now, fresh out of prison, he was back in Ireland; an uneasy Ireland, an Ireland with the republican forces smashed and beaten. He felt there was only one course and appealed to republicans to give up the armed struggle and undertake the constitutional one. Ten days later de Valera's famous message to "The Legion of the Rearguard" was issued ordering the republicans to "dump their arms". The civil war was at an end. The *Saorstát* Government required £17,000,000 and an army of 60,000 to crush the opposition to the Treaty. Ironically, Irishmen had achieved what Englishmen could not do. It was a hollow victory.

Although military causes led to the failure of the republicans, another basic factor led to their downfall. Dr. P. McCartan expressed it during the Treaty debate : "The reason for many young soldiers going wrong is that they never had proper grasp of fundamentals. They were absorbed into the movement and fight—not educated into it. Hence no real convictions." An army of the people cannot undertake a struggle without a strongly developed social awareness. The struggle of the Viet Cong is an example of an army soundly founded on an awareness of social philosophy keeping it united against impossible odds. The Irish national revolution failed to be a people's revolution because of the rapid

development of reformism and the adaptation of social democracy to the interests of the controlling bourgeoisie. The ICO
comments:

> The Irish national revolution was separated, isolated, from the
> democratic revolution. This happened because it was led in the
> interests of the bourgeoisie who, while they desired national
> independence (that is they desired to become the ruling class in
> Ireland) did not desire a thorough democratic revolution of the
> kind outlined in the 1916 Proclamation. Such a revolution would
> have drawn the masses of the Irish people into direct revolution-
> ary action, would have put an end to estate owning, would have
> confiscated imperialist property in Ireland and would have trans-
> ferred its ownership to the people. Such a revolution if carried
> out thoroughly would destroy the basis for capitalist development
> in Ireland and would lay the groundwork for Socialist develop-
> ment.
>
> The class interest of the national bourgeoisie demanded, there-
> fore, that democratic revolution should be separated from the
> national revolution instead of forming an integral part of it, and
> that it should be suppressed. (In this they found willing co-
> operators in O'Brien, O'Shannon and Foran.) The task of demo-
> cratic revolution was described as being "neither of a national nor
> a military character" and was suppressed. This brought about
> abortion of the national revolution.[15]

Connolly, as early as 1899, saw what would happen to a
national struggle which was separated from the social struggle.
In a biting article entitled *Let us Free Ireland!* he wrote:

> Let us free Ireland! Never mind such base, carnal thoughts as
> concern work and wages, healthy homes, or lives unclouded by
> poverty.
>
> Let us free Ireland! The rack renting landlord; is he not also
> an Irishman, and wherefore should we hate him? Nay, let us not
> speak harshly of our brother—yea, even when he raises our rent.
>
> Let us free Ireland! The profit grinding capitalist, who robs us
> of three fourths of the fruit of our labour, who sucks the very
> marrow of our bones when we were young, and then throws us
> out in the street, like a worn-out tool, when we are grown
> prematurely old in his service, is he not an Irishman, and mayhap
> a patriot, and wherefore should we think harshly of him?
>
> Let us free Ireland! "The land that bred and bore us." And

the landlord who makes us pay for permission to live upon it. Whoop it up for liberty!

"Let us free Ireland" says the patriot who won't touch Socialism. Let us all join together and cr-r-rush the br-r-rutal Saxon. Let us all join together, says he, all classes and creeds. And, say the town workers, after we have crushed the Saxon and freed Ireland, what will we do? Oh, then you can go back to your slums, same as before. Whoop it up for liberty!

And, say the agricultural workers, after we have freed Ireland, what then? Oh, then you can go scraping around for the landlord's rent or the money lenders' interest same as before. Whoop it up for liberty!

After Ireland is free, says the patriot who won't touch Socialism, we will protect all classes, and if you won't pay your rent you will be evicted same as now. But the evicting party, under command of the sheriff, will wear green uniforms and the Harp without the Crown, and the warrant turning you out on the roadside will be stamped with the arms of the Irish Republic. Now, isn't that worth fighting for?

And when you cannot find employment, and giving up the struggle of life in despair, enter the poorhouse, the band of the nearest regiment of the Irish army will escort you to the poorhouse door to the tune of "St. Patrick's Day". Oh! it will be nice to live in those days!

"With the Green Flag floating o'er us" and an ever increasing army of unemployed workers walking about under the Green Flag, wishing they had something to eat. Same as now! Whoop it up for liberty![16]

Thus did Connolly succinctly foretell the blindness of those who fought for the Irish Republic as against the *Saorstát*—they were fighting in fact over a word, a dictionary definition—and not for a new social order.

Larkin was now touring the ITGWU branches. From 5,000 members in 1916 the union had grown to the almost incredible figure of 100,000 members. But there was a split in the Labour Movement. O'Brien had consolidated his position not only as leader of the ITGWU, but as secretary to the Irish TUC. Irish Labour had become "imperialist and respectable" as Mellowes had said. There was now a Communist Party of Ireland, founded in Sepember, 1921, with the aid of Connolly's young son Roderick, who had fought in the GPO during 1916 as a boy. In their journal, *Workers' Republic*, they commented:

Jim Larkin has seen through the sorry pretence and camouflage of O'Brien, Foran and O'Shannon posing as revolutionaries. The clearout is coming.[17]

Larkin at first wanted to resign as general secretary of the ITGWU but was prevailed upon to go on a tour of the union's branches. He agreed, thinking he would appeal to the union's congress for support for his viewpoint. However, he discovered during the course of his tour, that O'Brien had appointed most of the union's delegates to congress and had thereby "fixed" the meeting. He was soon back in Dublin declaring war on O'Brien. O'Brien and the executive countered by suspending him. In the newly launched Larkinite *Irish Worker,* Larkin commented :

> We had the honour of initiating the Irish Labour Movement. We return to find a Labour Party lost to all sense of dignity, manipulated by ambitious self seekers, a feeble imitation of the English Labour Party, and which, parrot like, repeats the phrases of its prototype, but in a less vigorous manner.[18]

Taking advantage of the split in the Irish Labour Movement, the employers in the transport trade in Dublin announced on July 13, 1923, that dockers would have to take a reduction in wages... bringing the average wage to 16s a day. On July 16 Larkin led 1,500 men out on strike. It dragged on until October 26 when the ITGWU announced the strike over and refused to recognise a dockers' ballot of 687 to 443 for a continuation of the strike. Despite Larkin's attempts to hold the men together, however, many returned to work. Emmet Larkin writes :

> Was it time for attack or entrenchment? Could even a Larkin with a united Labour Movement solidly behind have effected a revolution? Hardly! The party of the revolution under de Valera, which had a wider and deeper support under the aegis of Nationalism among the Irish people, had just suffered a resounding defeat. The crest of the revolutionary wave had passed in Ireland, and none recognised this more than Larkin when he called on the Republicans to lay down their arms and come into the nation. Yet his own justification for splitting the Irish Labour Movement was that it was not a genuinely revolutionary movement, and to make it such he would have had to go out of the nation in order to achieve the Social Revolution. In short, Larkin's position in 1923, whether considered from a tactical, practical or ideological point of view, was untenable.[19]

Chapter 14

THE IRISH FREE STATE

IN THE LAST months of the Civil War, the Treatyite wing of
Sinn Féin had renamed itself *Cumann na nGaedhael* after
Griffith's original movement. De Valera's *Cumann na Poblachta*
then renamed itself *Sinn Féin*. In the general election of August,
1923, *Cumann na nGaedhael* won 63 seats while *Sinn Féin* increased their representation to 44. It was quite an achievement
because of *Cumann na nGaedhael's* attempts to dislocate *Sinn
Féin's* election campaign by using police, military, intelligence
services and propaganda that a vote for *Sinn Féin* would plunge
the country back into civil war. As well as this, most of the candidates were in jail or on the run. On July 1, 1923, there were
11,316 republican prisoners of whom 250 were women. A series
of hunger strikes managed to free most of them by 1924. *Sinn
Féin* decided on an abstentionist policy, maintaining that the
second *Dáil* was still the *de jure* legislature and that de Valera
was still "President of the Irish Republic". The only constitutional opposition to the new government was the Labour Party
with 14 seats led by its secretary, Thomas Johnson.

Cumann na nGaedhael had as its president William Thomas
Cosgrave, a former Dublin councillor, who, during the two
Republican *Dála* made his mark as Minister for the Local
Government. Cosgrave had no social ideology beyond the old
Sinn Féin national bourgeois demand. Only Ernest Blythe,
Minister for Finance, seemed a degree more progressive by harp-
ing on a hazy Celtic co-operatism. Joseph McGrath, a former
private secretary to Larkin, had been appointed Minister for
Industry and Commerce but had learnt nothing from Larkin. To
the extreme right of the government, opposing the old *Sinn Féin*
programme, was Kevin O'Higgins, vice-president and Minister
for Home Affairs. He had strong backing among government
members for his own views.

A parliament on the lines of Westminster had been established
consisting of a legislature, *an t-Oireachtas,* and an upper house,

an Seanad, to which members of the old (southern) Unionists
were included out of all proportion to their numbers as a segment
of the overall community. The significant appointment was that
of Governor General. The post went to T. M. Healy, the employers' advocate during the 1913 Lock-Out, and one of the extreme right wing members of the old Irish Nationalist Party.
O'Connor Lysaght comments:

> In these circumstances Irish policy under Cosgrave was con-
> servative at home as abroad. In the latter sphere it was circum-
> scribed by the Treaty; in the former by the social framework
> accepted by bureaucrats, ranchers and businessmen. Irish credit
> economy remained dependent on that of Britain. Irish credit
> had to be backed by British credit. Irish currency remained a
> prettier form of British currency. Irish exporters supplied the
> British market. To these aims the Irish power élite was en-
> couraged by various types of incentive given at the workers'
> expense, by the encouragement of foreign capitalists as examples
> and competitors, by agricultural aids benefiting, in the main, the
> ranchers, and, only when all else had failed, by a few faltering
> steps towards state sponsored enterprise.[1]

Cumman na nGaedhael had accepted *Saorstát* as the end.
Those republicans who had accepted the *Saorstát* simply as a
stepping stone to the republic were aggrieved and bitter. As
early as March, 1924, a mutiny occurred in the army. General
Richard Mulcahy, Minister for Defence, moved against the
mutineers without consultation with the government and was
therefore forced to resign. McGrath, who was in sympathy with
these mutineers, also resigned from the government and formed
a National Group of *Cumann na nGaedhael* T.D.s (*Teachta
Dála—Dáil* deputy) which drifted off into obscurity.

The fight between Larkin and the ITGWU came to a head
early in 1924 and on March 14 he was expelled from the union
he had created. He had been invited to attend the Fifth Congress
of the Third International in Moscow and, despite a refusal from
the *Saorstát* government to give him and his son passports, he set
off in June. In the meantime, on June 15, Larkin's brother, Peter
launched the Workers' Union of Ireland and within a month
16,000 men, two-thirds of the Dublin members of the ITGWU,
had transferred to the new union. Larkin was a popular figure in
Moscow. While in Sing-Sing he had been elected to the Moscow

Soviet by a group of Russian tailors. He spoke twice during the
Congress. G. Zinoviev, who at the time of Lenin's death was his
apparent successor, invited Larkin to speak on the national
question and Ireland. At the closing session on July 8, 1924,
Larkin was elected to the Executive Council of the
International. He stayed for the Third Congress of the Red
International of Labour Unions and spoke several times parti-
cularly in the debate on "The Strategy of Strikes". He returned
home to Dublin on August 25, 1924, bearing with him a scarlet
banner with the inscription "To the Revolutionary Transport
Workers of Dublin, Greetings—From the Moscow Transport
Workers".

He returned home to trouble. A series of disputes had broken
out between the ITGWU and the Workers' Union as to what
union would control what jobs. The Coal Merchants'
Association, upset at the continued unrest, decided to lock out
their men in July, 1925, and was backed by the Dublin
Employers' Federation Ltd. By 1926, however, the Irish trade
union movement was in decline. In 1923 there had been
130,000 trade union members but by 1926 there were only
95,000.

On November 25, 1925, the IRA split from *Sinn Féin,*
whose strength declined within the next two years from 1,500
branches to 303. In the local government elections of 1925 the
partly had been defeated, mainly due to the Local Appointments
Act which forced employees to swear an oath of loyalty to the
Saorstát. The party was also losing support because of its stead-
fast refusal to enter the *Dáil* and form an effective opposition,
despite pleas from the Labour Party to do so. On March 11,
1926, however, de Valera, at a special *Ard-fheis* of *Sinn Féin,*
proposed that the party should enter the *Dáil* if a way to eliminate the oath of allegiance to the English King could be
found. Meeting opposition he resigned from *Sinn Féin* and, on
May 16, announced the formation of a new party *Fianna Fáil*
(Soldiers of Destiny). The difference between *Fianna Fáil* and
Sinn Féin was purely one of constitutionalism. The IRA, now a
separate entity from *Sinn Féin,* aimed at making a thirty-two
county republic a reality in the shortest possible time. It
adhered to a republic of the workers as against the bourgeois
party politicians and thus provided a vehicle for such Socialists

as Peadar O'Donnell, George Gilmore, Seán MacBride and Michael Price.

Other parties were establishing themselves, however. In January, 1926, William Magennis, a professor of metaphysics, founded *Clann Éireann* (Irish People or People's Party) whose membership included Senator Maurice Moore who published a pamphlet attacking Land Annuities and encouraging a campaign to end them. *Clann Éireann* attracted the *Sin Féin* T.D. Dan Breen who entered the *Dáil,* took the oath to the King in order to move its abolition. The attempt was unsuccessful. In September of that year Captain Archer Redmond, founded a National League which was an attempt to revive his father's Irish Nationalist Party. After 1927 it broke up and its members merged with *Cumann na nGaedhael.* Also in existence was Larkin's Irish Workers' League, which had formed in September, 1923, to oppose the Labour Party.

Cumann na nGaedhael was proving to be a concessionist government. In 1924, under Article 12 of the Treaty, *Cumann na nGaedhael* demanded that a Boundary Commission be established to "determine in accordance with the wishes of the inhabitants as far as these may be compatible with economic and geographic conditions, the boundaries between Northern Ireland and the rest of Ireland." Everyone expected that the majority Nationalist counties of Tyrone and Fermanagh would, democratically, become part of the *Saorstát* and that the four Unionist counties would find their statelet uneconomic and eventually rejoin a united Ireland. They reckoned without the influence of the northern capitalists, hanging for dear life to their imperial markets. Professor Eoin MacNeill became the *Saorstát* delegate to the Commission, Mr. Justice Feetham, a judge of the South African Supreme Court, was appointed chairman, but Northern Ireland refused to appoint a representative. The English Government put through fresh legislation to enable them to appoint a representative on behalf of "Northern Ireland" as well as the chairman, giving a majority in their favour. A plebiscite on the boundary question was refused. On November 7, 1925, the *Morning Post* forecast that no territory would be transferred to the *Saorstát,* except strips of land in Fermanagh and Armagh while the Northern Ireland government would control not only the Nationalist counties of Tyrone and Fermanagh but have a tract of the richest land in Donegal as well. On November 21 Eoin MacNeill resigned from the Commission and from the *Cumann na nGaedhael* government. London was putting pressure on the *Saorstát* claiming, under Article 5 of the Treaty, an enormous tribute of £157,750,000 for the Public Debt of the United Kingdom and payment of war pensions.

Had the *Saorstát* government had one strong man in it perhaps London's bluff might have been called. However, Cosgrave, O'Higgins and Blythe rushed to talks in London where they signed an incredible agreement. The powers of the Boundary Commission were revoked and the whole six counties were signed over to Northern Ireland and the clause for a possible reunification of the country was abolished. In return the sum of £170,250,000 demanded by London from the *Saorstát* was "magnanimously" cancelled by the English government, despite the fact that Ireland, had *Cumann na nGaedhael* made counter claims, was owed far in excess of this sum by England. Apart from the wrong done to an invaded, occupied and misgoverned territory, Sir Anthony MacDonnell reported to the Primrose Commission in 1912 that Ireland had been overtaxed by £300,000,000 at that time. Instead of making a counter claim *Cumann na nGaedhael* calmly agreed to pay compensation to the English Government for costs incurred in maintaining their troops in Ireland during the War of Independence and to give compensation to Unionists and supporters of the Treaty. The sum was to be paid by £150,000 down and an annuity of £250,000 for the next sixty years. The agreement must surely rank as one of the most incredible ever made.

Apart from the pressures outside the party, *Cumann na nGaedhael* was suffering from the differing ideologies of Cosgrave and O'Higgins. O'Higgins was placing himself in a position where it seemed likely that he could oust Cosgrave as head of the *Saorstát* government. He was an efficient administrator who, despite his crypto-Fascist tendencies, maintained himself as a passionate believer in parliamentary democracy. He was trying to "pull the coals from the fire" by discussing with Sir Edward Carson a plan for the reunification of Ireland on the lines of Arthur Griffith's original idea of a dual monarchy ruling the empire.

This was the situation at the general election of June, 1927. *Cumann na nGaedhael* was returned with a decreased 47 seats but *Fianna Fáil* had won 44 seats with Labour holding 22, compared with 14 previously; the Farmers' Party, a right wing big farmers' group which merged with *Cumann na nGaedhael* in 1932, won 11; Independents and other parties, such as the National League, 15. The Labour Party now decided to try to form a coalition with Redmond and remove the oath. The plan failed when Major Bryan Cooper, a *Cumann na nGaedhael* T.D., caused Alderman John Jinks of Sligo, a Redmondite, to be drunk and incapable of going to the *Dáil* to vote. The result of the motion to form a new government was a stalemate and the *Ceann Comhairle,* chairman of the *Dáil,* cast his vote in favour of Cosgrave and a new election seemed likely. During the June election Larkin had fielded three candidates for his Irish Workers' League. His son, Jim, had split the vote causing Johnson, leader of the Labour Party, to lose his seat. Only Larkin was elected (for North Dublin) but he was debarred from taking his seat as it was claimed that he was an undischarged bankrupt. This arose because of his refusal to pay the costs of an action he had brought against the ITGWU. In the subsequent by-election he came third.

On July 10 O'Higgins was assassinated and his death remains a matter of speculation. Cosgrave immediately passed a new Public Safety Act and introduced a Bill where no one could stand for the *Dáil* unless he promised to take the oath. On August 10 de Valera led the *Fianna Fáil* deputies to the office of Colm Ó Murchadha, clerk of the *Dáil,* where a book containing the text of the oath of loyalty to the King was presented to him. De Valera addressed Ó Murchadha :

> *Ba mhaith liom a chur in iúl duit nach bhfuil mé le mionn a thógaint, ná aon gheallúint, dílseachta do Rí Shasana a thabhairt—ná d'aon chomhacht taobh amuigh de mhuinntir na hÉireann. Táim ag cur m'ainmse annseo chun cead fháil dul isteach imeasc na dteachta a toghadh ag muinntir na hÉireann, agus bíodh fhios agat nach bhfuil aon bhrí eile leis an rud atí a dhéanamh agam.*

I wish to inform you that I am not going to take an oath or give any promise of allegiance to the King of England or to any power apart from the Irish people. I am putting my name here to obtain permission to enter among the deputies elected by the Irish people. Understand that there is no other meaning to what I am doing.

The *Fianna Fáil* deputies were allowed to sign the book and take their seats for the first time in five years as opposition. A notable absentee was Countess Markievicz. She had died on July 15, 1927, after a short illness. True to her principles she was insisting to the last that she be placed in a general ward among the poor and not given preferential treatment.

In September, 1927, a new election took place. *Cumann na nGaedhael* was returned with 61 seats and *Fianna Fáil* gained 57 seats. Labour, led by T. J. O'Connell, dropped to 13 seats. Larkin and his party made no impression at all. The following year he made his second and last visit to Russia. The Stalin-Trotsky debate was going on and he was invited by Bukharin to speak on the issue. He refused as he felt that it was an internal struggle in the Russian Communist Party. He did, however, address a meeting of the Moscow Soviet. "The Russians looked upon Jim as some kind of enigma," wrote Jack Carney.[2]

Things were approaching a crucial state in the *Saorstát*. Patrick Hogan's Land Act of 1923 had furthered agricultural capitalism by transforming all remaining tenanted agricultural land from landlords via Land Commissions in order that tenants could buy easy land annuities. The legislation separated the farmer, however small, from the landless labourer. Conditions for the small man in the west of the country were impossible. Senator Moore of *Clann Éireann* tried to publicise the evils of paying land annuities to England and the Socialist IRA leader, Peadar O'Donnell, tried to get the Labour Party to campaign for the cessation of the annuities. The Labour Party refused fearing the effects of a "red scare" campaign. *Fianna Fáil,* however, promised to end the payments. In April, 1930, a Working Farmers' Conference in Galway, denounced annuities and associated itself with European movements with similar aims and with O'Donnell's Socialist *Comhairle na Poblachta* movement which was banned by the government in 1931 as "communist". In May, 1931, *Muintir na Tire* (People of the Land) was founded by Father John Martin Hayes, curate of Castleiney, Co. Tipperary. It was an organisation of peasants, both propertied and landless, to work out social problems. By 1949 it had 200 active "parishes" organising sewerage, building halls, planting trees, and organising the electrification of villages.

In the 1932 general election *Fianna Fáil* became the new government of the *Saorstát* winning 72 seats in the *Dáil* and backed by the Labour Party, with a drastically reduced number of seats totalling only 10. O'Donnell explained the left's attitude to *Fianna Fáil's* victory.

> To put *Fianna Fáil* in was the only way to put the Cosgrave gang out. *Fianna Fáil* was the flail to thrash the pious and illustrious William and Co. So *Fianna Fáil* goes in . . .
>
> The Communist vote was small; some thousand odd votes . . . Communists in Ireland have inherited no tradition of militancy, and are not seen as a head on crash with Capitalism and Imperialism. This vote must be a highly conscious one.
>
> The Labour Party resembles *Fianna Fáil* except in so far as it resembles the Cosgrave gang. It is absolutely innocent of the characteristics of a working class party . . . the working class movement in Ireland is surely at its low water level.
>
> The *Fianna Fáil* party cannot achieve the Irish Republic nor can it free the mass of the Irish people. These things are expected of them by the masses, and the task for us is to keep full light trained on their failure . . . These things the masses thought they were doing must be concretely stated and popularised in clear terms so that the shortcomings of the parliamentary machine may be clearly seen . . . It is important that we should keep minds trained on the parliament so that what will be seen is the failure of honest men to use such a machine except to do the work for which it is built—to enslave many and serve the few.[3]

Larkin had contested North Dublin again with little success. Since 1918 the Irish TUC and the Labour Party had been a single organisation. In 1930 they had split into two separate bodies. Membership of trade unions was declining rapidly and, in 1931, employers tried to force a reduction of wages which resulted in a big lock out of workers. The Labour Party, due to the defeat of O'Connell, was now led by William Norton, general secretary of the Post Office Workers' Union, who, supporting de Valera's move to form the new government, said :

> In the struggle for freedom the workers of Ireland did not join merely for the purpose of exchanging one capitalist system for

another. For ten years the Labour Party has pleaded with *Cumann na nGaedhael* to remember the Democratic Programme of the First *Dáil* and the pledges given to the workers by *Sinn Féin*. We have pleaded in vain. Now they are on the eve of going out of office and having regard to their record towards the workers there will be no tears shed and no regrets expressed. *Fianna Fáil* at least promises that it will tackle the social and economic problems pressing with so much rigour on the workers. It is because we in the Labour Party have hopes that *Fianna Fáil* will live up to their declared programme that we are going to vote for Deputy de Valera.[4]

De Valera gave encouragement to Labour when he told the *Dáil:*

> I never regarded freedom as an end in itself but if I were asked what statement of Irish policy was most in accord with my view as to what human beings should struggle for, I would stand side by side with James Connolly.[5]

De Valera's first act was the Constitution (Removal of Oath) Bill deleting the oath to the King of England. The "constitutional revolution" was followed by the enactment of acts abolishing the right of appeal to the English Privy Council and the Governor General's discretionary functions. In 1935 a new Citizenship Act was passed which England refused to recognise. Irish citizens resident in the U.K. were still regarded as British subjects. This attitude had serious practical consequences when the U.K. went to war and Ireland remained neutral. Those consequences are still felt by the U.K. today. The next change in constitution came with the abdication of Edward VIII in December, 1936, when de Valera's original idea of external association was passed and Ireland ceased to be one of His Majesty's Dominions but an Associated State, republic in form, but without a titular head. The new constitution was enacted by referendum held on July 1, 1937. Thus the Governor Generalship was abolished, providing for an elected president. Dr. Douglas Hyde was elected to this office. Also, it was decided to withhold from England the land annuities and other payments amounting to £5,000,000 a year. The English Government did not take these changes "lying down" and started an "economic war" against Irish goods and produce. This policy of sanctions lasted six years until, in 1938, the dispute was settled by Ireland agreeing to pay a lump sum of £10,000,000. However, the major concession was the withdrawal of all English troops from the *Saorstát* and the evacuation of naval bases, thus giving the *Saorstát* the means to stay neutral in the Second World War. The twenty-six counties was now a bourgeois republic in all but name.

Arising from the economic problems of the decade, between 1932 and 1943 *Fianna Fáil* organised a number of state sponsored bodies which paved the way towards the expansion of state services. *Cumann na nGaedhael* had been forced to establish the Shannon scheme, to provide hydro-electric power, because private enterprise was too weak or too unenterprising to tackle it, but it was *Fianna Fáil* who widened the scope of state sponsored enterprise, mainly due to the fact that capitalists saw little returns in investing in Ireland. *Bord na Mona* (the Turf Board), The Sugar Co., organised from the expropriation of a foreign private compaign, and the Cement Co. were all formed in 1934. *Monarchana Alcóil na hÉirean* (Industrial Alcohol Company), was formed in 1938; *Bord Fáilte* (Tourist Board) formed in 1939; *Mianrai Teoranta* (Irish mineral exploitation) formed in 1940 and the Irish Shipping Co. was formed in 1941.

In the north the same economic problems caused by the Great Depression were hitting the Six Counties. In 1921 the Unionist Party had won 40 seats in the 52 seat parliament. It immediately had to consolidate itself by the establishment of a system of ward rigging and voting qualifications, which disenfranchised many, and a partisan police force. Nevertheless, during the 1925 election its representation dropped to 32 seats, losing mainly to Independents, Farmers and Labour (who secured three seats). For the 1929 election the Unionists took steps to remedy the matter by abolishing proportional representation, which they had already abandoned in local government elections. They increased their seats to 37 in 1929 while Labour won only one or two seats during subsequent elections. The only constant factor was the Nationalist Party who held a steady 10 seats.

With the failure of the Boundary Commission, Joseph Devlin, the Nationalist M.P. for West Belfast, and the Nationalist M.P. for Antrim, took their seats in the Northern

Parliament. They were followed in 1926 by three more. By the end of 1928 Devlin led the party of ten members in the Northern Ireland Parliament. Sir James Craig, the premier, described the Northern Ireland parliament as "a Protestant Parliament for Protestant people." In 1925 an Amending Act to the Education Act ensured that Protestant children were taught by Protestant teachers. The Catholics then pressed that what was good enough for Protestants was also good for Catholics and the sectarian walls began to go up. The Unionists equated Catholicism with Nationalism and Nationalism with Disloyalty. A sectarian state had been established. The *Saorstát*, however, had not set a good example educationally. Although theoretically education is not given a sectarian basis in the twenty-six counties, in practice it is. School managers of National Schools, theoretically, can be anyone. They are almost invariably either the parish priest or, where numbers justify this, an Anglican Church of Ireland minister.

The 1930's were years of severe economic depression in the Six Counties; two great industries, linen and shipbuilding, were in decline and the number of unemployed jumped from 35,000 in 1929 to 72,000 in 1930. A cut in outdoor relief rates led to rioting in which two people were killed. During a rail strike Protestant trade unionists allied themselves with the IRA in a campaign of agitation and this brought condemnation from Catholic and Protestant alike. The 1922 Catholic Lenten pastoral warned of the dangers of communism while Bishop Meagher, in 1936, spoke of the dangers of communism "donning the cloak of patriotism". In 1931 sectarian rioting broke out in Armagh, Lisburn, Portadown and Belfast. Religious differences were once again made the scape-goat of the capitalist failure. In 1931 Catholic pilgrims travelling to the Dublin Eucharist Congress were attacked in Ballymena, Larne and Portadown. In 1934 more riots occurred and in July, 1935, the worst outbreak since 1922 took place. This resulted in 11 killings, 2 attempted killings, 574 cases of criminal assault, 133 cases of arson and 367 cases of malicious damage. The Northern Ireland government refused an official inquiry and Stanley Baldwin, the English Premier, refused all attempts to discuss the matter at Westminster. In 1934 the Council of Civil Liberties sent a Commission of Inquiry to the Six Counties and in 1936 reported :

Firstly, that through the operation of the Special Powers Act contempt has been begotten for the representative constitutions of government.

Secondly, that through the use of Special Powers individual liberty is no longer protected by law, but is at the disposition of the Executive. This abrogation of the rule of law has been so practised as to bring the freedom of the subject into contempt.

Thirdly, that the Northern Ireland Government has used Special Powers towards securing the domination of one particular political faction, and, at the same time, towards curtailing the lawful activities of its opponents ... the Government's policy is thus driving its opponents into the way of extremists.

Fourthly, that the Northern Ireland Government, despite its assurances that Special Powers are intended for use only against law breakers, has frequently employed them against innocent and law-abiding people, often in humble circumstances, whose injuries, inflicted without cause or justification, have gone unrecompensed and disregarded.[6]

A Catholic Social Conference was held in Belfast in 1937 and discussed some of the social evils of the time. A Social Service Bureau was established to deal with moneylenders and hire purchase sharks preying off the poor, and giving legal aid to those in difficulties with landlords and government. At the same time a Workers' College was established to give trade unionists a training in philosophy, economics and public administration. Elections of republicans pursuing an absentionist policy to the Northern Ireland parliament caused the passing of an Act in 1934 making it impossible for those standing for the parliament not to attend its sessions. However, Nationalist attendance after 1934 grew desultory.

Peadar O'Donnell summed up the situation.

In the North East the workers are collected around industries controlled by Imperial finance ... For the South the rulers are a mixed assortment of bankers, industrialists, upper-tier farmers and the backing they can attract. They have organised an army, police, jails etc. to put their will through and to maintain themselves; they bargain with British imperialism on terms where their state will hold Ireland for the Empire but get in return freedom to raise tariffs against imperialist industries breaking in on their markets.

Partition arises out of this uneven development of Capitalism in Ireland; sentiment won't remove it.

Beat the landlord out of life, beat the capitalist out of industry, smash the state machine, arm the workers. Rest in them, in alliance with the working farmers, all the powers of production.[7]

Internal politics in the *Saorstát* were now reaching a turbulent period. In 1931 a movement called *Saor Éire* (Free Ireland) had been formed as an offshoot from the IRA to create "an independent revolutionary leadership for the working class and working farmers towards the overthrow in Ireland of British imperialism and its ally, Irish capitalism". It was soon condemned as communistic by the Catholic Hierarchy and subversive by the then *Cumann an nGaedhael* government. It had lent its support to *Fianna Fáil* in 1932 but now *Fianna Fáil* found itself embarrassed by the republican left. *An Phoblacht* (The Republic) which had been started in June, 1925, as the journal of the republican movement, preaching a confused populist programme, was now under the editorship of Peadar O'Donnell, who took over in April, 1926. *An Phoblacht* urged the organisation of Workers' Revolutionary Groups and sent delegates to central European peasant worker movement meetings. It demanded "War on the ranches and banks . . . the banks to be taken over and made to serve the interests of the people. The ranches to be divided and distributed. Only when these things are done will the economic stranglehold of imperialism be loosened." Writing in November, 1933, Professor James Hogan stated:

> One thing, at all events, is certain. It was the growing menace of the Communist IRA that called forth the Blueshirts as inevitably as Communist anarchy called forth the Blackshirts in Italy.

The Blueshirts had been born in the spring of 1931 as the Army Comrades Association, formed by ex-members of the *Saorstát* army led by Dr. T. F. O'Higgins, brother of Kevin. Having opened its membership to the public in August, 1932, it soon stood at 100,000 strong, adopting a blue shirt, taking the name of the National Guard and being led by General Eoin O'Duffy, who had been sacked from his job as Commissioner of the *Garda Siochána* (police) in February, 1933. Political meetings were being broken up throughout Ireland by the militaristic Blueshirts on the grounds they "did not support the view Communists should be free to organise". The word Communist was allowed a wide interpretation. Like the European Fascists, the Blueshirts had youth organisations in which six-year-olds paraded and engaged in fisticuffs and there was also a girls' section. The rise of Blueshirtism was due to two main reasons: one, the emotional reaction to the "red scare" diatribes of Church and politicians; and, two, the support from farmers suffering under England's "economic war". Professor Hogan, the principal theoretician of *Fine Gael*, published a pamphlet in 1934, arising from a series of articles he had written the previous year, entitled *Could Ireland Become Communist?* All the republican movements were denounced as communistic. Welcoming the pamphlet Rev. P. J. Gannon, SJ, likened Lenin to "Attila, Genseric, Genghis Khan or Tamurlane" but Mussolini was "the shrewdest politician of the 20th Century". Blueshirt propaganda was loaded with intense racialism and bigoted chauvinism.

> The founders of Communism were practically all Jews. This can scarcely be a mere coincidence. It may appear singular that Marx, Engels, Lassalle and Ricardo were all Jews. Likewise such Communist leaders as Lenin, Trotsky, Zinoviev, Litvinov and Kakovlev are Jews, as well as the vast majority of the present rulers of Soviet Russia ... the Russian Government is not a national government, but a Jewish oligarchy imposed on a defenceless people.[8]

In the columns of a newspaper called *The Blueshirt,* launched in August, 1933, O'Duffy was described as "the symbol of the awakening Erin" provided by "a gracious Providence" to lead the Nation. The policy propounded was the Fascist Ireland of the corporate state. *United Ireland,* the journal of *Fine Gael,* pointed out:

> It is a complete mistake to suppose that Italian Fascism is merely a crude individual or party dictatorship ... it had gradually evolved a scheme of social and political organisation which is quite certain as time goes on to be adapted to the needs of every civilised country.[9]

A correspondent "Ogánach" writing in *United Ireland* in December, 1933, suggested that Blueshirts greet their leader,

O'Duffy, in the Nazi style. An ensuing issue bore a picture of O'Duffy with the caption "Hail O'Duffy!" O'Duffy announced the Blueshirt intention to hold a mass rally on Leinster Lawn, in front of the government building on August 12, 1933, to commemorate the deaths of Kevin O'Higgins and Michael Collins, Thousands of Blueshirts were expected to march on Dublin and the analogy to Mussolini's rise to power with the march on Rome was not lost. De Valera called O'Duffy's bluff, enforced the Public Safety Act, banned the parades, drafted in large contingents of *Gardaí* and waited. O'Duffy called off the demonstration and the Fascists reorganised themselves. The National Guard joined with *Cumann na nGaedhael* in a new movement called the United Ireland Party or *Fine Gael* and O'Duffy became president. The youth wing named the Young Ireland Association continued the military organisation of the National Guard, and, when it was banned in December, 1933, a League of Youth took over. The new movement, representing professional, commercial and big landowning interests as against the manufacturing capitalist and small farming interests represented by *Fianna Fáil,* did not lose faith in the idea of a coup d'état. In 1934, John Aloysius Costello, a leader of the new *Fine Gael* party, was warning the *Dáil*:

> The Blackshirts have been victorious in Italy; and Hitler's Brownshirts were victorious in Germany, as, assuredly, the Blueshirts will be victorious in the Irish Free State.

But the Blueshirts were on the decline and O'Duffy was forced to resign from the presidency of *Fine Gael.* A few years later, in 1936, O'Duffy resurrected the Blueshirts into a 700-strong Irish Brigade to go to Spain to aid Franco's Fascist rebellion. O'Duffy had the full blessing of the Catholic Hierarchy. Rt. Rev. Monsignor Ryan, Dean of Cashel, condoned Fascism in these words:

> The Irish Brigade have gone to fight the battle of Christianity against Communism. There are tremendous difficulties facing the men under General O'Duffy, and only heroes can fight such a battle. Those at home can help the cause in their prayers; the Rosary is more powerful than the weapons of war : in the presence of Our Lord Jesus Christ, let us promise that we will offer up a decade of the family Rosary daily, for poor suffering desperate battle against the horde that is threatening desecration

all over the world, let us pray that the destruction of civilisation may be averted and that Christ may live again and reign, and that Communism and the powers of darkness in it, can be brought to nought.[10]

Thus was the suppression of the Basque and Catalan nations, still fighting for their independence today, and the suppression of democracy in Spain condoned by the Irish Church. O'Duffy was to die in 1944 after trying to raise an Irish brigade to help the Nazis. The IRA saw through the "red scare" tactics and decided to support the Spanish Government in its fight against Fascism. An appeal was made for volunteers and Frank Ryan led 300 IRA men to Spain to join the International Brigade. They became part of the Lincoln Brigade. At the same time IRA units did their utmost to prevent O'Duffy's Fascist Brigade leaving Ireland but were outmanoeuvred. Ryan was to die in 1944. He had been taken prisoner by the Fascists but released at the request of the Germans after appeals from fellow Celtic Breton nationalist leaders. He suffered from ill health and acute deafness from his experiences.

Against the rise of Fascism in Ireland a united front was organised by the IRA leaders O'Donnell and Ryan but the Labour Party refused to have any connection with this. At the annual congress of the Labour Party, R. J. Connolly moved:

Believing that the dangers that face the workers of this and every other country from Capitalism, Fascism, International War and Imperialism, are too real and serious for us to remain parties to artificial divisions within the working class ranks, we call for a truce among all who stand for an Irish Workers' Republic and a united front against the common enemy. We recommend that in order to achieve united action the Administration Council invite members of the TUC, Republican Movement and other Republican bodies to exchange views with them on this question.

Labour rejected the idea. While claiming to derive their basic philosophy from Connolly, the Labour Party was never a Socialist party and, indeed, never called itself such. Its philosophy was vaguely the organisation of agriculture and industry on co-operatist lines with public control of banking and transport. During William O'Brien's chairmanship of the

party during 1933-38 there was a drift to the left when the
party proclaimed as its intention :

... the establishment in Ireland of a Workers' Republic founded
on the principles of social justice, sustained by democratic institutions and guaranteeing civil and religious liberty and equal opportunities to achieve happiness to all citizens who render service
to the community.

The Catholic Hierarchy objected to the term "Workers'
Republic", and William Norton, informing the Labour
Conference of this, asked the conference "to make up its mind
whether it is not wiser for the party to drop the term." It did so
by eighty-nine votes to twenty-nine votes. The left wing of the
IRA proposed to the IRA Convention of 1933 that it prepare to
make the IRA the alternative to *Fianna Fáil* by declaring "our
allegiance to the Republic of Ireland, based on production and
distribution for use and not for profit, in which the exploitation
of labour of human beings with all its attendant miseries and insecurity shall not be tolerated." The motion was strenuously opposed by the leadership. O'Donnell and Gilmore proposed the
establishment of a Republican Congress to rally opinion. The
majority of delegates were in favour, but voting by the leadership
turned down the idea. O'Donnell, Ryan, Price and Gilmore
walked out. O'Donnell wrote :

The IRA leadership is busy firing on its own left. IRA firing on
its own left has smashed the Dublin Brigade ...
The IRA leadership is not merely tardy about the revolutionary principles it professes; it is active on counter-revolutionary
lines. Its obstruction of the Congress is reactionary activity. Its
policy in the face of Fascism was a reactionary one. Its policy
during the Northern elections was a reactionary one. Its distrust
of the masses—"it is the masses who always let down the
revolution"—is a reactionary one. Even the very doctrine of physical force is used in a reactionary way, for it is used to screen the
desertion of revolutionary struggles. And it is against this leadership and not against the IRA organisation the Congress Groups
have to struggle.

The Republican Congress met in Rathmines Town Hall,
Dublin, on September 29 and 30; 186 delegates attended
representing Republican groups, the Communist Party,

Unemployed Workers' Movement, Tenants' League, and the newly reconstituted Irish Citizen Army, which was to have only a passing existence. There were two resolutions to be discussed. One resolution called for a united front for the Irish Republic while the other called specifically for a Workers' Republic. The second resolution, proposed by R. J. Connolly, Nora Connolly, O'Brien and Michael Price, held that the Congress should put the establishment of a Workers' Republic as an immediate aim. The Irish Republic Resolution, argued for by O'Donnell and Gilmore, held that while the establishment of the Workers' Republic was an ultimate aim the Congress should strive to unite all republican forces towards its achievement. This latter resolution was adopted by ninety-four votes to eighty-four. It was declared that "The Republican Congress, rallying centre for mass struggle capable of smashing imperialist and native exploiters, calls for a united front of working class and small farmers so that the submerged nation be roused to free itself and unite under the Irish Republic." The Congress carried on its activities in organising until 1936 when de Valera banned its weekly newspaper *The Republican Congress.* The same year the hard core of the Congress went to Spain's defence against Fascism.

The IRA began to conduct raids against the big property owners in Ireland. Many estates were still owned by absentee landlords and run through agents of the Captain Boycott variety. Evictions, sackings (for political beliefs) and other misuses of power took place. The IRA intervened, first by intimidation and then by more drastic measures. One estate manager, More O'Farrell of Sanderson Estate, Edgeworthstown, Co. Longford, had been warned a number of times by the IRA for evicting without just cause. On February 11, 1935, IRA men attempted to execute him but the bullet was deflected by a cigarette case. His twenty-one-year-old son was fatally wounded when he tried to attack the raiders. In March, 1935, a transport dispute took place in Dublin with the Dublin United Tramways. *The Saorstát* army were used in a strike-breaking capacity and the IRA issued the following statement :

The Army Council of the Irish Republican Army has had under consideration the dispute between the Dublin transport workers and the Dublin United Tramways Company. In the

opinion of the Army Council the situation is one in which more
than immediate causes are involved. The action of the Free State
Government in using army transport for strike breaking purposes
in the interests of the company to which the Government has
given a monopoly constitutes a definite challenge to all workers.
That the complete transport system of Dublin should be at the
mercy of a private company is a matter affecting the welfare of
all Dublin citizens.

The Army Council, realising the importance of the principles
involved, feels that the joint efforts of the Free State Government
and the Murphy combine must be defeated. For these reasons
the Army Council hereby expresses its willingness to assist the
workers in the struggle. Further, the Army Council is interested as
the Government programme on the question of transport
provides that railways, canals, airways, waterways, and all forms
of public inland transport shall be operated by a body set up by
the National Economic Council. The Army Council of the Irish
Republican Army offers its services to assist in mobilising the
maximum support for the Dublin transport workers in their
struggle . . .[11]

In 1936 *Fianna Fáil* moved against the IRA banning the
movement and arresting a great many. The same year Larkin
won a seat on the Dublin Municipal Council and the following
year North Dublin returned him to the *Dáil* as "independent
Labour candidate". Larkin had surprisingly little to say in the
Dáil; only now and again were there flashes of the old Larkin.
He died on March 30, 1947, aged 71. Labour had won 13 seats
in the 1937 election but *Fianna Fáil* had to go to the country
again in 1938 and Labour representation fell to 9. New parties
were springing up again. On August 15, 1938, representatives
from twelve counties met in Athenry, Co. Galway, and formed
Clann na Talmhan (Peasants' Party, literally—Children of the
Land) which was to win 14 seats in the 1943 election. On the
other hand, an ultra-right-wing *Ailtirí na hAiséirighe* (Brotherhood of the Rising) was formed and *Coras na Poblachta*
(Republican Organisation), made up of ex-IRA men and dis-
illusioned ex-*Fianna Fáil* men.

In September, 1939, war broke out in Europe. *Fianna Fáil* immediately declared the neutrality of the *Saorstát*. Indeed, with a
vulnerable coastline, no navy, no bomb-proof shelters, it would
have been a futile gesture to throw the country into a war.

Nevertheless the *Saorstát* put a very liberal interpretation on her neutrality in England's favour. Irish weather stations supplied the Allies with information; military aircraft, taking off from Northern Ireland, were allowed to violate *Saorstát* neutral skies with her blessing; a rescue ship at Killybegs, Co. Donegal, aided the Allies; Allied pilots shot down on *Saorstát* territory were allowed to cross the border while Axis pilots were interned. Thousands of Irish were allowed to enlist in the British Army and do important war work in U.K. factories. Some 97,800 English refugees were sheltered in Ireland.

Nevertheless, this liberal neutrality did not appease England. Winston Churchill maintained that the Irish ports of Berehaven and Lough Swilly were vital to English strategy and proposed an English expeditionary force be sent to seize them. In February, 1944, the U.S.A., backed by Churchill, issued an ultimatum to Ireland, denouncing its neutrality as pro-German support and demanding the expulsion of all Axis representatives from its soil. De Valera refused to accept this, mobilised the *Saorstát* army and all bridges to the Six Counties were mined against invasion. Although plans were ready in hand for the invasion the U.S.A. convinced Churchill that it would be futile to create another "front" in Ireland. The U.K. were contented in breaking every severable link with the *Saorstát*.[12] George Gilmore, the Socialist Republican, demanded that the *Saorstát* declared itself a republic and enter the war on the Allies' side.

On May 13, 1945, at the close of the war, in a radio broadcast, Winston Churchill vented his spleen over Irish neutrality.

Owing to the action of the Dublin Government, so much at variance with the temper and instinct of thousands of southern Irishmen, who hastened to the battle front to prove their ancient valour, the approaches which the southern Irish ports and airfields could so easily have guarded were closed by hostile aircraft and U-boats.

This was indeed a deadly moment in our life, and if it had not been for the loyalty and friendship of Northern Ireland, we should have been forced to come to close quarters with Mr. de Valera or perish for ever from the earth. However, with a restraint and poise to which I say history will find few parallels, His Majesty's Government never laid a violent hand upon them though at times it would have been quite easy and quite natural . . .

De Valera commented on *Radio Éireann*, May 17:

Mr. Churchill makes it clear that, in certain circumstances, he would have violated our neutrality and that he would justify his action by Britain's necessity. It seems strange to me that Mr. Churchill does not see that this, if accepted, would mean that Britain's necessity would become a moral code and that when this necessity became sufficiently great, other people's rights were not to count . . .

Chapter 15

THE DICTIONARY REPUBLIC

IN THE GENERAL election of June, 1943, the situation of the main parties was as follows : *Fianna Fáil*, 67 seats; *Fine Gael*, 32; Labour, 17 and *Clann na Talmhan*, 14. *Fianna Fáil* was now representative of a "constitutional centre" party while *Fine Gael* had gone very much to the right. It was in a stagnant state; until 1948 it did not win a single by-election. In January, 1944, Cosgrave resigned the leadership in favour of the extreme rightist General Richard Mulcahy. Mulcahy had lost his seat in 1943 and only just regained it in May, 1944. His one original proposal was the demand for an Anglo-Irish alliance which he quickly had to abandon in view of reaction within his own party. The other parties had little new to offer. Labour were preaching a modified state capitalism and *Clann na Talmhan* preached a vocationalism rather than Socialism. Much of the radicalness of Labour and *Clann na Talmhan's* programme was deflated when Seán MacEntee, of *Fianna Fáil*, enacted a children's allowances scheme.

The smallholders tended to vote for *Clann na Talmhan* or *Fianna Fáil*, while the large farmers and ranchers were behind *Fine Gael*. *Clann na Talmhan*, led by Michael Donnellan, was soon suffering from internal squabbles over such matters as rural distribution of land and fixity of tenure. In November, 1943, William Sheldon T.D. resigned from the party and, in the general election of May, 1944, when *Fianna Fáil* went to the country due to its parliamentary defeat over a co-ordinated transport issue, the party lost seats. Joseph Blowick became party leader in July that year and began to play down vocationalism, opening negotiations with Labour on joint welfare policies. But there was still dissension within the party and two of its deputies took prominent parts in land division agitation at Ballyhaunis, Co. Mayo. The deputy leader, Patrick Cogan, left the party with some colleagues in April, 1947, and formed a National Agricultural Party.

The Labour Party achieved its largest complement of seats in 1943, that it had held since the 1922 election. It also controlled Dublin Corporation where the Lord Mayor, Ald. Martin O'Sullivan, was the leader of the party. It was thought an alliance with *Clann na Talmhan* would bring power within its grasp. However, dissension was also splitting, the Labour Movement, the friction being caused between James Larkin and William O'Brien, now general secretary of the ITGWU. The ITGWU leadership were supporting *Fianna Fáil*'s Trade Union Act which the Labour Party and the Irish TUC were against. Larkin's Workers' Union of Ireland had now achieved recognition by the Irish TUC and Larkin was, of course, a member, albeit an "independent" one, of the Labour Party. O'Brien claimed there was a "Communist plot" to take over Irish Labour and, in January, 1944, the ITGWU's eight Labour deputies withdrew from the Irish Labour Party and formed a separate National Labour Party led by James Everett. The ITGWU affiliated itself to this party which acted purely as a *Fianna Fáil* subsidiary. The ITGWU left the Irish TUC after it had been defeated on a motion against entering the World Federation of Trade Unions. It claimed the TUC was full of "Communist influences from London and Belfast" and formed its own congress called *Comhar Ceard Éireann (Congress of Irish Unions.) Comhar Ceard Éireann* threatened to use the Trade Union Act to destroy English based unions in Ireland and also the Larkinite Workers' Union of Ireland. They based their threat on Part Three of the Trade Union Act which had a proviso for possible restriction of a firm's workers to the union of their majority. In July, 1946, however, the Irish Supreme Court declared this unconstitutional.

The ITGWU, *Comhar Ceard Éireann* and the National Labour Party were now racing towards the right wing. Frank Purcell, secretary of the National Labour Party, was demanding an episcopal inquiry into the "Communism" of the Labour Party. In January, 1948, the National Labour T.D., John O'Leary, was declaring: "only Communists would denounce Franco's Spain or ask for diplomatic relations with the USSR." But the Labour Party was showing similar reaction and many of its more convinced Socialist members, such as Peader Cowan who had started a movement to end partition on scientific Socialist principles, were being carefully "weeded out". However, the "red scare" tactics worked and the Dublin weekly *Standard* carried a series of headlines such as "Communist Victory Over Irish Labour" and "Red Coup in the Party". In April, 1945, the Irish National Teachers' Organisaion withdrew its support. Co-operation between the Labour Party and the National Labour Party was expedited by O'Brien's retirement in 1946 and the death of Larkin the following year. Deputy Jim Larkin Jnr. made an attempt to heal the split on the day of his father's funeral by writing to the *Irish Times*:

> The great mass of working men and women who constitute the Irish Labour Movement must ardently desire that their strength and purpose should be added to a thousandfold, by all that flows from unity ... Irish people are emotional and perhaps our common emotion this day may give us the unity we need, where reason and argument have failed in the past.
>
> I have no doubt of the truth of my statement when I declare that unity is the single quality sought for by the working men and women who constitute, and who are, the Irish Labour Movement, and why therefore when so little stands between them and the unity they desire should they be denied it?[1]

Within a year the Labour Party and National Labour Party had reunited but the ITGWU began increasingly to support *Fianna Fáil* and one of its leading figures William McMullan was elected to *An Seanad* for the party. This left wing support was rewarded by *Fianna Fáil* with a number of reforms such as a Social Welfare Act providing a single national insurance organisation.

In May, 1945, with the end of the war, the government ended most of its Emergency Powers, though not the Offences Against the State Act. They had been particularly active during the war years against republicans and had lost all credibility with republican groupings. The IRA on its part had also been active. In January, 1939, they had commenced a bombing campaign in England, issuing a statement to the English Government demanding the withdrawal of all English troops in Ireland or they would "be compelled to intervene in the military and commercial life of your country, as your government is now intervening in ours." At the expiration of the time allowed, a series of bomb explosions began in major English cities culminating with an explosion in Coventry on Friday, August 25, 1939. A bomb being taken to a generating station blew up prematurely killing 5, gravely injuring 20 and slightly injuring 40 more, Police eventually arrested 2 men, Peter Barnes and Frank McCormack, and, on extremely slender evidence, executed them. It was very much a sacrifice to the manifestation of popular hysteria rather than justice. The campaign in England ended with 2 executions; 23 men and women sentenced to 20 years penal servitude; 34 more to 10-20 years; 25 to 5-10 years and 14 to under 5 years. From a practical point of view the campaign can be condemned for it had no more than nuisance value. During the war years Seán Russell, chief of staff, tried to enlist German support but died of a ruptured ulcer, on his way back to Ireland in a U-boat. The *Fianna Fáil* government passed several acts which empowered them to imprison and execute republicans. On May 10, 1946, the ex-chief of staff of the IRA, Seán MacCaughey, died from a hunger strike in Port Laois jail. A campaign to free him had brought together many prominent Republicans, Socialists and other radicals who were to form a new political party called *Clann na Poblachta*.

The Irish petty capitalists had done well out of the war. Between 1938 and 1946 the money value of bank deposits rose by 103 per cent. By 1949 the total value of external assets rose to £400,000,000. Professor E. T. Nevin estimated that in 1953, 10 per cent of Ireland's population owned 66.7 per cent of the land and capital of Ireland. He added there was little change in the personal distribution of wealth. The Government had added to its state-sponsored bodies with such companies as *Coras Iompair Éireann* (Transport Company) in 1944; National Stud in 1945; Irish Steel Holdings in 1947; *Aramhara Teo.* (seaweed processing) in 1949; *Coras Trachtala Teo.* and the Voluntary Health Insurance Board. *Radio Éireann* was similarly transformed by Erskine H. Childers, Minister for Posts and Telegraphs in 1953. By 1951 Ireland's state-sponsored bodies controlled 25 per cent of Irish investment and employed 5 per cent of all employed workers at a wage 40 per cent more than average.

Following the end of the war, however, foreign capitalists began to move into the twenty-six counties buying native industries. A series of scandals were shaking *Fianna Fáil*. In July, 1946, Dr. Francis Ward T.D. was found to have connections with a bacon curing firm who were extremely evasive about their books. In October, 1947, Lemass and Boland were accused of conniving in a breach of the Control of Manufacturers Act in regard to Locke's whiskey distillery, Kilbeggan, Co. Westmeath. They were cleared of the charge but, nevertheless, disaffection was growing. However, there seemed little alternative to *Fianna Fáil*. In July, 1946, *Clann na Poblachta* had been formed by radical groupings led by Seán MacBride. It looked leftwards without being Socialist. In October, 1947, the new party won seats in two by-elections.

In February, 1948, a general election took place in which *Fianna Fáil* lost its overall majority but remained the largest party in the *Dáil*. *Clann na Poblachta* had won 10 seats. *Fine Gael* now proposed to the other parties that they form a coalition to oust *Fianna Fáil* from power. Labour, *Clann na Talmhan* and *Clann na Poblachta* decided to throw in with *Fine Gael*. The new "Inter-Party" government was led, not by Mulcahy (*Fine Gael's* president) but by John A. Costello, the former Fascist sympathiser, who became *Taoiseach* (Premier). William Norton of the Labour Party became *Tánaiste* (deputy premier) and Minister for Social Welfare. The other Ministers represented *Clann na Poblachta* and *Clann na Talmhan* with Dillon, an independent, becoming Minister for Agriculture. The "Inter-Party" government announced a ten-point programme which hardly differed from *Fianna Fáil*. There was an immediate reaction from the republican left. In 1948 the Communist Party of Ireland was revived as the Irish Workers' League and the IRA began to re-organise with *Sinn Féin*.

The new government, however, achieved initial success. It streamlined welfare benefits, continued a fairly progressive housing policy, organised the eradication of tuberculosis, initiated an economic drive, organised a land reclamation scheme, abolished compulsory tillage, expanded forestry and struggled to expand the sales of Irish produce at home and abroad. In 1950 it organised an Industrial Development Authority. Dr. James Ryan, the first Minister for Health under *Fianna Fáil*, had presented a Health Act, just before his party was swept from office, hinting at a British style Health Service. This had been attacked both by Irish Medical Association and the Catholic Hierarchy as "unChristian". When the "Inter-Party" government tried to implement its section on a free health scheme for mothers and children it was denounced by the Hierarchy. The Church claimed the right of parents to provide for their own children was "threatened" by this free scheme and that gynaecological care would mean birth control. In April, 1951, the Church were still negatively attacking the only scheme that would have reduced Irish mortality in childbirth. When *Fianna Fáil* returned to power and presented their Health Act of 1953, which included a more conservative mother and child care scheme, to overcome Church prejudice, the Hierarchy still attacked it but the Act became law and was the basis for future developments in the Irish health service. The doctors leaned heavily on the Church to denounce the scheme, basically because they felt that by coming under a state-sponsored scheme they would be under a much closer scrutiny as regards income tax.

In external affairs Ireland still pursued a neutralist policy. In June, 1945, Douglas Hyde had been succeeded by Seán T. Ó Ceallaigh as president of the state. Seán MacBride as Minister for External Affairs was insisting on Ireland's non-military alignment as against NATO's anti-Communist policies. He did this not for ideological reasons but because he was not prepared to accept the territorial status quo involved in the acceptance of the NATO Charter while England held on to the Six Counties. An all-party propaganda campaign against partition was initiated and, in 1949, a special Irish News Service was established for this purpose. Delegates to the Council of Europe took every opportunity to raise the issue. But no moves were made to try to heal the breaches created by years of religious propaganda in the Six Counties.

The 1930's had been bleak years for Northern Ireland. Some 37 per cent of the population of Belfast were still living in overcrowded or unfit houses and the rates of infant and maternal mortality were the highest in the United Kingdom.[2] Some 50 per cent of all houses in Co. Fermanagh were "unfit for human habitation". Frustration and increasing unemployment led many young Nationalists into the IRA while the unemployed Unionists could manage to live with mobilisation grants from the B Specials, the auxiliary police force recruited through the Orange Lodges. In the general election of 1938 Lord Craigavon (formerly Sir James Craig) did not draw attention to the Six Counties' 100,000 unemployed but to the fear of a "religious sell-out" because England was then negotiating trade agreements with de Valera.

With the outbreak of the war the northern capitalists had a

boom period with the shipyards, aircraft factories, engineering works, clothing factories increasing employment and profits. The dangers of war were alleviated by the sight of a regular pay packet for the working classes. In 1940 Craigavon died and was succeeded by J. M. Andrews. The war was now a reality and in June, 1940, it was found that there was not a single searchlight or mobile anti-aircraft battery in Northern Ireland and the only town to have defences was Belfast with seven heavy guns.

On April 7 a preliminary raid tested the Northern Ireland defences and, on the night of April 15/16 the raiders returned in force dropping 203 metric tons of bombs and killing over 700 people. On May 5, 96,000 incendiary bombs and high explosives were dropped on Belfast. On both occasions de Valera ordered the fire brigades of Dublin, Dun Laoghaire, Drogheda and Dundalk to the north. The action demonstrated the liberality of the twenty-six counties' neutrality. But 100,000 people had been rendered homeless in the raid. Unemployment was on the rise and by 1941 it rose to near its pre-war mark. Mounting criticisms forced Andrews from office and Sir Basil Brooke (later Lord Brookeborough) took over. It has been argued that had de Valera seized the opportunity of England's difficulty at Dunkirk, he could have seized control of the Six Counties. Whichever course subsequent events had taken, it has been argued, they would certainly have been more favourable than the drift policy that was followed regarding partition.

With the post-war Labour administration in England, Northern Ireland found itself having to institute schemes for housing, health, education and social security. The main body of Unionists were disturbed at this forced drift towards "Socialism". A number of them demanded that Northern Ireland be given dominion status. One of those attracted to the idea was Captain Terence O'Neill, later premier of the statelet.[3]

Costello had turned his "Inter-Party" government to the promise of an "official republic" by repealing the External Relations Act and declaring the Republic of Ireland on April 18, 1949. In retaliation to the declaration of a republic the London government had enacted that "in no event will Northern Ireland or any part thereof cease to be part of the

United Kingdom without the consent of the Parliament of Northern Ireland." Ireland was now considered to be "outside" the British Commonwealth. The truncated republic did not appease the republicans and the *Clann na Poblachta* T.D., Peadar Cowan, announced his intention of trying to create a rising in the north on Socialist principles. This provoked questions in the Northern Ireland parliament by irate Unionists. Cowan had been the only voice in the *Dáil* that squarely challenged the Catholic Hierarchy's intervention over the Irish Health Service Scheme for mothers and children. This made him an almost national (Protestant) hero overnight.

Despite the severance of links with the U.K., when the London Government devalued the pound on September 18, 1949, Ireland followed suit rather than break the financial link and so found that it was either dependent on U.K. produce or had to pay higher prices abroad. By 1951 Ireland was spending three times the dollars it was earning and found that it had to recall some £30,000,000 external holdings; for the first time, most Irish public assets were now in Ireland. A number of factors, apart from this, were shaking the Costello government. A bad harvest in 1950 was inevitably followed by bread rationing. A fuel shortage added to matters and new price controls were imposed. The opposition of the Catholic Church against the "unChristian" free health service for mothers and children caused the resignation of Dr. Noel Brown, *Clann na Poblachta* Minister for Health. Then two *Clann na Talmhan* deputies broke away and the dissidents threatened to ally with *Fianna Fáil*. In May, 1951, a general election was fought and *Fianna Fáil* gained only one seat but, backed by dissidents, it was able to form a government.

Fianna Fáil did not last long in office, however; MacEntee's budget of 1952 creating a slump in Ireland while the U.K. went into a period of "Tory Affluence" caused disaffection among the capitalists, who demanded a cut in direct taxation and reduction of social welfare schemes. In 1954 Costello headed his second "Inter-Party" government. Under his administration Ireland finally managed to enter the United Nations having been blocked since the end of the war by the USSR, partly as a retaliation for not giving the USSR diplomatic recognition; an irony, when it was the Russian Soviet Republic that first recognised the Irish Republic in 1919. The policies of the

"Inter-Party" government led to another economic crisis in 1956 and the following year *Fianna Fáil* were back in power to a country with 70,000 unemployed and the highest emigration figure since independence.

During this period Northern Ireland was becoming increasingly reactionary. In 1946 it had limited its local government franchise and indulged in jerrymandering in elections to maintain Unionist supremacy. In 1954 the Unionists banned the Irish flag, provoking a great deal of hostility. Such actions stimulated reaction from the republicans. The IRA and *Sinn Féin*, at the time, were led by three fairly moderate men, Anthony Magan, chief of staff; Patrick MacLogan, president of *Sinn Féin*; and Thomas MacCurtain. In November, 1953, a Co. Tyrone IRA leader, Liam Kelly, broke with the IRA and formed a movement called *Saor Uladh* (Free Ulster). He was elected to the Northern Ireland parliament but refused to take his seat, recognising only the *Dáil* and the national parliament. In December he renamed his movement *Fianna Uladh* (Soldiers of Ulster) but was subsequently imprisoned for "seditious statements". *Sinn Féin* was stimulated into running a candidate in Co. Louth in March 1954. They were unsuccessful.

Within a month of the general election of that year, Joseph MacCriostal, an IRA officer, made a successful raid on an arms depot in Armagh. Raids continued until 1956. In the meantime Liam Kelly was elected to the Irish *Seanad,* mainly due to *Clann na Poblachta* backing. In August, 1956, MacCriostal was expelled from the IRA with some colleagues and immediately joined Kelly's *Fianna Uladh* which declared war on the Northern Irish Government on November 11. This pressured the IRA into issuing its declaration of war on December 12, that year.

> ... the whole of Ireland—its resources, wealth, culture and history and tradition is the common inheritance of all our people regardless of religious belief. The division of this country by Britain, and its subjection to British political control in the north, and to British economic domination of the south, must now be ended for ever. It is up to this generation of Irish men and women to resolve for all time our unity, independence, and freedom from foreign domination. The alternative, if the present situation continues, is extinction as a nation...[4]

The government of the republic immediately denounced the IRA; nothing was done, however, until the Northern Ireland government blockaded the border and started to exert pressure. In December, 1955, the Offences Against the State Act was re-introduced and the *Gardai* started to round up IRA suspects. At the height of the troubles 210 men were interned in the notorious Curragh Camp detention centre compared with 187 interned in Crumlin Road Gaol, Belfast. The IRA "border war" lasted until 1962. The republicans had instigated some 600 "incidents", concentrating on destroying government property, and police and military installations. The size of the IRA at the time has not been estimated, it can hardly have been more than a few hundreds who were actively involved. Nevertheless, it kept 5,000 regulars, 5,000 territorials, 10,000 B Specials, 3,000 R.U.C. and 2,000 special security guards on full alert during this period. It left behind over £1,000,000 worth of damage and six R.U.C. dead, 32 soldiers wounded, compared with six IRA dead. During the 1957 election, *Sinn Féin*, now identifying itself as the political wing of the IRA, won 4 seats in the *Dáil*. These they lost in the 1961 election.

In June, 1959, de Valera succeeded Seán T. Ó Ceallaigh as president of the republic while Seán Lemass took office as *Taoiseach* to be succeeded by Jack Lynch in November, 1966. The trade union movement began to expand and consolidate. New unions such as the National Busman's Union (1963); the Irish Telephonists' Association (1965) and the Irish Post Office Officers' Association (1966) came into being while a Provisional United Trade Union Organisation finally united *Comhar Ceard Éireann* with the Irish TUC. In July, 1966, a Department of Labour was established with Dr. Patrick Hillery as minister. Nevertheless, high unemployment was still a feature of the republic with a figure of 59,000 in 1970.

Clann na Poblachta faded into obscurity in 1965 and their republican leftward looking role was taken over by *Sinn Féin*, under their new president Tomas Mac Giolla, who encouraged men with progressive social ideas to join the party. Cathal Goulding, chief of staff of the IRA, became editor of the *United Irishman*, making its appeal to Socialist intellectuals. The IRA started to become active against foreign capitalists and a number of German land and factory owners suddenly found their property burnt down in IRA raids. These attacks seemed to follow a tradition made by the *Lia Fáil* (Stone of Destiny) movement, founded by Father John Fahy in 1957 to agitate against foreign land purchases. At the 1969 *Ard-fheis* of *Sinn Féin*, 25 per cent of the delegates walked out and formed a "Provisional" group. Both groups avowed their belief in the establishment of a Socialist Republic in Ireland but the walk-out was basically over tactics. Mac Giolla and Goulding decided that *Sinn Féin* would enter into elections recognising the *Dáil*, Westminster and the Northern Ireland parliaments on the premises that their attendance would do more good than the old abstentionist policies. The "Provisionals", while agreeing that "the ultimate object is a Democratic Socialist Republic based on the 1916 Proclamation", adhered to the old absten-tionist policies. They held their own *Ard-fheis* in 1970, attended by 300 delegates, and Ruairi Ó Bradaigh, a former *Sinn Féin* T.D. for Longford-Westmeath, was elected president. P. Ó Domhnaill was named chief of staff of the "Provisional" IRA. The "Provisionals" resurrected *An Phlobacht* as their journal. In his first major public statement Ó Bradaigh claimed that the "Provisionals" had resisted an attempt at a take over by extreme Marxist elements who wished to establish a Marxist Socialist Republic. The "Provisionals" definition of their own Socialism :

> ... involved the nationalisation of the monetary system, commer-cial banks, and insurance companies, key industries, mines, build-ing land and fishing rights; the division of large ranches; an upper limit on the amount of land to be owned by any one indi-vidual; the setting up of workers-owner co-operatives on a wide scale in industry, agriculture, fishing, and distribution, but still leaving ample room for private initiative under state supervision. The extension and development of Credit Unions was also included.[5]

The *Sinn Féin* and the IRA of Mac Giolla and Goulding, with their *United Irishman* journal, have certainly come out more to the left. *Sinn Féin* president Mac Giolla, addressing a meeting at Oxford University in December, 1970, said:

> Republicanism is Socialist. It opposes the power of *élite* aris-tocracies of either wealthy privilege or class and advocates demo-cratic ownership and control by the people of both the political

and economic life of the nation. Republicanism is non-sectarian. It recognises the unity of interests of the mass of the Irish people irrespective of religion and is totally opposed to sectarian division or strife ... it consequently opposes all constitutional or legislative enactments or clauses which discriminate against or favour any particular religion ... Socialism and Republicanism are both international in concept. But we can best promote them internationally by promoting them at home. James Connolly defined International Socialism as a "Federation of free peoples". To be part of such a federation you must first be free.[6]

Clann na hÉireann, which describes itself as "The Irish Socialist Republican Organisation", is the branch of the Republican movement in England, Scotland and Wales. Could the "new image" IRA achieve enough support to turn it into an effective popular liberation front force? In January, 1969, such a Liberation Front was demanded by members of *Sinn Féin.* It is an interesting question, but the answer seems that such an achievement would be fairly unlikely, due to the prejudices and difficulties it would have to overcome and the fragmentation of the left. In January, 1971, another group broke away from Mac Giolla's *Sinn Féin* and formed the Socialist Party of Ireland. Led by Seán Ó Duinn and Seamus Ó Reachtagáin, the inauguration of the new party was a reflection of frustration with *Sinn Féin.* The party's manifesto stated : "In this most critical period in their history, the Irish people need clear and unequivocal leadership in the direction of national independence and socialism."[7]

On March 14, a united front called the Socialist Labour Alliance was formed by a number of Socialist groups. The main groups were the Belfast-based People's Democracy, League for a Workers' Republic, Young Socialist, Saor Éire and numerous local groups as well as disaffected Labour Party branches.

Apart from the Irish Communist Organisation, which has published some excellent Socialist literature, Communists in both north and south united in a Communist Party of Ireland on March 15, 1970. This was formed from the Irish Workers' Party, the traditional Marxist-Leninist party, which developed out of the Irish Workers' League in 1962, and the Northern Ireland Communist Party. In 1963 a Wolfe Tone Society was formed by Dr. Roy Johnson to work out a synthesis between traditional republican populism and Socialism. The Labour

Party's position was that of being on a big dipper. In the October, 1961, election, they won only 4 seats in the *Dáil*. Then, under the leadership of Brendan Corish, in the April, 1965 election, they won 22 seats. In a further election in 1969, they were again losing seats. This was mainly due to the old "red scare" bogey which seems an important part of *Fianna Fáil's* and *Fine Gael's* election platform.

The last twenty years of Irish government has been characterised by a return to economic unionism with the United Kingdom and thus the term neo-Unionists can aptly describe the *Fianna Fáil* and *Fine Gael* party establishment. This unionism is demonstrated by the belief that development can be obtained by enticing foreign capital (particularly Anglo-American, German and more recently, Japanese) investment. This has, however, resulted in a growth in metropolitan areas which has been accompanied by an unprecedented housing crisis and an inflation which has been the worst since pre-Hitlerite Germany. The housing question has led to the rise of militant housing action and squatters' groups.

Connolly's political ideology never formed any part of the political structure of the twenty-six county Irish state while Griffith's policies of native capitalist development did give the guidelines to the *Fianna Fáil* state. With the rejection of native capitalist development and encouragement of foreign capitalist investment, however, the twenty-six counties have returned to Redmondism, the ideology of Home Rule rather than independence. The change from a fairly independent policy to subservience on the Anglo-American economy and a commitment to the political and military defence of that economy occurred at the same time that the government of the U.S.A. changed their terms governing Marshall Aid grants and loans. They insisted that countries to which they had given such aid "without obligation" should give guarantees of political and military support for the Anglo-American bloc. The *Taoiseach*, Lemass, appealed to the Irish Chamber of Trade for help in maintaining Ireland's independence, to businessmen, "who wanted to see it able to stand alone and maintain its freedom." The Chamber of Trade did not evince much enthusiasm and Lemass gave in. In July, 1962, he announced in New York: "We are prepared to go into any integrated union without reservation at all as to how far this would take us in the field of foreign policy or defence commitments." President de Valera appeared to cling to the old *Fianna Fáil* policy by stating in October of the same year: "Neutrality remains constant national policy. We would never allow any foreign state to use our country as a base." Lemass immediately contradicted him: "In the East-West conflict we are not neutral . . . we have made it quite clear that our desire is to participate in whatever political union may ultimately develop in Europe. We are making no reservation of any sort including defence."[8] George Gilmore comments:

> The *Fianna Fáil* government in short, had attempted to maintain an independent foreign policy on the basis of the Griffithite State and had found that the structure would not support it, so now, in spite of some difficulties of re-adjustment that have become very obvious recently, we are back to Redmondism—to "a recognised national identity" accepting once again subservience to the British economy, and committed once again to the political and military defence of that economy. That, I contend, is the big issue in Irish politics today. Other dangers there are, but they are minor ones . . .[9]

It was whispered, in diplomatic circles of a reunited Ireland joining in some kind of federation within the United Kingdom.

Only agricultural prices, distorted by the English system of internal subsidies, have remained depressed. Much agricultural produce, notably butter, is exported at a loss as the English subsidy keeps the English price down. Irish farmers have been driven to militancy demanding a meat marketing board and incentive scheme for small farmers. To press their case they have even recoursed to strike action. The Government have tried to divide and rule by fostering an anti-farmer feeling among workers, pointing out that agricultural prices are a main element in the rising cost of living. Until the late 1960's the only course for small farmers was emigration. By 1970 they were beginning to fight back both as a mass organisation and by economic organisation, in co-operatives and communes. The success of farmers' co-operatives was mainly due to the inspiration of Father James MacDyer.

Fr. MacDyer, the priest of Gleann Cholmcille, Co. Donegal, was faced with a vanishing parish. By 1961 the last of the unmarried girls of the 16-35 age group had left. Fr. MacDyer, with the aid of the veteran Socialist, Peadar O'Donnell, supervised the organisation of a co-operative farming system, not only in his parish but neighbouring parishes. Life was brought back to the area as it developed into an economic unit. In September, 1966, Fr. MacDyer was released from his parish duties to devote full time to his scheme. His idea caught the imagination of farmers in similar plights throughout Ireland.

In 1970 there were about 500,000 workers, (200,000 in the North and 300,000 in the South) organised into numerous trade unions but there was a long tradition of non political control and lack of political education. The neo-Unionists therefore were still the main controllers among organised labour. The move by the Irish governments to establish bigger industries in Ireland based on foreign capital is, inevitably, increasing the number of industrial workers. Thus a stronger workers' element may be eventually created in the political sphere. At the moment the trade unionists are prepared to co-operate with the co-operative economic projects in rural areas (some working on them in their spare time and holidays). There is also an increasing support among young workers for the Irish language revival because of a realisation that this is bound up with economics, especially of the Irish-speaking areas in the West. *Scéim na gCeardchumann* is an inter-union organisation for workers' further education and which fosters the language among trade unionists.

On gaining independence, the *Saorstát* made Irish an official state language and, under the Minister of Education, Eoin MacNeill, provision was made for teaching it in all schools in the *Saorstát* territory. The position reached in the last census was that 700,000 people, 27 per cent of the population, registered themselves as Irish speakers, compared to 19 per cent in 1921. Superficially, this is the highest figure for seventy years. But on closer examination one finds that only 80,000 people are native speakers who live in areas (*Gaeltachtaí*) where Irish is the first language. Thus the Irish language revival when compared to the numerous other countries who have undertaken language revivals, is a definite failure. Take the Faroes, as a near example, where Danish had almost supplanted Faroese, which was not even a written language until the late 19th century. It was only in 1938 that Faroese was allowed to be taught during school hours and used as a medium of instruction. Today there are few monoglot Danish speakers in the Faroes. The Soviet Republic of Armenia restored her language in a series of five-year plans beginning in 1921. Other countries, ranging from Slovenia, Lithuania, Finland to Korea and Albania have also been successful. What then is the basic reason behind Ireland's failure? One reason is that the attitude of early governments to the revival was that by getting Irish taught in schools, the whole problem would be solved. No thought was given to creating an Irish environment outside of school hours in the English-speaking areas. Children were therefore instilled with the idea that they were being taught a dead language, and the system of education was such they were merely crammed with the language to get through an examination before passing on to more useful things. They resented and rejected the language and this inevitably led to an anti-Irish language movement being founded in 1966 under the name of the Language Freedom Movement, with whom *Fine Gael* flirted for a time before public opinion compelled them to desist.

At the same time the *Gaeltachtai*, or Irish-speaking areas, were disintegrating due to emigration arising from the lack of economic development. The humanitarian axiom that a society should be judged by the poorest of its members leads to a damning indictment of government neglect of the *Gaeltachtai*. Viewed in the light of each government's reiteration of the need to restore the language the indictment is equally damning. What should have been the bridgehead for the cultural reconquest has been allowed to all but vanish. Little has been done by private capital to develop the economy of such areas and when foreign capital has moved in, the English language has inevitably gone with it. Only Father MacDyer's scheme has put any life back into such an area. It can be pointed out that Mao Tse-tung came to power because he adapted Marxism-Leninism to Chinese conditions; that, in default of the government's development of the *Gaeltachtai*, the Irish Socialist movement should have concentrated on those areas which were both the most poverty-stricken and the repository of Irish culture instead of concentrating exclusively on the urban proletariat. Had they made this attempt they might well have harnessed the dynamism of nationalism to the gospel of Socialism and continued the tradition pioneered by Connolly.

However, the Irish government, while still paying lip service to the ideal of language revival in numerous reports and white papers, refused to take positive and strong measures, as taken in other countries, for such a revival. An English-speaking Ireland provides a reservoir of cheap labour for the English-speaking countries and emigration seems to be an essential part of the Irish economic programme. When Ireland enters the European Economic Community (the Common Market) on the coat tails of England, the anglicisation of Ireland will be given a further impetus. Whereas, when a country enters the EEC their national language becomes an official EEC language, the Irish government did not contemplate that Irish should be pressed as such. Only extreme pressure by language enthusiasts forced the issue. The move to enter the EEC began in 1961 but was held up to allow the U.K., on which Ireland had placed herself as an economy dependency, to enter first. This has led to the rise of several anti-EEC bodies. The Common Market Study group has produced several publications as to why Ireland should not join the community.

It can, of course, be validly argued that Irish participation in the EEC, on a cultural level, would broaden Irish horizons beyond those of England and America so that awareness that English is not the only language of any consequence would lead to an increased interest in Irish. The weakness of the argument lies in the fact that this would apply only in the context of a programmed, stage by stage, Irish revival policy. Projecting the existing linguistic *laissez-faire* into a European setting, the undoubted stimulus of interest by many individuals in their own language would have a minimal effect because it would be on an individual basis and would be more than counter-balanced by the inevitable acceleration of the present rural depopulation which is most marked in the *Gaeltachtaí*.

Inevitably, the Irish-speaking areas have not taken their destruction lightly and have, in the past few years, stirred into revolt. Out of Irish-speaking areas Socialist publications, such as *An Lamh Dearg* (The Red Hand) have begun to appear while from Dublin *Pobal*, a left-wing Irish language journal, has an expanding circulation. A Civil Rights for *Gaeltachtaí* Movement has emerged and, following a tradition of *Cymdeithas yr Iaith Gymraeg* (Welsh Language Society) a campaign of blacking out English road signs in Irish speaking areas took place. This resulted in the Government making assurances that it would put up Irish monolingual signs in such areas. Agitation against the Anglo-American-culture dominated *Radio Telefís Éireann* resulted in a pirate radio station being established in Irish speak-in Connemara, *Saor-radio Chonamara* (Free Radio Connemara). An obvious outcome of the illegal broadcasts was the government announcement that it would set up an Irish speaking radio station for *Gaeltachtaí* districts.

Perhaps inevitably, in view of their deprived position, the people of the *Gaeltachtaí* have not been unduly conspicuous in the national and social struggle. One definite exception was Máirtín Ó Cadhain, who died in 1970. While others committed to the language revival waited for the occasional governmental crumb, Ó Cadhain attacked the establishment with a vitriolic prose. A national teacher by profession, he was interned in the Curragh during the war years for his republican activities. When he died Irish Socialists and Communists united in their praise of his work. He was also regarded as one of the most significant of modern Irish writers.

There is now an interest in Socialist literature in Irish and the ICO recently reissued Padraic Ó Conaire's *Marxachas-Lenineachas* (Marxism-Leninism) and *Tuaisceart na hÉireann agus an Ghaedhilg* (The North of Ireland and Irish.) A major contribution to working-class literature was made in the 1960's with the publication of Donall Mac Amhlaigh's *Dialann Deoraí*, an account of life in construction gangs in post-war Britain. Mac Amhlaigh depicts the life of a modern *spailpín fanach* (wandering labour). The book was translated into English by Val Iremonger and published under the title *An Irish Navvy*. The life of Irish labouring workers in England was also recorded by Pat Magill of Donegal who published several books at the turn of the century. There is of course a strong social awareness among Irish emigrants in England and *Clann na h-Éireann* is an example. But the Connolly Association takes its place as the senior of the Nationalist left organisations in London, having been formed in 1938. It published a newspaper called *The Irish Democrat*, edited by Desmond Greaves who had published what can be regarded as the authorative life of Connolly.

Although there is considerable left wing activity taking place in the twenty-six counties today, given the present political and social framework and general lack of political education, there seems little chance of Connolly's Workers' Republic being established. Even if there were such a move supported by the people, there are greater forces which might lead to its destruction. In

December, 1970, the *Taoiseach*, Lynch, frightened by growing militancy from the republican left, reintroduced section II of the Offences Against the State Act. Irish Special Branch police started to conduct a series of raids on left wing organisations starting with the Connolly Youth Movement in Sligo. It was threatened that the old detention camps would be reopened for political prisoners. In fact, this brought the twenty-six counties into line with the Six Counties where the Special Powers Act enacted a similar legislation, all of which seemed to be an attempt to destroy the militant left.

The extreme right-wing English Tory Monday Club significantly produced a pamphlet in 1970 called *Ireland—Britain's Cuba*. O'Connor Lysaght points out the significance :

And it could never be ignored that a military attack could be made to prevent a Labour Government in Ireland. It may come from the Irish Army (as in Greece) or from abroad (as in San Domingo, Cuba or Vietnam). The latter possibility is likely to increase with foreign investment in Ireland.[10]

Only the Labour Party holds out any hope for constitutional radical change but this would not be Socialism but a pale pink liberalism. Even this liberalism has been denounced as "communism" by political leaders and Catholic Church leaders at election times, thus throwing into the Irish public the fear of a take-over by Moscow or Peking and relying on their nationalism to do the rest. This was shown in the 1969 election when charges of "Communism" and "Marxist infiltration" etc. were thrown at Labour. This was followed by Cardinal Conway who stated that Socialism was corrupting the minds of the young and hindering social evolution.

Until recent years, while homage was paid to Connolly as a leader of the 1916 Rising, little was known about his teachings. They were either directly suppressed or distorted. Books and pamphlets were issued to prove that he was not really a Socialist or that he had recanted his whole life's works and thought before his execution in 1916. There has been no greater insult to the memory of Connolly than this. Since the 50th anniversary of the 1916 Rising, however, there has been a greater awareness among the young Irish of Connolly and his socio-political philosophy. While there is still no complete collection of his writings nor an adequate bibliography, several small volumes of his writings have now been published and the Irish Communist Organisation have issued a number of his works under the title "Connolly's Suppressed Articles". The interest in Connolly and a swing towards radical politics by the Irish youth seems to be a hope for the future. But it is towards North-East Ulster that many people look, feeling that the north will—as it has before in Irish history—become the flashpoint to set in motion the wheels of social revolution.

Today, however, with almost two-thirds of Irish business land and capital being owned from outside Ireland, the twenty-six counties Irish Republic is an awful fulfilment of Connolly's prophecy :

> If you remove the English army tomorrow and hoist the green flag over Dublin Castle, unless you set about the organisation of the Socialist Republic, your efforts would be in vain. England would still rule you. She would rule you through her capitalists, through her landlords, through her financiers, through her whole array of commercial and individualist institutions she had placed in this country.[11]

Chapter 16

THE NORTHERN REVOLUTION

IN NORTHERN IRELAND Captain Terence O'Neill had succeeded Lord Brookeborough in 1963. O'Neill, who in terms of Northern Irish Unionism could be classed as reasonably "liberal", caused a great deal of mistrust in his party over his attitude. But, by occasionally making the usual anti-Catholic utterances expected of him, he displayed an amazing talent for political survival. Despite strong right-wing protests, he held a meeting with the republic's *Taoiseach*, Seán Lemass, in 1965, in an attempt to open a North-South dialogue. Under his premiership the Ulster Trades Union Movement gained legal recognition. But, apart from this, the daily life of Northern Ireland remained in much the same stagnant state. There were still high rates of emigration and unemployment while the same trickery and jerrymandering governed the political scene. The only "free elections" allowed were for the 12 imperial seats at Westminster. Hastings writes:

> There had never been the slightest difficulty about ensuring supremacy when in the great majority of parliamentary constituencies in Ulster, the Protestants were in a very safe majority. There being no call for gerrymandering or serious meddling to achieve the desired result, full adult suffrage had been in force at parliamentary elections for many years.[1]

At a local level, however, the Nationalists were a majority in some areas, ensuring domination of some of the Six Counties' seventy-one local authorities. The Unionist answer to this was a system of ward rigging, voting qualifications which disenfranchised a large number of Catholics so that in a city like Derry, where potential Nationalists (i.e. Catholics) numbered 36,000 to 18,000 Unionists (i.e. Protestants), the Unionists could gain control with 12 seats on the 20-seat council. Similar inequalities were evident in the Catholic towns of Armagh, Dungannon,

Fermanagh, Newry, Omagh, etc. Injustices were rampant, in particular, allocation of housing.

The Orange Order, numbering 200,000 members, still dominated political life. Every member of the Northern Ireland Cabinet was a member of it. Thayer comments:

> All the good government posts go to the Orangemen; not only in the Belfast bureaucracy but also in the local county offices. No job of any sensitivity or importance would go to someone not in the Order. Many liberal Protestants with passive disdain, regard the Orange Order as militant, dogmatic and out-dated, but they realise that it is still impossible to advance up the political and (to some extent) economic ladder in Northern Ireland without joining it. They also find that it is sometimes necessary to join more reactionary groups as well—those organisations whose membership overlap with that of the Orange Order—particularly the Black Preceptory and the Apprentice Boys of Derry.[2]

In 1967 Gerry Fitt, a Republican Labour M.P. for West Belfast, invited three Westminster M.P.s to go to Northern Ireland and investigate cases of discrimination against Catholics. They reported that they found strong evidence of such discrimination. "There is little doubt that this exists on a wide scale particularly where a dispersal of population would result in a changed political balance."[3] Their findings were later confirmed by a special survey in the London *Times* and a committee of the Society of Labour Lawyers, led by Sam Silkin, M.P. for Dulwich, went to investigate claims. O'Neill rebuked Westminster interference by saying, "there is really no acceptable or truly democratic alternative to letting us find the solution for our own problems." Hastings comments:

> One might have expected that in Northern Ireland, working class Catholics and working class Protestants would have felt unity of interest in reform and change. But working class Protestants were still far more afraid of Catholics than they were of poverty; they continued to vote for the reactionary, and by English standards, far right wing Unionists. They were willing to do anything to avoid rocking their Constitutional boat, so they preferred to suffer in Unionist silence. Thus, whatever the overall economic problems of Ulster, it was almost exclusively from the Catholics that political opposition to the forty-seven-year-old Government had to come.[4]

In February, 1967, a Campaign for Social Justice in Northern Ireland was established with its base in Dungannon, Co. Tyrone. It was non-sectarian and brought together a loose alliance of trade unionists, housing action groups, liberal Protestants and Catholics. This group sparked off the foundation of the Northern Ireland Civil Rights Association which came to the forefront of Northern Ireland politics in the spring of 1968. The flashpoint was Caledon, a village near Dungannon, in a Unionist dominated area. Two new council houses had been completed for "Protestant occupation" but two large Catholic families were aided to squat in the houses by a militant housing group. The police evicted the families and the new occupiers moved in . . . one of the houses went to a nineteen-year-old unmarried girl, Emily Beattie, who happened to be secretary to the local Unionist councillor's solicitor. Hastings comments: "like so many acts of Protestant injustice in Ulster, this one was a master-piece of ineptitude." Led by Austin Clarke, a Nationalist Stormont M.P., members of the CRA took over the house and held a token squatting demonstration.

On August 24 the first Civil Rights march to Dungannon was organised. Led by Currie, Gerry Fitt and Miss Betty Sinclair, chairman of the CRA a prominent figure in the Ulster Trade Union Movement and a veteran Communist, some 2,500 people marched. Protestant counter-demonstrators gathered in Dungannon carrying clubs and staffs while members of the Royal Ulster Constabulary, with riot tenders and shields, stood by. The RUC prevented the marchers from clashing with the counter-demonstrators and the march broke up without violence. In Derry, the Derry Labour Party, Young Socialists, Derry Housing Action Committee, Derry City Republican Club and James Connolly Society, under the auspices of the CRA, gave notice, in compliance with Six Counties' law, of organising a march through Derry from Waterside Station to the centre known as the Diamond, on October 5. The committee running the march was led by a twenty-six-year-old Socialist, Eamonn McCann, militant leader of the Housing Action Committee. A former Queen's University student, McCann had spent some time in England dabbling in labour agitation among the Irish on building sites. On October 3, however, the Minister for Home Affairs, William Craig, announced the banning of all marches in

Derry. The move was a moral victory for the CRA and showed to the world a "blatant suppression of civil rights". Nevertheless, it was decided that the march was to go on. Three English Labour M.P.s went to act as observers and the city soon filled with journalists, television men and armed police.

Some 2,000 gathered at Waterside the following day led by Gerry Fitt, Eamonn McCann, Austin Currie, Eddie McAteer, leader of the Nationalist opposition at Stormont, John Hume and Ivan Cooper, a prominent Protestant member of the Derry Labour Party. The three English M.P.s, Mrs. Anne Kerr, Russell Kerr and John Ryan, were also in attendance. The route of the march lay over the Craigavon Bridge entrance in Derry. Here the police were drawn up with revolvers, batons and with two platoons of special riot police. The marchers, finding their way thus halted, stood in confusion while the leaders addressed them. The police, however, were given the order to disperse them and, with batons, shields and water cannon, the squads went into action, clubbing at everyone in the vicinity. The marchers turned to flee in panic but found, behind them, more police squads had moved into the area to prevent their escape. Those caught in the crossfire were either batoned or hosed. Within half an hour the bloody and battered demonstrators were cleared off the streets.

As the news of the confrontation spread, men of the Catholic Bogside working-class district of Derry, decided that the attack had been a Protestant onslaught, a return to the pogroms of the 1920's and 1930's. They marched to a Protestant working class area waving republican banners and shouting Catholic slogans. It was a red rag to a bull, and soon the Protestants were flying out of their houses to meet them. Police squads moved in pushing the Catholics back into the Bogside where a guerilla battle continued for two days. The CRA's plan, to try to unite Protestant and Catholic into a non-sectarian civil rights movement, had misfired. Nevertheless, the riots in Derry sparked off the growth of the CRA all over the Six Counties and soon a definite programme of reform was drawn up.

1) A universal franchise in local government elections in line with the franchise in the rest of the United Kingdom, abandoning Ulster's proprietorial voting qualification.

2) The redrawing of electoral boundaries by an impartial Commission to ensure fair represenation, e.g. to eliminate

situations where Protestants could command disproportionate influence on councils.

3) Legislation against discrimination in employment at local government level and the creation of machinery to remedy local government grievances.

4) A compulsory points system for housing to ensure fair allocation.

5) The repeal of the special powers act.

6) The disbandment of the B Special Police Force.

7) The withdrawal of the Public Order Bill.

The B Specials were regarded with an almost paranoid terror by the Six Counties' Catholics. The 3,200 Royal Ulster Constabulary was formidable enough, with an armoury of water cannon, sub machine guns, armoured cars, heavy mounted guns and gas projectors. They were regarded (although 11 per cent of the force in 1968 were Catholics) as the military arm of Unionism. The B Specials, numbering about 8,000 in 1968, were different. They were recruited through the Orange Lodges and therefore were a Protestant élite fighting force of part-time volunteers, called up in special emergencies. They kept their weapons, such as sub machine guns, at home. Half trained, with no discipline, they were completely a sectarian military force. The Public Order Bill was a supporting legislation to the Special Powers Act which gave the police powers of search, arrest and detention without warrant or trial. It contravened twenty-one out of the thirty provisions of the Universal Declaration of Human Rights and its existence prevented the U.K. being a signatory of the declaration.

On October 9 about 1,000 students from Queen's University, Belfast, decided to hold a protest demonstration in favour of these aims. Many of the students, such as Bernadette Devlin, had been in the CRA marches. A Protestant extremist group held a counter-demonstration and police kept the two sets of demonstrators apart. "We are not here to support Catholics," explained one student, "but to draw attention to the social injustices that are common in this country." That night the students, with some of their lecturers and other sympathisers, held a debate at which the People's Democracy was born. Its leadership included Eamonn McCann, Bernadette Devlin, Cyril Toman, Kevin Boyle and a twenty-six-year-old lecturer of Belfast College of

Technology, Michael Farrell. It aroused instant support and 1,300 marched under its banner on October 16.

In Derry a Derry Citizen's Action Committee had been formed by a thirty-one-year-old businessman, John Hume. On October 19 he and a large numbers of supporters held a sit-down demonstration at the Diamond, followed, on November 2, by a march along the original October 5 route. Both demonstrations were peaceful and so Hume announced another march for November 12. Craig banned this march and riot police were moved into the city to quell the marchers. Incredibly 15,000 people gathered, outnumbering the surprised riot squads. Only Hume's brilliant diplomacy prevented bloodshed and the police refrained from interference. A week later the Unionists announced the first reforms: the corporation of Derry would be suspended and a Development Commission would replace it with more equal representation; housing allocation would be removed from the hands of local councillors and a fair system created; an Ombudsman would be appointed to deal with grievances against government or local councils; the company vote, by which businessmen were entitled to a special vote at local elections, would be abolished and, it was promised, the Special Powers Act would be reviewed "when circumstances allowed".

While the concessions would have quietened the more moderate civil rights advocates, the militants had the bit between their teeth. The cry was "one man, one vote". The left wing People's Democracy were enlarging their membership across the Six Counties while Protestant Unionist extremists tried to break up their meetings by force. The struggle now focused on Armagh where the CRA proposed to hold a march on November 30. The march was not banned despite protests from Protestant militants. These militants began to make their own plans, led by Ian Kyle Paisley, a nightmarish cross between Elmer Gantry and Benito Mussolini. He had taken degrees at some rather questionable theological colleges in America, including the Bob Jones University of South Carolina. He persuaded his father, a dissident Baptist minister to ordain him and, in 1951, set up his own "Free Presbyterian Church of Ulster" of which he pronounced himself Moderator. He also claimed to lead a paramilitary Ulster (Protestant) Volunteer Force, whose second in command was Major Ronald Bunting, a mathematics teacher who had headed a local ratepayers' association well known for progressive Socialist views. Paisley now established the Ulster Constitution Defence Committee and began to campaign for the removal of O'Neill because of his concessions to Catholics. On the morning of the CRA demonstration, Paisley and Bunting with some of their followers entered Armagh. They carried various clubs and weapons (police actually took some revolvers from them) but the CRA marchers, 5,000 strong, were kept away from them and the day passed fairly peacefully. O'Neill tried to move against the extreme right wing, arresting Paisley and Bunting for unlawful assembly. However, demonstrations, especially those held by the People's Democracy, were the subject of attack by extremists. On December 9, O'Neill called for moderation in a pseudo Churchillian-style television broadcast :

> What kind of Ulster do you want? A happy and respected province, in good standing with the rest of the United Kingdom? Or a place continually torn apart by riots and demonstrations, and regarded by Britain as a political outcast? As always in a democracy, the choice is yours . . .

He played for public support and won it; 135,000 signed a petition supporting his moderation. Thus armed he dismissed Craig, the most troublesome of the extreme right-wingers, who was now mooting the idea that the Six Counties might form a separate state and declare a Unilateral Declaration of Independence, cutting itself off from England and Ireland. Most of the CRA groups ceased their activities to see what O'Neill would do. A period of inactivity on the part of the Government followed and on December 20, 1969, the People's Democracy announced a civil rights march from Belfast to Derry beginning on January 1. Captain William Long, who had replaced Craig as Minister for Home Affairs, summoned the leaders and tried to dissuade them from marching but, trying to demonstrate the government's new liberal line, did not ban the march.

On January 1 some sixty marchers set off from City Hall, Belfast. Hastings comments :

> When the People's Democracy planned their march, they were doing so in the almost certain knowledge that it would be forcibly opposed. An admittedly left wing body, they are taking the road in a society in which Socialism is considered a form of the plague, and student protest something approaching treason.

Giving her reasons for the march, Bernadette Devlin says:

Our function in marching from Belfast to Derry was to break the truce, to relaunch the civil rights movement as a mass movement, and to show the people that O'Neill was, in fact, offering them nothing.[5]

Hastings adds:

People's Democracy sought to extend the nature of the Civil Rights struggle from a merely Catholic fight for legal justice to a broad cry for social reform; they demanded not only a bigger slice of the Ulster cake for Catholics, but a bigger cake; not only a share of the Protestant's economic and social problems, but general change on classic Socialist lines.

The march grew in strength until, on January 4, the demonstrators were approaching Derry. As they reached the Burntollet Bridge, across the river Faughan, the Protestant extremists attacked. They wore white armbands to distinguish them from the demonstrators. Marchers, men, women and young girls and boys were seized, kicked and beaten into unconsciousness. The police stood impassively by and no attempt was made to arrest the attackers or impede them. A number of the attackers were identified as members of the B Specials. It seems that the police were fully aware that the ambush was to take place.[6] The attackers retired and the police now even seemed reluctant to help the wounded. The Burntollet ambush was complete and devastating. O'Neill's liberalism was now a joke. The remnants of the marchers made their way into Derry to be attacked yet again before they reached the City Hall. Protestant gangs were attacking stragglers. Catholics from the Bogside now came to the aid of the marchers and the affair, once again, lapsed into a purely sectarian blood bath. Police joined in assaulting Catholics, even fighting their way into a department store and batoning customers. Bogsiders barricaded themselves in from the attack.

Government ministers were now resigning at O'Neill's inactivity in not teaching the "trouble makers", i.e. the civil rights marchers, a severe lesson, while Westminster was pressuring O'Neill to enact the reforms as quickly as possible. He was caught in a crossfire. On February 4, O'Neill dissolved the

Stormont parliament and declared a general election for February 24. Some thirteen parties put up candidates to contest the fifty-two constituencies. O'Neill found himself back in power but with eleven anti-O'Neill Unionists as an extreme right wing pressure group. Eddie McAteer, Stormont M.P. for twenty-two years, and a leader of the Nationalists had lost his seat while the CRA leaders, John Hume and Ivan Cooper, had been elected.

Demonstrations were turning into riots and battles across the Six Counties. On Saturday, April 12, a savage guerilla warfare took place in the Bogside and the police opened fire on the crowds. The new Home Affairs Minister ordered the police to withdraw. A series of bomb attacks took place throughout the Six Counties and, as usual, at the time, the IRA were blamed. But the explosions were perpetrated by the Ulster Volunteer Force.

On December 10, 1968, George Forrest, Unionist M.P. for Mid Ulster died, creating a vacancy in his marginally held seat at Westminster. A by-election was called for April 17, 1969, and the late M.P.'s widow, Mrs. Anna Forrest, was the Unionist choice. Bernadette Devlin, the twenty-one-year-old psychology student, and a People's Democracy leader, was chosen to fight the seat as a "unity" candidate. By a majority of 4,211 votes, which meant she had picked up 1,500 Protestant votes, Bernadette Devlin became the youngest woman M.P. to sit in the English House of Commons. On the day she made her maiden speech in the Commons, April 22, O'Neill and the Unionist Party were debating the advisability of allowing "one man, one vote". The following day they concluded their secret debate by supporting the proposal by twenty-eight votes to twenty-two. Immediately, James Chichester-Clark, Minister of Agriculture, resigned from the government. In despair, O'Neill announced his resignation as Prime Minister on April 28. On May 1, James Chichester-Clark, O'Neill's cousin, was elected Prime Minister by the Unionist Parliamentary Party by seventeen votes to sixteen. On May 6 he announced an amnesty for all political offences, thereby preventing any investigation over the Burntollet ambush.

An uneasy quiet descended. Then on July 12, Protestant demonstrations set off rioting throughout the Six Counties. In despair Eamonn McCann said: "This has nothing to do with

Civil Rights. The old primeval instincts have come to the surface. This is a holy war." During the next two weeks the situation worsened. Against this background the Derry Apprentice Boys were allowed to hold their annual Protestant demonstrations on August 12. A group of Catholic youths started to throw stones at the parade and the police, in full riot gear, began to move against the Catholics, pushing them back into the Bogside area. The Bogside Catholics began to throw up barricades and organise defences against the invading police. They were under no illusions what would happen if the police entered the Bogside. Petrol bombs and paving stones met gunfire, tear gas and batons. Bernadette Devlin raced around the area trying to organise the defences. She felt "the revolution had come". She phoned the Dublin Minister for Defence to plead that 1,000 gas masks be sent to protect the children, but the Dublin Government refused to become involved. Later Bernadette Devlin was imprisoned by the Northern Ireland Government for the part she played in the defence of the Bogside. By nightfall police and Protestant civilians were wreaking havoc on any targets they could find. The siege of Bogside was on.

The CRA tried to organise demonstrations in other towns to relieve the pressure on Derry and calls were made to Dublin to intervene, as well as to the Northern Ireland Government and to Westminster. People looked on in horror as 600 fully armed police, backed, in many cases, by armed civilians, attacked and re-attacked the barricaded Bogside. The twenty-six-county *Taoiseach*, Jack Lynch, in a television speech, announced the setting up of Irish Army field hospitals near the border and the Minister for External Affairs, Dr. Hillery, was sent to the United Nations to demand that a United Nations peace-keeping force be sent to the Six Counties. The trouble spread to Belfast, Armagh, Dungiven, Dungannon, Enniskillen and Coalisland; in Dungannon and Dungiven shootings took place. Several times the police at Bogside fired on the crowds. Thousands of Catholics were fleeing from Northern Ireland in the biggest exodus since the pogroms of the 1920's. The feared B Specials were mobilised and, armed with rifles and submachine-guns, they were moving into Derry.

On Thursday, April 14, on the orders of the U.K. Home Secretary, English troops moved into Derry in full battle kit and placed themselves between the Bogside and other Catholic areas and the police. As the police and B Specials withdrew the fighting ceased. In Belfast and other areas similar action was taken. Hastings comments:

> After Thursday night, there was no shadow of doubt that without the army, the Protestants would have totally overwhelmed the Catholic areas given a few more hours, and the police would have done little to stop them.

By the morning of Saturday, August 16, Belfast was under control. English troops were rushed into the Six Counties, commanded by General Sir Ian Freeland, Commander-in-Chief of the Army in Northern Ireland. The barricaded areas, such as Bogside and Falls Road, Belfast, formed "communes" run, in the case of Falls Road, by a Citizen's Defence Committee led by Jim Sullivan. The committee was composed of representatives from every street in the barricaded zone. Guards were on watch twenty-four hours and Radio Free Belfast broadcast from the headquarters of the Citizen's Defence Committee. Likewise, in Bogside, a Radio Free Derry took to the air.

The English troops were welcomed by the Catholics for they had saved them from immediate massacre. The army fulfilled its position in a peace keeping role quite adequately at first, incurring the wrath of the Protestants. On September 7 gas was used to disperse a Protestant mob attacking Catholics. On September 10 the army set up their own barricades between Catholic and Protestant areas and on September 28 enraged Protestants attacked the troops, also setting fire to five Catholic houses.

Lord Cameron chaired a commission on the cause of the civil strife and found proved all the Catholic grievances, such as discrimination and unfairness of the electoral system. Burntollet also made an impact on the commission, causing it to advise the disbandment of the B Specials and the civilianising of the RUC. The Northern Ireland Government replied by announcing the reforms that it had underway... none of which had been enacted. One of the oddest things about the Government's declaration is that they maintained they had long foreseen the civil unrest coming from:

> ... some genuinely held grievances; of the formation of well meaning organisations to ventilate those grievances but also of

the prompt exploitation of those organisations by ill disposed persons for their own ends, the least of which is a systematic attempt first to discredit and then to undermine all constituted authority—the local authorities, the police, the Ulster Special Constabulary, and ultimately the Parliament and Government of Northern Ireland—in a determination to achieve either the merging of this State into the Irish Republic or the setting up of a new Irish Workers' Republic.[7]

On October 10 Chichester-Clark announced that the police would no longer carry firearms and that armoured cars and machine guns would no longer be part of their weaponry. A reserve force would replace the B Specials in the form of an Ulster Defence Regiment in which Catholics would be encouraged to enlist and this would be under command of the British Army Commander in Northern Ireland and its functions would be determined by Westminster. It would seem, however, that many B Specials re-enlisted into this new part-time defence force.

By 1970 the role of the army in the Six Counties began to change, significantly it would seem, following the 1970 U.K. General Election in which the Conservative and Unionist Party came to power. The troops had arrived in the Six Counties ostensibly to protect the Catholic communities from attack by the Protestant extremists. Now the Nationalist Catholic communities found themselves the object of searches and harassment by the army while the Protestant Unionist extremists, such as the UVF, banned in 1966 and described by South Antrim's Unionist M.P. James Molyneaux as "a frankly terrifying force", were ignored. No move was made to decrease the number of guns in the hands of the Unionist extremists despite the fact that Westminster had been told that the Protestant communities had 102,000 licensed weapons with which they could practise legally at "gun clubs" throughout the Six Counties. The Catholics turned to the "Provisional" IRA, now commanded by 42-year-old Seán Mac Stiofáin, for protection rather than to Cathal Goulding's "Official" IRA. Many people resented the fact that IRA leadership, so concerned with pursuing a political programme, had apparently been unprepared and so unable to protect them during the attempted pogrom of 1969, and this criticism had, in fact, been one of the main reasons for the

"Provisional" breakaway in late 1969. Thus, with a fairly sound popular basis, the "Provisionals" became active. In 1970 there were 170 bomb attacks while in the period January-July 1971, the figure was 298. By August 1971, fifty-nine people had been killed, including ten soldiers, while sixty-seven soldiers had been wounded. A familiar pattern of guerilla warfare was emerging. The "Official" IRA were also active, co-operating with the "Provisionals" at "grass roots" level but only in defensive and retaliatory actions. According to Cathal Goulding: "Our attitude is that the first problem is to organise the people in civil agitation, whether concerning housing or civil rights or issues like that. Our job is to defend these people. Our philosophy is that physical force has its greatest justification when it is used in defence of the people. It should be the last phase of a revolution." This was the basic tactical difference between the two IRAs: the "Provisional" tactics were offensive while the "Officials" were defensive and retaliatory. Another breakaway group of militants called *Saor Éire*, a Marxist group, some of whom had received training in Algeria, were conducting raids for money and arms mainly in the twenty-six counties. The image of liberal Unionism was no longer feasible and right wing pressures forced the resignation of Chichester-Clark in March 1971. The former Home Affairs Minister, Brian Faulkner, became premier. To counteract the growing IRA campaign during early 1971, a number of intelligence officers, drawn from MI5, Special Air Services, Royal Military Police and Manchester City Police, established a headquarters on the top floor of Churchill House, in Belfast's Victoria Square, the home of the Northern Ireland section of the GPO. One small branch of this unit became known as the "Aden Gang" which, according to one English publication, was led by agents who had experience in instigating differences between rival nationalist groupings during the last days of imperial rule in Aden. Their task in Northern Ireland was a similar one, i.e. to further the split between the "Official" and "Provisional" IRA and between Catholic and Protestant groupings.

George Gale, editor of the London *Spectator,* published on May 15, 1971, a blood curdling IRA oath which he claimed he had received from "an army source". It was pointed out that the oath was entirely bogus, one which had, in fact, been faked in 1920 to justify the activities of the Black and Tans. In the subsequent issue Mr. Gale "regretted" its publication. When Lt.

Reid, of the "Provisional" IRA, was shot dead in an engagement with troops and buried in the "Republican Plot" in Belfast's Milltown Cemetery, a statement was "issued" in the name of the "Official" IRA to the effect that Reid's body would be dug up and removed from the "Republican Plot". Although the "Official" IRA denied this, the *Belfast Telegraph* banner headlined the story. There have been many similar incidents.

On Monday, August 9, 1971, Faulkner announced the re-introduction of the Civil Authorities (Special Powers) Act (Northern Ireland) 1922 and, for the first time since 1962, internment without trial was brought in to try to contain the IRA campaign. As the army made dawn arrests of suspected IRA men and civil rights leaders in the Catholic communities, the UVF felt they had received *carte blanche* for an all-out attack against the Catholic communities, and within a week 8,000 Catholics had been forced to flee to refugee camps in the south. To the Catholic communities it appeared as if the UVF and British Army had united in action against them and their only hope of defence was the IRA. On August 9, alone, fourteen people were killed and over 100 wounded. Although the British Army chief-of-staff, Brigadier Marston Tickell, admitted that "Protestant gunmen" were active between August 9 and August 11 and were responsible for a number of deaths, the authorities refused to move against the UVF, showing their claim to be acting against extremists of all political persuasions to be ridiculous. In spite of the fact that Brigadier Tickell claimed, on August 13, that 70 per cent of the IRA leadership had been imprisoned, that the IRA had suffered heavy losses and had been "virtually defeated", the guerilla warfare increased in intensity.

In the south the *Taoiseach*, Jack Lynch, found himself in a difficult position. In June 1970 he had dismissed two of his Ministers, Charles Haughey and Neil T. Blaney, who were arrested and charged with gun-running to the north. They were subsequently found not guilty. A third Minister, Kevin Boland, resigned in protest over the trial and, on September 18, 1971, formed his own political party *Aontacht Éireann* (United Ireland). Lynch was pressured by public opinion to take a strong stand over the northern situation and suggested that a United Nations peace-keeping force should take over the role of the British Army. Conferences betwen the British Prime Minister, Edward

Heath, and tripartite talks with Heath and Faulkner did not lead to an easing of the situation. After repeated protests at the incursion of armed British soldiers into the Republic's territory, Lynch threatened, on October 20, to ask for a United Nations force to patrol the border without consulting the U.K. Many members of *Fianna Fáil* felt he was not being firm enough with Heath and, on November 10, he survived a motion of no confidence by 72 votes to 69.

In the north the seventeen Stormont Opposition M.P.s, united in the Social Democratic and Labour Party, launched a civil disobedience campaign urging no payment of rents and rates to local authorities. The majority of Catholic local councillors withdrew from their respective councils. The campaign became widespread and on October 26, the date of the re-opening of Stormont, the Opposition M.P.s and councillors established their own parliament, the Assembly of the North, with John Hume M.P. as president. Strikes in support of the civil disobedience campaign took place despite appeals from the British and Northern Irish TUCs to trade unionists not to strike for political aims. The entire opposition to the Unionists was no longer calling for reforms but the total abolition of the Stormont régime.

By the third week of November, 14,500 regular troops, commanded by Major General Harry Tuzo, had failed to crush the escalating urban guerilla campaign and political sops, such as Faulkner's proposal of proportional representation on October 26, had failed to win the support of the Stormont Opposition M.P.s and the people they represented. In March 1970, David Bleakley, a member of the Northern Ireland Labour Party, had been appointed as Minister for Community Relations to win over the anti-Unionists; but as Bleakley was not even an elected M.P. the appointment was an ineffectual one. Bleakley resigned after his six-month term of office expired and a Unionist M.P., William McIver, took over on October 26. In a determined effort to win Catholic suport, Faulkner appointed a leading Belfast Catholic, Dr. Gerard Newe, as a Stormont Minister to establish contact with the Catholic communities. Again Dr. Newe was not an elected M.P. and the appointment was also meaningless. By the third week of November, thirty-eight regular soldiers had been killed and 197 wounded; fourteen members of the Ulster Defence Regiment and the now rearmed RUC had been killed and an unspecified number wounded. The civilian death toll, including

IRA and UVF, according to official sources, was 111. In reality it was probably closer to 180. The escalation of the guerilla campaign was formidable in spite of the fact that between August 9 and October 31 some 882 suspects were arrested of whom 476 were interned. The situation continues at the time of writing and it would be futile to try to keep pace with current events. So far, the familiar pattern of guerilla warfare as witnessed in such countries as Palestine and Cyprus has emerged. Perhaps a more accurate parallel of the Northern Ireland situation (because of the "loyalist" population) would be the Algerian war of independence. History again repeats itself with terror, counter-terror and the usual flood of propaganda. Only time will tell if this is yet another chapter of the still uncompleted story of Ireland's struggle for national and social liberation or whether the Westminster and Stormont concern for a "military solution"—in spite of the British Labour Party's proposal for a united Ireland within the British Commonwealth—will simply fend off a proper solution of the problem until another generation.

Despite the undoubted non-sectarian intentions of protagonists, both the CRA and the Republican movements tended to move back willy-nilly to the atavistic Protestant versus Catholic track. It is hoped that from previous chapters it has been demonstrated that Northern Ireland was not created out of religious bigotry but that religious bigotry was fostered as a weapon by which to create it. The basis of Northern Ireland's creation was the uneven development of capitalism in Ireland, the fear of the northern capitalists of losing their imperial markets. Since the establishment of the Six Counties statelet had its basis on a real conflict of class interests it will only be moved on that basis.

There are perhaps two bases on which Irish unity could be founded. Firstly, it could come from strong political development of the Irish working classes, irrespective of the carefully fostered religious bigotry. Such a development has not occurred and seems unlikely. The failure of the CRA and People's Democracy have already given a demonstration of the difficulties. Nevertheless, the nettle must be grasped. In Derry, before the confrontation, the Credit Union movement had provided a basis for the inter-denominational co-operation. Credit must also go to trade union officials who have managed to avert the attempt to repeat the 1920's and 1930's clearances of Catholic workers from the

Belfast shipyards. In Belfast, agitation for slum clearance could provide a common meeting point for Catholics and Protestants while agitation against the foreign eel-fishing monopoly on Lough Neagh provides something of a rural basis for a common standpoint. It must also be pointed out that partition has become one of the main obstacles for preventing the development of working-class political consciousness in Ireland as a whole by subordinating the workers politically to one or other section of the Irish bourgeoisie.

The second basis would be a change in the position of capitalism in Ireland; either a run down of northern capital or a build-up of southern capital could bring the two sections closer together.

To take the second basis first: the past fifty years have seen a development of southern capitalism geared solely for the English economy. Despite the fears of the northern capitalists, who established the Six Counties statelet purely to maintain their links with an imperial market, the rest of Ireland has become practically 100 per cent culturally, politically and economically subservient to England. Today Ireland is growing to a stage when partition ceases to become economically necessary. As soon as it ceases to be economically necessary, it ceases to be politically desirable. It was only while it served a sound bourgeois concept that it was worth the friction which created it. The hope for a move towards such unity by a balancing of capitalist interest was illustrated when the twenty-six county *Taoiseach,* Jack Lynch, commenting on Ireland's attempt to join the EEC, pointed out: "One of the effects frequently mentioned in connection with entry into Europe is that of the reunification of Ireland proceeding from a dilution of the Border's divisive effects within a larger unit."[8] But, because of the frictions and myths invented to establish the Six Counties, there can be no simple transition from partition to unity. The northern capitalists are now the prisoners of the monster they created. In view of the Fascist nature of the politics required in the Six Counties to maintain it apart from the rest of Ireland, it could not be expected that political change would come about without major social struggles.

The sectarian political machine developed by the northern ruling class to defend its capitalist interests cannot be dismantled overnight. The machine itself would, as we have seen, resist democratisation and the ruling class could not afford to come into direct antagonism with it without the risk of self-destruction (as in the cases of O'Neill and Chichester-Clark). The reform of the machine has to be gradually changed in case it turns on the ruling class and destroys it, like Frankenstein's monster, creating a more ultra-right corporate state. A leader for such an ultra-right coup could be found in Paisley, now an M.P. both at Stormont and Westminster.

The ruling class realise that in order to safeguard their future they must change their methods of rule in North-East Ulster. Safeguarding their future does not necessarily mean "Unionism" with England but to be able to place themselves in a position which safeguards their capitalist interests and markets. If they can do this under the banner of a united Irish Republic they will do so. Far sighted Unionists have already seen the need to run down their statelet and bring it into line with England's parliamentary democracy. *The Belfast Telegraph*, mouthpiece of the Unionists, stated:

> The Unionist Party is in the course of finding the best equilibrium between the old and the new. The process is a painful one as Paisleyism has shown, but it is none the less necessary and it has to be faced and not run away from.[9]

Paisley is the old style Carsonite Orangeism trying to maintain its position in the North East while the ruling class are trying to discard it. Unless a situation arises where Paisleyism will benefit the northern capitalists, his movement will inevitably fail.

Ireland was witnessing under O'Neill a liberalisation and the first tentative steps towards unification of the Irish ruling classes. The long term effect of reuniting bourgeois Ireland under one ruling class would have the effect of the unification of the Irish working classes; but if it is to be reunited as a by-product of bourgeois politics it must rid itself of the religious and racial myths, now a reality in the minds of the people, which have kept it divided for so long. Connolly was, perhaps, too optimistic when he wrote sixty years ago:

> ... the Irish Socialists are wiser today. In their movement the North and South will again clasp hands, again will it be demonstrated, as in '98, that the pressure of a common exploitation can make enthusiastic rebels out of a Protestant working class, earnest

champions of civil and religious liberty out of Catholics, and out of both, a united social democracy.

But there is hope for the future. Owen Dudley Edwards has recently pointed out :

> It is in Northern Ireland that the real industrial wealth is centred and hence the basis for class conflict was always stronger there. And working class solidarity is no Utopian left wing dream in the Northern Ireland context. It has existed before, within living memory, and there is little valid reason to assume it cannot be born again.[10]

Notes

Chapter 1

1. *Labour in Irish History.* James Connolly. 1910.
2. *The Brehon Laws,* Laurence Ginnell. 1894.
3. *Land Tenure in Ireland,* William E. Montgomery. 1889.
4. *Celtic Scotland,* Vol. III, W. F. Skene. 1876-80.
5. *Liberty, Order and Law Under Native Irish Rule,* Sophie Bryant, Harding & More, 1923.
6. *Land Tenure in Ireland,* William E. Montgomery.
7. *The Brehon Laws,* Laurence Ginnell.
8. *Land Tenure in Ireland,* William E. Montgomery.

Chapter 2

1. *Short History of the Irish People,* Mary Hayden and George Moonan, Talbot Press, 1921.
2. *History of Medieval Ireland,* Edmund Curtis, Methuen, 1938.
3. *Labour in Irish History,* James Connolly, Three Candles Press, 1910.
4. *Land Tenure in Ireland,* William E. Montgomery.
5. *History of Medieval Ireland,* Edmund Curtis, Methuen, 1938.
6. *Land Tenure in Ireland,* William E. Montgomery.
7. *History of Medieval Ireland,* Edmund Curtis, Methuen, 1938.
8. *The English in Ireland,* J. A. Froude. 1881.
9. *Land Tenure in Ireland,* William E. Montgomery.

Chapter 3

1. *History of Land Tenures,* George Sigerson. 1871.
2. *The Scotch-Irish,* James G. Leyburn, University of North Carolina, 1962.
3. *History of the Presbyterian Church in Ireland,* James Seaton Reid. 1853.
4. *The Scotch-Irish,* James G. Leyburn, University of North Carolina, 1962.
5. *History of Land Tenures,* George Sigerson.
6. *The Scotch-Irish,* James G. Leyburn, University of North Carolina, 1962.

7. *The Cromwellian Settlement of Ireland*, J. P. Prendergast. 1865.
8. *Re-conquest of Ireland*, James Connolly, Mauricel, 1915.
9. *The English in Ireland*, J. A. Froude.
10. *A short History of Ireland*, Roger Chauviré, Devin Adair Co., 1956.

Chapter 4

1. *The War for the Land in Ireland*, Brian O'Neill, Martin Lawrence, 1933.
2. *Tour in Ireland*, Vol. II, Arthur Young. 1892.
3. *The Rise of the Irish Linen Industry*, Conrad Gill, Clarendon Press, 1925.
4. *The Hedge Schools of Ireland*, P. J. Dowling, Talbot Press, 1934.
5. Ibid.
6. Ibid.
7. Edmund Burke Correspondence i-45.
8. *History of Ireland*, ed. T. W. Moody and F. X. Martin, Mercier, 1967.
9. *The Ulster Land War*, F. J. Bigger, Sealey, Bryen & Walker, 1910.
10. *History of Ireland*, Vol. II, Gordon.
11. *An Phoblacht*, February 7, 1931.
12. *The Rise of the Irish Linen Industry*, Conrad Gill, Clarendon Press, 1925.
13. *An Economic History of Ireland*, D. A. Chart, Talbot Press, 1920.
14. *The Rise of the Irish Linen Industry*, Conrad Gill, Clarendon Press, 1925.
15. *The History of Ireland from the Union with Great Britain*, E. Plowden, Vol. I. 1811.
16. *Orangeism in Ireland and Britain 1795-1836*, Hereward Senior, Routledge, 1966.
17. Ibid.

Chapter 5

1. *History of the Working Classes in Scotland*, Thomas Johnson, Forward Press, 1920.
2. Trial of the Rev. William Jackson, 1795.
3. *The Making of the English Working Class*, E. P. Thompson, Gollancz, 1963.
4. *Life of Theobald Wolfe Tone*, written by himself and continued by his son, 2 vols. 1826.
5. *The Making of the English Working Class*, E. P. Thompson, Gollancz, 1963.

6. *The Great Mutiny*, James Dugan, Deutsch, 1966.
7. *Orangeism in Ireland and Britain 1795-1836*, Hereward Senior, Routledge, 1966.
8. Castlereagh, Correspondence i. 219.

Chapter 6

1. *The Making of the English Working Class*, E. P. Thompson, Gollancz, 1963.
2. *The Unfortunate Col. Despard*, Sir Charles Oman, Arnold, 1922. *Secret Service Under Pitt*, W. J. Fitzpatrick. 1892.
3. *History of Ireland*, Martin Haverty. 1860.
4. *Literary Remains of the United Irishmen*. Vol. III, R. R. Madden. 1887.
5. *Personal Recollections of the late Daniel O'Connell M.P.*, W. J. O'N. Daunt. 1848.
6. *William Thompson: Geschichte der sozialistischen*, von H. S. Foxwell. Berlin, 1903.
7. *The Revolt of the Bees*, J. M. Morgan. 1826.
8. *William Thompson 1775-1833*, Richard K. P. Pankhurst, Watts & Co., 1954.
9. *A History of British Socialism*, M. Beer, Bell, 1929.
10. *Co-operative Magazine*, Vol. I, No. 10.
11. *Robert Owen: Letters*, No. 211.
12. *An Irish Commune: History of Ralahine*, E. T. Craig, Martin Lester, 1920.
13. Ibid.
14. *A Memoir of E. T. Craig*.

Chapter 7

1. *The Fall of Feudalism in Ireland*, Michael Davitt, Harper, 1904.
2. Ibid.
3. Ibid.
4. *House of Commons Papers*, July 7, 1834.
5. *James Stephens and the Fenians*. 1866.
6. *Fortunes of the Irish Language*, Daniel Corkery, Mercier, 1954.
7. *The Fall of Feudalism in Ireland*, Michael Davitt, Harper, 1904.
8. *An Economic History of Ireland*, D. A. Chart, Talbot Press, 1920.
9. *Fortunes of the Irish Language*, Daniel Corkery, Mercier, 1954.
10. *Freeman's Journal*, November 5, 1830.
11. *Ibid*, March 20, 1848, Also "The artisans of Dublin and Daniel O'Connell: 1830-47: an unquiet liaison", by F. A. D'Arcy, *Irish Historical Studies*, Vol. XVII, 66.
12. Ibid., *Irish Historical Studies*.

13. *Freeman's Journal*, January 9, 1838.
14. *Hansard*, 3 XL 1097.
15. *Irish Historical Studies*, Vol. XVII, 66.
16. *Leaders of Public Opinion in Ireland*, Lecky.
17. *Friedrich Engels*, G. Mayer, Martin Lawrence, 1936.
18. *British Imperialism in Ireland*, Elinor Burns, Workers' Books, 1931.
19. *Contemporary Ireland*, Paul Dubois.
20. *The Making of the English Working Class*, E. P. Thompson, Gollancz, 1963.
21. *The Fall of Feudalism in Ireland*, Michael Davitt, Harper, 1904.
22. *The Great Hunger*, Cecil Woodham Smith, Hamish Hamilton, 1962.
23. *The Fall of Feudalism in Ireland*, Michael Davitt, Harper 1904.
24. *The Times*, June 26, 1845.
25. *Life of Mazzini*, Bolton King, Everyman Library, Dent, 1919.
26. *Writings of James Fintan Lalor*. 1895.
27. *Italy in the Making 1846-1848*, Vol. II, G. P., H. & J. Berkeley, Cambridge University Press, 1936.
28. *The War for the Land in Ireland*, Brian O'Neill, Martin Lawrence, 1933.

Chapter 8

1. *Fall of Feudalism in Ireland*, Michael Davitt, Harper, 1904.
2. "Marx and Engels on Ireland", T. A. Jackson, *The Labour Monthly*, October, 1932—January, 1933.
3. *Capital*, Karl Marx, Vol. I. (The General Law of Capitalist Accumulation; Ireland).
4. *New York Tribune*, January 11, 1859.
5. *Fall of Feudalism in Ireland*, Michael Davitt, Harper, 1904.
6. *New York Tribune*, June, 11, 1853.
7. *Fall of Feudalism in Ireland*, Michael Davitt, Harper, 1904.
8. *History of Ireland*, F. Engels, ICO pamphlet. 1965
9. *Fall of Feudalism in Ireland*, Michael Davitt, Harper, 1904.
10. *Recollections of an Irish Rebel*, John Devoy. 1929.
11. *Marx and Engels on Ireland*, Jackson: Marx to Engels, December 17, 1866.
12. *The Phoenix Flame*, Desmond Ryan, Arthur Barker, 1937.
13. "My Connections with Fenianism", Cluseret, *Frazer Magazine*, July, 1872.
14. *The Fall of Paris*, Alistair Horne, Macmillan, 1965.
15. *Recollections of Fenians*, John O'Leary, University of Ireland, 1969.

16. The Phoenix Flame, Desmond Ryan, Arthur Barker, 1937.
17. *The Fall of Feudalism in Ireland*, Michael Davitt, Harper, 1904.
18. *New York Herald*, October 25, 1878.
19. *James Larkin*, Emmet Larkin, Routledge, 1965.
20. *The Phoenix Flame*, Desmond Ryan, Arthur Barker, 1937.
21. *The Irish Tangle*, Sir Shane Leslie, Macdonald, 1946.
22. *The Times*, December 3, 1867.
23. *History of the Internationals*, William Foster, Lawrence & Wisha, 1935.
24. *Marx and Engels on Ireland*, Jackson.
25. *The Making of the English Working Class*, E. P. Thompson, Gollancz, 1963.
26. *The Fenians*, Karl Marx, ICO pamphlet.
27. *Marx and Engels on Ireland*, Jackson : To Marx, May 8, 1870.
28. *My Years in English Jails*, O'Donovan Rossa. 1874.
29. *Ireland Her Own*, T. A. Jackson, Cobbett Press, 1946.
30. *History of the First International*, G. M. Stekloff, Martin Lawrence, 1928.
31. *Marx, Engels, Lenin and the Irish Revolution*. 1932.
32. *Karl Marx, Robert Payne*, W. H. Allen, 1968.

Chapter 9

1. *The Land Monopolists of Ireland and a Plan for their Gradual Extinction*, Spencer Jackson. 1880.
2. *The Land League Crisis*, N. D. Palmer, Yale Historical Publications, 1940.
3. *Ireland Her Own*, T. A. Jackson, Cobbett Press, 1946.
4. *Evening Mail*, June 7, 1879; November 20, 23, 29, 1880; and June 19, 1881.
5. Irish Land Committee Pamphlet. 1880.
6. *Evening Mail*, March 12, 1880.
7. *New York Herald*, January 2, 1880.
8. *History of Ireland*, James O'Connor, Benn Bros., 1929.
9. *Socialism Made Easy*, James Connolly. 1917.
10. Report of H.M. Commission of Inquiry into the Working of Landlord and Tenant (Land) Act, 1870. Bessborough Commission.
11. *The Land League Crisis*, N. D. Palmer, Yale Historical Publications, 1940.
12. *British Imperialism in Ireland*, Elinor Burns, Workers' Books, 1931.
13. *Fall of Feudalism in Ireland*, Michael Davitt, Harper, 1904.
14. *Ireland Her Own*, T. A. Jackson, Cobbett Press, 1946.

15. *British Imperialism in Ireland*, Elinor Burns, Workers' Books, 1931.
16. *Scottish Nationalism*, H. J. Hanham, Faber, 1969.

Chapter 10

1. *Co-operative and Nationality*, George Russell, Maunsel, 1921.
2. Ibid.
3. *My Story*, Patrick Gallagher, Cape, 1939.
4. *The Republic of Ireland*, D. R. O'Connor Lysaght, Mercier, 1970.
5. *The Irish Labour Movement*, William P. Ryan, Talbot Press, 1919.
6. *Irish News*, May 9, 1907.
7. *Ibid*, January 15, 1908.
8. *Ibid*, July 3, 1907.
9. *Ibid*, July 4, 1907.
10. *Ibid*, July 12, 1907.
11. *Northern Whig*, August 12, 1907.
12. *Irish News*, August 14.
13. *James Larkin*, Emmet Larkin, Routledge, 1965.
14. Irish TUC 15th Annual Report.
15. *Cork Constitution*, November 11, 1908.
16. *Freeman's Journal*, November 19, 1908.
17. *Ibid*, November 30, 1908.
18. *Ibid*, December 12, 1908.
19. *Ibid*, December 1, 1908.
20. *Rule Book of the Irish Transport and General Workers' Union*, 1909.

Chapter 11

1. *James Larkin*, Emmet Larkin, Routledge, 1965.
2. *Cork Constitution*, June 19, 1909.
3. *Workers Control*, eds. Ken Coates and Tony Topham, MacGibbon & Kee, 1968.
4. *Axe to the Root*, James Connolly. 1921.
5. *James Larkin*, Emmet Larkin, Routledge, 1965.
6. *Freeman's Journal*, August 29, 1911.
7. *Irish Worker*, July 29, 1911.
8. *Watchword of Labour*, October 30, 1920.
9. *Sinn Féin*, September 30, 1911.
10. *Workers' Republic*, December 18, 1915.
11. *Ibid*, April 8, 1916.
12. *The Harp*, April, 1907.

13. *Workers' Republic,* March, 1903.
14. *The Irish Labour Movement,* W. P. Ryan, Talbot Press, 1919.
15. *Freeman's Journal,* September 4, 1913.
16. *Severnaya Pravda,* September 11, 1913. (Lenin on Ireland, 1970.)
17. *50 Years of Liberty Hall,* C. O'Shannon, ITGWU, 1959.
18. *Daily Citizen,* November 12, 1913.
19. *Severnaya Pravda,* September 16, 1913. (Lenin on Ireland, 1970.)
20. *Workers' Republic,* September 30, 1915.
21. *Irish Times,* February 3, 1914.
22. *Forward,* February 7, 1914.
23. *The Working Class in the Irish National Revolution 1916-23,* (ICO).
24. *Irish Churchman,* November 14, 1913.
25. *Put Pravdy,* March 12, 1914. (*Lenin on Ireland,* 1970.)
26. *Green Banners,* R. M. Fox, Secker & Warburg, 1938.
27. *Put Pravdy,* April 23, 1914. (*Lenin on Ireland,* 1970.)
28. *History of the Irish Citizen Army,* R. M. Fox, J. Duffy, 1943.
29. *Irish Worker,* February 22, 1913.
30. *Workers' Republic,* November 6, 1915.
31. *Irish Worker,* July 25, 1914.

Chapter 12

1. *Forward,* August 15, 1914.
2. *The Making of 1916,* Kevin B. Nowlan, Gill & Macmillan, 1969.
3. *Ireland Her Own,* T. A. Jackson, Cobbett Press, 1946.
4. *Workers' Republic,* March 18, 1916.
5. *History of the Irish Citizen Army,* R. M. Fox, J. Duffy, 1943.
6. *Workers' Republic,* November 27, 1915.
7. *Political Writings and Speeches,* Padraic Pearse, Talbot Press, 1966.
8. *Workers' Republic,* November 13, 1915.
9. *Ireland Her Own,* T. A. Jackson, Cobbett Press, 1946.
10. *The Worker,* January 30, 1915.
11. Documents Relating to the *Sinn Féin* Movement, H.M.S.O. 1921.
12. *Workers' Republic,* January 29, 1916.
13. *The Making of 1916,* Kevin B. Nowlan, Gill & Macmillan, 1969.
14. *Republic of Ireland,* O'Connor Lysaght, Mercier, 1970.
15. *Irish Freedom,* October, 1913.
16. *Labour and Nationalism in Ireland,* J. D. Clarkson, Columbia University Press, 1925.
17. *Workers' Republic,* April 8, 1916.

18. *The Easter Rebellion*, Max Caulfield, Muller 1963.
19. Ibid.
20. *Daily News,* May 19, 1916.
21. *Nashe Slovo,* July 4, 1916. (*Lenin on Ireland.*)
22. *Shornik Sotsial Demokrata,* October, 1916. (*Lenin on Ireland.*)
23. *The Masses,* July, 1916.
24. *The Irish Working Class in the Revolution,* ICO.
25. 22nd Report of the ITUC and Labour Party, Sligo, 1916.
26. *Labour and Nationalism in Ireland,* J. D. Clarkson, Columbia University Press, 1925.
27. *The Republic of Ireland,* O'Connor Lysaght, Mercier, 1970.
28. *James Larkin,* Emmet Larkin, Routledge, 1965.
29. Ibid.

Chapter 13

1. *Watchword of Labour,* September 27, 1919.
2. *The Irish Republic,* Dorothy Macardle, Gollancz, 1937.
3. Ibid.
4. *The First Dáil,* Maire Comerford, Joe Clarke, 1969.
5. Ibid.
6. *Westminster Gazette,* July 24, 1920.
7. *A Plea for Justice,* George Russell. 1920.
8. *The Irish Republic,* Dorothy Macardle, Gollancz, 1937.
9. Ibid.
10. *Republicanism, Christianity and Marxism,* Derry Kelleher. 1970.
11. *The Irish Republic,* Dorothy Macardle, Gollancz, 1937.
12. *Echo de Paris.*
13. *Voice of Labour,* June 14, 1922.
14. *History of the Irish Citizen Army,* R. M. Fox, J. Duffy, 1943.
15. *Irish Working Class in the National Revolution.*
16. *The Workers' Republic,* 1899.
17. *Workers' Republic,* June 3, 1922.
18. *Irish Worker,* June 5, 1925.
19. *James Larkin,* Emmet Larkin, Routledge, 1965.

Chapter 14

1. *Republic of Ireland,* O'Connor Lysaght, Mercier, 1970.
2. *James Larkin,* Emmet Larkin, Routledge, 1965.
3. *An Phoblacht,* March 12, 1932.
4. *The Years of the Great Test,* edit. MacManus, Mercier, 1968.
5. Ibid.
6. Ibid.

7. *An Phoblacht,* February 7, 1931.
8. *Catholic Mind,* May, 1934.
9. *United Ireland,* December 16, 1933.
10. *The Easter Lily,* Seán O'Callaghan, Allen Wingate, 1956.
11. Ibid.
12. "How Britain nearly Invaded Ireland in 1939", Nicholas Bethell, *The Times,* January 1, 1970.

Chapter 15

1. *Irish Times,* February 5, 1947.
2. *The Government of Northern Ireland,* R. J. Lawrence, Clarendon Press, 1965.
3. *Ireland in the War Years and After,* Nowlan and Williams, Gill & Macmillan, 1969.
4. *The British Political Fringe,* George Thayer, Anthony Blond, 1965.
5. *An Phoblacht,* November, 1970.
6. *United Irishman,* December, 1970.
7. *Irish Times,* January 26, 1971.
8. *Irish Press,* October 24, 1962.
9. *The Relevance of James Connolly in Ireland Today,* George Gilmore. 1970.
10. *The Irish Republic,* O'Connor Lysaught, Mercier, 1970.
11. *Shan Van Vocht,* January, 1897.

Chapter 16

1. *Ulster 1969,* Max Hastings, Gollancz, 1970.
2. *The British Political Fringe,* George Thayer, Anthony Blond, 1965.
3. *Herald of Wales,* May 20, 1967.
4. *Ulster 1969,* Max Hastings, Gollancz, 1970.
5. *Price of My Soul,* Bernadette Devlin, Pan Books, 1970.
6. *Burntollet,* Bowes Egan and McCormack. 1970.
7. Commentary by the Government of Northern Ireland to Accompany the Cameron Report.
8. *Unity,* December 12, 1970.
9. *Belfast Telegraph,* September 26, 1966.
10. *The Sins of Our Fathers,* Owen Dudley Edwards, Gill & Macmillan, 1970.

Select Bibliography

The volumes listed here are a selection of major source material. References to works quoted are given in the notes and these include newspapers, periodicals and pamphlets not listed below.

AKENSON, Donald H., *The Irish Education Experiment*. 1970.
ATKINSON, Norman, *Irish Education*. 1969.
BEER, M., *A History of British Socialism*. 1929.
BIGGAR, F. J., *The Ulster Land War*. 1910.
BLUNT, Wilfred S., *The Land War in Ireland*. 1912.
BOYLE, J. W. (editor), *Leaders and Workers*. 1967.
BRYANT, Sophie, *Liberty, Order and Law Under Native Irish Rule*. 1923.
BURKE, John F., *Outlines of the Industrial History of Ireland*. 1940.
BURNS, Elinor, *British Imperialism in Ireland*. 1931.
CAIRD, James, *The Plantation Scheme*. 1850. *The Irish Land Question*. 1869.
CAMERON, John, *Celtic Law*. 1937.
CAULFIELD, Max, *The Easter Rising*. 1963.
CHART, David A., *Ireland from the Union to Catholic Emancipation*. 1910. *An Economic History of Ireland*. 1920.
CLARKSON, J. D., *Labour and Nationalism in Ireland*. 1925.
COMERFORD, Maire, *The First Dáil*. 1969.
CONNOLLY, James, *Labour in Irish History*. 1910. *The Re-conquest of Ireland*. 1915. *The Rights of Ireland*. 1910. *Socialism Made Easy*. 1917. *The Axe to the Root*. 1921. *Labour and Easter Week 1916*. 1916. *Socialism and Nationalism*. 1948. *The Workers' Republic*. 1951.
CONNOLLY, Nora, *The Unbroken Tradition*. 1918.
CORKERY, Daniel, *Fortunes of the Irish Language*. 1954.
CRAIG, Edward T., *An Irish Commune : History of Ralahine*. 1920. *The Irish Land and Labour Question*. 1882. *Memoir of E. T. Craig*. 1885.
CURTIS, Edmund, *A History of Medieval Ireland*. 1923.
DAUNT, William J. O'Neill, *Personal Recollections of the late Daniel O'Connell M.P.* 1848.
DAVIES, Noelle, *Connolly of Ireland*. 1946.
DAVITT, Michael, *The Fall of Feudalism in Ireland*. 1904. *Some*

Suggestions for a Final Settlement of the Land Question. 1902.
The Land League Proposal. 1882.

DEVLIN, Bernadette, *The Price of My Soul.* 1970.

DEVOY, John, *The Land of Eire.* 1882. *Recollections of an Irish Rebel.* 1929.

DE LAVERGNE, Leonce, *The Rural Economy of England, Scotland and Ireland.* 1885.

DOOLEY, Pat, *Under the Banner of Connolly.* 1945.

DOWLING, P. J., *The Hedge Schools of Ireland.* 1934.

DUBOIS, Paul, *Contemporary Ireland.*

DUGAN, James, *The Great Mutiny.* 1966.

EDWARDS, Owen Dudley, *The Sins of Our Fathers.* 1970.

ENGELS, Frederick, *History of Ireland* (unfinished ICO edition 1970.) *The Origins of the Family, Private Property and the State.* 1902.

FOSTER, William, *History of the Internationals.* 1935.

FOX, Ralph W., *Marx, Engels, Lenin on the Irish Revolution.* 1932.

FOX, R. M., *History of the Irish Citizen Army.* 1943. *Green Banners.* 1938. *Years of Freedom.* 1948. *Jim Larkin.* 1957.

FOXWELL, H. S. *William Thompson : Geschichte der sozialistischen.* Berlin, 1902.

FROUDE, J. A., *The English in Ireland.* 1881.

GALLAGHER, Patrick, *My Story.* 1939.

GILL, Conrad, *The Rise of the Irish Linen Industry.* 1925.

GILMORE, George, *Labour and Republicanism in Ireland.* 1967.

GINNELL, Laurence, *The Brehon Laws.* 1894.

GORDON, *History of Ireland.*

GREAVES, Charles D., *The Life and Times of James Connolly.* 1961. *Liam Mellowes,* 1971, and *Marx and Engels on Ireland* (ed.) 1971.

HANHAM, H. J., *Scottish Nationalism.* 1969.

HASTINGS, Max, *Ulster 1969.* 1969.

HAVERTY, Martin, *History of Ireland.* 1860.

HAYDEN, Mary and MOONAN, George, *Short History of the Irish People.* 1921.

HYDE, Douglas, *A Literary History of Ireland.* 1899.

JACKSON, Spencer, *The Land Monopolists of Ireland ... 1880. Landlord Abuses : and a plan for the extinction of Landlordism.* 1885.

JACKSON, Thomas A., *Ireland Her Own.* 1946.

JOHNSON, Thomas, *History of the Working Classes in Scotland.* 1920.

JOYCE, P. W., *The Story of Ancient Irish Civilisation.* 1907.

KANE, Robert J., *The Industrial Resources of Ireland.* 1844. *Statutes Relating to the Law of Landlord and Tenant.* 1898.

KING, Bolton, *Life of Mazzini.* 1919.

LALOR, James F., *Writings of James Fintan Lalor.* 1895.

LARKIN, Emmet, *James Larkin: Irish Labour Leader.* 1965.

LAWRENCE, R. J., *The Government of Northern Ireland.* 1965.

LECKY, William E. H., *The Leaders of Public Opinion in Ireland.* 1861.

LENIN, V. I., *Lenin on Britain.* 1936. *Lenin on Ireland.* 1970.

LEYBURN, James G., *The Scotch-Irish.* 1962.

LYSAGHT, D. R. O'Connor, *The Republic of Ireland.* 1970.

MACAONGHUSA, Proinsias and Ó RÉAGÁIN, Liam, *The Best of Connolly.* 1967.

MAC AN BHEATHA, Prionsias, *Tart na Córa—Séamus Ó Congaile, a shaol agus a shaothar.* 1963.

MACARDLE, Dorothy, *The Irish Republic.* 1937.

MACAULIFFE, M. J., *Gaelic Law.* 1924.

MCMANUS, Francis (editor), *The Years of the Great Test 1926-39.* 1967.

MACNEILL, Eoin, *Phrases of Irish History,* 1919. *Early Irish Law.* 1935. *Celtic Ireland.* 1921.

MADDEN, Richard R., *Literary Remains of the United Irishmen.* 1887.

MARX, Karl, *Capital.* Trs. S. More and E. Aveling. Allen & Unwin, 1938.

MAYER, G., *Friedrich Engels.* 1936.

MINS, L. E., *Founding of the First International.* 1939.

MONTGOMERY, William E., *Land Tenure in Ireland.* 1889.

MURPHY, John N., *Ireland, Industrial, Political and Social.* 1870.

NEVINSON, Henry W., *Why Irish Labour Failed.* 1923.

NOWLAN, Kevin, *The Making of 1916.* 1969.

NOWLAN, Kevin and WILLIAMS, T. Desmond, *Ireland in the War Years and After 1939-51.* 1969.

O'BRIEN, R. B., *Select Committee on Unlawful Combinations.* 1871. *Parliamentary History of the Irish Land Question.* 1880.

O'BRIEN, William, *Christmas on the Galtees.* 1878.

O'BRIEN, William and RYAN, Desmond, *Devoy's Post Bag 1871-1928.* 1953.

O'CATHASAIGH, P., *The Story of the Irish Citizen Army.* 1919.

O'CONNOR, Sir James, *History of Ireland.* 1929.

O'FAOLAIN, Seán *Constance Markieviecz.* 1934.

O'LEARY, John, *Recollections of the Fenians.* 1969.

O'NEILL, Brian, *The War for the Land in Ireland.* 1933.

O'SHANNON, Cathal (editor), *Fifty Years of Liberty Hall.* 1959.

PALMER, N. D., *The Land League Crisis.* 1940.

PANKHURST, Richard K. P., *William Thompson, 1775-1833.* 1954.

PAYNE, Robert, *Karl Marx*. 1968.

PEARSE, Padraic, *Political Writings and Speeches*. 1966.

PHILLIPS, W. Alison, *History of the Church of Ireland*. 1933/4.

PLOWDEN, F., *History of Ireland from the Union with Gt. Britain*. 1811.

POMFRET, John E., *The Struggle for Land in Ireland 1800-1923*. 1930.

PRENDERGAST, J. P. *The Cromwellian Settlement of Ireland*. 1865.

RICHARDS, M., *The Laws of Hywel Dda*. 1954.

REID, James Seaton, *History of the Presbyterian Church in Ireland*. 1853.

ROSE, Paul, *The Manchester Martyrs*. 1970.

RYAN, Desmond, *The Phoenix Flame*. 1937. *James Connolly: His Life and Work*. 1924. *The Fenian Chief, a biography of James Stephens*. 1967.

RYAN, William P., *The Irish Labour Movement*. 1919. *The Labour Revolt*. 1913.

RUSSELL, George, *Co-operation and Nationality*. 1921.

SENIOR, Hereward, *Orangeism in Ireland and Britain 1795-1836*. 1966.

SIGERSON, George, *History of the Land Tenures and Land Classes of Ireland*. 1871.

SHEEHY-SKEFFINGTON, Francis, *Michael Davitt*. 1908.

SKENE, W. F., *Celtic Scotland*. 1876-80.

SMITH, Cecil Woodham, *The Great Hunger*. 1962.

STELKOFF, G. M., *History of the First International*. 1928.

STEPHENS, James, *James Stephens and the Fenians*. 1866.

THAYER, G., *The British Political Fringe*. 1965.

THOMPSON, E. P., *The Making of the English Working Class*. 1963.

TONE, T. Wolfe, *Life of Theobald Wolfe Tone*. 1826.

Index